Performing Qualitative Cross-Cultural Research

Cross-cultural research is rife with ethical and methodological challenges but, despite the increased demand for such research, discussions on 'culturally sensitive methodologies' are still largely neglected. Consequently, researchers often find themselves faced with difficulties but lack information on how to deal with them. This text provides an in-depth discussion on how to perform qualitative research in cross-cultural contexts with an emphasis on a more ethical, sensible and responsible approach. Pranee Liamputtong suggests culturally sensitive and appropriate research methods that would work well with cultural groups. She offers thought-provoking perspectives and diverse cultural examples that will be of value to both novice and experienced cross-cultural researchers. Throughout the volume there are references to the excellent work of many cross-cultural researchers who have paved the way in different social and cultural settings.

Pranee Liamputtong is a professor in the School of Public Health at La Trobe University.

Performing Qualitative Cross-Cultural Research

Pranee Liamputtong

CAMBRIDGE
UNIVERSITY PRESS

CAMBRIDGE UNIVERSITY PRESS

Cambridge, New York, Melbourne, Madrid, Cape Town, Singapore,
São Paulo, Delhi, Dubai, Tokyo

Cambridge University Press
The Edinburgh Building, Cambridge CB2 8RU, UK

Published in the United States of America by Cambridge University Press, New York

www.cambridge.org
Information on this title: www.cambridge.org/9780521727310

First published 2010

Printed in the United Kingdom at the University Press, Cambridge

A catalogue record for this publication is available from the British Library

Library of Congress Cataloguing in Publication data
Liamputtong, Pranee, 1955–
    Performing qualitative cross-cultural research / Pranee Liamputtong.
       p.   cm.
    ISBN 978-0-521-89868-3 (hardback) – ISBN 978-0-521-72731-0 (pbk.)
    1. Cross-cultural studies – Research.   2. Qualitative research.   I. Title.
    GN345.7.L53 2010
    301.072–dc22   2009053755

ISBN 978-0-521-89868-3 Hardback
ISBN 978-0-521-72731-0 Paperback

To my parents
Saeng and Yindee Liamputtong
and
To my children
Zoe Sanipreeya and Emma Inturatana Rice

Contents

Preface

The reasons I wrote this book are many. For one, I am the product of cross-cultural identity. My grandparents, apart from my paternal grandmother, were migrants who escaped poverty from the south of China and settled in the south of Thailand, where I was born and raised. Throughout my childhood, I was constantly made aware of my 'alien' status within the local Thai community. It was not only my 'ethnicity' but also my 'poverty' that continued to plague my childhood. We were misunderstood about so many things, and often people would look down on us – the alien and the poor family. I survived all of this and I have always vowed to myself that I would write something about cross-cultural issues when I had the chance, and that chance has arrived. This is the reason for the birth of this book.

Second, because of my own cultural identity, I have great interest in the lives of 'cultural Others' who are also marginalised in society. In particular, I have been touched by writers who come from non-Western societies or those who have been marginalised due to their race and ethnicity. The story that I found most touching was when the tennis star Arthur Ashe announced that he had AIDS, a *People* magazine reporter asked him: 'Mr Ashe, I guess this must be the heaviest burden you have ever had to bear, isn't it?' Ashe said: 'It is a burden, all right. But AIDS isn't the heaviest burden I have had to bear … Being black is the greatest burden I've had to bear' (in Ashe & Rampersad 1993: 139). Because of my interest, I wanted to learn how cross-cultural researchers perform their research. Once I started, I couldn't stop. I found more and more interesting aspects of cross-cultural research and this prompted me to write this book.

Third, I have been doing research with ethnic minority groups in Australia. Often, I come across issues that I think researchers who wish to carry out their work in different cultures ought to know, not only for their projects to become a success, but also for the well-being of the research participants. Cross-cultural researchers must do their research sensibly and responsibly. What they do should not further marginalise people or harm them in any way. This book deserved to be born, since there is no other book which dedicates the entire discussion to how to do research in cross-cultural settings.

This book is written so that more justice will result in many research projects and hence we will no longer see the exploitation of our research participants in this world. To be more ambitious, my wish is that this book will help to address what Martin Luther King wrote in his *Letter From the Birmingham Jail* (1994: 2–3): 'Injustice anywhere is a threat to justice everywhere.' Perhaps, 'justice anywhere is a path for justice everywhere' will be what we see in the future!

I realise that what I write in this book may not please everyone because there is no way that I can cover every angle of performing cross-cultural research. However, there is a need for me to speak about what I believe is important in this volume. As Audre Lorde (1984: 40) says: 'I have come to believe over and over again that what is most important to me must be spoken, made verbal and shared, even at the risks of having it bruised or misunderstood.' This is because if we do not speak out or share with others, as Trinh T. Minh-Ha (2006) warns, people will speak for us and our work will be criticised and misinterpreted. This is not a self-indulgence, I can assure you. Rather, it is the way for me to bring forth troubling issues that have always stayed in my heart. I believe that it is also important for other social scientists to appreciate these issues.

I would like to express my gratitude to several people who have helped to make this book possible. First, I thank John Haslam, acquisitions editor at Cambridge University Press, who believes in the virtue of this book and contracted me to write it. I thank him wholeheartedly. I wish to thank Rosemary Oakes, my dearest friend, who would diligently read through, comment and edit my chapters before I sent them to John. She sacrificed much of her time to assist me with the final touches of this book. Rosemary's help is greatly appreciated. I also want to express my thanks to Carrie Cheek, assistant editor at Cambridge University Press, who worked with me on the book cover and the production of the book. Last, I thank my two daughters, Zoe Sanipreeya Rice and Emma Inturatana Rice, who put up with my busy writing tasks. Bringing both of you up cross-culturally has also been an inspiration for me to write this book.

Pranee Liamputtong
Melbourne, March 2009

About the author

Pranee Liamputtong is a Personal Chair in Public Health at the School of Public Health, La Trobe University, Melbourne, Australia. Pranee has previously taught in the School of Sociology and Anthropology and worked as a public health research fellow at the Centre for the Study of Mothers' and Children's Health, La Trobe University. Pranee's particular interests include issues related to cultural and social influences on childbearing, childrearing and women's reproductive and sexual health.

Pranee has published several books and a large number of papers in these areas. These include: *Maternity and Reproductive Health in Asian Societies* (edited with Lenore Manderson, 1996); *Asian Mothers, Western Birth* (1999); *Living in a New Country: Understanding Migrants' Health* (1999); *Hmong Women and Reproduction* (2000); *Coming of Age in South and Southeast Asia: Youth, Courtship and Sexuality* (edited with Lenore Manderson, 2002); *Health, Social Change and Communities* (edited with Heather Gardner, 2003). Her more recent books include: *Reproduction, Childbearing and Motherhood: A Cross-Cultural Perspective* (2007); *Childrearing and Infant Care Issues: A Cross-Cultural Perspective* (2007); *The Journey of Becoming a Mother amongst Thai Women in Northern Thailand* (2007); *Population, Community, and Health Promotion* (edited with Sansnee Jirojwong, 2008); and *Infant Feeding Practices: A Cross-Cultural Perspective* (to be published in 2010).

Pranee has published several research methodology books. Her first was titled *Qualitative Research Methods: A Health Focus* (with Douglas Ezzy, 1999; reprinted in 2000, 2001, 2003, 2004); the second edition of this book is titled *Qualitative Research Methods* (2005, reprinted in 2006, 2007, 2008); and the third edition, *Qualitative Research Methods*, is authored solely by herself (2009). Pranee has also published a book on doing qualitative research online: *Health Research in Cyberspace: Methodological, Practical and Personal Issues* (2006). Her new books include: *Researching the Vulnerable: A Guide to Sensitive Research Methods* (2007); *Undertaking Sensitive Research: Managing Boundaries, Emotions and Risk* (with Virginia

Dickson-Swift and Erica James, 2008); *Knowing Differently: Arts-Based and Collaborative Research Methods* (edited with Jean Rumbold, 2008); and *Doing Cross-Cultural Research: Ethical and Methodological Issues* (2008). Two further methodology texts include *Research Methods in Health: Foundations for Evidence-Based Practice* and *Focus Group Methodology: Principles and Practices* will be published in 2010.

About the book

This book comprises nine chapters. In the first chapter, I discuss the necessity of performing qualitative cross-cultural research. As in any good methodology textbook, I provide some theoretical standpoints that I believe sit neatly within the framework of cross-cultural research. Chapter 2 introduces crucial issues regarding ethical and moral perspectives in performing cross-cultural research. Some general discussions on ethical and moral issues which have been debated in the literature, historical examples of research which have exploited many individuals and communities, and issues relating to ethical principles and informed consent are presented. This chapter also includes discussions on the risk and harm which may befall cross-cultural researchers themselves.

In Chapter 3, issues relevant to accessing potential research participants are raised. I point to some strategies which will assist researchers to gain access and to maintain relationships with their participants so that their research projects may run successfully. Chapter 4 discusses cultural sensitivity in cross-cultural research. I argue that cultural sensitivity is an important issue in conducting research with people from different cultures. This chapter provides some suggestions about how to become a responsible researcher when working with cultural groups.

I introduce the issue of the insider and outsider status of cross-cultural researchers in Chapter 5. I suggest that the insider and outsider dichotomy based on cultural attributes 'remains contested', as there are other issues at hand and these include gender, social class, age and other social characteristics. These issues are covered in this chapter. In Chapter 6, I point to the importance of language and communication in cross-cultural research. Often, researchers and their participants are from different linguistic backgrounds. This can have a great impact on the research process and its success. In this chapter, I discuss issues pertaining to language and relevant to bicultural researchers, and working with interpreters and/or translators. I also introduce forward- and back-translation issues in this chapter. Last, discussions on the transcription in its original language and a translation method which cross-cultural researchers may adopt in their qualitative research are provided.

Chapter 7 begins the discussion of qualitative research methods which represent personal and collective testimonies: oral/life history and focus group methods. The essence of oral/life history and focus group methods and some examples of cross-cultural research which make use of these methods are detailed. Chapter 8 continues people's testimonies in cross-cultural research, but it emphasises personal and collective testimonies within a collaborative effort. This chapter is dedicated to the methodology of community based participatory research (CBPR), and includes discussions on CBPR, participatory action research (PAR) and the photovoice method.

In the last chapter, I discuss the way we write to represent the voices of our research participants in cross-cultural research. There are several salient issues that I believe deserve great attention. For example, how do we write our research findings in a way that what we write will not further marginalise our participants, in what language should we write our findings, and who owns the research findings? Ways in which we can write up the findings sensitively and make use of innovative writing strategies are suggested. The last section is on the dissemination of research findings. How do we do this in cross-cultural research so that the findings can be fed back to our participants and reach a wider audience?

Performing qualitative cross-cultural research: an introduction

From the vantage point of the colonized, a position from which I write ... the term 'research' is inextricably linked to European imperialism and colonialism. The word itself, 'research', is probably one of the dirtiest words in the indigenous world's vocabulary ... It stirs up silence, it conjures up bad memories, it raises a smile that is knowing and distrustful.

(Smith 1999: 1)

Research by its very nature is inherently political; it is about the nature of power as well as access to power ... The academy has been dominated by White middle-class and/or male researchers, whose political values and commitments have influenced social research, leading it to be predominantly Eurocentric, bourgeois and patriarchal in its agenda ... This agenda has been informed primarily by the dominant groups, such that the 'marginal', the 'powerless' and the 'oppressed' have been the excessive object of study.

(Mirza 1998: 80)

Introduction

Historically, cross-cultural research has been an important part of the anthropological discipline. Researchers within this discipline have worked with people in different social, cultural and geographical settings, using mainly ethnography as their method of data collection. They are known as ethnographers. They have tried to conduct their research with the hope that they can 'interpret what is on the "inside", through the voices of informants' (Adler 2004: 107). This tradition continues. Although the ethnographers are performing cross-cultural research, in the past they have also been seen as the 'takers and users' who 'exploit the hospitality and generosity of native people' (Trask 1993: 7; see also Minh-Ha 1989, 2006). Through their ethnographic gaze, anthropologists have collected information from native peoples, classified the people, and then represented them as the 'Others' to the extent that they are often seen by native people as 'the epitome of all that is bad [about] academics' (Smith 1999: 67). Surely, we need to undo this perception of indigenous/native people, and this is why we need a book about performing qualitative cross-cultural research. This book may help cross-cultural researchers to avoid repeating our history of treating local people badly.

The presence of indigenous populations in countries such as Canada, the United States, New Zealand and Australia has a great ramification for social science researchers. These indigenous people have been colonised and have become marginalised in their own native lands. More disturbingly, their traditional knowledge and ways of living have been stolen, damaged and destroyed by the colonising process (Smith 1999, 2006a, 2006b, 2008; Iwasaki *et al.* 2005; Walker *et al.* 2006; Aspin & Hutchings 2007; Bartlett *et al.* 2007; Salmon 2007; Bishop 2008; Denzin *et al.* 2008a, 2008b; Cram 2009). Inequalities in education, employment, health, living conditions and opportunities among indigenous people (in comparison to white, dominant groups) continue to exist while the 'mainstream' societies have become even wealthier. Indigenous people continue to disproportionately represent those who are poor, sick and disadvantaged in health, welfare and opportunity in nations such as Australia, Canada, New Zealand, the United States (see Rock 2003; Iwasaki *et al.* 2005; Walker *et al.* 2006; Bartlett *et al.* 2007; Bishop 2008; Smith 2008; Cram 2009). Rates of imprisonment, suicide and alcoholism are disproportionately high among indigenous populations around the globe (Smith 1999). Deaths in custody of indigenous Australian men are well known and continue to the present time. This has led some social science researchers to suggest that indigenous groups live in the *fourth world* (O'Neil 1986; Bartlett *et al.* 2007). It has been suggested that dealing with these problems among indigenous people should be seen as 'a top priority', not only in policy making and service provision, but also in research (Bartlett *et al.* 2007: 2372).

Because of concern about reducing inequalities between the indigenous peoples and the 'white' populations, there have been attempts to include these vulnerable people in the research arenas. But as we have witnessed, research concerning indigenous people has been intensely biased by Eurocentric philosophies and paradigms (Smith 1999, 2008; Edwards *et al.* 2005; Walker *et al.* 2006; Bartlett *et al.* 2007; Robinson & Trochim 2007; Bishop 2008; Denzin *et al.* 2008a; Cram 2009). Linda Tuhiwai Smith (2008: 116) points out that indigenous people around the world become people who are 'the "most researched" people in the world', but that the research has not improved their lives and well-being. Indigenous peoples have often voiced their concerns about the 'problem of research'. In Aotearoa/New Zealand, for example, Māoris have been heavily researched by Pakeha (non-Māori) researchers, who not only neglected to involve Māoris in the development of their research (Walsh-Tapiata 2003: 55), but also have marginalised them as people who have problems and who cannot cope or deal with their problems (Bishop 2008; Smith 2008; Cram 2009). Pakeha researchers gain great benefit from their research, but not for Māoris. This has happened similarly to indigenous people in other parts of the world, too. From the indigenous perspectives, Linda Tuhiwai Smith (2008: 116) contends, research is 'so deeply embedded in colonization that it has been regarded as a tool only of colonization and not as a potential tool for self-determination and development'. It has now been realised that research in a number of areas, including social welfare and health needs, is crucial (Walsh-Tapiata 2003; Bishop 2008; Smith 2008; Cram 2009). But this research must employ culturally sensitive and empathetic approaches which take into consideration the issues and problems which are important for the people who are being 'researched' (Smith 1999; Cram 2009).

There are also those ethno-specific groups who have lived for long periods in some Western societies, such as African Americans in the United States and Caribbean-born people in the UK. These people have also been marginalised by social, cultural and political factors. Many of them have been caught in research endeavours carried out by researchers who exploited and abused them or who had little or no regard for the cultural integrity of these people. This has tremendous implications for cross-cultural research at the present time.

Multicultural societies such as the UK, the USA, Canada, New Zealand and Australia contain an increasing number of people from different cultural, ethnic and linguistic backgrounds. These people may arrive as immigrants (legal and illegal) or as refugees who have fled war-torn countries. Many of them have health problems and no access to social benefits. Their health and well-being have implications for the provision of culturally sensitive health and social care in the host societies. Hence, the provision of culturally sensitive care has become 'a necessity' (Dunckley et al. 2003; Tsai et al. 2004: 3; Barata et al. 2006).

Globally, too, we have witnessed many poor people become vulnerable to health and social issues. These people have also been subject to abuse and exploitation in intervention and experimental research (see Macklin 2004). Because of their poverty and powerlessness, many have been coerced into research endeavours which render them more vulnerable. At the present time, we are still witnessing this. Do we, as social science researchers, have a moral obligation to provide culturally competent care to these marginalised people?

The need for culturally competent social and health care requires knowledge of the social and cultural contexts of the people, and this can be obtained by research, and particularly by the qualitative approach (Esposito 2001; Papadopoulos & Lees 2002; Hall & Kulig 2004; Tillman 2006; Smith 2008; Liamputtong 2008, 2009). Many researchers have started to conduct projects with vulnerable and marginalised people in a cross-cultural context. But it is crucial that the researchers ensure that their research is conducted ethically and that they take into account the cultural integrity of the participants. As a result, their research may not harm but benefit local people who take part in it (Smith 1999; Borkan *et al.* 2000; Liamputtong 2008; Smith 2008; Chilisa 2009; Cram 2009).

Despite the increased demands on cross-cultural research, as Esther Madriz (1998: 7) contends, discussions on 'culturally sensitive methodologies' are still largely neglected in the literature on research methods, including qualitative methods. As a result, people who are working within socially responsible research in cross-cultural settings often confront many challenges with very little information on how to deal with these difficulties. Conducting cross-cultural research is rife with ethical and methodological challenges (Small *et al.* 1999a, 1999b; McDonald 2000; Best 2001; Hall & Kulig 2004; Mkabela 2005; Bishop 2008; Hennink 2008; Liamputtong 2008). This book is born out of this need.

In this first chapter, I shall introduce the case with which I wish to start the discussion about the necessity of performing qualitative cross-cultural research. Then, I shall proceed to stage the essence of qualitative research in cross-cultural research. As in any good methodology textbook, I shall then provide some theoretical standpoints that I believe sit neatly within the framework of cross-cultural research.

Before proceeding further, I must make it explicit that individuals or groups that I will refer to in this book include those who are indigenous populations, ethnic minority groups in Western societies and those living in non-Western societies who are also poor and vulnerable socially, culturally, politically and economically. Hence, my discussions may at times refer to indigenous people, immigrants, refugees, ethnic minorities, Aboriginals and cultural groups interchangeably.

A case in point

I wish to commence this chapter with a case study that stems from my own ethnographic research with the Hmong community in Australia as a way of illustrating the challenges of research and the debates about working with ethnic minority populations in cross-cultural research (see also Liamputtong Rice *et al.* 1994; Liamputtong 2009).

The story of Mai

Mai was thrity-four years old, married and had six children. Four children were born in a refugee camp in Thailand and two in Australia. Five of her children were born naturally. However, when Mai had her last child she was advised that she needed a caesarean section since the baby was in a transverse lie. Mai refused the caesarean and insisted that she could give birth naturally. She was told that if she attempted a vaginal birth the baby might not survive. Because of her concern about the survival of her baby, Mai agreed to a caesarean. However, the caesarean was carried out under a general anaesthetic and she was alone in the operating theatre as her husband was not allowed to stay with her. Since the birth of that child, Mai had been physically unwell. She saw a number of specialists about her health, but they were not able to find anything wrong with her.

Mai believed that while she was unconscious under the general anaesthetic one of her souls, which takes care of her well-being, left her body and was unable to re-enter. Because she was moved out of the operating theatre and regained consciousness in a recovery room, she believed that her soul was left in the operating theatre. She strongly believed that the departure of this soul was the main cause of her ill health because she frequently had bad dreams in the following ten months. The dreams occurred two or three times a week. Each time, after the dream, she felt very ill and had bad pains. In her dreams, she wandered to far-away places. She did not know where she was going since she had never seen these places before. It was as if she just had to keep walking and there was no ending. Mai believed that this was a sign that her lost soul wandered in another world.

The Hmong believe that each person has three souls. A soul is called 'plig' in Hmong. One soul is to look after the body when a person is still living. When the person dies, this soul travels to the other world and awaits the opportunity for rebirth. A second soul stays to look after the grave of the person after his/her death and is not reincarnated. A third soul travels to live with the ancestors in the other world. If all souls reside in the body, a person is well and healthy. A soul may wander off occasionally, but is usually able to return to its body. Ill health occurs when a soul leaves the body because it is frightened away for various reasons and is unable to find its way home. The causes of soul loss are many, for example injury and wounds, a great fall, a loud noise, being alone in darkness, feeling sad and lonely, and being unconscious. Common symptoms include tiredness and weakness, headaches and fever, loss of appetite but increased thirst, insomnia, and frequent dreams of being in a strange place with a stranger.

In order to regain her health, Mai believed that she must undergo a soul calling ceremony and that this would have to be performed at the operating theatre in which the caesarean had been done, and where her soul would still be waiting to be called back. I asked her if she had approached the hospital, but her instant response was that it would not be possible since the hospital staff would not understand her customs and would refuse the request, since the ceremony involved a live chicken and the burning of an incense stick. Her husband made the comment that it was hard enough to accompany his wife into the operating theatre, so it would have been impossible to perform a ceremony which is alien to Western health care providers. Because Mai felt unable to perform a soul calling ceremony at the operating theatre, the family believed that her soul had transformed into another living thing because it had left her body for a lengthy period of time. Thus, as a consequence, her health continued to deteriorate.

Concerned about the well-being of Mai, I promptly had a meeting with my superior and discussed the possibility of taking Mai back to the hospital to perform a soul calling. My superior immediately contacted one of the hospital staff. Through this person the Deputy Chief Executive Officer of the hospital agreed to the request. Her positive response was that 'the hospital is more than happy to do anything for the woman if this can help her'. She then left the name of a person to contact for making the arrangements.

I approached the operating theatre manager to arrange the soul calling ceremony. I was told the operating theatre was quite busy during the week, so I suggested that Mai had it done at the weekend. Since the date was not important, Mai agreed to have the ceremony performed on a Sunday morning. At eight o'clock one Sunday morning, Mai, her husband and a shaman met us on the ground floor of the hospital with the essential ingredients, including a live chicken in a cardboard box. We reached the operating theatre, where the charge nurses were expecting us. They were very helpful and supportive. They showed Mai where she was put to sleep and where she regained consciousness. They also showed her the path along which she was carried to the operating theatre, because they wanted to ensure that the ceremony was performed appropriately. At half past eight the shaman performed the soul calling ritual in the operating theatre. There, it took him about twenty minutes to persuade Mai's soul to come home with her. However, to ensure that the soul would not be confused with the body and where it belonged, the shaman also performed the same ritual at the spot where Mai regained consciousness in the recovery room. This took him only ten minutes. Then we all went back to Mai's house to perform another ceremony. This was to welcome the soul back to its home.

Could this situation have been avoided? I believe it could if the cultural beliefs and practices of the Hmong women had been taken into account. No doubt, in this particular case, a caesarean section was essential for the survival of the infant. However, it could have been managed differently. For example, an epidural anaesthetic could have been used, and Mai's husband should have been with her in the operating theatre so he would be able to call her soul into the recovery room for her.

The positive aspect of this ceremony was the agreement of the hospital to allow Mai and her family to perform a soul calling ceremony in the operating theatre, in addition to the concerns about her well-being by hospital staff. This illustrates how mainstream health services can provide culturally sensitive care to consumers from different cultural backgrounds, if they are informed of these cultural beliefs and practices.

Within multicultural societies such as Canada, New Zealand, the UK, the United States and Australia, different cultural sensibilities need to be understood not only as a matter of cultural tolerance, but because they may have a direct effect upon the health and well-being of a mother and her newborn, as well as on the use of health services. A knowledge of existing patterns of childbirth beliefs and practices amongst Hmong women should be a prime concern in establishing maternal health programmes in Australia. This knowledge can improve our understanding of women's acceptance or rejection of certain practices and health resources. When misunderstanding and mismanagement are eliminated, there will be better health care delivery for consumers from different cultural backgrounds. This is particularly important among the Hmong, since the majority of Hmong women are of childbearing age. Because the Hmong put a high value on having many children, they will be major users of mainstream health services, and health care providers will have more contacts with Hmong women.

But how we do acquire this culturally appropriate knowledge from individuals who come from different cultural backgrounds? It is only through qualitative enquiry which allows the researchers to work closely with the participants, and which allows them to build trust and rapport with them; the participants have their opportunities to articulate their needs and concerns in great depth. This is what I advocate in this book, and I shall come back to this point in the latter part of it.

Participation in research and cultural groups: suspicion and fears

> It is important to avoid causing suspicion and fear, and thereby maintain the trust of … broader communities, for it is from a position of trust that we are able to continue the work that we – and hopefully others – value. (Israel & Hay 2006: 5)

History is filled with the abuse and exploitation of ethnic, non-Western and indigenous people which was calculatedly carried out by Western researchers in experimental or intervention research. It is not surprising that this has resulted in suspicion and fears among these groups (see also Chapter 2).

Increasingly, the literature has pointed to the reluctance and low participation in biomedical and positivist research of indigenous, non-Western and ethnic minority groups. Several indigenous writers (Smith 1999, 2008; Lomawaima 2000; Aspin & Hutchings 2007; Bartlett *et al.* 2007; Salmon 2007; Bishop 2008) have shown that indigenous peoples around the globe are very suspicious of research, particularly positivist projects which have placed them as the 'Others' and socially pathologised them. As Russell Bishop (2008: 147) points out, Māori people in Aotearoa/New Zealand have been researched by the colonisers using 'colonial paradigms':

> A social pathology research approach has developed in Aotearoa/New Zealand that has become implied in all phases of the research process: the 'inability' of Māori culture to cope with human problems and propositions that Māori culture was and is inferior to that of the colonizers in human terms.

Similarly, studies which examined perceptions of medical research among ethnic minorities have shown that these people generally 'have more negative feelings towards research than their White counterparts' (Robinson & Trochim 2007: 523; see also Mouton *et al.* 1997; Kressin *et al.* 2000; Shavers *et al.* 2002). Participation rates in prevention trials in particular have been significantly lower among ethnic minority populations (see Giuliano *et al.* 2000).

What is more disturbing, to me and many others, is that the low participation rates of ethnic minority groups may lead to the negative assumptions that indigenous and ethnic minority groups are not willing to participate in research. For example, there is an assumption that parents of children from ethnic minority groups 'are uncaring or lack the education to understand the value of the research' (Fisher & Ragsdale 2006: 6). However, the reality of their refusal is that these parents do not 'trust the motives of the researchers, do not believe the research goals will benefit their communities, are fearful that the research will further stigmatize their children, or are concerned that confidentiality breaches will lead to unnecessary government intrusion' (Fisher & Ragsdale 2006: 6; see also Fisher & Wallace 2000; Fisher 2004).

A recent survey undertaken by Corbie-Smith *et al.* (2002) with 1,000 African-American and white adults showed that African Americans were more likely to say that individuals from their ethnic groups would be used as 'a guinea pig' without their consent. They were also likely to state that doctors often gave out medications for conducting experiments on people without their consent, or provided treatment as part of their experiment without getting their permission. Sengupta *et al.* (2000) carried out a survey of thirty African-American adults in order to examine factors which might affect their participation in AIDS research. More than half of them said that black people are very suspicious of research that is undertaken in their communities. They also believed that the African-American community had not benefited from any AIDS research with which the US government had been involved. Vicki Freimuth and colleagues (2001) also found that the lack of trust in the informed consent procedures and the researchers among African Americans was a great barrier to recruitment in their research.

Similar suspicion and fear have also been reported in studies concerning HIV and mental health among black women (see Tharao & Massaquoi 2002; Onwumere *et al.* 2002; Mills *et al.* 2006; Suite *et al.* 2007; Williams *et al.* 2009). This is not surprising when one listens to folklore within the African-American communities: 'The legend was that unsuspecting Black people would be kidnapped, usually at night, and taken to hospitals to be killed and used in experiments' (Wallace 2006: 68). This suspicion and distrust is born out of the ethical horror story of the Tuskegee syphilis experiment (see Chapter 2). As Tovia Freedman (1998: 945) succinctly puts it: 'As long as the Tuskegee Experiment is imprinted in the concerns of Black persons, no matter what their educational background and training, the fear of "becoming guinea pigs for White people" will be difficult to dispel' (see also the recent discussion provided by Susan Reverby (2008)).

In some Asian countries, according to Eun-Ok Im and colleagues (2004: 897), surveys and interviews were once used to enforce taxes on lay people by government officials. Hence, in certain situations, researchers may find that their attempts to gain trust from potential research participants can be problematic. Im *et al.* (2004: 897) point out that 'the difficulty that researchers face in developing a sense of trust from participants can be even more pronounced when the researcher does not speak the same language, or is of a different ethnicity [from] the participants' (see also Chapters 5 and 6 in this volume) .

But this does not mean that indigenous and ethnic minority people do not wish to participate in research. Wendy Wendler *et al.* (2006) have shown that although ethnic minority people have lower participation rates, they are as willing as their white counterparts to participate in research. Sengupta *et al.* (2000) also show that they wish to help their community by taking part in research. And Freimuth *et al.* (2001) have also suggested in their study that African Americans see the value of some types of research.

Because of a negative perception of the research process, which is based on the history and personal experiences of indigenous, ethnic minority and cultural groups, researchers need to reconsider their research design to make it more culturally appropriate for these groups (G. Smith 1992; Rigney 1999; L. Smith 1999, 2008; Lomawaima 2000; Robinson & Trochim 2007; Tillman 2006; Bartlett *et al.* 2007; Bishop 2008; Dillard 2008; Liamputtong 2008). This is particularly so for the design and implementation of a research project, including recruitment, methodology, the process and the outcomes of the research. If the researchers pay more attention to the social and cultural needs of these people, and employ culturally appropriate research methodology in a manner that reduces or eliminates their suspicions and fears about the research, then they may be more willing to participate in the research (see Smith 1999; Tillman 2006; Bishop 2008; Dillard 2008; see also later sections on theoretical frameworks). Most qualitative approaches, which are based on the methodology of healing, love, compassion and the decolonisation of hegemony of positivist science, permit this.

Qualitative methodology and cross-cultural research

Qualitative research is known for giving voice to people, to hearing people's own personal narrative and using the language of our participants in research. (Munhall 2006: 4)

In this book, I advocate the use of qualitative research inquiry. Qualitative research is essential when there is little knowledge of a research area which deals with 'the questions of subjective experience and situational meaning' (Davies *et al.* 2009: 6). A qualitative approach provides 'a better opportunity for conveying sensitivity' (p. 6). As such, it helps to eliminate or reduce the distrust that individuals from ethnically diverse communities may have towards research and the researchers (Skaff *et al.* 2002; Levkoff

& Sanchez 2003; Liamputtong 2007a; Davies *et al.* 2009; Liamputtong 2009).

I contend that cross-cultural research cannot be too rigid and too 'object-ive', as in positivist (quantitative) science. As Russell Bishop (2008: 171) suggests, much positivist research has insisted on using 'researcher-determined positivist and neopositivist evaluative criteria, internal and external validity, reliability, and objectivity' and this has 'dismissed, marginalized, or main-tained control over the voice of others'. It is impossible to 'measure' people, or to 'generalise' about people, if the researchers wish to understand people within the context of their own society and culture. We are at a juncture of social turmoil in the twenty-first century, when too many people struggle with health and social difficulties and inequalities in their lives. Social sci-entists have a moral obligation to do something to improve the lives of many marginalised people in different cultures, and it is more likely that a qualita-tive approach will allow us to accomplish this task.

Qualitative research relies heavily on 'words' or stories that people tell researchers. The focus of this approach is on the social world instead of the world of nature. Fundamentally, researching social life differs from research-ing natural phenomena (Liamputtong 2010). In the social world, we deal with the subjective experiences of human beings, and our 'understanding of real-ity can change over time and in different social contexts' (Dew 2007: 434). Essentially, qualitative research aims to 'capture lived experiences of the social world and the meanings people give these experiences from their own perspective' (Corti & Thompson 2004: 326; Liamputtong 2009).

Qualitative research emphasises interpretation and flexibility. The inter-pretive and flexible approach is necessary for cross-cultural research because the focus of such research is on meaning and interpretation (Denzin & Lincoln 2008; Liamputtong 2007a, 2009). As Martyn Hammersley (1992: 45) suggests, qualitative data are reliable because they 'document the world from the point of view of the people … rather than presenting it from the perspec-tive of the researcher'. For most qualitative researchers, it is accepted that in order to understand people's behaviour, we must attempt to understand the meanings and interpretations that people give to their behaviour.

Because of its flexibility and fluidity, qualitative research is suited to under-standing the meanings, interpretations and subjective experiences of indi-viduals (Liamputtong 2007a; Denzin & Lincoln 2008; Dickson-Swift *et al.* 2008; Liamputtong 2009). Qualitative inquiry allows the researchers to be able to hear the voices of those who are 'silenced, othered, and marginalized by the dominant social order', as qualitative methods 'ask not only "what is it?" but, more importantly, "explain it to me – how, why, what's the process, what's the significance?"' (Hesse-Biber & Leavy 2005: 28; Denzin & Lincoln 2008: Liamputtong 2009). The in-depth nature of qualitative methods allows the researched to express their feelings and experiences in their own words (Liamputtong 2007a; Bryman 2008; Padgett 2008; Liamputtong 2009). This approach is particularly appropriate and essential for researching those communities 'who have historically been described as oppressed but who are wanting to take control of their situation and move towards social change' (Walsh-Tapiata 2003: 60). Here, I refer to many indigenous communities in the world. Linda Tuhiwai Smith (2008: 136) writes:

Qualitative research is an important tool for indigenous communities because it is the tool that seems most able to *wage the battle of representation* ... to weave and unravel competing *storylines* ... to situate, place, and contexualize; to create spaces for decolonizing ... to provide frameworks for hearing silence and listening to the voices of the silenced ... to create spaces for dialogue across difference; to analyse and make sense of complex and shifting experiences, identities, and realities; and to understand little and big changes that affect our lives.

In their research on drug use and risky sexual behaviour with young, low-income Latina women, Cathy Lindenberg and colleagues (2001) used a qualitative approach. Lindenberg *et al.* (p. 134) tell us that 'through the use of qualitative research methods and talking directly with clients and providers, we gained understanding of the beliefs, knowledge, practices, and social context in which young, Latina, low-income, immigrant women make their drug use and sexual behavioural choices'. In this study, they adopted focus group methodology and individual ethnographic life stories. They say that these methods were 'indispensable to understanding the contextual and cultural realities in which Latinas make their alcohol, drug use, and sexual decisions'.

Paul Jackson (2000: 347) tells us about a research project in which he had been involved in Zimbabwe in 1998. The project adopted a methodology referred to as an 'enabling state assessment methodology' (ESAM). It was developed because of a general dissatisfaction with conventional (positivist) methodologies in the African context. Often, surveys were used to obtain information from local people. Jackson (p. 348) contends that positivist methodologies do not fully capture the views or agendas of local people. On the contrary, participative research methodology 'relies upon local people to formulate ideas and then to test them against their own experience'.

The opinions of Zimbabwean entrepreneurs about the traditional methodologies of questionnaires and the more participatory-based approach were markedly different. The participatory approach allowed many participants to express and explore their own ideas, which they felt would have been missed by positivist methodologies. One participant who has been subject to numerous research projects said that none of the approaches in which he had been asked to participate 'had allowed him to actually get his views across. He had filled in numerous questionnaires, but had received very little feedback or interaction with the research team'. On the contrary, the 'hands on' approach of the participative research 'had allowed him not only to express and develop his opinions, but also to meet and discuss these issues with other stakeholders' (p. 356).

Qualitative research, Edward Morris (2007: 410) contends, has functioned as 'the sociological vanguard' for exploring cross-cultural issues. Because of the ability of qualitative approaches to closely follow social processes as they emerge and change, the inquiry is particularly useful for examining race, culture and ethnicity as 'the product of social interaction'. In her research regarding women's experiences of education with South Asian girls and women, Mehreen Mirza (1998: 82) adopted a qualitative approach. She articulates on her choice of methodology:

I chose to pursue a qualitative research methodology in order to explore the girls' and women's lives from their own perspectives. I felt that the interview technique would best allow social process to be examined and questions of 'how' and 'why' to be answered. Thus the methodology would provide an informal environment which would encourage the women to discuss 'their experiences, beliefs and values, and the social meaning they attach to a given phenomenon' (Brah & Shaw 1992: 53). This was especially important as I sought to explore sensitive issues such as sexism, racism and culture, as well as the area of 'non-traditional subjects', which can be difficult. Interviewing enables respondents to move beyond answering the questions asked, to raising other issues and concerns which the researcher may not have considered or seen as relevant, thus providing considerable opportunity for respondents to control the interview and hence to dictate the content and form of the data.

In the case study of Mai I have presented above, what can we say about qualitative research? According to Robert Stake (2008: 134), ethnographic materials 'parallel actual experience, feeding into the most fundamental processes of awareness and understanding'. In particular, when the researcher provides a narrative account of the story, he or she allows an 'opportunity for *vicarious experience*, [and then] readers extend their perceptions of happenings' (original emphasis). In the case of Mai, readers are told some new things in a convincing manner, as if they had experienced them. Qualitative researchers posit that knowledge is socially constructed, and that qualitative materials help readers in the construction of that knowledge (Schwandt 2000; Stake 2008). For a qualitative research community, Stake (2008: 120) asserts, a case story focuses on 'experiential knowledge of the case and close attention to the influence of its social, political, and other contexts'. To this I would add 'the cultural context'.

The example of Mai permits readers to experience the real life of the story. This is largely done by the provision of 'narratives and situational descriptions of case activity, personal relationship and group interpretations' (Stake 2008: 134) by the researcher. Readers come to know about the experience of a Hmong woman and how she sees health and illness in the context of Hmong culture. It is powerful enough to make policy makers listen and find the solution to improve her health.

Methodologically, what can we say about this story? Mai's story was found because of the nature of the qualitative methodology: a process of discovery. Would her story be found in quantitative research such as randomised controlled trials or other standardised measurements used in positivist science, which are seen as 'strong' or 'hard' methods? The answer is probably 'no'. It was only through the processes of in-depth discussion and a good relationship between Mai and me as a researcher that the story unfolded. And this is the beauty of qualitative inquiry.

In sum, qualitative research is an essential approach for performing cross-cultural research. We, as cross-cultural researchers, need to cast the net of our approach wider because we are now living in 'an era when the diversity of human experience in social groups and communities, with languages and epistemologies, is undergoing profound cultural and political shifts' (Smith 2008: 137).

Embracing healing methodology

It is important to 'drink from our own wells', from our own experience not only as individuals but also as members of a people. (Gutierrez 2003: xix)

In the time of global uncertainty and crisis that we are now facing, 'a methodology of the heart, a prophetic, feminist postpragmatism that embraces an ethics of truth grounded in love, care, hope and forgiveness, is needed' (Denzin et al. 2008a: 3). Hence, I am introducing the 'healing methodology' in this section.

Healing methodology is theorised by Cynthia Dillard (2008: 286), who argues that the approach is an essential ethic and methodology for working with indigenous and African women. Healing methodology, accordingly, is 'a form of struggle against domination'. The methodology is 'consistent with the profound indigenous pedagogical tradition of excellence in the history of African people' (see also King 2005: 15). Healing methodology involves action; the researchers must 'engage and change' with situations which they encounter in their research endeavours. Dillard (2008: 286) asserts:

We must fundamentally transform what research is and whose knowledge and methodologies we privilege and engage … In this spirit, there must be a 'letting go' of knowledge, beliefs, and practices that dishonor the indigenous spiritual under-standings that are present in African ascendant scholars, given our preparation and training in predominately Western, male, patriarchal, capitalist knowledge spaces and the manner in which our spiritual understandings are negated, marginalized, and degraded.

The essence of healing methodology is 'spirituality and transformation' (Dillard 2008: 287). This methodology can work to counteract the negative attitudes of many African Americans towards research which was due to 'abusive hegemonic structures that have characterized the methodologies and practice of research in the Western academy' (see also Chapter 2, this volume).

Healing methodology encompasses the principles of 'unconditional love, compassion, reciprocity, ritual and gratitude'. Dillard (2008: 287) also refers to these principles as 'methodologies of the spirit'. These components are proposed as 'a way to honor indigenous African cultural and knowledge pro-duction and as activist practice designed to acknowledge and embrace spir-ituality in the process of all of us becoming more fully human in and through the process of research'. The first three principles are essentially relevant to performing cross-cultural research involving indigenous and marginalised ethnic communities. Hence, I shall focus my discussion on these three issues in the following paragraphs.

Love is the first principle of healing methodology. Too often, as bell hooks (2000: 287) says, researchers do not consider love as the wisdom which can produce 'reciprocal (and thus more just) sites of inquiry'. Love as knowledge will allow the practice 'of looking and listening deeply'. Thus, the researchers will 'know what to do and what not to do in order to serve others in the pro-cess of research'. Love also includes carefully seeking understanding of 'the needs, aspiration, and suffering of the ones you love' (Hanh 1998: 4). Deeply understanding the humanity of the individuals with whom we engage in the research process is 'a necessary prerequisite for qualitative work in the spirit' (Dillard 2008: 287; see also Chapter 4 in this volume).

The second principle of healing methodology is to embrace compassion. According to Dillard (2008: 288), compassion is about 'the intention and capacity to relieve and transform suffering through our research work'. It is 'a form of struggle against dehumanizing contexts and conditions'. Compassion as a methodology requires the researchers to 'relieve communities of their suffering through the process of activist research'. It means that the researchers must have serious and ongoing concerns for the research participants and want to bring benefits to them through their research. As researchers, Dillard (p. 288) contends, 'we must be culturally and historically knowledgeable about and aware of suffering, but retain our clarity, calmness, our voices and our strength so that we can, through our practice, help to transform the situation and ourselves' (see Chapter 4 in this volume).

Seeking reciprocity is the third principle of healing methodology. Within this principle, the researchers must have their 'intention and capacity to see human beings as equal, shedding all discrimination and prejudice and removing the boundaries between ourselves and others' (p. 288). If the researchers continue to perceive themselves as 'researchers' and the others as the 'others' (the 'researched'), or if they continue to see their own research agenda as more crucial than the needs and concerns of the research participants, they 'cannot be in loving, compassionate, or reciprocal relationships with others' (p. 288; see also Chapter 3 in this volume).

Healing methodology (love, compassion and reciprocity) allows us to see those with whom we do our research as human beings, and this will have a profound impact on our ways of performing cross-cultural research. The methodology may be seen as less rigorous from the positivist perspective because it involves emotions and feelings towards the research participants. However, as I have suggested, the healing methodology is essential for culturally sensitive research and when we work with marginalised and vulnerable people in cross-cultural settings.

Relational ethics: collaboration with local people

Community participation is a scientific, as well as an ethical imperative in working with Hispanic and other racial or ethnic minority communities. (Castro *et al.* 2006: 147)

In working with ethnic minority groups, Scyatta Wallace (2006: 67–68) proposes that the researchers may adopt 'relational ethics' if they wish to have more responsibility towards the people they research. Relational ethics is based on 'a mutual and respectful' dialogue between the researchers and the prospective individuals and communities of research in order to ensure that 'the values, hopes, and concerns of participants will be reflected in the design, implementation, and interpretation of research'. Through the relational ethics approach, the research participants will learn how the research can be used to improve the health and well-being of themselves and of their communities. At the same time, the researchers will become knowledgeable about the expectations and concerns of the individuals and community which may smooth or hinder the research process. Relational ethics also takes into account 'historical memories, attitudes toward research, and notions of ethical principles' amongst the participants and communities of research.

An essential component of relational ethics is community consultation. The aim of community consultation is to include 'potential participants as partners in solving the ethical dilemmas posed in designing research' (Wallace 2006: 72). In research involving African Americans, Scyatta Wallace (2006: 73) contends that the researchers should not underestimate or dismiss their suspicion and fears about research (see earlier section and Chapter 2 in this volume). For the researchers who claim to be 'relational ethicists', they are very 'proactive in addressing scientific mistrust'. Relational ethicists attempt to reduce the power imbalance between the research participants and the researchers by establishing relationships between the community and research institutes. Relational ethicists 'espouse the values of significant involvement and functional relevance, which call for members of the group under study to have a central role in the entire research process'. They also 'dictate that studies promote the expressed needs and perspectives of the study population'. Community consultation is used by relational ethicists before they begin the process of recruitment in order to understand/examine 'community conceptions of the ethical principles that guide the research process, to deliberate risk and benefits, and to enhance participants' understanding of research procedures, including informed consent'.

Community consultation situates the researchers within the context of the research community. It requires the researchers to make decisions whilst taking consideration of the cultural relevance of the research groups (see Fisher & Wallace 2000). Potentially, then, it can gain the trust of individuals and communities in the research. Through community consultation, people can increase their understanding about the research process, which can enhance their participation rates, particularly in biomedical and behavioural research. This in turn may 'help to decrease the disparities' in social and health outcomes amongst African Americans (Wallace 2006: 73).

Based on relational ethics, the concept of collaborative research has emerged. Cross-cultural researchers have called for a collaborative approach in research concerning ethnic minority and indigenous groups (Beauvais 2006; Vannini & Gladue 2008; Battiste 2008; Bishop 2008). As Gerald Mohatt and Lisa Thomas (2006: 95) suggest, 'failure to use a collaborative approach often results in published data with scant useful feedback to the communities of concern, as well as intentional or unintentional exploitation of community knowledge'. This is referred to as the process of colonisation by Linda Tuhiwai Smith (1999; see also later section in this chapter). Research evidence has pointed to the fact that collaborations between the researchers and the communities are likely to produce research which is 'appropriate, relevant, and respectful' as well as provide research findings which are more 'accurate and effective' (Mohatt & Thomas 2006: 95; see Edwards *et al.* 2000; Fisher & Ball 2002; Beauvais 2006; Denzin *et al.* 2008a).

According to Marie Battiste (2008: 508), research carried out with indigenous communities must be structured/set within the principles of collaborative participatory research. It is a research process which endeavours to empower the communities through their own knowledge as a final research outcome. As I shall show in Chapter 8, participatory action research (PAR) and the photovoice method are particularly linked to this standpoint.

Collaborative research, Fred Beauvais (2006: 243) points out, is characterised by equal relationships in the planning and management of the research between the researchers and the communities. The methodology is indeed distinctive from other research frameworks where the researchers have more or sole power and control over the research process, and the communities are treated as only passive recipients in the research. As such, collaborative research can address 'ethical pitfalls' which have occurred in the research regarding ethnic minority communities.

Culturally Sensitive Research Framework

Culturally Sensitive Research Framework is theorised by Linda Tillman (2006) for undertaking culturally sensitive research with minority groups. This framework posits 'the cultural standpoints' of both the researchers and the research participants 'as a framework' for designing research and collecting and interpreting the data.

Culturally Sensitive Research Framework, according to Tillman (p. 265, original emphasis) 'not only recognize[s] race and ethnicity, but position[s] *culture* as central to the research process'. Culture, as defined by Tillman (2002: 4), refers to both the 'individual and collective ways of thinking, believing, and knowing' of a group. This culture may include the 'shared experiences, consciousness, skills, values, forms of expression, social institutions, and behaviors' of the group. When research is taken from a culturally sensitive perspective, the researchers acknowledge 'the complexity of an ethnic group's culture, as well as its varied historical and contemporary representations' (Tillman 2006: 266). Culturally sensitive research approaches which are adopted for research with cultural groups enhance the 'telling' of people's 'stories within a cultural and conceptual framework' which would honour the local communities (Carter 2003: 36).

A framework for culturally sensitive research incorporates five key components: 'culturally congruent research methods, culturally specific knowledge, cultural resistance to theoretical dominance, culturally sensitive data interpretations, and culturally informed theory and practice' (Tillman 2006: 269). The framework embodies the concept of culturally nurturing research (Hill & King 2005: 367), which advocates that researchers 'produce knowledge and understanding of ways to dismantle aggressive beliefs, behaviors, and strategies of domination through an affirmation of voices and perspectives of those who share a commitment to (Black) people's survival and advancement'. The framework represents 'epistemological and methodological possibilities' which 'have the power to produce culturally informed research, theory and practice' (Tillman 2006: 269).

Culturally sensitive approaches employ qualitative methods including individual interviews, focus groups, life history, participant observation and reflective journaling. Qualitative approaches are essential for capturing 'holistic contexualized pictures of the social, political, economic, and educational factors that affect the everyday existence of African Americans' (Tillman 2002: 6). In her research, Linda Tillman (2005a) used interviews, observation and reflective journaling to examine social and educational factors in the urban school context which have impacted the professional development of a first-year African-American teacher. In another study, Tillman (2005b) carried out focus groups with twelve African-American principals to understand about teacher mentoring and the roles of principals in the arrangements of both formal and informal mentoring programmes. The use of focus group interviews permitted these principals to be able to articulate both their individual and collective stories.

Culturally sensitive research approaches make use of 'the particular and unique self-defined (Black self-representation) experiences of

African-Americans'. The researchers must be responsible for, and have their commitments to, sustaining the cultural virtue of their research participants (as well as of other community members). The researchers need to also carefully examine how their own cultural knowledge and their insider/outsider statuses may have an impact on the research process (Tillman 2006; see also Chapter 5 in this volume). It is crucial that in adopting culturally specific knowledge, the researchers do not compare their findings with other individuals or communities. The cultural knowledge of a particular group is counted in its own right. In Tillman's study with African-American principals (2005b), the culturally specific knowledge of the principals was privileged. As such, she avoided comparing their self-defined experiences with those of white principals.

These approaches aim to 'reveal, understand and respond to unequal power relations that may minimize, marginalize, subjugate or exclude the multiple realities and knowledge bases of African-Americans' (Tillman 2006: 270). Research situated within this framework will question any 'claims of neutrality and objectivity of research' as are practised in positivist science. The framework also challenges research inquiries which marginalise the standpoints of African Americans. It fosters the cultural knowledge of individuals who have witnessed the social and cultural legacies of 'unequal power relationships' rather than 'the assumed knowledge of those who are positioned outside of these experiences' (Tillman 2006: 270). The framework rejects any pre-existing theories which fall outside the boundary of the specific groups of research participants.

Culturally sensitive research approaches privilege 'the experiential knowledge of African-Americans as legitimate, appropriate and necessary for analyzing, understanding and reporting data'. The analysis and presentation of research findings is co-constructed by the researchers and the participants. Hence, the framework promotes the presentation of data as storytelling, family histories, biographies and narratives, and other alternative forms of data presentation such as poetry and short stories (see Tillman 2003, 2005b). Vanessa Siddle Walker (2003), for example, carried out many in-depth interviews with an African-American principal in the South, and chose to tell his story using a narrative format. Siddle Walker (p. 59) contends that her research would 'expand the narrow lens through which Black leadership has historically been viewed'.

These approaches will result in the construction of 'theories and practices' which can be used to represent the culturally appropriate situations of the lives of African Americans (Tillman 2006). The researchers develop their theory(s) from the participants' lived experiences and their cultural understandings of the issues being researched. The culturally informed knowledge can then be applied to promote changes for the communities concerned. The research findings can also be used to establish more meaningful and productive relationships with the communities (Tillman 2006). Christopher Dunbar (2001), for example, undertook his research with African-American male adolescents who enrolled in alternative educational settings. Dunbar continued his contact with the participants even after he had finished his research. He also used his results to carry out further research and develop new theoretical knowledge which would enhance educational change for young people and help him (as a university professor and researcher) to establish meaningful relationships with the school systems.

Although Tillman (2006) proposes the framework for researching African-American communities, I contend that it is essentially applicable to other cross-cultural groups. If we replace the words 'African Americans' with other groups such as refugees, indigenous or ethnic minorities, and the word 'education' with 'any social and health issues', the framework can be applied to other cultural groups including ethnic minorities and those in non-Western societies.

Decolonising methodology

Decolonization is about the process in both research and performance of valuing, reclaiming, and foregrounding indigenous voices and epistemologies. Thus, we see decolonizing research resisting the lures and mires of postcolonial reason that position certain players within postcoloniality as more 'valid' postcolonial researchers/ scholars. (Swadener & Mutua 2008: 31)

Research has been referred to as 'a colonising construct' (Mutua & Swadener 2004: 1; Cram 2009), with a legacy of which Linda Tuhiwai Smith (1999: 80) writes: 'They came, they saw, they named, they claimed'. Colonising refers to a process where a foreign settler creates a new colony in a new land and, over time, takes away the livelihood and suppresses the identities of many native peoples (Smith 1999; Chilisa 2009; Cram 2009), and this has resulted in significant loss of culture and ways of life impacting on the health and well-being of local people (Bartlett *et al.* 2007; Cram 2009). Smith (2008: 126) says that in the process of colonisation 'something gets lost'. The 'something lost' for indigenous peoples includes 'indigenous knowledge and culture'.

Rey Chow (1993) terms this 'something lost' as 'endangered authenticities'. Smith (2008: 126) puts it thus:

In biological terms, the 'something lost' is our diversity; in sociolinguistics, it is the diversity of minority languages; culturally, it is our uniqueness of stories and experiences and how they are expressed.

Linda Tuhiwai Smith (1999, 2008) and Beth Swadener and Kagendo Mutua (2008) argue that through the refusal to recognise non-Western perspectives as 'legitimate knowledge', the colonial research traditions have made cultural knowledge silent (see Sandoval 2000; Subedi 2007; Cram 2009). This is referred to as the 'methodology of imperialism' by Edward Said (1995: 21). To counteract this hegemony, the perspectives of indigenous people must be 'adopted and valorized in the research process' (Bartlett *et al.* 2007: 2372). Indigenous researchers such as Linda Tuhiwai Smith (1999, 2008), Fiona Cram (2009) and Bonnie Duran and Eduardo Duran (2000) call for decolonising methodology to recognise and undo the damage caused by the colonial authority. Decolonising methodology, Smith (2008: 117) suggests, requires 'the unmasking and deconstruction of imperialism, and its aspect of colonialism, in its old and new formation alongside a search for sovereignty; for reclamation of knowledge, language, and culture; and for the social transformation of the colonial relations between the native and the settler'.

Decolonising methodology questions colonial models of understanding the indigenous reality and 'challenges dominant modern methods of knowing and reinforces Indigenous identity and discourse' (Habashi 2005: 771). This methodology accepts indigenous standpoints, processes and ways of learning and knowing (Smith 1999; Bartlett *et al.* 2007; Brooks *et al.* 2008; Vannini & Gladue 2008; Cram 2009). It aims to create research which allows for indigenous self-determination. As Julie Kaomea (2004: 43) says: 'Indigenous research should be about healing and empowerment. It should involve the return of dignity and the restoration of sovereignty, and it should ultimately bring formerly colonized communities one step further along the path to self-determination.'

Decolonising methodology is guided by the values, knowledge and research of indigenous people (Smith 1999; Bartlett *et al.* 2007; Prior 2007; Cram 2009). Therefore, the methodology can begin to address the suspicion and harm that previous research has created in indigenous communities. Decolonising discourse assists in developing trust in the researcher and the researched relationship through respect, reciprocation, collaboration and cooperation throughout the research (Prior, 2007; Brooks *et al.* 2008; Vannini & Gladue 2008; Cram 2009).

Thus, decolonising methodology attempts to change research practices which have damaged indigenous communities in the past. Rather than accepting traditional scientific methodology and research, from design to dissemination, the methodology deconstructs research to reveal hidden biases (Brooks *et al.* 2008). This methodology strives to empower indigenous communities and respect their culture and traditions (Brooks *et al.* 2008). To impart a decolonising methodology to the research, the voices of indigenous researchers, those who live and work in indigenous communities, are privileged (Bartlett *et al.* 2007; Cram 2009).

Methodologically speaking, traditional positivist research has often denied the agency of indigenous (colonised) populations. This has led to methodological resistance among decolonising researchers. Norman Denzin and colleagues (2008a: 11) say this clearly: 'Indigenists resist the positivist and postpositivist methodologies of Western science because these formations are too frequently used to validate colonizing knowledge about indigenous peoples.' Instead, decolonising researchers advocate 'interpretive strategies and skills fitted to the needs, languages, and traditions of their respective indigenous community. These strategies emphasize personal performance narratives and testimonies.' Thus, the use of qualitative research inquiry and more innovative methods are promoted in decolonising methodology (see Bartlett *et al.* 2007; Bishop 2008; Brooks *et al.* 2008; Smith 2008; Vannini & Gladue 2008).

Importantly, Judith Bartlett *et al.* (2007: 2376) contend, community-based participatory action research (PAR) is an important method within the framework of the decolonising methodology. The principle of PAR makes it likely that the research process and its outcomes will be more related to and beneficial for indigenous individuals and communities. The research process and sequences also provide empowerment among those individuals involved (Park 2006; Reason & Bradbury 2006a; Brooks *et al.* 2008; Conrad & Campbell 2008; Kemmis & McTaggart 2008).

Decolonising methodology also allows collaboration among the native researchers themselves and with outside researchers. Within decolonising research, Beth Swadener and Kagendo Mutua (2008: 31) contend, 'the possibilities of forging cross-cultural partnerships with, between, and among indigenous researchers and "allied others" and working collaboratively on common goals that reflect anticolonial sensibilities in action are important facets of decolonization'. Collaboration with others requires that decolonising researchers 'acknowledge and interrogate theories that inform our research agendas and the ethical and moral issues embedded in them as part of making this a reality' (Jankie 2004: 101–102). More importantly, it requires that research is carried out in ways which are sensitive and culturally appropriate for both the research participants and the decolonising researcher.

Indigenous and postcolonial (decolonising) researchers are part of a 'cacophony of subaltern voices' (Gandhi 1998). Such subaltern voices, Swadener and Mutua (2008: 39) remind us, speak many languages and communicate through oral storytelling, song, poetry, dance and rituals. These voices make use of 'performative styles' which reflect a wide range of 'indigenous epistemologies that go far beyond prevailing Western academic styles and venues for dissemination'. Such subaltern voices reject 'external definitions of what is of worth', and often mirror 'relational versus individualistic constructions of human beings and other creatures'. As such, decolonising methodology supports the use of alternative and performative styles such as storytelling, narratives, music, drama and art 'as vehicles of growing resistance to Western, neoconservative, and positivist paradigms' (p. 41).

Decolonising methodology, according to Swadener and Mutua, does not only apply to researching 'exclusively in contexts where the geopolitical experience of colonization happened, but indeed among groups where colonizing research approaches are deployed' (p. 35). To them, decolonising methodology applies to those who are non-Western, marginalised people such as those living in poverty and ethnic minority groups. Decolonising methodology offers indigenous cultural ways of undertaking research for other researchers (Bartlett *et al.* 2007). For Julie Kaomea (2004: 43): 'We should think on these factors as they apply to our own research, and if and when we decide to proceed, we should do so humbly, in an effort to serve.' This is the stance that I am advocating in this book.

Kaupapa Māori research methodology

Kaupapa Māori research methodology sits neatly within the framework of decolonising methodology. Kaupapa Māori research has emerged from a broader movement by Māoris to question the Westernised frameworks of culture, knowledge and research (Smith 1999, 2008; Walker *et al.* 2006; Bishop 2008; Carpenter & McMurchy-Pilkington 2008; Cram 2009). Kaupapa Māori research has been adopted as a form of resistance to positivist biomedical science as well as a methodological framework which emphasises that research is initiated, managed and undertaken by Māoris, and the end results are to benefit Māori people. Kaupapa Māori research aims to promote the self-determination of Māori people (Smith 1999, 2008; Walker *et al.* 2006; Bishop 2008; Cram 2009).

Kaupapa Māori research is referred to as research by Māori, for Māori and with Māori people (Walker *et al.* 2006: 333; see also G. Smith 1999; Pihama *et al.* 2002; Bishop 2008; Cram 2009). Kaupapa Māori research, Russell Bishop (2008: 152) asserts, is 'collectivistic and is oriented toward benefiting all the research participants and their collectively determined agendas, defining and acknowledging Māori aspirations for research, while developing and implementing Māori theoretical and methodological preferences and practices for research'.

Shayne Walker and colleagues (2006: 333) say that as a research strategy, kaupapa Māori research is concerned with 'Māori ownership of knowledge', and acknowledges 'the validity of a Māori way of doing'. It is suggested that kaupapa Māori research can be seen as 'a paradigm, a form of resistance and agency, and a methodological strategy' (Walker *et al.* 2006: 333; see also Smith 1999; Barnes 2000; Gibbs 2001; Bishop 2008; Cram 2009). However, according to Walker *et al.* (2006: 333), kaupapa Māori research embraces the following salient features:

- it fully recognises the 'cultural values and systems' of Māori people;
- it provides a strategic ground to challenge 'dominant Pakeha (non-Māori) construction of research';
- it defies 'the assumptions, values, key ideas, and priorities of research';
- it warrants that Māori people 'maintain conceptual, methodological, and interpretive control over research';
- it is a philosophical and strategic framework which 'guides Māori research and ensures that Māori protocol will be followed during research processes' (see Bishop 1996; Smith 1999; Cram 2001; Powick 2003; Cram 2009).

To Smith (1999), kaupapa Māori research aims for emancipation and empowerment. Hence, it can be seen as a 'localized critical theory' that permits kaupapa Māori researchers to resist 'dominant, racist, and westernized hegemonies' as well as to argue for 'Māori to become more self-determining' (Walker *et al.* 2006: 333). Kaupapa Māori research is 'based on the assumption that research that involves Māori peoples, as individuals or as communities, should set out to make a positive difference for the researched' (Smith 1999: 191; see also Aspin & Hutchings 2007; Bishop 2008; Cram 2009).

Methodologically, according to Walker *et al.* (2006: 336), data collection methods in kaupapa Māori research are not specifically fixed for Māoris. However, qualitative research methods including oral histories, narratives, in-depth interviews and focus groups sit neatly within 'a Māori way of doing'. Bishop (2008: 159) also suggests that the approaches adopted by kaupapa Māori research are similar to participatory action research, which has emerged 'more or less deliberately as forms of resistance to conventional research practices that were perceived by particular kinds of participants as acts of colonization' (Kemmis & McTaggart 2003: 345, 2008; see also Smith 1999, 2008; Cram 2009). The emphasis of PAR is on 'self-emancipation' (Bishop 2008: 159). This, too, is the focus of kaupapa Māori research.

There are several research projects which are based on kaupapa Māori research methodology. Here, I shall provide some discussions on the work of Edwards and colleagues as an example.

Māori researchers have begun to challenge the way in which research had unfavourably compared Māori with non-Māori people, which has resulted in deficit-based approaches to seeing Māori (Bishop 1996; Powick 2003; Edwards *et al.* 2005; Carpenter & McMurchy-Pilkington 2008). For example, research regarding sudden infant death syndroms (SIDS) among Māori infants has been undertaken to compare Māori with non-Māori infants. Māori babies are 3.81 times more likely to die of SIDS than non-Māori. The high risks among Māori infants are reported to be due to several factors: higher rates of maternal smoking, prone sleeping position, co-sleeping and bottle feeding (see Mitchell *et al.* 1991; Scragg *et al.* 1993, 1995). Because of the higher rates of SIDS among Māori babies, Māori parents have been marginalised through their ways of life. The cot death prevention campaign, which went against bed sharing, was undertaken in New Zealand in 1991. The campaign was not only unpopular among Māori people, it also had great ramifications for the promotion of other aspects of SIDS prevention in Māori communities (Tipene-Leach *et al.* 1999; Abel *et al.* 2001). The inherent message of the research findings and health promotion to reduce SIDS suggests that Māori parents (read mothers here) are to be blamed for their cultural practices. As Māoris will continue to experience disproportionately high rates of SIDS, they will continue to be pathologised by positivist science.

The lack of progress in reducing the rate of SIDS among Māori infants has led to the development of Māori-led research at the University of Auckland. It was seen that Māori understanding and experiences regarding childrearing, grief and life course, which could have great implications for advancing knowledge and the prevention of SIDS, have not been given enough attention (McCreanor *et al.* 2004; Edwards *et al.* 2005). Shane Edwards and colleagues (2005: 92) undertook kaupapa Māori research to examine the experiences and worldviews of Māori SIDS parents (MSP), caregivers and whânau (extended family). It was a collaborative, qualitative approach carried out by the MSP team and Māori university researchers. Within this research, life stories are gathered on the contexts within which Māori SIDS occurred from Māori parents (mainly mothers). They are seen as the 'neglected holders of experiential data'. The project privileges the oral stories 'as testimony that gives voice to marginalised experiences' (Edwards *et al.* 2005: 92). This is in contrast to those positivist research projects that I mentioned earlier on.

Clive Aspin and Jessica Hutchings (2007: 421) point to the issue of Māori sexuality within the colonising gaze, that the traditional perceptions and understandings of Māori sexuality 'have become blurred, misinterpreted or lost completely' because of 'the imposition of a colonialist view of sexuality'. Aspin and Hutchings undertook the Māori Sexuality Project in New Zealand, and the data gathered from this project are very important because they do not only represent the understandings of different individuals within the Māori community, but they 'serve to refute some of the narrow views of sexuality that have developed since the onset of colonisation over two hundred years ago' (p. 416). Aspin and Hutchings say: 'Sexual cultures of indigenous societies throughout the world have been subjugated by colonising influences that have assumed that non-Western forms of sexual expression were somehow inferior to those that the colonisers brought with them' (p. 421).

The project is based on kaupapa Māori research methodology. By positioning Māori at the centre of the research, Aspin and Hutchings tell us that the findings would yield 'a more accurate and appropriate reflection of Māori views than an approach that depended on non-Māori views of the world' (p. 416). Through the use of culturally appropriate research methods employed in kaupapa Māori research, accurate information about issues which are more relevant to, and of great concern to, Māori people are more likely to be discovered. The findings of a kaupapa Māori research project would be better understood and adopted by Māori communities, as 'they are more likely to have a beneficial impact on the health and well-being of the Māori community'.

It is clear that kaupapa Māori research provides a paradigm which offers 'new ways of asking, seeing, and doing' (Walker *et al.* 2006: 342). It can remedy some of the past damage that has occurred to Māori people. Kaupapa Māori research has also helped the Māori people to restore their faith in research. Māoris have begun to have more trust in Māori researchers, and they can see that kaupapa Māori research can result in beneficial outcomes for Māori people (Walsh-Tapiata 2003; Walker *et al.* 2006; Cram 2009). According to Walker *et al.* (2006), the principle of kaupapa

Māori research can also be adopted to other indigenous peoples in a global context.

Tutorial activities

You are a PhD student who intends to undertake your research with a minority group in your local area or country. You are interested in how these people deal with racism and discrimination in their everyday lives. You wish to know how these issues impact on their personal lives and families. You also want to ensure that the results of your research will provide benefits to these people. How will you design your research? What methodological and theoretical frameworks will you be selecting to ensure that you can do this project appropriately and sensitively?

Chapter summary

Doing cross-cultural or cross-national work in neo-colonial settings presents many ethical and methodological dilemmas, particularly when there is a conscious attempt to decolonize the research. (Swadener & Mutua 2008: 35)

Cross-cultural research has become hugely important in this postmodern world, where many people have been, and still are, marginalised and vulnerable to others in more powerful positions, such as colonial researchers. In this chapter, I have suggested that qualitative research is particularly appropriate for cross-cultural projects because it allows us to find answers which are more relevant to the research participants. I have also provided a different theoretical framework that cross-cultural researchers may adopt. By now, as readers may have realised, most methodological frameworks I have proposed are based on love, compassion, reciprocity, respect for culture and people's dignity, and a call for collaborative efforts with local people. They are methodologies that will allow us to see the world through the eyes of the research participants. They are methodologies that will ensure that our research products provide benefit to the participants instead of harming them.

Performing qualitative cross-cultural research is exciting but, as I shall show in the chapters that follow, it is also full of ethical and methodological challenges. It is crucial that we, as qualitative researchers, speak out loudly about the challenges and rewards that we come across in our research endeavours, and continue to do so, so that new researchers and students can learn from our experiences. This is my intention in this book.

This volume will encourage readers to start and continue to perform qualitative research in cross-cultural settings. I hope that it will be useful for many of you in the field.

We all have the power to listen to 'voices' that are seldom heard. If we choose to make the time, to learn, to listen and to struggle with the pain and frustration that disempowered people feel, we will see new visions, feel new energy and find hope in our future. (Pearpoint 1989: 503)

SUGGESTED READING

Bartlett, J. G., Iwasaki, Y., Gottlieb, B., Hall, D., & Mannell, R. (2007). Framework for Aboriginal-guided decolonizing research involving Métis and First Nations persons with diabetes. *Social Science and Medicine* **65**(11), 2371–2382.

Bishop, R. (2008). Freeing ourselves from neocolonial domination in research: A kaupapa Māori approach to creating knowledge. In N. K. Denzin & Y. S. Lincoln (Eds.), *The landscape of qualitative research,* 3rd edition (pp. 145–183). Thousand Oaks, CA: Sage Publications.

Cram, F. (2009). Maintaining indigenous voices. In D. M. Martens & P. E. Ginsberg (Eds.), *The handbook of social research ethics* (pp. 308–322). Thousand Oaks, CA: Sage Publications.

Davies, B., Larson, J., Contro, N., Reyes-Hailey, C., Ablin, A. R., Chesla, C. A., Sourkes, B., & Cohen, H. (2009). Conducting a qualitative culture study of pediatric palliative care. *Qualitative Health Research* **19**(1), 5–16.

Dillard, C. B. (2008). When the ground is black, the ground is fertile: Exploring endarkened feminist epistemology and healing methodologies in the spirit. In N. K. Denzin, Y. S. Lincoln, & L. T. Smith (Eds.), *Handbook of critical and indigenous methodologies* (pp. 277–292). Thousand Oaks, CA: Sage Publications.

Harrison, E. V. (Ed.) (1991). *Decolonizing anthropology: Moving further toward an anthropology for liberation*. Washington, DC: Association for Black Anthropologists, American Anthropological Association.

Liamputtong, P. (2007). *Researching the vulnerable: A guide to sensitive research methods.* London: Sage Publications.

(2009). *Qualitative research methods,* 3rd edition. Melbourne: Oxford University Press.

Mkabela, Q. (2005). Using the Afrocentric method in researching indigenous African culture. *The Qualitative Report* **10**(1), 178–189.

Sandoval, C. (2000). *Methodology of the oppressed: Theory out of bounds*. Minneapolis: University of Minnesota Press.

Smith, L. T. (1999). *Decolonising methodologies: Research and indigenous peoples*. London and Dunedin: Zed Books and University of Otago Press.

(2008). On tricky ground: Researching the native in the age of uncertainty. In N. K. Denzin & Y. S. Lincoln (Eds.), *The landscape of qualitative research,* 3rd edition (pp. 113–143). Thousand Oaks, CA: Sage Publications.

Swadener, B. B., & Mutua, K. (2008). Decolonizing performances: Deconstructing the global postcolonial. In N. K. Denzin, Y. S. Lincoln, & L. T. Smith (Eds.), *Handbook of critical and indigenous methodologies* (pp. 31–43). Thousand Oaks, CA: Sage Publications.

Tillman, L. C. (2006). Researching and writing from an African-American perspective: Reflective notes on three research studies. *International Journal of Qualitative Studies in Education* **19**(3), 265–287.

Walker, S., Eketone, A., & Gibbs, A. (2006). An exploration of kaupapa Māori research, its principles, processes and applications. *International Journal of Social Research Methodology* **9**(4), 331–344.

Wallace, S. A. (2006). Addressing health disparities through relational ethics: An approach to increasing African American participation in biomedical and health research. In J. E. Trimble & C. B. Fisher (Eds.), *The handbook of ethical research with ethnocultural populations and communities* (pp. 67–75). Thousand Oaks, CA: Sage Publications.

2 Moral and ethical perspectives

Many shameful events in the history of clinical research testify to the ease with which researcher-participants have exploited the vulnerability of oppressed or devalued members of society for the ultimate benefit of others.

(Baylis *et al.* 1998: 244)

The principle that underlies problems of ethics is respecting the humanity of others as one would have others respect one's own. If field [researchers] genuinely feel such respect for others, they are not likely to get into serous trouble. But if they do not feel such respect, then no matter how scrupulously they follow the letter of the written codes of professional ethics, or follow the recommended procedures of field [research] manuals, they will betray themselves all along the line in the little things.

(Goodenough 1980: 52)

Ethics is a set of moral principles that aim to prevent research participants from being harmed by the researcher and the research process. Ethical and moral responsibility is essential in any research, but when it comes to cross-cultural research it is even more important, as the researchers deal with individuals who have been exploited, who are more marginalised and vulnerable in so many ways. Often, they are people living in poverty, who do not have enough education to deal with the formality of research, and who feel too powerless to express their concerns or to resist the power of researchers. If we look at the history of research in this world, and I shall point out some examples later on, we will see that the researchers must be more responsible when they perform cross-cultural research. It is crucial that researchers take their ethical responsibilities seriously (Israel & Hay 2006; Liamputtong 2007a).

In this chapter, I shall discuss some crucial issues regarding ethical and moral perspectives in performing cross-cultural research. I first introduce some general discussions on those ethical and moral issues which have been debated in literature. I then move on to present some historical examples of research which has exploited many individuals and communities. Issues relating to ethical principles and informed consent are then presented. I finish the chapter with some discussions on the risk and harm which may befall cross-cultural researchers themselves.

Ethical and moral issues: introduction

Researchers have questioned the ethical and moral conduct of researchers in cross-cultural settings (Macklin 2004; Marshall & Batten 2004; Smith 2008). Some of the major concerns regarding cross-cultural research include exploitation, damage of the community group and the reporting of inaccurate research findings (Freimuth *et al.* 2001; Leaning 2001; Corbie-Smith *et al.* 2002; Macklin 2004; Fisher & Ragsdale 2006; Shah 2006; Wallace 2006; Bishop 2008; Kissell 2008; Smith 2008). Although these moral issues can be applicable to people in general, individuals from different cultural settings may be affected more due to many complicated historical, political, social and cultural agendas (Mulder *et al.* 2000; Freimuth *et al.* 2001; Macklin 2004; Birman 2006; Smith 2008; Barata *et al.* 2006; Kissell 2008). For example, Dina Birman (2006) points to the ethical and moral issues in research involving undocumented immigrants in the US, and that these people may be identified by the authorities because of their involvement in research. This can lead to their prosecution and deportation.

The question is then: Is it ethically and morally just that researchers should include these people in their research? When embarking on any cross-cultural research, but particularly on research concerning historically marginalised groups, Joy Adamson and Jenny Donovan (2002: 822) argue that the most important thing that researchers need to question is the relevance of their research to the cultural groups and its likely outcomes. Research can only be justified if the outcome will benefit the community rather than further damaging it (Benatar & Singer 2000; Leaning 2001; Macklin 2004; Smith 2008).

In some cases, the researchers may have to weigh the potential harm to individual participants against the possible benefits which may apply to a larger group of people or communities. Lisa Fontes (1998) tells us that one Indian researcher decided not to pursue the experiences of women who had been burned by their husbands because of dowry disputes. She did not wish to cause further risk to the women. However, according to Fontes, there were costs relating to the decision of this researcher. It prohibited a 'possibility that the women interviewed – and women like them – might benefit from an end to their isolation and vulnerability' (Israel & Hay 2006: 108). But I query whether the results of this Indian researcher would really help the majority of Indian women to end their miseries from their husbands. This is an ethical issue that we need to carefully examine.

Ethical issues: historical perspective

I shall begin my discussion on ethical considerations by referring to several historical records of abuse in research. There have been many research experiments that were clearly instances of the abuse of other human beings. The message that emerged from these experiments was a distrust of the values and ethics of medicine and science.

African Americans have had to endure many negative experiences with health research. Scyatta Wallace (2006: 68) bluntly says that, 'medical and scientific history in the United States has a dark past when it comes to the professions' involvement in and support for racist social institutions. Theories developed by the medical and scientific community were used to perpetuate stereotypes proposing the racial inferiority of African Americans. These scientific theories and studies were often used as justification for the mistreatment and misuse of African Americans during slavery periods' (see also Guthrie 1998). Too often, slaves were used as the subjects of medical experiments. Dr J. Marion Sims, the father of modern gynaecology, for example, used slave women for his experiments to develop an operation to repair vesicovaginal fistulas between 1845 and 1849. Without anaesthesia, these women were between them subjected to thirty painful and dangerous operations. Disturbingly, it was only after the experiments with the slave women were successful that he started the procedure with anaesthesia on white women volunteers (Gamble 1997; Wallace 2006).

But the most famous exploitative research project that people from minority groups have had to deal with is the Tuskegee syphilis study. This was a forty-year research study sponsored by the US Public Health Service. Beginning in 1932, researchers examined untreated syphilis among rural black men in Alabama. In this study, 399 African-American men infected with syphilis were used as research subjects, and 201 as a control group. The men were not told that they had syphilis, nor were they offered appropriate treatment. Thus, potential sexual partners were left unprotected. The men were never asked to give their consent to participation in the study (Trimble & Fisher 2006a). In fact, they were deceived by being told that they were recruited for the treatment of their 'bad blood' (Jones 1993). Before the advent of penicillin, the men were inexplicably given only about half of the then usual dose of medication. By the early 1940s, when penicillin had become the standard treatment for syphilis, the men were still denied effective treatment. The study was initiated before the Nuremberg Code, so it was not subjected to any 'ethical' review. No informed consent was received from the subjects (Gray 1998). The study lasted for more than forty years and was terminated only in 1972. It was only because the details of the study were picked up by the media in the 1970s that the experiment was stopped.

The risks of untreated syphilis, and later the benefits of penicillin, were simply not discussed with the men in the study. These black men were clearly denied the specific information required to make informed risk–benefit analysis (Heintzelman 1996; Gray 1998; Freimuth *et al.* 2001). By the time this study was stopped, at least twenty-eight of the men had died from untreated syphilis (Jones 1993; Heintzelman 1996; Freimuth *et al.* 2001). It was also estimated that as many as 161 may have died because of their untreated syphilis (Chin *et al.* 2006).

The purpose of this experiment was to confirm research results on the long-term effects of untreated syphilis. This study clearly showed the racist attitudes and behaviours of white researchers towards African Americans (Heintzelman 1996; Hesse-Biber & Leavy 2005). No doubt the Tuskegee syphilis study, as Joseph Trimble and Celia Fisher (2006a: xviii) point out, is 'one of many instances in which scientists have exploited historically oppressed groups, ostensibly to advance an understanding of the human condition'. Indeed, the name 'Tuskegee' has become a 'code word' for the exploitation of individuals who are poor and helpless for the benefit of those who are in power and who would not tolerate such treatment if it happened to them (Kissell 2008: 331).

This study is a graphic example of research that today would be considered unethical. Whatever the potential benefits to the wider community, the way the studies were carried out was clearly harmful to the participants. The men concerned had little opportunity to make an informed decision as to whether or not they would take part in these studies. Indeed, as Marcia Angell (1997: 847) puts it, 'they were deliberately deceived'. They were also denied treatment and as a result many of them died or were severely affected.

As a result of this history of abuse and exploitation that I have outlined above, there have been numerous important developments in international and national guidelines. The Nuremberg Code, established in 1947, was the first international code of ethics set up to protect people from research abuse (Greig *et al.* 2007; Miller & Boulton 2007). Other codes of agreement include the World Medical Association's Declaration of Helsinki in 1964 and the Belmont Report in 1979 (Israel & Hay 2006). In addition, the Council for International Organisations of Medical Sciences (CIOMS) was established in 1949 for researchers working in developing countries (Beyrer & Kass

2002). There are also the International Ethical Guidelines for Biomedical Research Involving Human Subjects (Greig *et al.* 2007; Miller & Boulton 2007; Carpenter & Suto 2008). Nowadays, there are committees established worldwide whose aims are to protect research participants: the Institutional Review Boards (IRBs) in the US; the National Research Ethics Service, formerly referred to as the Central Office for Research Ethics Committees, in the UK; the Medical Research Council of Canada's Tri-Council Policy Statement for the Ethical Conduct for Research Involving Humans; and the Human Research Ethics Committees (HRECs) and the Australian Health Ethics Committee (Israel & Hay 2006; Miller & Boulton 2007; Carpenter & Suto 2008). The new codes were developed so that potential participants in any research project would have the right to know what was required of them. They would also need to be informed of the actual consequences of their participation. Under the new codes, potential research participants must formally agree to their participation.

One would like to believe that all these codes would prevent any more exploitation and abuse of human beings in research. I certainly hope so. But some more recent research projects have not proved this. This is particularly so for clinical and drug trials research. The use of non-Western women as 'guinea pigs' in medical research – that is without a sound ethical base and without informed consent – has also been a problem and serious harm has resulted (see Liamputtong & Dwyer 2003; Macklin 2004; Shah 2006). The original testing of oral contraceptives with unsuspecting Puerto Rican women was an example of 'blatant disregard for women', particularly impoverished non-white women (Ruzek 1978: 44). As recently as 1970, Joseph Goldzieher, a gynaecologist at the Southwest Foundation for Research and Education in San Antonio, and his colleagues conducted a double-blind experiment on the side effects of birth control pills among poor Mexican-American women (see Goldzieher *et al.* 1971a, 1971b). They were interested in testing whether depression and nervousness were side effects of oral contraceptives. The women were recruited when they came to the clinic for contraceptives. They were told neither of the experiment, nor that some of them would receive a placebo rather than a contraceptive. Four months later, eleven of the seventy-six women (ten while on placebo) became pregnant (Seaman 1972; Stevens & Pletsch 2002).

This kind of abuse also occurs in the Third World. Norplant studies, for example, were conducted without informed consent on women in Bangladesh, Sri Lanka, the Philippines, the Dominican Republic, Chile and Nigeria (Hamilton 1996). The experimental AIDS vaccine was tested in high-risk groups of women in the Third World, including prostitutes in Thailand (Hamilton 1996).

A more recent study that is seen as another disturbing example of abuse and deception by the research team is the clinical trials of the anti-retroviral drug zidovudine (AZT) in developing countries where most people were poor and had no access to medical care. In 1994, a large randomised trial study had been conducted in France and the United States and it was reported that the 076 regime of AZT was able to reduce HIV transmission from mother to child (Connor *et al.* 1994). However, this therapy was prohibitively expensive; it was estimated at $800 per patient (Orentlicher 2002). This meant that many poor women, and particularly those in resource-poor countries, would not be able to access the treatment. In response to this, other researchers carried out studies that involved a less aggressive, less expensive course of AZT treatment in order to test if it would also decrease the risk of HIV transmission from mother to child. These studies involved pregnant women and they were put into two groups: one received the less aggressive treatment, the other received a placebo (Orentlicher 2002). However, this type of study was prohibited by US government regulations from being undertaken in the United States. As the drug has been known to be effective, the use of placebos in such trials was not permitted. Hence, the researchers carried out their studies in developing countries, mainly in Africa, where HIV/AIDS had become epidemic and where the provision of expensive AZT therapy (which was available in the United States) could not be made. In one study, according to Schensul and Le Compte (1999: 186–187), the researchers recruited their participants by suggesting to the women who had just been tested for pregnancy and HIV infection that their participation in the study 'could help their baby remain healthy'. Most of the women who consented to participate expressed their concerns later on that 'they were too confused and frightened at their diagnosis – and at finding out simultaneously that they were to become mothers – to understand clearly what the study was about. Most – even those in the control group – believed that they were receiving real drug therapy'.

The researchers who conducted trials in poor countries were heavily criticised for two reasons: 'for implementing in a poor, nonwhite country a study that they could not have done in their own country, and for not obtaining truly "informed" consent from the participants' (Schensul & Le Compte 1999: 187; see also Lurie & Wolfe 1997; Levine 1998; De Zulueta 2001; Orentlicher 2002). Their critics asked an ethical and moral question: Why should researchers carry out research in poor countries which would have been unethical in the United States (Orentlicher 2002: 404)?

Other researchers also critiqued these studies on the grounds that they were experimental research and the outcomes would only benefit developed countries. Although the less aggressive therapy would be much less expensive than the more aggressive one, it would still be too expensive for the local people who resided in the countries where the AZT trials took place and who were also in desperate need of the therapy. David Orentlicher (2002: 404) points out that, 'under such circumstances, the research subjects were assuming the risks of research solely for the benefit of people living in developed countries, a situation that clearly constitutes exploitation' (see also De Zulueta 2001). Accurately, Marcia Angell (1997: 848) points out, the justifications of the AZT trials are 'reminiscent of those for the Tuskegee study'.

What are the implications of these clinical trials for the health and well-being of women in Third World countries? Is it an abuse of human (women's) rights? Or is it just another ethnocentric view that the women of the poorer nations are not worth as much as those in the Western world? See the recent writings of Ruth Macklin (2004) and Sonia Shah (2006) for clinical trails in poor nations which, for many sensitive cross-cultural researchers, would be seen as unethical and abusive.

Primum non nocere – first do no harm

> Ethical research should not only 'do no harm', but also have potential 'to do good', to involve 'empowerment'. (Madge 1997: 114)

The principle of *primum non nocere* (first do no harm) has now become an accepted ethic in all research disciplines. When undertaking research that involves ethnic minority people, Nancy Busch-Rossnagel (2006) contends, researchers must keep the aim of 'first, do no harm' in mind at all steps of the research process: from the selection of the methodology through the data collection process and the dissemination of the research findings. However, Svetlana Shklarov (2007: 533) suggests that 'the interpretation of what is harm and for whom, and the decisions on what procedures should be employed to avoid harm, remain culture specific and context related'. She warns us that harm and strategies to avoid harm can be different in different cultural contexts. Hence, researchers must be vigilant about harm that may befall their participants in cross-cultural research.

Researchers have a responsibility to ensure the physical, emotional and social well-being of their research participants. Researchers must ensure that they will not be adversely affected by participating in their research (Sin

2005: 279). As Margaret Melrose (2002: 343) contends, 'researchers have a duty to ensure that no harm comes to their subjects, whatever their ages, as a result of their agreement to participate in research. If we cannot guarantee that such participation may improve their lives, we must ensure, at least, that our scrutiny of them does not leave them worse off.'

Conducting research may lead to unintentional danger to the participants (Sin 2005; Liamputtong 2007a). Hence, special attention needs to be paid to risks to the participants throughout the research processes. By taking part in our research, some participants may have to deal with the consequences of our research actions as well as with the disclosure and publishing of our research findings (Carter 2004; Sin 2005; Liamputtong 2007a). For example, in research with pulmonary tuberculosis (TB) patients in northern Thailand conducted by Jintana Ngamvithayapong-Yanai and colleagues (2005), one potential participant refused to take part as she was afraid that she would lose her employment at a restaurant if her TB became known to her employer through a research publication or any other means.

In his study in Brazil, Patrick Peritore (1990) interviewed members of the Communist Party and found that his participants were subsequently re-interviewed by security forces. Hammed Shahidian (2001: 59), in his study of Iranian underground political activists in exile, contends that his study was sensitive as 'it reveals information that could be potentially harmful to (former) activists'. In the course of undertaking his study, Shahidian was concerned about 'the danger potentially caused by revealing sensitive information'. During the interviews, the participants disclosed 'information regarding networking in prison, preparation for smuggling out of and into countries, and mechanisms that refugees have developed to deal with various institutions in host countries such as immigration or welfare offices'. Shahidian realised that by the time he published his work, the data would be too old to cause any threat to the participants. However, he argues, 'there was no guarantee that all people involved would be out of danger before publication. Political prisoners were particularly concerned.' Therefore, Shahidian omitted or kept to an absolute minimum many details to protect his participants. As I suggested earlier, researchers have advocated that we must make sure that what we find in our study will not further marginalise our participants.

John Carter (2004), in his research on the experiences of ethnic minority nurses in the UK, found that many people were extremely cautious about talking to him about their views of the impact of the equal opportunities policy within their organisation. Carter points out that, when researching topics where participants are likely to reveal sensitive information, it is crucial that the researchers make sure that the participants are 'protected from the possible negative consequences' of their participation in the research (p. 349). To Carter, 'the standard research practice is to make data from interviews anonymous. However, in some cases, the highly individual nature of biographical material may mean that the data are unusable if the identity of the respondent is to be successfully protected.' For this reason, in his research, Carter tells us that there were many interviews that he could not use in the final published findings.

This was also my experience in my research with Hmong people in Australia (see Liamputtong Rice 2000). The Hmong culture adheres to beliefs and practices regarding shamanic healing rituals. During the course of my research, I was asked not to write about certain aspects of Hmong rituals, as to do so could harm the cultural integrity of the community. Consequently, when I was writing up my findings, I did not elaborate on some issues in any great depth. My ethical dilemma was that it might be suggested by some colleagues that my description of Hmong rituals lack depth, but I chose to adhere to my moral obligation to the community.

Apart from physical and social harm, psychological and emotional distress can also happen to the participants in cross-cultural research. As Chih Hoong Sin (2005: 279) points out, 'the experience of participating in research may cause some participants to feel disturbed and anxious. It may also give rise to uncalled for self-knowledge with adverse psychological implications.' In Sin's study on social networks and social support amongst older ethnic groups in Britain, one woman disclosed that her son was in jail and her daughters had suffered mental illnesses. She talked about her sense of guilt, hopelessness and depression and blamed herself for the problems that her children had. During the interview, she broke down many times and shed tears. This has also happened in my own research with refugee women in Australia. In the course of our conversations, painful memories of their lives in their home countries, difficult journeys when they tried to escape and harsh lives in refugee camps brought tears from many women. I, too, often cried with them.

One of the ethical considerations in conducting research is the well-being of the participants. Researchers have to be sure not to cause harm to those who agree to take part in the study. However, sometimes the researchers may do the wrong thing out of their ignorance. The following is an example. In a small-scale society such as the Hmong, individuals rely heavily on traditional healers. Some people may become healers by the wish of supernatural beings, as in the case of shamans. However, other healers, such as medicine women, have to acquire knowledge by learning, and must pay a fee to their teacher. When passing on their healing knowledge, they must also be paid. This payment is to honour the teacher who passes on the knowledge. Without it, a medicine woman may become seriously ill and perhaps die. This is a serious matter in Hmong culture.

In my research, when I interviewed several traditional healers, I had the privilege to interview two medicine women. Because I had learned what I must do to obtain knowledge from medicine women (see Chapter 4), I asked them what particular things I should do to prevent ill health befalling them. I was told to perform certain rituals to honour them. On one occasion, the medicine woman asked for Aus$300 as a fee for learning about Hmong medicines. On another occasion, I had to prepare a bunch of incense sticks tied with a piece of red cloth, $25 cash and a live chicken. I had to kneel in front of the medicine woman's altar and ask her and her 'teacher' to teach me about Hmong herbal medicines. With this ritual, I was then able to acquire the knowledge I needed for the project. Without the knowledge of what must be done before I interviewed the healers, I would have caused ill health or death to some of them. This would have been a disaster for me, as a researcher who had promised not to cause harm to their community, because they still rely on these healers even though they are now in Australia and have more access to Western medicines. A similar practice was carried out when I interviewed a Hmong medicine woman in the northern part of Thailand.

'Cause no harm' applies to how the researchers present their findings, too. In writing their findings, researchers have a moral obligation to not present the participants in a way that readers will be able to identify them. Researchers must ensure that these people or their community will not be easily identified by the research findings (Liamputtong 2007a; Morse 2007; Dickson-Swift *et al.* 2008). In reporting their findings, researchers may adopt different methods to protect the true identity of their research participants. For example, the sites where the research was conducted can be disguised by giving them fictitious names (Hancock 2001; Melrose 2002). When presenting the participants' verbatim explanations, pseudonyms can be used rather than their real names (Hess 2006; Liamputtong 2007a). This is what I have done in my writing, and many other qualitative researchers have also adopted a similar practice.

But we have also seen that the attempts of some researchers can be harmful to the participants. This tends to occur with prevention research, which often involves the collection of data which might be very sensitive. If used inappropriately, this sensitive data could 'reflect negatively on the reputation of the community' (Beauvais 2006: 251). In one unfortunate circumstance, a research team published data which were collected from a community that had experienced a tremendous problem with alcoholism. The community's real name was published with the data. The story was picked up by the national media, and as a result, 'the community experienced severe embarrassment and financial setbacks'. Fred Beauvais contends that, 'Needless to say the interpersonal dynamics in the community were negatively affected, and extreme anger at the author and other community outsiders seeking information resulted' (p. 251). It is his view that, 'before all else we must protect the reputation and integrity of the community' (p. 251). Researchers may write to provide sufficient information to portray the research participants, but they should stop short of anything which might reveal their identities.

Last, I should like to provide a warning from Lynne Brydon (2006: 31–32) about the 'deception' of the researcher. During her eighteen months of fieldwork, Brydon had an opportunity to attend the staple crop cultivation ritual, which is organised only once a year. However, the presence of women of menstruation age is a curse to the gods in whose names the rituals are performed. She was told by the priests that she could attend the ritual if she underwent 'a special dispensation'. This involved 'a journey to a sacred place in the bush, libation pouring and prayer there, and a joyful return to the village with the assurance of a good harvest for the current year'. But at the time, she must not be actually menstruating. Brydon was in fact menstruating, but she decided to go, as she would have missed the special ritual that she had been waiting for all the time of her fieldwork. She took many slides during the ritual so that she could use them with her field notes. But none of the slides she took from the ritual 'worked'. All photos were out of focus: 'every one was blurred and its contents indistinct'. Brydon admits that it was 'the result of my deception! The Western rational social science explanation might be that I was feeling so embarrassed at being there and taking photographs when I had promised that I wouldn't go and pollute the ceremonies, that I did not hold the camera steadily enough to take the photographs, but another part of me suspects that perhaps the gods had something to do with it and I was merely being punished for my unethical behaviour!' (p. 32). So be careful with what you do in your fieldwork – no deception, of course!

Embracing the ethics of care

I wish to promote the 'ethics of care' theorised by Carol Gilligan (1982) for performing qualitative cross-cultural research. Gilligan proposes an ethics of care which emphasises care, compassion and relationships. An ethics of care demands that 'the search for just outcomes to ethical problems takes account of care, compassion, and our interpersonal relationships, and ties to families and groups' (Israel & Hay, 2006: 22). This ethics of care has marked ramifications for the moral and ethical issues in the performing of cross-cultural research. It dictates how the researchers relate to individuals with whom they come into contact during their research and their lives (Israel & Hay 2006).

One ingredient of morality, according to Gilligan (1982), is that individuals have responsibilities towards others. A moral person will be concerned about the well-being and reputation of others (see also Gilligan 2003). Following Gilligan's position, Joseph Trimble and Gerald Mohatt (2006: 333) recommend that researchers must seriously consider framing their research 'around the formation and maintenance of responsible relationships'. They maintain that 'one takes the time to nurture relationships, not merely for the sake of expediting the research and gaining acceptance and trust but because one should care about the welfare and dignity of all people'. One way to do this is by establishing community partnership and collaborative arrangements with the participants.

This principle is critically important in research regarding indigenous people around the world. Due to the fact that most indigenous people have for centuries been exploited, abused and robbed of their knowledge, researchers have the moral responsibility to ensure that indigenous people will not be further marginalised. As Marie Battiste (2008: 503) contends, 'ethical research systems and practices should enable Indigenous nations, peoples, and communities to exercise control over information relating to their knowledge and heritage and to themselves'. Ethical research projects need to be conducted collaboratively with indigenous peoples. Additionally, the researched communities should receive benefit from the opportunities generated by the research, such as training and employment. Battiste writes: 'It is vital that Indigenous peoples have direct input into developing and defining research practices and projects related to them. To act otherwise is to repeat that familiar pattern of decisions being made for Indigenous people by those who presume to know what is best for them' (p. 503). And she means white researchers.

According to Battiste, most research on indigenous peoples is 'contaminated by Eurocentric biases'. Ethical research 'must begin by replacing Eurocentric prejudice with new premises that value diversity' (p. 503). Norman Denzin and colleagues (2008a: 15) call for an indigenous ethical and moral model: 'a collaborative social science research model' which obliges the researchers to be more responsible toward their research participants. This model, according to Denzin *et al.*, emphasises 'personal accountability, caring, the value of individual expressiveness, the capacity for empathy, and the sharing of emotionality' (p. 15). The Māori moral position, for example, 'privileges storytelling, listening, voice, and personal performance narratives'. This moral pedagogy is based on 'an ethic of care and love and personal accountability that honours individual uniqueness and emotionality in dialogue' (p. 14).

The indigenous ethical and moral model promotes 'collaborative, participatory performative inquiry. It forcefully aligns the ethics of research with a politics of the oppressed, with a politics of resistance, hope, and freedom.' The model compels researchers to 'take up moral projects that respect and reclaim indigenous cultural practices'. The end result of this model is the production of 'spiritual, social, and psychological healing'. And healing, in turn, 'leads to multiple forms of transformation at the personal and social levels' (p. 14).

Informed consent in cross-cultural research: a thorny issue!

Informed consent has become a crucial part of cross-cultural research (Israel & Hay, 2006; Trimble & Fisher 2006a; Adams *et al.* 2007). There are many issues regarding informed consent that we need to take into account when performing cross-cultural research. I shall point to some salient issues in this section.

Informed consent, according to Miller and Boulton (2007: 2202), is grounded in the 'ethical principles of respect for the dignity and worth of every human being and their right to self-determination'. Informed consent 'serves as a sign that individual autonomy is respected' (Mani 2006: 6). It must be seen as integral to the research process if a researcher wishes to 'maintain a respectful stance with a participant by viewing individuals as deserving of respect' (Mani 2006: 6; cf. Adams *et al.* 2007; Parker 2007). It is recognised as the chief means of protecting research participants from being harmed and exploited. Informed consent has been defined as 'the provision of information to participants, about the purpose of the research, its procedures, potential risks, benefits, and alternatives, so that the individual understands this information and can make a voluntary decision whether to enrol and continue to participate' (Emanuel *et al.* 2000: 2703). The principle of informed consent, as Jean Chin and colleagues (2006) point out, is based on an assumption that people have enough knowledge and also understanding about the consequences of their participation in a research project, about the procedures being carried out and about potential harm that may come to them.

Obtaining informed consent from participants is now required before conducting any research and, of course, this includes cross-cultural research (Hoeyer *et al.* 2005; Sin 2005; Israel & Hay 2006; Trimble & Fisher 2006a; Mani 2006; Adams *et al.* 2007; Parker 2007; Miller & Boulton 2007; Christians 2008). However, in cross-cultural research, gaining informed consent can sometimes be a challenging task, because 'issues of culture come into play' (Mani 2006: 6). Informed consent can often be difficult for potential participants to understand in any research but, in the case of cross-cultural research, Mani contends that 'it is even more difficult, as cultural differences might emerge regarding the purpose and outcome expectations of research' (p. 6). It is important that the researchers make every effort beforehand to ensure that the research participants have a clear understanding about their engagement in the research. Priya Mani also suggests that 'not having adequate information can result in the participant's having unrealistic expectations regarding how research will be represented' (p. 7). As with any other research participants, those in cross-cultural research also have the right to know about the 'benefits, risks, and limitations associated with research' (see also Wallace 2006; Adams *et al.* 2007).

Informed consent and current practices

In current practice, a signed consent form is required from individual participants (Hoeyer *et al.* 2005; Israel & Hay 2006). However, in certain circumstances and with some cultural and ethnic groups, obtaining a signed consent form can be a challenging task. And in some cases, it can be problematic (Liamputtong Rice, 1996; Wendler & Rackoff 2001; Macklin 2004; Dawson & Kass 2005; Birman 2006; Tindana *et al.* 2006; Adams *et al.* 2007; Smith 2008). It is also a moral and ethical issue, particularly in research concerning ethnic minorities and indigenous people (see Gostin 1995; Smith 1999, 2000, 2008; Barata *et al.* 2006). Linda Tuhiwai Smith (2008: 131) puts it clearly:

One concern of indigenous communities about the informed consent principle is about the bleeding of knowledge away from collective protection through individual participation in research, with knowledge moving to scientists and organizations in the world at large. This process weakens indigenous collectively shared knowledge and is especially risky in an era of knowledge hunting and gathering.

In cross-cultural research, according to Jean Chin and colleagues (2006: 129), language factors play a major role in the construction of informed consent and in the understanding of potential participants (see also Chapter 6 in this volume). In some ethnic minority groups, particularly those who are recent arrivals, according to Trimble and Fisher (2006a: xix), the participants 'may not understand the reason behind the use of consent forms, the technical words and scientific jargon used to describe aspects of the forms, the flow and length of the sentences and paragraph structure, and the implications if they refuse to sign'. These individuals may have to rely heavily on interpreters/translators to make the decision as to whether they wish to take part in a research project. Informed consent may also be 'poorly translated, or not translated, such that the true intent of the study is not known'. This can have a great impact on the well-being and dignity of research participants.

Written consent can be intimidating to many cultural and ethnic groups, particularly those who are doubly vulnerable, like refugees (Fluehr-Lobban 1994, 1998, 2003; Liamputtong Rice 1996; Hennings *et al.* 1996; Birman 2006; Liamputtong 2008). As Hennings and colleagues (1996: 15) argue, 'in a culture where the spoken word is taken as a binding legal contract, to ask for signed consent would be to imply mistrust'. Vicki Freimuth and colleagues (2001: 802) suggest that many African-American participants in their study expressed difficulty understanding the study consent forms. One told them that: 'You sit there and you read it but you don't necessarily understand what you're reading when you sign the paper'. They also thought that signing informed consent was 'signing away your rights', and that the process was done mainly to protect the research team from legal responsibility.

Dina Birman (2006) contends that, for refugees, the promise of anonymous participation is taken away by the need to sign informed consent forms, and that this may create fears about the loss of confidentiality among research participants. Elana Yu and William Liu (1986) had great difficulties in securing informed consent from Vietnamese refugees even though they were willing to participate. Their fears came from their experiences of living under the communist regime in Vietnam. They believed that communist spies would be able to trace them once they signed the document. One participant in Yu and Liu's study asked for the form back from the researcher so that she could destroy it. Another three participants had problems with sleep after signing the form, as they were afraid of the repercussions.

I had a similar problem when I conducted research with Cambodian, Vietnamese and Laotian refugees in Australia. Their reluctance to sign an informed consent stemmed mainly from their negative experiences of living under the communist regimes and their difficulties in attempting to resettle in a third country, when they had to sign countless forms, and when their attempts were often not successful. Before I asked them to sign the consent form, I had to explain clearly that the signing of a consent form was something that would protect them, not jeopardise them. I suggest that, even though this is stated on the consent form, and even if it is translated into their languages, it is better if we explain it again before we ask them to sign.

Some cultural and ethnic groups may be illiterate even in their own language (see Fluehr-Lobban 1998; Benitez et al. 2002; Winslow et al. 2002; Dawson & Kass 2005; Lu et al. 2005; Barata et al. 2006; Adams et al. 2007). Hence, signing an informed consent form can be difficult for them, as they may not fully understand what is said on the form. In international collaborative research, where cultural differences and language barriers exist, obtaining informed consent is particularly challenging (Dawson & Kass 2005; Adams et al. 2007). These types of problems may result in a refusal from potential participants to take part in the research (Macklin 2000; Molyneux et al. 2004, 2005; Adams et al. 2007). Worse, it may affect the well-being of some individuals who may have fears about signing the form (Macklin 2000; Liamputtong 2007a; Dickson-Swift et al. 2008). Researchers need to take this into consideration when working with people from a cross-cultural perspective.

Some writers point to the fact that within some cultural groups, an informed consent has to be obtained from significant others rather than from the individual research participants. For example, women in some cultures cannot participate in research unless their husbands give consent for them to do so (see Loue et al. 1996; Leflar 1997; Macklin 2000, 2004). In other cultural groups (such as in villages or tribes where traditional chiefs are influential), consent may have to be obtained from community leaders (Meadows et al. 2003; Macklin 2004; Marshall & Batten 2004; Dawson & Kass 2005; Molyneux et al. 2005: Israel & Hay 2006; Tindana et al. 2006; Bishop 2008). This has led to some heated debate over the rights of an individual in cross-cultural research. However, researchers have argued that such a practice is justified by the social and cultural context of the country where the research is being undertaken (Macklin 2000, 2004). Natalie Piquemal (2001) points to potential problems in attempting to identify the legitimate person who can give informed consent for all members within an aboriginal nation. Anne Marshall and Suzanne Batten (2004: 3) point out that some tribal councils are distanced from and mistrusted by members of the community. In cases like these, it is unethical and illegitimate for researchers to obtain consent from the authority of the community.

But within indigenous research ethics, particularly those of the kaupapa Māori research, collective consent is more culturally appropriate than individual consent (Smith 2000, 2008; Israel & Hay 2006; Bishop 2008). This is obviously not in line with the principle of informed consent that is based on the right of individuals to give consent (Smith 2008). Research ethics with indigenous people like the Māori, Smith (2000) asserts, go beyond individual consent and confidentiality. As Clifford Christians (2008: 210) puts it, 'the characters of various indigenous peoples are rooted in a participatory mode of knowing and presumed collective, not individual, rights'. The collective rights, Norman Denzin (2003: 257) suggests, include 'control and ownership of the community's cultural property … and the rights of indigenous peoples to protect their culture's new knowledge and its dissemination'. This characteristic has ramifications for the way in which sensitive researchers may secure informed consent within indigenous communities.

Paulina Tindana and colleagues (2006) contend that in certain cultural groups, such as the group in which they did their research in northern Ghana, permission from the relevant elders or hierarchy serves as a 'visa' for undertaking research within the community. Individual consent to participate in research is not permitted unless the researchers have received this 'visa' from those in authority.

The ability to carry out research can be jeopardised if the process of gaining consent is done insensitively. Darou *et al.* (1993) tell us about the rejection of one research assistant who attempted to obtain access to participants in a remote Cree village in Canada without involving and gaining permission from the tribal leader. This attempt was met with negative responses and it was seen as 'divisive for the village'. The researcher was 'warned to "take the next plane out of the village or sleep in a snow bank"' (cited in Israel & Hay 2006: 71).

What is needed to make consent more culturally appropriate?

For any ethically grounded cross-cultural research, Solomon Benatar and Peter Singer (2000: 825) advocate that informed consent must be obtained in the local language of the participants and 'with an understanding of their world view or value system' (see also Adams *et al.* 2007). In Kathleen Ragsdale's research in Belize with sex workers (cited in Fisher & Ragsdale 2006), informed consent was administered in Spanish with a clear indication that the women could refuse to answer any question and terminate the interview at any time. She made sure that the women were fully informed about their rights as research participants and she made a special effort to inform her interpreter not to rush this process.

In some circumstances, when consent forms in English are translated into other languages, Joseph Trimble and Celia Fisher (2006a: xix) point out that 'the meaning of terms and the sentence do not accurately translate into words and sentences found and used in the native language of the participants'. Hence, cross-cultural researchers need to ensure that the translation is carried out appropriately. In their research in Tibet, Vincanne Adams and colleagues (2007) worked with local researchers to ensure that the translation of their informed consent was done not only accurately but also culturally appropriately. The word 'placebo', for example, is very new in Tibet. It is literally translated as *sems gso'i sman* ('mind healing medicine'). The translated word is borrowed from the Chinese word *an wei ji*, which has similar meaning. This literal translation of this word would create some confusion, particularly when it needed to be back translated. Adams *et al.* adopted a 'meaning-based' approach in their final consent form which indicated that 'placebo is a pill with no medicine in it, but that helps put patients at ease during research' (p. 461).

It is suggested that informed consent in cross-cultural research should be written simply (Crigger *et al.* 2001; Meadows *et al.* 2003; Birman 2006). Nancy Crigger and colleagues (2001: 463) tell us that researchers have come across research participants who had problems understanding 'a gauge to measure the hydrostatic pressure', but they could perfectly understand 'an instrument to see how hard your heart is working'. In Lynn Meadows and colleagues' (2003) study with aboriginal women, they sought permission from their institutional ethics review board to use a simple, one-page informed consent form. The form essentially contains study information which was written in an easy-to-read format and omitted some standard clauses required by the university regarding injury and liability. They argue that these standard clauses 'are awkward and at times disconcerting, raising issues such as harm from the research and cost of subsequent treatment' (p. 5). They have adopted a similar approach in other studies concerning vulnerable groups, including immigrant women and women with disabilities (see also Laverack & Brown 2003; Eide & Allen 2005; Birman 2006).

In the case that the participants are illiterate, it would be appropriate and sensible if the details of the consent were read out to the participant and an oral consent secured, and this can be done by recording into a tape-recorder prior to the interview (see also Liamputtong Rice, 1996; Glantz *et al.* 1998; Winslow *et al.* 2002; Benitez *et al.* 2002; Meadows *et al.* 2003; Scheyvens *et al.* 2003; Dawson & Kass 2005; Eide & Allen 2005; Lu *et al.* 2005; Molyneux *et al.* 2005; Barata *et al.* 2006). The Emirati women in Winslow *et al.*'s (2002) research were illiterate, and hence oral informed consent was given by them. In Meadows *et al.*'s (2003) study with aboriginal women, they adopted oral consent. They followed the oral traditions of aboriginal peoples. The aboriginal committee also required them to make the process of securing informed consent as unobtrusive as possible. In their research on spousal abuse with Bangla women, Andrea Shelton and Nahid Rianon (2004) tell us that due to the sensitive nature of the study and the lack of privacy within the research setting, they used a verbal consent procedure in their research. They prepared the oral consent wording in both Bangla and English. The women approved of the verbal consent as they believed it protected their confidentiality better than signing a written form. In their study of the meaning of death as experienced by the elderly women of a Korean clan, Kyung Rim Shin and colleagues (2005) also used verbal consent. As most of the elderly women were illiterate due to their lack of formal education, permission for the researchers to undertake interviews and to participate in their live events was given verbally in preference to writing. Jenny Littlewood and Jenny Harrow (1999), from their supervision of a Saudi student, tell us that the student understood the notion of informed consent as it is practised in the Western context, but to obtain a signed consent from the women in the study was not feasible. In Saudi society, women do not usually sign documents. Most women in this study were also illiterate, hence their verbal agreement was treated as consent from them.

Some cross-cultural researchers recommend the use of audiovisual aids and images such as still photographs, pictures, drawings, diagrams and films to explain the research aims, methods and procedures and to obtain informed consent from the participants (see Benitez *et al.* 2002; Flory & Emanuel 2004; Adams *et al.* 2007). Oscar Benitez and colleagues (2002) argue that the use of audiovisual documentation of oral consent (video recording and photography) is particularly useful for research concerning illiterate participants. Vincanne Adams and colleagues (2007: 447) contend that these alternative methods will 'help to render research in coherent, ethical, and culturally contextual ways that augment written documentation'. Adams *et al.* used drawings to accompany their simple written information sheet and consent form in their attempt to secure culturally appropriate consent forms for their research regarding the feasibility of traditional Tibetan medicine (*Zhi Byed 11*) to prevent postpartum haemorrhage among pregnant women in Tibet.

Yun Lu and colleagues (2005: 1152), in their research on AIDS in rural China, learned that their potential participants were illiterate. Hence, they developed 'a voice signature consent system' to go with their written consent form. The Chinese research assistants read the consent form to the participants and, once they agreed, they were asked to speak to the video camera with the message 'I agree to participate in this study'.

Nevertheless, in cross-cultural research, some researchers would argue for more emphasis on trust building, reciprocity and rapport than the mechanistic process of securing informed consent (see Fluehr-Lobban 1994, 1998, 2003; Denzin 2003; Scheyvens *et al.* 2003; Barata *et al.* 2006; Parker 2007; Christians 2008; Smith 2008). Indeed, in cross-cultural research examining people's perceptions of research participation and informed consent with Portuguese-Canadian and Caribbean-Canadian immigrants in Canada conducted by Paula Barata and colleagues (2006), trust and mistrust emerged as the most important theme recognised by the participants. The participants expressed their concerns regarding fear of exploitation and issues of mistrust which would deter them from participating in research. They also wanted to have more information before agreeing to take part and signing the consent form. A similar type of concern has prompted Carolyn Fluehr-Lobban (1994, 1998, 2003) to advocate an open and sincere process of securing informed consent from research participants in cross-cultural research. Fluehr-Lobban (1998: 185) contends that 'the genesis of informed consent and its guiding spirit is that of openness and disclosure in research practice'. When applying the spirit of informed consent to cross-cultural research, it requires that the researchers openly discuss the methods and likely research outcome with the research participants. This will allow the establishment of an open relationship between the researcher and the researched. Ideally, informed consent opens a two-way channel of communication, and once open, information and ideas will continuously flow. Through her twenty-five years of research experiences in the Sudan, Egypt and Tunisia, Carolyn Fluehr-Lobban tells us that:

I came to understand that being open about research is a way to keep open the lines of communication throughout the course of research, to allow negotiation of terms of research as it progresses through its various stages. Informed consent doesn't translate literally and directly into Arabic, or I suspect, many other languages. But making honest attempts to talk about the nature, course, and research funding and allowing a relationship to unfold that may even permit a participant's withdrawal from research is more ethical and probably results in better research. (p. 187)

Safety and well-being: the vulnerable researcher

Thus far in this chapter, I have only discussed issues relevant to the research participants. However, in any piece of research, there is another side to the coin, that is the researchers themselves. I am unable to cover all of the issues relevant to the researchers in this chapter (space won't permit), but I wish to suggest one aspect which sits neatly within the ethical and moral issues of undertaking cross-cultural research; that is the safety and well-being of the researchers in the field.

Carrying out cross-cultural research can sometimes have negative impacts on the researchers' physical and emotional well-being (Scheyvens *et al.* 2003; Simmons & Koester 2003; Singer & Easton 2006). In dealing with human beings, regardless of social and cultural backgrounds, we may have to deal with some unpleasant situations. It is worse in cross-cultural settings due to language and cultural differences. Rachel Hall (2004: 136) tells us about her negative experience in her research with South Asian women in West Yorkshire. Due to her own ethnicity as a white British woman, some women referred to her in a derogatory term. On one occasion, she met a woman during a *mela* festival celebrating International Women's Day and invited her to participate in her research. Whenever Hall asked the woman to commence the interview, she would continue to say 'do it later'. But then she began talking in Punjabi and kept referring to Hall as a *gori*, which can be translated literally as 'fair' as in 'fair-skinned'. However, it also carries an insulting meaning and is used to refer to white people or South Asians who are seen to have adopted Western ways of life. Hall tells us:

This negative experience certainly affected me, particularly by causing me to feel powerless and rather self-conscious about my ethnicity … I left the *mela* feeling confused and slightly upset as to why this woman acted the way she did towards me. Nonetheless, after calling me a *gori* she let me interview her. This was the first and only time in the research project where an interviewee has acted in this way towards me. Reviewing this has forced me to acknowledge that I have an ethnicity, which I bring to bear in the context of the interview, even though I want to keep it outside of the interview setting. As a member of the majority-ethnic population I must accept that some people will look at me as a 'white person', and attach assumptions to this. (p. 136)

Culture shock is the most common negative experience that most fieldworkers have to deal with in their cross-cultural research (see Bradburd 1998; Leslie & Story 2003; Caufield 2006). Culture shock can begin from the very first day that the researchers leave their own familiar homeland and enter their fieldwork site (Gokah 2006). Not being familiar with the physical, social and cultural environments of the field can produce physical and emotional turmoil in researchers. Catherine Caufield (2006), in her research with traditional midwives in Guatemala, provides a good example of this problem. There are two main challenges that Caufield articulated in her recent writing: an adaptation to poor living conditions and how white people, including herself, are stereotyped by local people. Poor living conditions were difficult to deal with for a long period of time in her fieldwork; she could only tolerate a week or so. Frequently she had to bathe with cold water and she longed for a hot bath back home. Ill health was a main concern for Caufield. She elaborates:

As usual for me in the tropics, I was frequently ill. I acquired diarrhea every 2 or 3 weeks, and contracted some sort of skin infection, a tooth infection, and, the *coup de grace*, hepatitis … It was a bit scary being sick, because there were no information sheets available, and I could not go to the library to look things up. It was then, when I was ill, that I found the slapping sound of women making tortillas and the smell of maize cooking over a wood fire repugnant. Walking along certain streets in which the daytime heat brought out the stench of corners that were stained with the darkened reminds of where people urinated nauseated me … I did not want to look at the woman who just spat a great yellow gob onto the street. I did not want to see the boy stretched out, drunk, on the sidewalk beside the cantina [bar]. I did not want to see where the sex workers were, and, furthermore, I did not want any more fried chicken with rice and beans. I longed for the soda biscuits and Cheez Whiz that my mother used to give me when I was sick.

Caufield's experience is not uncommon in cross-cultural research. I am not suggesting that this will happen to all researchers. Rather, I am saying that it can happen to novice researchers who may not have made good preparations for their fieldwork in a strange land. See more discussion on this issue in the writing of Helen Leslie and Donovan Storey (2003).

Risks faced by researchers during their fieldwork is another real issue for cross-cultural researchers (Sampson & Thomas 2003; Gokah 2006; Singer & Easton 2006). During fieldwork, researchers, both male and female, may have to deal with sexual harassment or assault (Warren 1988; Bourgois 1995; Jacobs 1998; Coffey 2002; Liamputtong 2007a). As Theophilus Gokah (2006) tells us, in his PhD thesis investigating children's rights and well-being policy in sub-Saharan Africa (Ghana, Uganda, Ethiopia and South Africa), there are many types of risk that he was exposed to. These include: 'risk from armed banditry (Uganda and Ethiopia), risk based on social crime which sometimes involves armed robbery (South Africa), and an invisible risk environment (Ghana)'.

In one incident in Uganda, Gokah tells us:

After my contact with a church-based organisation I returned to find a crowd gathered around the vehicle I was using. I was told by an on-looker that my driver and one other escort in our company were under arrest by armed security personnel (not the police), the reason being that the security apparatus in the local district had received information about a 'strange' car with four occupants ... In Uganda, security agents are suspicious of any vehicle carrying more than two or three men, so I was told. The security personnel warned we were under strict surveillance and could not leave the district where I was operating as a researcher. My visibly shaken driver told me his car was carefully inspected and he was asked for the whereabouts of the remaining occupants. Fortunately, one occupant knew one of the security operatives and explained that his organisation had received a visitor (myself) from the UK studying children's welfare and that I was talking to people in the church nearby. The commander of the group ordered his men to put away their guns before I returned to the car. One of the security men said within hearing: 'You are lucky, if it were the police you would have been shot on sight'. (p. 65)

Gokah's experience is very similar to that of Ross-Owens (2003), who was accused of being a spy in Zanzibar during his fieldwork at a solar New Year festival. John McCall (2000) was also suspected of being an American spy among the Ohafia Igbo.

Sometimes, the processes involved in collecting data in their daily lives could also lead to dangers in fieldwork. For example, the difficulties and dangers may come merely when researchers are trying to get to their fieldwork or research sites. Sam Punch (personal communication in Lee-Treweek and Linkogle 2000: 2) was physically attacked by dogs as she walked to remote households in villages when researching childhood in rural Bolivia. I, too, was attacked by a dog when I went to interview a Thai mother in a suburban area in Bangkok. This incident left me with open wounds on one of my legs which took a few months to heal.

Those who conduct research in other cultural and social settings, apart from having to deal with the feelings of dislocation and isolation, may also experience some physical dangers due to the political and physical environments. Stephanie Linkogle (2000), while carrying out her fieldwork in Nicaragua, had to deal not only with the dangers due to political violence within the country, but also with some day-to-day hazards. In their research with AIDS victims in rural China, Yun Lu and colleagues (2005) had to travel by foot, bicycle or by *beng-beng che* ('a riding cart pulled by a motorcycle-bike'). However, very often they had to walk to the village as no *beng-beng che* drivers wanted to get into what they called 'the village of plague'. There was one occasion that they managed to rent a *beng-beng che*, but the driver stopped five miles away from the village and told them that he would not go any further. Hence, once again they all had to walk to their research site.

Recent writing by Sabina Rashid (2007), who undertook her research regarding reproductive health with poor women living in a slum in Dhaka, is a good example of the issues I have mentioned in this section. In the slum where Rashid did her research, violence, fear and a sense of insecurity are part of the everyday life that people experience. The violence in this slum involves domestic abuse, fights between neighbours, fights among gamblers and drug addicts, gang warfare, police raids and the overt oppression of residents by local leaders and the state. Doing fieldwork in a slum was very stressful for her and her research team, but she had to continue negotiations with gatekeepers at both individual and community levels so that she could carry out interviews with the women.

The physicality of the slum is not conducive to human health either. Rashid tells us:

The alleyways were tiny and congested, rooms had no fans, and drains overflowed with water, sewage, and excrement, particularly during the rainy season. Skin infections were rampant. During interviews with young women, I often saw rats and cockroaches run across the floor. The women had few possessions, sometimes only a jute mat to sleep on and utensils for cooking. (p. 370)

During the fieldwork, Rashid came across several examples of threatening behaviour from the husbands of her participants. Normally, the husbands would be informed about the project and permission was sought from them before their wives were interviewed, but in four incidents, the men denied Rashid and the team permission to talk to their wives. Rashid says:

One of the men just said no. In another case, a husband walked into the room to find his wife in an interview with me and proceeded to hit her. I ran outside to get help, and the landlady [a senior leader's wife] intervened, calling the husband 'a heroin addict' and threatening to slap him. He left the room quickly, and I ended the interview, not wanting to cause any further trouble for the young woman ... In another case, the husband stood in the doorway while I was conducting the interview and glared at us, forcing me to end the interview quickly; in another case, the husband walked in halfway through an interview and began asking me about family planning methods I could give him. He then took off his shirt and lay down on the bed. I was uncomfortable and ended the interview. In both of these last cases, the women avoided me whenever we saw each other and I was never able to interview them again. (p. 378)

Rashid contends that an important concern for her and her research assistant was their personal safety. This was particularly so when there was a police raid or the outbreak of gang violence. Throughout their fieldwork, she and the research team 'remained anxious because we were women working in a completely unfamiliar territory' (p. 380).

I wish to briefly point to another contentious issue with which some cross-cultural researchers may have to deal. Many researchers work for governments, private corporations, tribes, ethnic and indigenous communities or receive funding from agencies. Their responsibilities toward the research participants may be mediated and compromised by their obligations towards their employers or funding agencies. The research they are doing may conflict with the ambitions of governments, business and other vested political interests. Hence, cross-cultural researchers must acknowledge the political traps that may arise in their research and find ways that they can negotiate prior to and throughout the research process. If the interests of the employers and funding agencies outweigh the safety and well-being of their participants, the researchers may have to seriously consider the implications of their research on their participants and themselves. I believe this is a moral and ethical issue that some of you need to think about carefully before embarking on your cross-cultural research.

Tutorial activities

(1) You have been asked to undertake a research project on issues relating to alcohol consumption among young indigenous men. You have been told that these men are likely to be homeless or living in poverty. What moral and ethical issues will you need to consider to do this piece of research? How will you overcome some of these moral and ethical issues? Discuss some of these with your research team or supervisor.

(2) As a researcher who will be performing cross-cultural research on domestic violence with women in a poor nation, what issues will you be likely to face in your fieldwork? How will you deal with them? Will this stop you from doing this research? Discuss this in detail.

Chapter summary

The ethical choices we make as researchers are motivated by an underlying morality (for example, a desire to: respect and care for others; promote justice and equality; protect others' freedom and avoiding harming others), which guide our behaviour, not just during the course of our research, but in all of our social interactions. (Hallowell *et al.* 2005: 149)

In planning cross-cultural research, it is essential that the researchers must balance the risks against the benefits by thinking carefully about whether their research is morally justified, or if it is ethical to carry out their research, and whether their research results will further marginalise the group of people. Clearly, there are moral and ethical issues that cross-cultural researchers must consider before embarking on their research. In this chapter, I have discussed some ethical and moral issues in doing cross-cultural research. I have included a suggestion for the inclusion of an 'ethics of care' when undertaking cross-cultural research, particularly with indigenous people. The thorny issue of informed consent in cross-cultural research is also discussed in great depth.

Within this chapter, I have not only discussed issues of risk and harm which the participants may experience in participating in research, but also pointed to the risk and harm and political traps that may befall the researchers during their fieldwork. Undertaking cross-cultural research can place a great many demands, physically and emotionally, on the researchers.

Although there has been increasing attention paid to the ethics of carrying out cross-cultural research, particularly within ethnic communities and indigenous groups, Fred Beauvais (2006: 253–254) says that 'the dialogue, of course, must go on. Ethical issues are rarely completely solved; rather they are the subject of continuing refinement and deeper understanding.' I agree entirely on this point. We do not wish to see any of the historical exploitation happening again in the near future, do we?

SUGGESTED READING

Battiste, M. (2008). Research ethics for protecting indigenous knowledge and heritage. In N. K. Denzin, Y. S. Lincoln, & L. T. Smith (Eds.), *Handbook of critical and indigenous methodologies* (pp. 497–509). Thousand Oaks, CA: Sage Publications.

Caufield, C. (2006). Challenges for a North American doing research with traditional indigenous Guatemalan midwives. *International Journal of Qualitative Methodology*

5(4), Article 4. www.ualberta.ca/~iiqm/backissues/5_4/pdf/caufield.pdf Accessed: 10 January 2007.

Denzin, N. K., Lincoln, Y. S., & Smith, L. T. (Eds.) (2008). *Handbook of critical and indigenous methodologies*. Thousand Oaks, CA: Sage Publications.

Price, D. (2004). *Threatening anthropology: McCarthyism and the FBI's investigation of American anthropologists*. Durham, MD: Duke University Press.

Rashid, S. F. (2007). Accessing married adolescent women: The realities of ethnographic research in an urban slum environment in Dhaka, Bangladesh. *Field Methods* **19**(4), 369–383.

Trimble, J. E., & Fisher, C. B. (Eds.) (2006). *The handbook of ethical research with ethnocultural populations and communities*. Thousand Oaks, CA: Sage Publications.

3   The research participants: accessing and reciprocity

Gaining access into marginalized communities is not an innocent undertaking; such entries are always fraught with ethical considerations.

(Subedi 2007: 56)

Gaining access to potentially hard to reach populations is a great challenge. Some groups are not only hard to reach geographically but may also be culturally, socially, or developmentally resistant to participating in ... studies'.

(Lindenberg *et al.* 2001: 135)

How do we make contact with individuals and ask them to participate in our research, particularly if they do not wish to be found? Locating potential research participants can be a challenging and often problematic task. Many people are reluctant to enter the research field, as they do not 'trust the researchers', and may have other priority concerns (Liamputtong 2007a). Some groups, such as Hispanic Americans, have high mobility rates due to their employment and other issues and hence locating these groups can be a great challenge to researchers (Lange 2002). Because of this, recruiting research participants can be a formidable task for those carrying out cross-cultural research, and particularly so when the research is involved in sensitive issues.

In this chapter, I shall discuss several issues relevant to accessing potential research participants. I also provide some strategies which will assist researchers to gain access to and maintain relationships with the participants, so that their research projects may run successfully.

Gaining access to participants

Gaining access to any research participant can often be problematic (Liamputtong, 2007a, 2009). It is even more so when attempts are made to recruit research participants in cross-cultural research (Brown *et al.*, 2000; Lindenberg *et al.* 2001; Preloran *et al.* 2001; Rodríguez *et al.* 2006; Subedi 2007; Liamputtong 2008; Topp *et al.* 2008; McMillan *et al.* 2009). In cross-cultural research, it can also be more problematic because of language and cultural differences.

Quite often, people have negative experiences with previous research (Salmon 2007) and are suspicious of research projects (Freimuth *et al.* 2001; Preloran *et al.* 2001; Carter 2004; Rashid 2007; Subedi 2007). As I pointed out in Chapter 1, local people in poor nations and indigenous people have been exploited by Western researchers who come and take their knowledge for their own advantages. Despite this knowledge that they pass on to the researchers, native people have often not been respected by outside researchers. This has resulted in negative experiences and resentment among local people in many parts of the world. In many African nations, as Paul Jackson (2000: 349) suggests, people have 'a deep suspicion of any agenda which is either not perceived to be sufficiently transparent, sufficiently beneficial to them, or to come from any political hierarchy'. And the most commonly held view is their 'lack of faith in anything happening'. This has led to their reluctance in participating in research, particularly in research that adopts positivist science, a quantitative questionnaire, and which does not permit local people to express their own concerns or make their voices and needs heard (Subedi 2007).

In their study with at-risk young Amerasians, Rita Chung and Fred Bemak (1997: 470) suggest that recruiting research participants can be a problem due to cross-cultural differences, and there may be other issues influencing people's decisions. Chung and Bemak point out that at-risk young people may have to deal with the legal authorities or they may come from politically oppressed countries where persecution is common. This may make the young people suspicious about many aspects of the inquiries, particularly if the research is sponsored by the government. Even the use of the term 'investigation' may bring back memories of previous extremely negative experiences with government officials, which in some cases can be linked with life-threatening circumstances. In their study, the mistrust and suspicion of the young people was one of the difficulties of conducting research with at-risk youth. Very often, the young people became resistant and this led to low participation rates in the study.

Sabina Rashid (2007: 379) undertook her research with women in a Dhaka slum. She and her research team were introduced by the health workers and obtained permission from some leaders in the slum. One persistent problem was that some of the slum dwellers, and many of her participants, did not believe that she and her research assistant were interested in learning about women's health. They suspected that Sabina and the team were spies from the government, planning to steal their land. Others thought that they were journalists who were trying to get information about illegal activities and the drug business. One young woman said during the interview: 'Apa, are you sure you are not from the DB [detective branch]? Lots of people come here and try and take information from us. Often police informers come and pretend to be working elsewhere. They get friendly with the families and then try and get inside information about this area' (p. 379).

In Mehreen Mirza's (1998) study with South Asian women, the women had their concerns about the motivations of the research, the research process and confidentiality. They questioned Mirza about the reason she was undertaking the research, what angle she was coming from, where she obtained her funding and how the research findings would be used. The women even wanted to know about the questions that she asked. Kalwant Bhopal (1997: 31–32) says this:

Asian women are a very difficult group to study, based upon their cultural definitions and strong views regarding male and female roles within their communities.
They are very close knit groups who portray a very strong, cohesive sense of belong-
ing and security. Their cultural identity is reinforced and regarded as essential to
the well-being of the community, culture and individuals. Outsiders who do not
identify with the group are viewed with suspicion and seen as a threat. Members of
the community question what the outsiders want and how they may affect the daily
lives of the individuals who live in the culture.

It is often suggested that people from immigrant or minority groups do not understand the nature of research and hence tend to refuse to participate in any research project (Preloran *et al.* 2001). As Beth Brown and colleagues (2000: 155) point out, special groups, such as ethnic minority women, are seen as people who are more resistant to research recruitment efforts. To be able to recruit them successfully requires 'customized approaches'. However, I con-tend that there are many salient issues that may prevent or prohibit people from immigrant and minority groups from participating in research.

Language barriers tend to be the main problem for most people who do not use English as a first language (Berg 1999; McMillan *et al.* 2009; see Chapter 6 in this volume). In a study by Jennifer Harris and Keri Roberts (2003: 8), 'linguistic barriers to participation in the interviews were minimized by the use of first-language interviewers and the provision of sign language inter-preters for deaf interviewees'.

Potential participants may not perceive research as having any benefit to them (Preloran *et al.* 2001). Higher priority or other more important com-mitments may also prevent people from taking part in research. Due to family and work commitments, many women and men, as shown in Mabel Preloran and colleagues' (2001) study, declined or were reluctant to partici-pate. Qualitative research tends to require a long-term relationship between the researcher and the participant and this may be seen by the potential participants as a time-consuming task.

There are also other important issues. Jennifer Harris and Keri Roberts (2003: 7–8) suggest that venues traditionally used for research, which require asking the participants to travel to a university or to an office of the researcher, can be inaccessible to many people. Hence, selecting a venue for research needs to take into consideration the 'potential social and physical barriers to participation'. In their study, the participants were invited to choose an interview venue, and this included their own home, a local community centre or refugee community group. They also reassured their participants that the alternative venues would be 'culturally appropriate and physically accessible for people with impairments'. The participants were also provided with transport costs if they decided to be interviewed outside their own homes. Most participants, however, wanted to be interviewed in their own homes, but some wished to be interviewed at disabled refugee organisations (see also Liamputtong 2007a, 2008).

Strategies for accessing research participants in cross-cultural research

There have been a number of strategies which researchers have adopted in gaining access to research participants in different social and cultural settings. I shall highlight several strategies in the following sections.

Relationship/Collaboration with community leaders and stakeholders

Very often, researchers gain access to their potential participants through relationships with community leaders or stakeholders. Stakeholders may include formal and informal group leaders, service providers, business people and residents who have an interest in the particular community (Sixsmith *et al.* 2003; Hall & Kulig 2004; Sin 2005; Rashid 2007; Salmon 2007). These stakeholders help researchers to develop important links with the community and to identify and respond to important issues and situations within the community (Rashid 2007). To recruit women to participate in their focus group research, Wendy Winslow and colleagues (2002) approached the Abu Dhabi Women's Association, an organisation that provides the education and domestic skills for family care to Emirati women who left school early. The Association was a place where these women congregated for their educational and social activities. It was an ideal place for focus groups, as it reduced problems with transportation for the participating women.

Cathy Lindenberg and colleagues (2001: 133) worked with gatekeepers, the director of health education and a maternal/child physician in recruiting and conducting a prevention intervention to reduce substance use and risky sexual behaviour with young low-income Latina women. They tell us that 'identifying key "gatekeepers" was central to our success. As community-based service providers, gatekeepers understand community needs and traditions and, in our case, also acknowledged the need for and complementarities of talents and resources from academic settings ... Extremely knowledgeable about the needs of young Latinas, both gatekeepers were highly respected and valued health care providers. Our shared values, common goals, and complementary talents drew us together.'

Lynn Meadows and colleagues (2001) gained their access to ethnic communities in Canada through key contacts in the ethnic communities. But in their recent work with aboriginal women (2003: 10), they had to expand their recruitment strategies. They tell us:

We were successful in recruiting participants in a series of steps that provided opportunities for the community to become familiar with our research team. These included working with reserve health committees, attending health fairs and visiting the reserves on multiple occasions; depending on the circumstances we provided refreshments and/or contributed a door prize to the event. Having gained a level of community acceptance, we then planned several field trips as opportunities for casual encounters to introduce the research to women and to offer appointments to potential participants. In this way we were successful in recruiting over 50 midlife aboriginal women who lived on three reserves and in two urban locations for either group or in-depth individual interviews.

In their research with at-risk youth, Rita Chung and Fred Bemak (1997: 470) worked through bilingual/bicultural community leaders and members to gain access to these young people. These key people were instrumental in helping the research team to make contact with and inform potential participants about the study. Chung and Bemak suggest that it was crucial that the study was supported by the community and agencies serving Amerasians. These people must also have a clear understanding of the purpose of the research, its intended outcomes and what the research could potentially contribute to the community. It was also crucial that the research team had extensive experience working with Amerasians and a good knowledge about the culture, as this would allow them to develop a good rapport with the communities and agencies.

In their intervention research with hard-to-reach Latina women, Cathy Lindenberg and colleagues (2001: 135) worked with community leaders, groups and institutions (such as schools, churches, Latino clubs, and health and social service institutions) organised for and committed to serve the women. This was essential for the success of their study. They tell us that the key to their success for accessing the young people was to develop 'relationships with community leaders and institutions who are trusted by young Latinas'.

In their study on the initiation of HIV prevention methods among female sex workers in Southern China, Margaret Weeks and colleagues (2007) worked closely with Centres for Disease Control (CDC), the provincial and county/municipal-level centres, known by the Chinese as 'anti-epidemic stations'. This allowed access to hard-to-reach women. Weeks *et al.* explain: 'CDC staff and local health workers provided input on recruitment procedures and incentives, recruited and screened participants, got informed consent, and conducted all interviews and surveys. This close working relationship between the researchers and the site-based health educators and health workers was crucial to the study' (p. 192).

Amy Salmon (2007: 984) carried out her research with Aboriginal mothers who have experienced foetal alcohol syndrome (FAS/FAE) in Vancouver. She eventually formed a trusting relationship with Mary, a native activist. Mary assisted Salmon with her recruitment. Salmon elaborates on this:

On my behalf, Mary offered to approach the women who were participating in her program (to protect their confidentiality), explain the project, and provide them with my contact information if they were interested in participating. I provided notes outlining what the research was about, the participation criteria, and the research procedures. Mary also communicated to the group that this research was 'a good thing to be part of because it would go into a book that people would read and might somewhere down the line help other women in their situation' … and that I could be trusted to be respectful of and sensitive to their concerns.

After the women had received initial information from Mary about Salmon and her research, the women invited Salmon to attend one of their regular meetings to discuss her project, her intentions in carrying out the research and their potential participation. Mary enthusiastically told the women that:

This is your chance to tell it like it is. Amy will bring the policies to you, and you can take this chance to give your opinions about them. She will put it in a book, and lots of people will read it. Then people can use what they read to make changes, to make things better. This can be a really important thing to be a part of. What you know could make a difference. (p. 984)

In carrying out cross-cultural projects, researchers need to obtain permission from community leaders or those who are influential in the local area. Without permission, the research project may not be able to run successfully (see Walsh-Tapiata 2003; Tindana *et al.* 2006). In my study with Hmong women in Melbourne (Liamputtong Rice 2000), entry into the community was sought from community leaders. Prior to entering the Hmong community for my fieldwork, I attended one of the community's fortnightly meetings and sought permission from the community leaders. The Hmong community was aware and informed of my presence and of the purpose of my research. This greatly facilitated the smooth running of my data-collection process.

Sabina Rashid (2007) conducted her research on reproductive histories with poor adolescent women in an urban slum in Dhaka, Bangladesh. She had to obtain permission from key members of the community. Because people were suspicious of her role (they thought she and her research assistant belonged to authorities who wanted to evict them from the slum area), she learned that she needed to gain trust from people and this could only be done through gatekeepers. Rashid tells us that:

I began by introducing myself and my research assistant … to the three health workers … who worked in the clinic … These health workers lived in the slum and were well known and well liked by everyone. Initially suspicious of our intentions, over the course of a month, as we visited the clinics regularly, the health workers warmed to us and agreed to introduce us to potential respondents … Just as important, they would also introduce us to the real leaders of the community, the mastaans, on whose permission our research program depended. Each section of the slum had its own mastaan (with various factions) who controlled law and order, meted out justice, and collected money for water, electricity, and other services, to which tenants and landlords were forced to contribute. The mastaans had both the power and the right to permit the people in their area of the slum to be studied. (pp. 374–375)

Rashid was later advised by one of the health workers that she needed to introduce herself to the main leader of the slum, Kabir, who was very influential and feared by the local community. Eventually, she and the team met with him in a nearby teashop. After hearing Rashid's explanation about her research, he said this to her: 'Sister, as long as you study what you say you are interested in, then there should be no problems. But if you do have any problems, just let [X] know. He will sort it out for you. We will learn from you, and you will learn from us.' However, Rashid tells us that his permission for her to work in the local community 'came with warning "not to investigate anything other than women's health"'. Otherwise, she and the team 'could be in trouble' (p. 375). Rashid later learned that the leaders of this section of the slum ran a heroin business and they were supported by the police and other local political leaders. But, as Rashid and the team sought their permission and adhered closely to the topic of reproductive health, they were provided with support and protection. And this became a significant step for her and her research team. Rashid writes, 'one of the main leaders had given us permission to work and had provided protection from harassment by their gang's members or by other household residents' (p. 375).

However, stakeholders may also act as gatekeepers who control access to community members (Thomas 1990; Groger *et al.* 1999; Sixsmith *et al.* 2003; Carter 2004). When Thomas (1990: 8–9), in her study with older Afro-Caribbean people, attempted to recruit people at a West Indian centre, the supervisor of the centre told her that these elders were fed up with researchers who came to ask them about their life histories, because there had been too many who had done so. One member of the centre even said to her: 'We hope you are not one of those who want to come and ask endless questions. If you are, forget it! We have given enough already.' This has been my recent experience with the work of one of my postgraduate students. The student wished to examine the sexual health needs of young Vietnamese immigrants in Melbourne. She sought assistance from one of the Vietnamese organisations working with young people with the hope that this gatekeeping agency would help her to make contact with several young Vietnamese girls. After several meetings, the gatekeeping agency declined to do so and the reason was that young Vietnamese girls would be exploited by the research project and that the community had been over-researched, despite the fact that the proposed research topic had not been carried out among young Vietnamese in Australia and we were hoping that this study would contribute to greater knowledge of young people and their sexual needs within an ethnic community. I suggested to my student that we had to respect the decision of the gatekeeping agency and find other avenues for accessing these young people, which she was eventually able to do.

Knowing the person concept

Collaborating with a local community, Phyllis Eide and Carol Allen (2005: 2) suggest, can be made easier when 'the researcher knows and is known by community members and leaders'. Having good connections with community members or the culture is extremely beneficial. This is particularly so when researchers work with an indigenous group. This can be seen in the example of Amy Salmon (2007), which I discussed above.

Phyllis Eide (Eide and Allen 2005) undertook research on aboriginal Hawaiian women and breast cancer in the state of Hawaii. Originally, she planned to recruit potential participants through the orthodox means of letters and posters/flyers, but this proved to be inefficient. Fortunately, her supervisor introduced her to the clinic nurse, who was known and trusted by her targeted group. Eide contends that, 'without her brokering between the cultures of university and researcher (me) and Native Hawai'ians and breast cancer population (clinic), the study would have not been accomplished with the 1-year time frame that it encompassed' (p. 3). Eide relied on the 'knowing the person' concept for her recruitment (p. 5). She strongly suggests that 'not only must the researcher know about the group being studied, he or she must be known by at least some group members in order to gain access that allows for trust building'. In Eide and Allen's study, very often the participants would say things like 'I know her auntie', 'He knows the governor' or 'He knows my uncle' (p. 2). These comments 'reveal the truth of the adage' that 'it's not what you know but who you know' in many cultures, including the Hawaiian.

More often, potential research participants would want to identify a common person whom they themselves and the researcher know as a way for them to check the researcher's credibility and trustworthiness. This is also what Cathy Lindenberg and colleagues (2001) recommend. In their study concerning the development of services to prevent and reduce substance use and risky sexual behaviour among low-income Latina women, they employed many strategies to recruit the women. However, the most effective way was personal interactions between bilingual researchers and the women and by word of mouth.

John Carter (2004) wanted to have access to ethnic minority nurses to speak about their experiences within an organisation. He attempted to access his potential participants through working with senior managers of the organisation and found that people were reluctant to talk to him. Carter spent many months trying to get in-depth information from potential participants but he only obtained short answers. He then met a black African ward manager within the organisation where he was doing his research, and he started to talk informally about the problems he had encountered in trying to access ethnic minority nurses. The ward manager had worked in that organisation for a while. He knew most of the ethnic minority nurses and had a good working relationship with them. During the course of their conversation, Carter's near desperation at failing to persuade people to speak openly was obvious to the manager. The manager offered to help

Carter by putting him in touch with ethnic minority nurses that he knew within that organisation. The manager also volunteered to approach the nurses before the interview to explain to them that Carter was genuinely interested in their experiences and not a 'management spy' (p. 348). After this introduction, the nurses' attitudes towards Carter changed markedly. Carter contends that 'a halo effect had been conferred on me by a key gate-keeper whose intervention gave me a credibility among ethnic minority staff that I had previously lacked. I was certainly no longer regarded as a management spy' (p. 350).

Culture broker

Potential participants may be recruited by a 'culture broker' (Eide & Allen 2005). Culture brokers are people who serve as 'links between individuals or groups who are culturally different' (p. 6). They have an understanding and sympathy for the cultural values and social issues of the relevant cultures. As such, culture brokers 'bring people together and reduce misunderstandings and conflict'. Culture brokers can assist the researcher in making contact with potential research participants. Janice Crist and Socorro Escandón-Dominguez (2003: 267) also suggest that the knowledge of the culture brokers 'are valuable in helping the researcher enter the culture, learn how to understand behaviors, avoid social errors, and sustain good relationships'. Culture brokers can act as translators about the behaviour and meanings of local people for researchers who are outsiders of the social and cultural groups. They also help to refer potential participants for the study.

In a study which attempted to improve equity of services for older Mexican Americans in southern Arizona, Janice Crist and Socorro Escandón-Dominguez (p. 267) tell us that the culture brokers in their research were two nurses who had Mexican and Mexican-American backgrounds. They had advanced degrees and had collaborated with the researchers in previous research projects. The culture brokers suggested a number of people with whom the researchers could make contact. They tell us: 'Some of the suggested contacts became valuable partners for the research project, some were helpful in referring the researcher to other partners, and some were not relevant for current projects, although they may be helpful in future projects' (p. 268). The two culture brokers provided advice to the researchers from the beginning of the study and continued to do so when the need arose.

Bicultural research assistants

Researchers may have better access to participants if they work with bicultural research assistants (Schoenberg *et al.* 2005). Mable Preloran and colleagues (2001: 1832) suggest that working with recruiters who are from the same ethnic background as the participants can assist the researchers with access to potential participants. Judith Berg (1999: 240) notes that research assistants who are representative of the same culture as the potential participants can greatly enhance the response rates. Berg (1999: 240) suggests that 'culturally matched research assistants may have an increased ability to establish rapport with minority or immigrant participants and thus encourage participation'.

In their research on cervical cancer screening among central Appalachian women in Kentucky and West Virginia, Nancy Schoenberg and colleagues (2005: 93) required the assistance of bicultural researchers who were middle-aged women and had been living locally for their entire lives. Identifying women who declined screening was not a simple process. They had to rely on 'the trustworthiness and reputations' of their bicultural researchers. The bicultural researchers recruited the hard-to-reach women through several means: by snowballing (see below) and by 'posting themselves' in different locations that would allow them to meet a wide range of women, and these locations included 'a community college cafeteria, a low income housing project, and a senior citizen centre'. Living locally and being local people, these bicultural researchers knew where they would be likely to have access to these difficult-to-reach women.

This has been a strategy in all of my cross-cultural research projects in Australia. A bicultural researcher from each of the ethnic communities in which I have carried out my research (for example, the Cambodian, Hmong, Iraqi, Lao, Philippine, Turkish and Vietnamese communities) was employed. Because of their knowledge of their own communities, they were able to access potential participants and build good rapport and trust with their community members (see also Chapter 6).

It is worth mentioning here that working with culture brokers and bicultural research assistants may also restrict the recruitment efforts of the researchers. Small minority communities may distrust cultural insiders because they fear that their issues may be gossiped about by the researchers within their community. Some people may find it better to talk to people outside rather than inside their community. This insider/outsider issue will be discussed in great length in Chapter 5.

Snowball method

As in the recruiting strategy with vulnerable people (Liamputtong 2007a), snowballing seems to be appropriate for cross-cultural research, particularly when researchers work through cultural brokers or community leaders (Adamson & Donovan 2002; Lu *et al.* 2005; Liamputtong 2008). The researchers or the culture brokers may commence with a group of people they know and then recruit more potential participants through contacts of the original group members (Eide & Allen 2005). The potential pool of research participants can be enlarged this way (Liamputtong 2009). Eide and Allen (2005: 6) remark that 'this is an effective method of helping the researcher to be known to others by the process of positive recommendation ... Snowballing provides opportunities for the culture broker and participants to vouch for the cultural competency of the researcher to new contacts'. Yun Lu and colleagues (2005: 1152) conducted research with rural Chinese who contracted AIDS through selling blood. Lu, as a principal researcher, made contact with an advocate for AIDS orphans through the Beijing Research Office. He was then introduced to five key persons in the village and three became gatekeepers who assisted him with access to potential participants within the village. Their initial recruitment led to snowball sampling groups; villagers heard about the research and were invited to participate. When the researchers arrived at the home of the first participant, about thirty people were waiting to take part. The potential participants told Lu and colleagues that when they learned from the gatekeepers that some 'kind-hearted, learned people' needed villagers to help them with their research, they wanted to be included because 'they wanted their stories to be heard'.

In their study on cervical cancer and pap tests with Appalachian women who were rarely or never screened, Nancy Schoenberg and colleagues (2005) had to rely heavily on the snowball method to recruit the women. They tell us:

Since identifying women who are rarely or never screened is not a straightforward process (such individuals are often described as the 'hard to reach populations'), we relied on the trustworthiness and reputations of the local interviewers, all of whom had lived in their communities for their entire lives. These interviewers recruited the women through a snowball sampling approach.

In her research relating to the experiences of British immigration control with South Asian women in West Yorkshire, Rachel Hall (2004: 130) used the snowball technique to recruit the women. She contacted the women 'informally through local South Asian organisations, women's groups, playgroups, friends, acquaintances and local authority departments mandated to work with West Yorkshire's South Asian communities'. These initial contacts permitted Hall to speak to potential participants directly or over the telephone. From these initial contacts, the snowballing technique was used to recruit more women into her research. Hall contends that this approach seems to be a common technique in research projects concerning South Asian women (see Egharevba 2001). In Hall's research, the snowballing technique occurred when the women she had previously interviewed told their friends or relatives about it. Hall (2004: 130–131) elaborates:

I found these recommendations of my research and myself particularly encouraging. Perhaps this suggests that these South Asian women regarded me positively, or at the very least felt comfortable with me to allow me access to their friends and family. The snowballing technique proved to be indispensable for accessing participants, as without recommendations from people known to the interviewees I would certainly have had problems accessing South Asian women. My contacts were a crucial link to the South Asian community, a link which, as a white woman, I simply did not possess. The outcome of this snowballing technique allowed me to interview sisters, mothers, and daughters, thus providing a rich source of data relating to the range of immigration experiences within one family.

Paul Maginn (2007: 436–437) refers to the snowballing method as 'sponsorship'. He argues that gaining access to people who are reluctant to participate in research necessitates an alternative strategy. Previous participants with whom the researchers have established particularly strong links are asked if they could recommend the research to others and also introduce the researchers to them. In his own research, this approach helped him to access many hard-to-reach participants across the study areas and provided a cross-section of male and female and black and white research participants. Maginn tells us: 'My first contact in London, recommended to me by a former colleague from Northern Ireland, was with an Afro-Caribbean male who worked at a black-led housing association. From this initial contact, a network of contacts engaged in urban regeneration, community development, and race and ethnic issues across London quickly snowballed' (p. 430).

But the snowball method has its own limitations. One is that it tends to result in individuals who 'resemble each other'. This can limit 'the diversity' of the research participants (Eide & Allen 2005: 6; see also Sixsmith *et al.* 2003; Mani 2006; Liamputtong 2007a, 2009, 2009). In her research with Indo-Canadians, Priya Mani (2006: 4) recruited her potential participants via the snowball sampling method. Her initial participants suggested others they knew who might be interested in participating in her study. The snowball sampling technique was effective, but 'the individuals selected were similar in acculturation levels to themselves. The result was a very select sample of individuals.'

Cultural scripts as motivation

This approach is very interesting. It is based on cultural ideology within a social group that the researchers attempt to access. I shall refer to the work of Mabel Preloran and colleagues (2001) here. Their research involved a group of women of Mexican origin who had screened positive on an α–foetoprotein (AFP) test, a routinely offered prenatal blood test, and were offered amniocentesis.

Preloran *et al.* (2001) attempted to recruit an immigrant group who customarily had a low rate of participation in social research. The researchers were also trying to recruit couples, not just individuals. These couples were also approached at a very sensitive time, in a medical setting and without offering any medical incentives.

Preloran *et al.* attempted to include male partners in their study of amniocentesis decisions to fill a gap in the literature which had focused almost exclusively on women. They argued that little is known about men's values, attitudes and needs in relation to foetal diagnosis, or how men influence the decision of women. It was crucial for them to talk to the men, as 'evidence suggests that men's wishes can be decisive in women's fertility decisions' (p. 1833).

They tell us that they had to find ways which could motivate the women and the men, as most were not interested in participating in the research. As other researchers working with ethnic minorities have found, they worked with bilingual, bicultural recruiters and it was very helpful in building trust with the participants. However, they went further. Taking a cue from the participants, they found that they could motivate the participants by 'appealing through aspects of the "traditional" gender roles found in Latino culture' (p. 1834).

Preloran *et al.* offered to do some small favours, such as helping the women communicate with hospital staff, completing hospital forms or watching their children while they were busy with medical or administrative matters. They listened sympathetically to complaints about the long hours of waiting. Occasionally, they would offer emotional support to women who became upset with the prenatal genetic testing decisions with which they were dealing. Often, they tried to develop 'friendly ties' by offering help or giving some information even before they introduced themselves as researchers. Preloran *et al.* suggest that 'these interactions followed a "cultural script" that we came to call *comadrismo*, a term derived from *madre* or mother that is commonly used by Latinas to describe relationships of trust and mutual support among women' (p. 1835).

Preloran *et al.* worked via the women in order to recruit their husbands or partners in the study. From the women's perspectives, there were two themes which could be used to persuade the men to participate in the study: 'altruism toward the child they were expecting or toward the community and home security' (p. 1836). When contacting the men, they underscored 'the altruistic aspect of collaborating with the research for the good of the children and the Latino people'. They also tried to allay the men's security concerns by telling them that they would only send a female interviewer who could be trusted. Preloran *et al.* elaborate:

> We sought to couch our approaches to Latino men in a cultural script that was familiar to them. We developed an approach that we termed *poderismo* ('powerism'), in which men were assured that they would retain control of the research process at all times, deciding when and where to meet and, should they wish, when to withdraw from the study. Under *poderismo*, men were encouraged to express their concerns about participating and to suggest ways to resolve these concerns. Instead of anticipating problems and offering solutions, as we often did with the women, we would pose the questions, 'What should we do about this?' (p. 1836)

By adopting the *poderismo* approach, Preloran *et al.* were able to recruit many reluctant men in their study. They conclude that:

> By framing our requests in terms of *comadrismo* and *poderismo*, we encouraged our male and female candidates into roles that were familiar and perhaps even comforting to them. Many female participants felt close enough to us to talk very openly about what it meant to them to have their pregnancies declared high-risk and what was involved in their decision to accept or decline amniocentesis. Likewise, by putting men 'in charge' of the research proceeding, *poderismo* gave men a reassuringly familiar role in an otherwise unfamiliar domain. These approaches were successful in raising the recruitment rate. (p. 1839)

Advertisements and making oneself seen and known

Researchers have also made use of advertisements in their attempt to recruit potential participants. It is crucial that the advertisement of a research project must be done in the native language of the targeted participants. More often, in order to reach potential participants, Western researchers will need to translate the project detail into the local language.

In a study carried out by Jennifer Harris and Keri Roberts (2003: 7), they tell us that it was clear when they were recruiting their potential participants that the material advertising the research and inviting people to participate needed to be produced in a number of languages and formats to reach those individuals who might find printed English-language material inaccessible. Therefore, brochures in English, Tamil, Sorani, Vietnamese and Somali, with Braille versions, were developed and distributed to relevant refugee community groups across Britain. Harris and Roberts also placed translated advertisements in minority ethnic newspapers and audio and visual advertisements on minority ethnic radio and TV stations. In the advertisements, they particularly emphasised that the interviews would be undertaken by interviewers from minority ethnic communities, and that the participants would be able to select whether they wanted to speak to a woman or a man.

Harris and Roberts and their first-language interviewers also participated in a number of cultural and disability events in order to promote awareness of their project and to encourage people to participate. From these methods, they were able to recruit thirty-eight participants in their study.

However, Priya Mani (2006) suggests that advertising may sometimes not work well. Judith Berg (1999: 241), for her study of midlife Filipinos, advertised the project in a Filipino community newspaper called *Philippine News*. The newspaper published two press releases about the study. Both were front-page articles. One article contained a call for interested women in the specified age range to contact the principal researcher for more information about the study or to volunteer as a research participant. However, through this means, only one woman was recruited into the study.

In Mani's research (2006: 4) with Indo-Canadians, she employed a Sikh Indo-Canadian research assistant to help with recruitment. The assistant made contact with a number of individuals she knew in the community. The participants told her that they would have been reluctant to take part in the study if 'they had been left with an advertisement and had had no opportunity to meet the researcher'.

Making use of different and innovative strategies

More often, researchers make use of different ways to recruit their potential participants. In their study with young Latina women, Cathy Lindenberg and colleagues (2001: 135) used a number of ways to recruit the women. They suggested that public communication strategies were crucial to attract the young Latina women into this programme of research:

We used multiple strategies including a catchy, colourful logo, and posters and flyers containing simple, short messages in Spanish at a fifth-grade literacy level. We used multiple sites for disseminating information. Recruitment efforts might include movie theatres, shopping malls, Hispanic supermarkets, Laundromats, community centres, and Hispanic churches, especially in residential areas where Latinos predominate. Community health and social service providers also distributed recruitment materials. Hispanic radio and Hispanic newspapers were also sources used to disseminate information and encourage participation in the research.

Nevertheless, Lindenberg *et al.* also admit that the most effective means of recruiting their participants was through personal and one-to-one interaction. The recruitment was 'most successful when conducted by well-trained recruiters who were bicultural and bilingual and who identified with the clients' (p. 135). They also made use of the telephone as a means of recruiting participants, finding that 'the telephone was another important avenue for working with Latino populations because it provided a confidential, private, and caring avenue for communication related to these sensitive topics of substance use and sexual risk-taking behaviors'. Finally, 'word of mouth' was also adopted as a means of recruitment of the women.

Interesting recruitment strategies adopted by Beverly Leipert and Linda Reutter (2005) deserve our attention here. In their study exploring how women in geographically isolated settings in northern Canada maintain their health, Leipert and Reutter recruited the women by television and radio interviews because of logistical constraints caused by distance, terrain and weather. They also placed advertisements about the research in local newspapers, and posters were displayed in tack-and-feed stores and auction markets, and they used word of mouth to recruit the participants. With these efforts, more than 100 women from across the north responded in order to take part in the study.

Andrea Shelton and Nahid Rianon (2004) provide an interesting recruitment strategy in their research on spousal abuse with Bangladeshi immigrants living in Houston. Shelton and Rianon conducted three stages of preparation, contacting and following up in their attempt to recruit Bangladeshi women to take part in their study. Initially, they were not able to obtain any participation from the women despite attempts made to meet their needs and despite the fact that Rianon is a Bangladeshi woman who speaks the same language and shares the cultural background of the women. But through the outreach efforts of the first two stages, they decided that recruitment had to be done at a large social gathering where the whole family would attend. They suggested that the interviews conducted in this setting were about their immigrant experiences, the quality of life, physical and mental distress, and suffering. After these, information about spousal abuse might be volunteered. Most women suggested that 'there would be less attention given to them individually and that they would feel less intimidated at a social outing with their husbands and peers in the midst of a large group of people engaged in the same activities (eating, watching a band, listing to music)'. In the end, twenty-nine women were recruited during three cultural events held in January and February 2000 with the approval of the Bangladeshi Association. More women were invited to take part in the study, but most declined as their husbands did not approve. It took the researchers a year of repeated efforts to engage the women in their research.

An innovative recruitment strategy that I wish to point out here is the use of beauty salons as a site for recruitment and advertising for the research project. This strategy has been adopted successfully by those in health promotion areas (Linnan *et al.* 2005). Beauty salons are settings where most people have time to talk to their cosmetologists and other customers. It presents an ideal place for the recruitment of potential participants. The researchers may work with the owners of the beauty salons or the cosmetologists and invite them to act as a recruiter for their research, or to simply ask them to give out information sheets about the research project to their customers. A number of researchers who have carried out their research with ethnic minority women have successfully used this strategy to recruit their research participants (see Key & Marble 1996; Ferdinand 1997; Kong 1997; Sadler *et al.* 2000).

I wish to add another salient issue relevant to accessing the participants. Although the researchers may be able to recruit their respondents, for some research projects, such as longitudinal research, it is crucial that they follow up these people. The researchers need to consider ways in which they might maintain the involvement of the participants. In their research with Latinos, Cathy Lindenberg and colleagues (2001: 135) employed several strategies to reduce their attrition. They tell us:

As the Latino population with whom we work is extremely mobile, it was also important to verify the current address and phone number of the participants and a close friend or relation at *every* client encounter as well as to inquire about possible moves. Personalized follow-up letters, with little gifts such as a bookmarker, birthday and other holiday cards, transportation incentives, tee shirts, and mugs, as well as financial incentives were also used to promote retention for follow-up measures.

In my own research with Filipina Turkish and Vietnamese women, we provided the women with a fridge magnet which contained the bicultural research assistants' telephone numbers. We asked the women to put the magnets on the refrigerators so that they could see them clearly and they would remind them to inform one of us if they moved from that address. We did a similar thing in my recent research with Cambodian and Iraqi mothers, but this time we made a multi-coloured postcard which the women displayed on their refrigerators.

Strategies for keeping the participants and maintaining relationships

As can be seen, it is often problematic and not easy to recruit and maintain participants. Researchers need to seek ways to make this happen. I offer a few strategies here.

Incentives/Compensation

Compensation or payment for participating in a research project is a controversial issue. Some argue that payment is not appropriate, as the participants may 'skew responses' (Booth 1999: 78). Payment can also be seen as 'coercion' if researchers work with certain groups of people, such as those who are extremely poor, homeless or using drugs (and so need money to buy drugs) (Liamputtong 2007a). Nancy Crigger and colleagues (2001: 464), for example, point out that potential participants from poor countries are indeed vulnerable to coercion. The income level (if there is any) is very low compared to the Western standard. Ten US dollars may be equivalent to a week's income for a worker in Honduras. Thus, these poor people may try to be included in research and this is seen as coercion. Some researchers view this as unethical (Paradis 2000), but others assert that researchers need to 'value the contribution, knowledge and skills' of the participants and payment should be provided to them, particularly if they have no or little money (Booth 1999: 78), for example homeless and poor people (Beauchamp et al. 2002; Umaña-Taylor & Bámaca 2004; Liamputtong 2007a). It is also a symbol of the researchers' respect for the participation of these people. This stance is applicable to researching many groups, such as ethnic women, homeless persons and the mentally ill, who tend to be poor and the money may assist them with their daily living (Madriz 1998; Umaña-Taylor & Bámaca 2004). Additionally, we have asked the research participants to sacrifice their time to participate in our research. Some feminist researchers have argued that money given to research participants should be perceived as the compensation for being research partners in the research project (Landrine *et al.* 1995; Paradis 2000).

Many Aboriginal women and the service providers who work with them see researchers as 'people who collect information and "data" from Aboriginal people but don't give anything back' (Salmon 2007: 983). One Aboriginal woman explained to Salmon that:

> I've been part of lots of research. They come, talk to us, do their research, write our names in the report like we supposedly contributed. Then they go away and we never hear from them again. Or we never see what they've written until it's been sent out all over the country. That's what researchers do all the time to the women here.

Because of this, Aboriginal community leaders have requested more reciprocal research relationships, and this can be done by the researchers providing compensation to individuals who participate in the research. Salmon contends that this was 'one of the ways in which the immediacy of such an acknowledgment often ensures that participants benefit from their involvement in research in a tangible and meaningful way … Moreover, because most Aboriginal people live well below the poverty line, even a small honorarium can significantly enable a person's participation, for example by allowing them to pay for child care, transportation, or a meal' (p. 983). In her research, Salmon gave each woman US$25 per interview as a way of acknowledging her contribution and compensation for any costs she might have incurred because of her participation in the research (p. 985). Salmon also paid for bus travel to and from the interview, and arranged on-site refreshments and child care for the women.

Offering monetary compensation can be effective in accessing potential participants (Preloran *et al.* 2001; Liamputtong 2007a, 2008). As Culhane (2004: 11) suggests, 'if the research was seen as worthwhile, if they felt respected when they participated, if honoraria and food were provided, then women would be more likely to make and keep appointments for interviews'.

Valerie Martinez-Ebers (1997) argues that compensation or monetary incentives are essential in securing hard-to-reach populations. In her study of the analysis of the effects of monetary incentives on the response rate and composition of respondents with Latino groups, Martinez-Ebers found that 'monetary incentives clearly play a vital role in securing the cooperation of the targeted population' and 'monetary incentives do not encourage panel respondents to provide more favourable answers to subjective questions' (p. 80). In their study on the connection of religion and health among African-American church members, Cheryl Holt and Stephanie McClure (2006) gave the participants US$20 at the end of the interview. The participants were not informed about these incentives when they were recruited. Two participants did not wish to take the money, and one actually returned it to the researchers while the other one donated it to the church. Holt and McClure contend that their participants were 'intrinsically interested in participation', not because of the incentive (p. 271).

In Preloran *et al.*'s (2001) study with Latinas in California, they provided financial compensation, which they referred to as a small amount, as a gesture of appreciation for the participants' time. They paid US$20 per person. The participants were only given the money after the interviews had been done. Some participants who were initially reluctant expressed more interest when they were informed about the compensation. Their research required the participation of the women's partners, who were also paid, and many women continued to express their interest but could not decide without discussing the matter with their husbands. Preloran *et al.* state that:

Becoming *comadres* (i.e., offering resources and services, including the monetary compensation) appears to have been significant in motivating some women who had been otherwise reluctant to enroll. The financial incentive was not the decisive factor in most cases, but it did make a difference for women who seemed less inclined to participate and who may have been politely trying to refuse by saying they would think about it or call back. (p. 1835)

More and more cross-cultural researchers have practised giving compensation in their research. Varas-Diaz *et al.* (2005) paid US$50 to their Puerto Ricans living with HIV/AIDS. Romero-Daza *et al.* (2003: 240) paid US$10 incentive and tokens for transportation to the Hispanic Health Council to poor Hispanic women who took part in their study of violence, drugs and street-level prostitution in Hartford, Connecticut. In my own research with women living with HIV/AIDS in Thailand (Liamputtong *et al.* 2009), we gave 200 Thai baht to each woman. We learned that the amount we gave was enough for the women to feed their families for at least two days.

Nonetheless, David Langford (2000: 139) contends that when giving an honorarium to the participants, cash should be provided and the respondents should not be required to sign a form, as this signed document could be traced and therefore the participants' confidentiality breached. He argues that this is essential in a study involving sensitive issues and vulnerable populations, such as in a domestic violence study. He suggests that researchers and their institutions should pay their participants with petty cash for the participants' parking and honorarium. The participants in his study were paid from a petty cash account so that there would be no record linking them with the study, medical centre or university. Lynn Meadows and colleagues (2003) contend that the requirement of an ethics committee to obtain a signature for the receipt of compensation might compromise the confidentiality of the research participants. This has to be discussed carefully in researching groups such as Aboriginal people. Adriana Umaña-Taylor and Mayra Bámaca (2004: 265) assert that obtaining personal information for payment, such as a social security number from Latinos in the US, may cause a feeling of vulnerability amongst these groups, as most of them are undocumented immigrants. This could discourage them from taking part in the research. Dina Birman (2006) gives a similar warning to researchers who work in cross-cultural research. In her inquiry with former Soviet immigrants, the respondents were given some cash and the university required not only signed receipts from these people but also their social security numbers. The participants were very uncomfortable with this process. They felt that it completely undermined the assurances of confidentiality from the researchers. Because this was attempted, the participants became suspicious that their social security number was being used by the researcher to obtain personal information for the state office of refugee resettlement.

Incentives or compensation may not need to be in cash. Umaña-Taylor and Bámaca (2004: 265) suggest that if personal information is needed for compensation, researchers may provide other means of incentives, such as gift vouchers. They supplied the participants with US$20 gift vouchers from a local general store. In their study on breast cancer screening among African-American women, Husaini *et al.* (2001) gave all the women grocery gift certificates worth US$30. In Shelton and Rianon's (2004: 377) study of spousal abuse within the Bangladeshi community in Houston, the participants were given a gift bag that included sample products and coupon vouchers donated by local shops. A meal, food vouchers or bus tokens rather than cash were given to homeless participants in Unger *et al.*'s (1997) study. Takahashi and Kai (2005) gave a prepaid, public telephone card worth 1000 yen (US$9.00) as a thank-you gift to their participants. In their study, Bender and colleagues (2001) gave a gender- and language-neutral baby toy to Latina immigrant women as a way to thank them for their participation. Romero-Daza *et al.* (2003) provided educational material on HIV/AIDS and referrals to drug treatment, health and social services for the women in their study. As Kathleen Ragsdale and her co-researcher (in Fisher & Ragsdale 2006: 16) had a limited budget for their research with sex workers in Belize, monetary incentive was not provided to the women. Through the process of learning from the research participants, nail polish was suggested as a culturally appropriate token of appreciation for the participants. Nail polish was perceived as an 'extra' by these young women, as they did not have easy access to it. The women received a few bottles of nail polish and they were allowed to choose their own colours.

However, this can be assessed on an individual case. Lynn Meadows and colleagues (2003) intended to buy traditional offerings of tobacco for the Aboriginal women in their study, but were informed by their Aboriginal assistant that the women preferred cash as they had more need of money than tobacco. In Margaret Weeks and colleagues' (2007) study with female sex workers in southern China, all participants were provided with free transportation to the interview and were given a small gift package containing toiletries and other health items and free condoms. The gift package was worth about 20 Chinese yuan (about US$2.50). This was seen as more appropriate by the local team.

Also, there is always another side to the coin. As Cathy Lindenberg and colleagues (2001: 136) point out in their study of Latina women, the participants felt 'uncomfortable receiving financial cash incentives (they felt that they were being "bought") and that they would prefer coupons or gift certificates for grocery or department stores'. In Betty Davies and colleagues' (2009) research with Mexican Americans and Chinese Americans, the community advisory group and bicultural research assistants advised that offering the families a small food gift, such as fruit or cookies, was 'an important gesture of gratitude and respect' and 'establishes rapport'. It is so 'culturally significant' that their research assistants did not feel comfortable arriving at the participants' homes empty-handed. They were also informed that 'offering money would be inappropriate and offensive in both cultures'. Some Alaska Native participants in the People Awakening project declined a US$25 honorarium as they considered that their stories were a gift for their communities (Mohatt & Thomas 2006).

Reciprocity

Not only must we provide financial compensation to our participants, it is also essential that the researchers give something back to participants for their time and valuable knowledge. By giving something in return for receiving information, researchers can reduce the power inequality between themselves and the researched (Liamputtong 2007a). More importantly, the participants will be able to see that the researchers have genuine concerns about their lives and well-being.

Reciprocity can include providing information useful to the participants. Harris and Roberts (2003) prepared information about entitlements to welfare services in England for their participants, as many of them lack knowledge about their rights and entitlements. In Pauw and Brener's (2003) study with female street sex workers in Cape Town, the women were provided with AIDS education as well as HIV/STD educational material after their participation in in-depth or focus group interviews.

Very often, researchers will find that participants may request some form of help during or at the end of the interviews. Many people from ethnic minority groups have limited English. They may ask the researchers to help with filling in forms, writing a letter to the social security department, phoning the school principal about a letter that one of their children has brought home and so on. Children who are in school may ask the researchers for help with an essay or homework. This was often my experience in research with some ethnic groups in Australia. It is usual for cross-cultural researchers to respond to any request for help, as very often the participants lack the knowledge, skills or support for what they need to do. In Harris and Roberts's (2003: 8) study, their participants asked for help with clarification and understanding of official letters they received after the interviews. The researchers 'responded positively to requests to write letters, for instance, requesting that service providers correspond with the interviewee in accessible formats'.

Rachel Hall's (2004: 137) research was with South Asian women in Great Britain. One woman said that she would only participate in the project if Hall helped her with an immigration application that she was making. Hall did so. She explains that:

Had she consulted a solicitor she would have been charged for the advice, whereas I gladly gave the advice freely as a way in which I could give something back to the researched beyond the interview situation … On at least one other occasion I have sent an interviewee who hoped to enter politics, information on minority-ethnic parliamentary candidates. Hopefully, these acts helped to establish a reciprocal, albeit minimal relationship between the interviewees and myself, whilst demonstrating that I did not forget about the South Asian women as soon as the interview finished.

It is also crucial that, following the completion of the research project, arrangements are made for each participant to receive a report of the research findings in a culturally and appropriate format so that it is more accessible to the participants (Harris & Roberts 2003: 9). In her research with Aboriginal mothers who experienced FAS/FAE, Amy Salmon (2007: 985) tells us that the women were frustrated with their experiences with researchers in the community who would 'come, do the research, and then it's months or years before we hear from them again'. Salmon was keen to bring the findings of her research back to the women as quickly as possible. She did so when she conducted the second interview with the women, which was about six weeks after the first interview.

Some researchers may go further than this. Reciprocity may include some form of social action or social change as part of the project. This can be seen in my own research with the Hmong ethnic community in Melbourne, when I brought one Hmong woman, who strongly believed that her ill health following her last childbirth was due to the loss of one of her souls following a caesarean section. During the course of my research, I took her back to the maternity hospital to conduct a soul-calling ritual to regain her health (see Liamputtong Rice *et al.* 1994; Liamputtong 2009, and Chapter 1 in this volume).

Theophilus Gokah (2006: 70) also behaved as more than a mere researcher. He asserts that 'for me as a researcher, I see my role as going beyond my immediate locale. Thus, as a social researcher my contribution to knowledge, awareness creation and practice are synonymous. Hence, turning a blind eye to urgent needs (in spite of the researcher's financial and physical ability to deal with the situation) such as those I encountered is hypocritical.'

In one community where he conducted his research, Gokah was told about a child who was a clever boy but, due to poverty, his mother could not afford to keep him in school. As a result, the boy was wandering about in the village. Gokah was very sympathetic to the child's condition and, without losing the focus of his research, he paid a fee for the boy to return to school the next day. But Gokah cautions us that he is not saying that all 'researchers in the field must take "action". This is purely a moral issue and its judgement rests with the researcher' (p. 70). In another case, he came across two children who were affected by malaria, but the parents could not afford medication and treatment. He, of course, supported the children, who then received treatment. He also tells us that when he returned to the UK, his colleagues organised some financial contributions to make sure that more children could go to school. He contends that the step taken by him as a researcher in poor countries is not only a reciprocal effort but a practical one.

In her research with poor women living in a slum in Dhaka, Sabina Rashid (2007) was asked by many women to help them. As with Gokah, Rashid admits that, as a researcher, it is difficult for her to be 'objective or invisible' (p. 380). Rashid comes from a different social class from her participants and she had never 'seen or imagined the poverty in the slum'. She therefore did many things to help the women.

I took some women to a charity clinic in the city for health care and paid the local NGO clinic fee (TK20) for others. I paid for the treatment of one adolescent woman's husband, who had been ill for some time. My research assistant and I shared our lunches and brought gifts of fruit, vegetables, and meat to the families with whom we were close and on whose discretion we could rely. Toward the end of my field-work after the eviction, I financially helped a few of the most vulnerable women – the abandoned, the widowed, and the extremely poor. I struggled with whether this would compromise my objectivity, but in the end, I could not remain aloof and was convinced of the instrumental value for my own work of intervening – that any loss in objectivity would be more than offset by the trust gained, the close relationships formed, and the depth of the information gathered.

When I was writing my book on childbirth and Asian mothers (Liamputtong Rice 1999), I asked one of my participants to be photographed for the cover of the book. In return, the woman and her family received a small sum of money from the publisher and a copy of the book. I also gave her a small sum from my own pocket. Even though the sum was not large, it helped the whole family, since they had only recently arrived and relied on social security benefit for survival in Australia. The book was also a great honour for the family for a long time. Whenever they had visitors, the woman and her family would show the book to their guests, and everyone would congratulate them for being on the book cover. I believe that even little things such as what I have done for my participants provide reciprocity that our participants greatly value.

Tutorial activities

You are a new researcher who will be doing your research with an ethnic community in your area. You have been told in previous research that it has been very difficult to recruit members of this ethnic community.
- How will you go about this?
- What will be the best possible strategies for you to access this community?

• What important issues do you need to consider in your attempt to recruit them?

Chapter summary

In this chapter, I have discussed salient issues relevant to the research participants in cross-cultural research. I have pointed to accessing issues: how we can find our research participants, particularly when they do not wish to be found or when they are very suspicious of the research project or the researchers. It can be problematic for many researchers to try to enter into the community. Hence, gaining access to potential participants or research sites can be a challenging task. I have therefore suggested several strategies that cross-cultural researchers may adopt in their attempts to access their potential participants and to maintain relationships with those participants so that their research can be done successfully. As Paul Maginn (2007: 438) contends, 'gaining access to culturally diverse sites to ask sensitive questions means that researchers will need to be prepared to assert a range of strategies and tactics to win over the trust and confidence of gatekeepers and informants … This means initiating, developing, and solidifying relationships with a diverse range of people.'

You need to bear in mind that what I have suggested cannot guarantee that you will be able to enter successfully. There are many other issues that researchers need to consider, and these will be discussed in the chapters that follow.

SUGGESTED READING

Berg, J. A. (1999). Gaining access to underresearched populations in women's health research. *Health Care for Women International* **20**, 237–243.

Crowley, J. E. (2007). Friend or foe? Self-expansion, stigmatized groups, and the researcher-participant relationship. *Journal of Contemporary Ethnography* **36**(6), 603–630.

Liamputtong, P. (2007). *Researching the vulnerable: A guide to sensitive research methods*. London: Sage Publications.

Maginn, P. (2007). Negotiating and securing access: Reflections from a study into urban regeneration and community participation in ethnically diverse neighborhoods in London, England. *Field Methods* **19**(4), 425–440.

Preloran, H. M., Browner, C. H., & Lieber, E. (2001). Strategies for motivating Latino couples' participation in qualitative health research and their effects on sample construction. *American Journal of Public Health* **91**(11), 1832–1841.

Rashid, S. F. (2007). Accessing married adolescent women: The realities of ethnographic research in an urban slum environment in Dhaka, Bangladesh. *Field Methods* **19**(4), 369–383.

Rodríguez, M. D., Rodríguez, J., & Davis, M. (2006). Recruitment of first-generation Latinos in a rural community: The essential nature of personal contact. *Family Process* **45**(1), 87–100.

Salmon, A. (2007). Walking the talk: How participatory interview methods can democratize research. *Qualitative Health Research* **17**(7), 982–993.

4 Cultural sensitivity: a responsible researcher

> Researchers doing research with ethnic minorities should be cognisant of the customs, values, and beliefs of the target group(s) before designing any project.
>
> (Hunt & Bhopal 2004: 621)

Cultural sensitivity is an important issue in conducting research with people from different cultures (Weinfurt & Maghaddam 2001; Papadopoulos & Lees 2002; Walsh-Tapiata 2003; Hall & Kulig 2004; dé Ishtar 2005a, 2005b; Birman 2006; Liamputtong 2008). Cultural sensitivity, according to Joan Sieber (1992: 20), is 'the understanding and approaches that enable one to gain access to individuals in a given culture and to learn about their actual lifestyles (beliefs, habits, needs, fears and risks)'. In Phylis Eide and Carol Allen's terms (2005: 4), this is referred to as knowing the cultural context of the group that the researchers wish to work with. The researchers exhibit 'cultural sensitivity and competence' through their knowledge of the key values of the social groups. They also need to demonstrate 'culturally appropriate communication and willingness to learn'.

Without appropriate cultural sensitivity, misunderstanding or (worse) racist attitudes may surface and this will jeopardise the progress of research, or at the extreme level, the termination of your project. Bahira Sherif (2001: 444) tells us about her experiences while conducting research in Egypt. Some of her American colleagues who dressed in 'a very provocative manner' repeatedly said that they were extremely displeased with 'the unwanted attention' from the men on the streets. After a particularly unpleasant incident, Sherif advised them to 'tone down their appearance', but her suggestions were responded with negative comments such as, 'I am free to dress and do as I please'. A number of American researchers and students exhibited a 'rebellious attitude' which was similar to racism. Sherif (2001: 444) comments that 'because they did not feel connected to any part of the culture and lacked an understanding and appreciation of the society, a certain percentage of the American scholarly community decided that it was useless to try to assimilate. Instead, it was easier to adopt a supercilious attitude and point out that the reason for the many obvious problems in a country such as Egypt had to do with the incompetence of the people.'

This example is an extreme case of cultural insensitivity, but it demonstrates how such insensitivity might prohibit researchers from successfully carrying out their project. In conducting cross-cultural research, there are many forms of cultural sensitivity to be carefully considered (Laverack & Brown 2003; Liamputtong 2008). I shall point out several salient issues in this chapter.

The acquisition of cultural knowledge

Performing cross-cultural research necessitates the acquisition of cultural knowledge of the social group that the researchers wish to learn from (Papadopoulos & Lees 2002; Hall & Kulig 2004; Struthers & Peden-McAlpine 2005; Birman 2006; Liamputtong 2008; Topp *et al.* 2008). This means researchers need to have a thorough understanding of the culture, which includes extensive knowledge of 'social, familial, cultural, religious, historical and political backgrounds' (Jackson & Mead Niblo 2003: 24). Eun-Ok Im and colleagues (2004: 895) refer to this as 'culturally competent knowledge', which 'provides a context for the phenomenon, the research questions, the results, and the interpretations'. Context, according to Im *et al.*, is an important part of cross-cultural research. Context, accordingly, 'includes sensitivity to structural conditions that contribute to participants' responses and to the interpretations of situations informed by experiences, by validation of perceptions, and by a careful review of existing knowledge. Without contextual understanding, cross-cultural … phenomena cannot be fully understood' (p. 895).

A good example of this issue is discussed by Ponce and Comer (2003), in their review of studies on acculturation in the United States. Ponce and Comer assert that most acculturation studies ignore the socioeconomic contexts which hinder the everyday lives of ethnic minority people. They refer to two studies which suggested that Mexican Americans were people who had low aspirations and no interest in education. But the reality was that children of poor Mexican-American peasants were restrained by educational opportunities; their teachers discouraged them and they were sometimes needed by their parents to start working at a young age. Without a cultural context, studies such as these will surely misrepresent ethnic minorities and contribute to negative stereotypes of these poor people (Im *et al.* 2004).

My point is that sensitivity to the culture is good, but this is still not good enough. Knowledge of the culture is essential so that the researchers can work more effectively with members of the community. Sabina Rashid (2007: 377), in her research on the reproductive health of poor women living in a slum in Dhaka, Bangladesh, was very particular about obtaining cultural knowledge in working with the community. She and the research team learned about the importance of mothers-in-law in Bangladeshi culture. Their strategy was then to establish a rapport with the mothers-in-law so that they would grant permission to Rashid to interview their daughters-in-law. Rashid contends that: 'In patrilocal households in Bangladesh, newlywed women are expected to obey their in-laws and to accept restricted mobility outside the household, and indeed, we had easiest access to married adolescent women who lived either with their own mothers or in neolocal households.' Knowing this cultural concept allowed Rashid and her research team to successfully access many women.

There are many ways in which researchers can acquire cultural knowledge. Some intensive training on cross-cultural issues will help a great deal (Russon 1995; Laverack & Brown 2003), but I contend that it is only by immersion in the culture that researchers may have an in-depth and accurate understanding of the cultural groups. This necessitates a long-term relationship or a long stay within the group (Corbie-Smith *et al.* 2002; Meadows *et al.* 2003; Sixsmith *et al.* 2003; dé Ishtar 2005a, 2005b; Eide & Allen 2005). For researchers who share social and cultural characteristics, this may not be too problematic, but there are many subtle issues that they may need to take into consideration (see Douglas 1998; Madriz 1998; Izugbara 2000; Papadopoulos & Lees 2002; Ezeh 2003).

Individually, cross-cultural researchers need to have the following skills and qualities in order for the success of their research: 'tolerance for ambiguity, patience, adaptiveness, capacity for tacit learning and courtesy' (Laverack & Brown 2003: 334). As Eide and Allen (2005: 6) suggest, the researchers need to know the culture as well as the individual participants. This is a time-consuming process and requires the researchers to have flexibility and a willingness to learn (see also Hall & Kulig 2004). Eide and Allen (2005: 4) suggest:

When researchers and participants have widely disparate cultural norms, the researchers' humility, cultural sensitivity, and caring contribute to building a bridge of trust among them. The researcher demonstrates cultural sensitivity and competence through knowing key values and stakeholders, and exhibiting culturally appropriate communication and willingness to learn.

It is also imperative to have a team that includes members of the local community. A person who is working closely with the local people will be the most suitable person for cross-cultural research (see Benatar & Singer 2000; Lindenberg *et al.* 2001; Michaud *et al.* 2001; Laverack & Brown 2003; Redmond 2003; Hall & Kulig 2004; Birman 2006). As Eide and Allen (2005: 2) contend, research which will have benefit for the local group must be developed and carried out in collaboration with local members. This can be done when the researchers get to know, and are also known by, community members and their leaders. Eide and Allen suggest that in some aboriginal communities, such as Hawaiians and Micronesians, 'knowing and being known are crucial to every activity'. This 'knowing and being known' will accommodate research entry and success in recruiting potential participants in these cultural groups. I have discussed this in Chapter 3.

In their cross-cultural research on the health and behaviour of young people, Pierre-André Michaud and colleagues (2001: 1237) suggest that researchers may come across different aspects of traditions, beliefs and behaviour amongst group members even though these young people are from within a particular cultural group. Researchers need to work collaboratively with local people in order to interpret their data correctly. They suggest that the interpretation and dissemination of research findings must be carried out sensitively and that it should be done with the assistance of experts from the cultural or ethnic groups with whom the researchers have worked. Michaud *et al.* contend that, in cross-cultural research, the research team must facilitate 'attention to complex cultural data by providing the expertise in instrument design ... as well as providing different perspectives during interpretation' (p. 1242).

Some researchers have tried to acquire cultural knowledge in order to overcome cultural insensitivity by establishing an advisory committee for the research project consisting of members of the cultural groups or of people who have extensive knowledge about the group. This committee can assist the research team with a range of issues including cultural knowledge (Small *et al.* 1999a, 1999b; Hall & Kulig 2004; Gibson *et al.* 2005; Molzahn *et al.* 2005; Topp *et al.* 2008). Nancy Gibson and colleagues (2005) also worked with what they called the Community Advisory Committee (CAC) in their research on the prevention and treatment of tuberculosis in immigrant and aboriginal communities in Canada. Members of the CAC were sought from existing organisations 'with a view to ethnic origin, networking experience, leadership skills and knowledge of community health in its broadest sense' (p. 933). These members helped them in the planning and conduct of the study, and guided and contributed to the overall research process. They participated in the recruitment, selection and training of the community research assistants. CAC members were also instrumental in providing 'advice on how research in their cultures should be conducted in a sensitive and appropriate manner' (p. 933).

A study on beliefs about organ donations amongst Chinese Canadians was carried out by Anita Molzahn and colleagues (2005). They were assisted by a Chinese Canadian advisory committee which was formed essentially because all members of the research team were white. The committee provided culrurally appropriate advice on the selection of research participants, strategies to recruit the participants, how to elicit good information from the participants, data analysis and validation of the results. In their study on smoking behaviour in a remote indigenous Australian community, Vanessa Johnson and David Thomas (2008: 1709) set up a reference group that included representatives from the community. The reference group offered guidance on the research process, including advice on questions to be used, crucial cultural protocols and the need to employ a cultural broker in the community who could introduce potential research participants to the researchers.

I was one of the chief investigators in the Mothers in a New Country (MINC) project conducted with immigrant women in Melbourne, Australia (Small *et al.* 1999a, 1999b). We established a Reference Group to advise us on our project. The Reference Group broadened the research team's expertise in researching three immigrant groups of women: Filipino, Turkish and Vietnamese. The Group comprised advocates from all three immigrant groups and one invited community member. The Reference Group assisted us with the selection of bicultural researchers, the translation of research tools, the training programme, the interpretation of research data and the dissemination processes. Indeed, the Group proved to be an invaluable part of the success of our cross-cultural research.

Cross-cultural research and sensitivity: practical issues for consideration

Researchers need to prepare for some practical issues, and I shall point to some important ones in the following sub-sections.

Respect for cultural norms

Respect for the cultural values and practices of the research participants is a crucial part of performing cross-cultural research (Walsh-Tapiata 2003; Chin *et al.* 2006; Bishop 2008). For example, in a group discussion in Fiji, research participants may be seated according to their status. This means that those with a higher status will be seated at the front and those with less status will be placed at the back. This may create some problems with interaction in the group but it is up to the skill of the moderator to ensure full participation from all members of the group.

Participants may turn up at the interview sites late and the procedure may go slowly, and this may be due to the perception of time in a cultural setting; in their research, Glenn Laverack and Kevin Brown refer to it as 'Fiji time'. Laverack and Brown (2003: 340) elaborate: 'Fiji time means that priorities are different in different cultural contexts. The social ceremonies and customs of Fiji are of great importance and can take precedence over "just getting things done". A casual pace is taken as a normal part of rural Fijian life, and plans can be changed at short notice' (see also Madriz (1998) with her research with Latina women for a similar situation). Laverack and Brown suggest that researchers working in a cross-cultural context must be flexible in order to accommodate an uncertain and different time frame in the local cultural group. The following occasion is a good example of 'Fiji time':

During the fieldwork the participants arrived around mid-morning after travelling to the community or after completing their domestic duties. The research was preceded by the ceremony of *sevusevu*, which took between 30 and 45 minutes, and this was then followed by tea and snacks. Starting the research midday resulted in the cool of the morning's being lost, and sometimes the work had to be conducted under rushed circumstances.

In their conclusion, Laverack and Brown (2003: 341) suggest that Western researchers need to have a good 'understanding of the fluid social dynamics and complex balance of relationships that occur between research participants in a cross-cultural setting'. Some local practices may be seen as non-significant by researchers, but they can have a great impact on the research participants. In their research, the practice of the seating arrangement for different groups of people was important for the Fijians, and they had to observe this rule when carrying out their project.

In Japanese culture, there is a tradition of *omiyage*. It is the custom that a visitor will bring a gift for a person whom he or she visits to show an appreciation for being welcomed into the home. This tradition was honoured by Gayle Iwamasa and Kristen Sorocco (2002) during their fieldwork at a Japanese-American senior citizens' centre in Los Angeles. They provided gifts such as artworks, flowers, plants, and photography supplies for their participants and the staff of the centre as a way of showing respect for the Japanese culture and appreciation for being accepted to do research with them. See also the writings of Wheturangi Walsh-Tapiata (2003) and Russell Bishop (2008), who provide the cultural practices of the Māori that researchers need to be familiar with before they can commence their research with Māori people in New Zealand.

In Wendy Winslow and colleagues' (2002) study of women in the United Arab Emirates, they used a focus group method to elicit information from the participants. They point out that selecting an appropriate time for the group discussion is essential. As many Emiratis rest during the intense heat of the afternoon, focus groups should be conducted during the morning or evening. Additionally, Muslim women pray five times each day and hence the time chosen for research should not interfere with these daily prayers. However, Winslow *et al.* also contend that the prayer time can be seen as a natural break during a group discussion, as women in their study were able to resume the group discussion easily as they perceived prayers as part of the natural rhythm of their day. A group moderator must also be female, as this would be appropriate to the culture. It is important that the seating arrangements in focus groups need to be culturally considered. Women in the Arab world are accustomed to sitting cross-legged in a circle on a rug with shoes off. In Winslow *et al.*'s study, they point out that this allowed the women to have a natural involvement and interaction which might not have occurred if the women were sitting at tables on chairs.

Neil Spicer (2005: 2167) provides another interesting angle in performing cross-cultural research. Spicer interviewed a number of both sedentarised and semi-nomadic families in the northeast Badia of Jordan. His position as an Anglo white male has implications for the conduct of a study in an Islamic society. In this study, he could interview only male parents. He laments, 'not interviewing women limits the study since mothers tend to be the principal child carers in the northeast Badia'. However, as adult male family members tend to accompany their wives when the children were taken to health services, he believed that these men could provide him with a useful set of perspectives on the heath of their children. Spicer was not allowed to tape-record the interviews as the men believed it might jeopardise their anonymity and he had to take extensive notes, including verbatim quotes. He initially aimed to examine differences in how these men seek health for their male and female children. But this issue had to be abandoned, as the topic 'offended and in some cases incensed' the participants. Others indicated emphatically that boys and girls are 'treated equally with respect to health and illness'.

Within the Pacific Island groups, cultures are likely 'to be high context and collectivistic' (Eide & Allen 2005: 4). These cultures are more homogeneous. Interactions between members of the cultural group are dictated by norms and expectations which are positioned within the social context of the culture. Communication between members is 'implicit, and meanings are interpreted primarily from the context and from nonverbal cues'. Often, these cultural norms and expectations complicate matters and make it difficult for outside researchers who do not share the same cultural values. High-context cultures such as the Pacific Islanders' are collectivist and the needs and concerns of the group, including the family and the clan or the social unit are emphasised and are more important than the individuals' needs and concerns. These cultural values are in contrast with Western cultural norms, which honour explicit communication and an individualistic pattern. This can create misunderstanding among researchers who are not familiar with the culture, and if the researchers do not respect the cultural norms and expectations of the group, it can jeopardise their research progress.

When Sahar Al-Makhamreh (in Al-Makhamreh & Lewando-Hundt 2008: 18) interviewed elderly Jordanian participants, she used fictive kinship terms such as 'father' or 'mother' or 'grandfather' or 'grandmother' to address them in order to show respect. Often, she would recite a poem to honour their status. This proved to be very helpful for obtaining acceptance as an insider from her participants so that she could carry out interviews in their households after they had been discharged from hospital.

Even though Al-Makhamreh is a Christian, in her interviews with the participants who were Muslim she cited many well-known vernacular phrases relating to Allah, such as 'Allah kareem' ('God is generous) and 'Destinay' ('Naseeb or Kader'). These formulaic greetings and wishing people comfort and relief were crucial in her interactions with the participants. They were important for the opening and closing of conversations, and they were used when listening to the stories told by the participants.

Asking questions and recording conversations

In some situations, communication styles such as the wording of questions may also impact on the data collected (see Redmond (2003) for his example of using the simple question 'Why?' in cross-cultural research). The acquisition of cultural knowledge will prevent researchers asking insensitive questions or using culturally inappropriate (insensitive) words.

Some questions can also be problematic with certain groups in cross-cultural research. Christopher Dunbar and colleagues (2002: 294) assert that researchers need not only to ask culturally sensitive questions, but also to 'ask questions in a culturally relevant and explicit manner'. If researchers are not cautious about this, it can jeopardise their research project and, worse, the data collected may be inaccurate. In his research on education with young black people in the US, Dunbar tells us that when he asked Bobby, one of the participants, if anyone at home helped him with his homework and to prompt him to go to sleep at a reasonable time, Bobby said, 'Wat yu trying to say, Mr. Dunbar, dat dare's somtin' wrong with my family?' (p. 294). Dunbar points out that the majority of poor African-American children have been 'interviewed, tested, incarcerated, restrained, denied, abused, lied to, and misled' so often that they learn to have 'a keen ear for what is being asked *implicitly*' (p. 294). Some children will question what they have been asked, but others might say what they think the researchers want to hear.

If the research project involves discussion about sexual matters, the researchers need to be cautious about asking questions. In most Asian cultures, sex is regarded as taboo, a personal matter, not something that should be talked about with other people. However, it is possible to discuss it with caution, and particularly with a person of the same gender. Many years ago, when I was working as a research assistant, I had to interview Cambodian refugees about their health beliefs and practices. One of the scales that I had to use contained a question on sexual interest or pleasure. I had to say to the participants: 'I have to ask you the following question in order to complete our questions. Please do not feel offended by it or feel that I am rude, and please forgive me if you feel that the question is too intrusive.' Then, I proceeded, and it worked well. This usually works as long as we are careful and let the participants know that we are aware of and respect their customs.

When I was collecting data on childbearing and reproductive health among Southeast Asian women, I needed to obtain some information related to cultural practices during pregnancy and a period after birth (confinement). One sensitive question was about sexual intercourse during these periods. I again used the apologetic approach before asking the question. More often than not, the women felt that I understood their cultural norms and values. As a result, they were willing to tell me about their practices, often with laughing and giggling.

It is typical in qualitative research that conversations are recorded for detailed analysis. Often, this may not be a problem as long as researchers ask for permission from the participants. But with certain groups in cross-cultural research, this may pose difficulties (Gokah 2006; Poulin 2007; Subedi 2007). This can have great impact on our research as it could terminate the research or have a marked impact on the interview process. The danger exists, as Steen Mangen (1999: 117) cautions, 'that recording can inhibit respondents or cause them to decline to participate: Some cultures are not attuned to non-official interviews at all, especially when they are being recorded; and in "expert" interviews there may be the added possibility of respondents' concern about the attribution of material being collected.'

In their work with Kanadier Mennonites (religious groups living in Canada but originating from Mexico), Barry Hall and Judith Kulig (2004: 365) did not tape-record the interviews. This was because, when viewed from a biblical perspective, the use of technology was seen as 'being too worldly and deemed inappropriate'. Notes were taken during the interviews and, soon after the session, the research assistants tape-recorded a summary of the interview so that other research teams were able to examine the data. Although some of the data were lost in this process, it was a way to show respect to the cultural group with whom they worked.

In my work, I occasionally came across this problem. I interviewed several women from Muslim backgrounds. The women did not want me to tape-record our conversation and the reason they gave was their husbands did not wish them to record their voices in any form. Some said that it is prohibited in Islam for a woman's voice to be recorded. In these situations, I had to take extensive notes and write them up soon after I returned home when my memory was still fresh. I had to respect the women's cultural needs and find other ways to do my work.

In his research in sub-Saharan Africa, Theophilus Gokah (2006) suggests that there were occasions when asking permission to tape-record conversations met with difficulty. Despite his reassurance of anonymity to the participants, some of them could not overcome their fear of being taped. One informant in Gokah's research became nervous about this; 'she jerked backwards, panicky and requested to seek further clearance from her boss' (p. 68). Another participant 'spoke very low and carefully. No amount of prompting will make him speak up as if to say he did not want those nearby to hear what he was saying … I literally had to push my microphone under his chin to ensure that I had recorded his voice' (p. 68).

Michelle Poulin (2007: 2385), in her research on sex in Malawi, did not record the conversations during the interviews, as she believed that it would cause discomfort to the young women. As premarital sexual relationships are often secretive, 'a sexually active 15-year-old girl may feel less comfortable speaking about her relationship were she asked to record her words into an unfamiliar looking machine'. In order to prevent or minimise any undue anxiety, Poulin took notes. However, she performed extra steps to overcome a limitation of note taking, which tends to be the 'potential loss of important, translatable information'. Based on the notes, the bicultural research assistant immediately reconstructed each interview and translated it into English. Poulin then read through each interview and checked the reconstruction and translation. Poulin asserts that:

These steps allowed for quick clarification of any confusion with the translation or with uncertainties over the meaning of any of the interviewer's writing; more broadly, this process also allowed me to respond more efficiently to general problems with the interviews. The speed of the verification process improved the interviewer's ability to remember certain details and thus made it easier for me to address a concern. (p. 2385)

Poulin also acknowledged that the translated data depended on what the assistant could remember. Hence, there might be some subtle losses in the transcripts. But she also said that conversational interviews without the use of recorders have permitted many researchers to access local understandings, and this is what ethnographers do when they are in the field and writing field notes. During her fieldwork, Poulin also undertook many informal conversations with key informants and acquaintances, colleagues and/or strangers. These informal conversations, made without recording, have provided her with invaluable knowledge for the interpretation of her data in Malawi.

According to Binaya Subedi (2007: 63), resistance to conversations being recorded has implications for the development of a culturally appropriate research approach. He contends that 'the discourse on the resistance to being tape-recorded cannot be seen in isolation since marginalized communities may have legitimate concerns over data being misused' (see also Abu-Lughod 1988; Anderson 1993; Freimuth et al. 2001). Recording may be seen as 'a form of surveillance' by the participants (see Gwaltney 1981). Hence, the resistance of participants to the audio-recording of interviews must be recognised by the researchers. The willingness or resistance of the participants to being recorded can have a great impact on the nature of the data being collected. This was the experience of Subedi in his research with Asian Americans.

Subedi says that we should not be too surprised when our participants tell us not to record the conversations. In his own research, Subedi (2007: 64) admits that:

Athough my intention in audio-recording the conversations was an effect of my desire to 'get it right' ... I had not taken into consideration what the teachers felt about being recorded. Too often I was consumed by the thought that I could not have the 'real' data or that my research would not be interpreted as compelling or valid if I did not record the conversation. Was I exerting a form of research authority by insisting on archiving the teachers' voices? This has much to do with the ways in which I interpreted recorded data as a form of 'evidence' and as proof of my field-work – perhaps to claim that my participants were visible and 'real' and that they spoke to me.

As with the examples I have given above, Subedi took notes of the conversations he had with his participants who did not wish to be recorded.

Developing a trusting relationship

Instilling trust is crucial in cross-cultural research (Preloran *et al.* 2001; Walsh-Tapiata 2003; Liamputtong 2008; Topp *et al.* 2008). To collect excellent and reliable data from individuals of different cultures, researchers need to develop a trusting relationship with their research participants in order to establish a good rapport and maintain cultural sensitivity. This should be developed before any data collection takes place and should continue throughout the life of the research (Corbie-Smith *et al.* 2002; Papadopoulos & Lees 2002; Ryen 2002; Laverack & Brown 2003; Walsh-Tapiata 2003; Hall & Kulig 2004; Sin 2004; Fisher & Ragsdale 2006; Salmons 2007; Weeks *et al.* 2007; Smith 2008). It is suggested by Chih Hoong Sin (2004: 266) that when undertaking research with older ethnic minority people, researchers must spend time building up trust and rapport with the participants. Similarly, Phyllis Eide and Carol Allen (2005: 5) point out that developing trust is crucial, but it can also be more difficult when the researcher and the participant do not share the same culture. This is particularly so if the researcher is from a group that has historically been an oppressor or coloniser of the potential participant group. In this case, building up trust can be difficult and requires more time (Lindenberg *et al.* 2001; Corbie-Smith *et al.* 2002; Walsh-Tapiata 2003; Salmon 2007).

Amy Salmon (2007), in her research with Aboriginal women who had experienced substance use and foetal alcohol syndrome (FAS/FAE), had some difficulties in accessing the women, and this was mainly due to their negative experiences with previous research. While she was working on another community-based health project, she came to know Mary, who was a well-known Aboriginal community leader and activist. The discussion that Salmon had with Mary often pointed to the impact of research on the lives of Aboriginal women in the local area. Mary would often say about university-based researchers in her community that 'It's more of the same, it's colonization all over again'. Salmon was also very clear about her personal politics and commitments to feminist and anti-colonial research, and she shared this with Mary. Salmon held similar personal views to Mary regarding their mutual commitment to help Aboriginal women who had experienced substance use and FAS/FAE. This opened up an opportunity for Salmon to develop a trusting relationship with Mary. From then on, Mary assisted Salmon with recruitment and became actively involved in the research.

In their research with female sex workers in Southern China, Margaret Weeks and colleagues (2007: 192–193) tell us that one of the research team had worked on the study sites for many years, carrying out sexually transmitted infection (STI) and HIV prevention and epidemiological research, collaborating with local health promoters and health care providers to gain entry to sex work establishments. She had built rapport and trust with many sex workers and the owners of brothels. Weeks speaks Mandarin and had also previously carried out extended research in Beijing. This assisted her in building her rapport with some of the brothel owners. In order to establish and maintain the trust (which was particularly needed in her study), the research team and local research staff adopted 'a non-judgmental approach' towards the sex workers and the owners. They clearly stated that the purpose of their research was to obtain information on issues relevant to the health of the women and their clients. With each visit, they also provided the women and the brothel owners with health promotional information and materials, for example free condoms. Because of their ongoing work in the community, many of the local health promotion staff were known to the women and the owners.

Weeks *et al.* also ensured that their research protocols would protect the identity of the participants and all research activities were done in private. This was another attempt by them to build up rapport with the participants. Before any interview was conducted, research staff would obtain informed consent from the women. They were told that no identifying information would be recorded on any data forms. Interviews were carried out in private rooms away from their work place, but the venues were within easy travelling distance.

There are several practical approaches that researchers can adopt to build up this relationship. Respect for the research participants is one essential issue (Smith 1999, 2000, 2008; Walsh-Tapiata 2003). Linda Tuhiwai Smith (2000: 242) asked researchers to show respect for indigenous people such as the Māori by showing their willingness 'to listen, to be humble, to be cautious, to avoid flaunting knowledge, and to avoid trampling over the *mama* of people'. For indigenous and other marginalised people, Smith (2008: 128–129) contends that:

Research ethics is at a very basic level about establishing, maintaining, and nurturing reciprocal and respectful relationships, not just among people as individuals but also with people as individuals, as collectives, and as members of communities, and with humans who live in and with other entities in the environment. The abilities to enter preexisting relationships; to build, maintain, and nurture relationships; and to strengthen connectivity are important research skills in the indigenous arena. They require critical sensitivity and reciprocity of spirit by a researcher.

Similarly, in native societies such as the Ojiwi, elders have a respected position. Mary Hermes (1998) suggests that researchers must seek elders' consent and advice before undertaking their research. Ojiwi elders would talk about the issues of concern through stories during their conversations. As European Americans have exploited indigenous knowledge through research, Hermes contends that researchers need to engage in collaborative and ethical research. They need to recognise that not all stories should be recorded, transcribed and written. Native people may wish to discriminate between knowledge that can be shared with the dominant society and that which should remain within their own communities. The researchers need to carefully consider these ethical issues when working with indigenous communities as a way to build rapport and a trusting relationship with the communities. See also Walsh-Tapiata (2003) and Walker *et al.* (2006) for similar issues among Māori communities in New Zealand.

According to Janice Crist and Socorro Escandón-Dominguez (2003: 269), effective cross-cultural research requires the use of '*personalismo*' and '*respeto* (respect)'. In community-based research projects, for example, researchers need to use '*personalismo*' by making all interactions with the participants as pleasant as possible. Greeting the participants with warmth when they arrive, showing them how important it is that they attend the research meetings and providing food afterwards will all help to create this atmosphere.

They also contend that showing *respeto* to the participants will provide 'a safe environment', allowing them to contribute freely in the group meeting. The simple act of inviting the participants to introduce themselves or any new members of the group will show respect towards them.

Researchers need to be conscious about the way we present ourselves in cross-cultural research, particularly with certain groups who are more strict with their social codes (I have pointed this out at the beginning of this chapter). Itohan Egharevba (2001: 237) suggests that how we dress can show respect for our participants. In her study with South Asian women, she tells us, 'I also gave consideration to my clothes, being aware that all except one of the women I interviewed were practicing Muslims. I therefore chose to dress conservatively for my meetings with the women, wearing clothes which covered my arms and legs and were not too tight fitting or revealing'.

Researchers should be dressed neatly and formally, as this is a way of showing respect. In particular, a female researcher should dress so as not to reveal too much of her body, for example by wearing shorts or a miniskirt. It can be seen as 'rude' by many cultural groups. This can jeopardise the research relationship and, worse, the researcher may be expelled from the community.

The presentation of self, Mehreen Mirza (1998: 83) contends, is very important in research. It can have an impact on the attempt to recruit potential participants. It can also affect the actual data collection process. Mirza paid special attention to how she dressed during her research fieldwork. But in her case, it was problematic for her. She needed to dress up formally so that she would look respectable to the teachers from whom she needed to gain support in order to access students in the schools. But in order to fit in with the students, she had to wear a less formal outfit which would allow her to gain access to the world of the students as well as to build up rapport in order to do her research. Importantly, the clothes she had to choose 'would not cause offence or upset their sensibilities' (p. 84). Eventually, Mirza decided to wear trousers and blouse. This did not really work either. She tells us:

It became apparent that my garb and the amount of make-up I wore was not acceptable, as the respondents commented negatively upon them. They would have found a more 'traditional' South Asian form of dress more acceptable (such as a *Shalwar kameez*). Often, the students would make comments like 'my parents wouldn't let me wear that', and 'that outfit is indecent'.

Observing some day-to-day practices which are commonly carried out in the culture can also show respect to the members of that particular culture. For example, when the researchers enter the house, they should take notice of how the participants arrange their household. Taking shoes off before entering the house is very common in many cultures. The researchers need to respect that culture by also taking their shoes off. When I went to interview women from Southeast Asia in Melbourne or Thai women in Thailand, I would take my shoes off at the front door of their house. Even if the participants insist that we can leave them on, we should nevertheless take them off, like the owner of the house. I believe this is more respectful. When the researchers enter the house, they should also find out if the older family members, such as parents or grandparents, are at home. If they are, the researchers should ask to see them and pay their respects, or at least greet them. In this way, the researchers show that they respect their family.

Some practical aspects, such as sharing meals, involment in family activities and doing things with participants are good strategies for establishing rapport and a good relationship (Sieber, 1992; Liamputtong Rice, 2000; Quraishi 2008). William Shaffir and Robert Stebbins (1991) argue that the researchers who avoid participating in the informants' activities, when it is possible to do so and use that participation to good ends in their research, lose the opportunity to gain rapport and promote good field relations.

In my work, after our interviews with ethnic women in Melbourne, I was often invited to stay on to share meals with the women and their families. I accepted their invitations without reluctance. As Juliene Lipson and Afaf Meleis (1989: 112) suggest, 'accepting such hospitality moves the researcher into a different kind of relationship', often into a more trusting relationship. This has been my real-life experience. Many times I would be invited to travel with the women on their community outings. Women would also ask me to be more involved in their daily lives, particularly when it was something to do with children, not only theirs but mine, too.

Another good example from my own research deserves to be mentioned here. The Hmong grow several herbs in their gardens, and these play a crucial role in maintaining and restoring health, particularly women's health during childbirth. During the confinement period, Hmong women only eat a chicken soup cooked with several kinds of green herbs. These have several functions: restoring the heat lost in childbirth, washing out what may be left in the uterus, stimulating lactation and restoring strength (Liamputtong Rice 2000). Since I was a married woman, many Hmong women gave me the herbs and instructed me on how to grow them in my garden in case I needed them in the future. They insisted that I would have to look after my own health by taking the herbs, in the same way as all Hmong women do. I did grow the herbs in my garden and used a lot in my cooking, even though I was not pregnant. And the women knew about this. This example illustrates that simple actions can build up rapport and trusting relationships between the researcher and the researched.

In Devika Chawla's (2007: 11) research, her interview with one participant, Sonia, occurred over many cups of tea, which her older daughter prepared for them. She says:

Drinking tea was a very large part of my experience of interviewing, because in North Indian homes, tea is brewed almost every hour. Most of my audiotaped interviews unfolded over many cups of *chai* (tea). I came to see the drink [as] a necessary condiment to the interview events and sites. Even when I did not feel like drinking it, I would agree to have a cup, because I knew it would make my participants comfortable and feel in charge in terms of hospitality (which is a cultural marker for the Punjabi community, as we are known mainly for our hospitality, love of entertaining, song and dance, and loudness).

In his research with Muslim prisoners in the UK, Muzammil Quraishi (2008: 460) established his rapport and trust with the participants by joining them during Friday prayers. Friday prayers were the only time that Muslim prisoners could gather in large numbers. He tells us: 'I was invited by the temporary Imam and prisoners in Prison 2 for their *Eid-al-Adha* [the Feast of Sacrifice] prayers and to eat with them following prayers. This represented a sacrifice for me since *Eid* is normally spent with family, but I felt it was necessary to maintain rapport with my prisoner respondents.'

One way that researchers can develop trust is by 'being there and being seen', and this can be done by 'immersing oneself in the community and contributing to the community' (Eide & Allen 2005: 5; see also Villenas 1996; Meadows *et al.* 2003; Sixsmith *et al.* 2003; Jeffries *et al.* 2005). In her study on coping with trauma and hardship among unaccompanied refugee youths from Sudan, Janice Goodman (2004) did volunteer work with the resettlement of Sudanese refugees and facilitated a support group for the youth. Her volunteer work, she claimed, contributed to the young people trusting her and this led to their enthusiasm for participating in the study.

In one of the prisons that Muzammil Quraishi (2008) did his research (see above), there was no full-time Imam. Because of this, a wrong day for *Eid* was scheduled. Because of his own religious background, Quraishi was able to point this out to the management team of the prison and it was quickly rescheduled to the right date (p. 460). Without the observation of Quraishi, the prisoners would not have been able to celebrate on the right date.

As part of the daily social exchanges in Muslim society, men greet other men by not only a verbal greeting but also by other physical contacts, which include a firm handshake and hugging. This became problematic in the prison setting. Quraishi needed to establish rapport with the men by following these social exchanges, but he became aware that the greeting practices would create suspicion from the officers in charge in the prison, who might not know about or appreciate the symbolic significance of greeting between fellow Muslims. In the prison setting, Quraishi tells us, 'security considerations dictated that physical contact should be kept to a minimum. This was to avoid accusations of prohibited articles being exchanged between persons as well as to guard against potential outbursts of violence from prisoners' (p. 462). He had to constantly deal with this greeting dilemma when seeing Muslim prisoners. Because of this, Quraishi developed ways in which he could greet the prisoners. He says, 'I would place my outstretched palm to them and wave by way of "salaam"'. He goes on to tell us:

Whilst this technique seemed to be reciprocated, I soon developed a more heart-felt greeting. This greeting begins with the same outstretched right palm but then involves folding the arm inwards to rest on the heart. This removed the need to physically touch but maintained sincerity. (p. 462)

Such incidents, I contend, have helped Quraishi to be able to develop good rapport and a trusting relationship with the participants in prisons.

Developing trust relations is not an easy task in any research, and even more so when the researcher and participant have different cultural norms and expectations. Very often, researchers have to deal with hostility and even danger. Eide and Allen (2005: 5) contend that 'when the researcher is a member of a group that has historically been an oppressor or colonizer of the potential participant group, then trust building is more complicated and difficult and requires more time' (see also Lindenberg *et al.* 2001; Corbie-Smith *et al.* 2003). This can be clearly seen in Ilse Pauw and Loren Brener's (2003) study of female street sex workers in Cape Town, South Africa. Their initial fieldwork was undertaken prior to data collection using in-depth interviews and focus groups. The researchers argue that this 'initial fieldwork allowed the research team to gain access to the population, establish legitimacy for the project and initiate relationships with key informants'. The initial fieldwork took nine months. Pauw and Brener (p. 467) tell us that the sex workers were initially suspicious of the researchers. Their suspicions were formed by their negative past experiences with the police, church groups, reporters or health and welfare agencies. But after regular visits, the researchers became known and accepted. As the researchers were ethnically similar to and spoke the same language as the sex workers, this helped to increase the establishment of rapport and trust. When trust had been developed, the sex workers actually looked for the researchers and had longer conversations with them. The sex workers also asked the researchers for advice and counselling in addition to seeking help with arrests, court appearances and bail applications. The fact that the sex workers perceived the researchers as 'wise' assisted the establishment of trust and provided the researchers with great opportunities 'to gain insight into the otherwise hidden worlds of the sex worker. The role of confidant and counsellor alerted researchers to the range of issues faced by sex workers in their working and private lives.'

It is important to take the time to build trust and get to know the participants, as this will provide researchers with a better understanding of their social and cultural situations (Corbie-Smith *et al.* 2002; Walsh-Tapiata 2003; Sin, 2004; Eide & Allen, 2005). It is likely that the participants will share their lived experiences, that they have previously never shared with anyone, with the researchers if they feel that they have a good relationship with them and that they can trust them (Egharevba 2001; Meadows *et al.*, 2003; Goodman, 2004).

Phyllis Eide and Carol Allen (2005) warn us that things can go wrong at any time. Although the researchers may make their best efforts and have good intentions, trust may not be established or (worse) is sometimes destroyed. If this occurs, it may not be possible for the researchers to continue, or they might have to spend a lengthy period of time and effort to rebuild trust. And if rebuilding trust is not feasible, the researchers need to re-evaluate the situation and perhaps change the research sites and groups.

Considering the needs of participants: place of research

Researchers need to carefully consider the place where they will carry out their research so that the needs of their participants can be taken into account (Liamputtong, 2007a; Topp *et al.* 2008). Participants tend to be more comfortable being interviewed in their own homes. They do not have to travel and they may have young children to take care of. They may not have enough time to allow for travelling. I often find this in my own research with women from ethnic minorities. I normally ask the participants where they would feel most comfortable for me to talk to them and the answer is usually their own home. Rachel Hall (2004: 132) reported that in her research with South Asian women in West Yorkshire, the women were offered interviews in community centres, work places and her office at the university. Most of the women, however, preferred to have the interviews carried out in their own homes. The home interviews gave the women more confidence because the interview was done in a familiar environment.

But sometimes this may not be the case. Some participants may prefer not to be interviewed at home for many reasons, including privacy. Cross-cultural researchers have conducted interviews in cafés, libraries, health care centres, parks, playgrounds and supermarkets, wherever participants suggest. Itohan Egharevba (2001: 239) also tells us of an interesting incident concerning the location of interviews. She asked all the women if they wanted to be interviewed at home, but they all, except one, rejected the option. Rather, they wanted to be interviewed in public places such as their colleges or local premises. Initially, Egharevba thought that the women were not happy to bring a stranger into their private spaces. However, she later found out that the public spaces were more 'private' for them. She tells us: 'In meeting in their colleges or at the local base, they could ensure private, uninterrupted time to a greater degree than they could in their homes where family members and neighbours were likely to be present, vying for their attention.'

This is also my recent experience with research in Thailand. My colleagues and I interviewed many women who were living with HIV/AIDS. We suggested to the women that we could travel to their homes so that they did not have to travel. Most, however, wanted to meet us elsewhere. They did not want their family members to know about their 'secret' illness. Many of the women we interviewed had not disclosed their illness status to all family members, at most only their mothers and husbands. By talking about the illness experience, other family members and neighbours would learn about their illness. This could have a detrimental effect on them as HIV/AIDS is still seen as a stigmatised illness and people do not want to disclose their condition to outsiders. Some women, however, said that they were too poor and they were ashamed of me seeing their houses.

One of my students did her research on sexuality with young female Vietnamese. She carried out her in-depth interviews in cafés around Melbourne, Australia, because the young girls did not wish to be interviewed at home in case their parents heard their stories. Many of these young girls have very different ideas about sexuality from those of their parents (Rawson 2007; Rawson & Liamputtong 2009).

Being happy about where interviews take place not only makes the participants feel more comfortable, it also permits them to feel more in control and this may allow the participants to speak more openly or in detail. Penny Rhodes (1994: 354) contends that 'where interviews take place in respondents' homes, familiar territory generates confidence, the interviewer is invited in as a guest and the balance of power is more likely to tilt in the interviewee's favour'. This was also the experience of Egharevba (2001) in her research with South Asian women. Despite problems accessing potential participants at the beginning of his research, John Carter's (2005) later interviews with retired African-Caribbean nurses revealed that these participants talked openly about their experiences. Carter believes strongly that this occurred because of '*where* the interview was taking place'. Carter elaborates: 'The venue in which the interview took place seemed to have an effect on the willingness of respondents to talk openly' (p. 350).

In carrying out research in some ethnic communities, researchers may find that extended family members may wish to be present during the interviews. In her research, Ann Phoenix (1995: 59) points out that ethnic minority women sometimes asked if their male partners could also attend the interview, and often the men would answer some of the questions. Phoenix contends that this can be an awkward situation because she wants to hear the women's stories. But in Rachel Hall's (2004) study, this did not occur. Hall tells us that 'at no stage in any of the interviews did a male relative want to sit in on the interview. Rather male relatives appeared eager for me to hear the woman's narrative, particularly if her immigration history was complex' (p. 132).

My recent experience in Thailand mirrors that of Hall. I carried out in-depth interviews with women living with HIV/AIDS and often I would meet the women in a café. The women's partners would be present, and they might sit near us, but never once would they answer the questions or ask anything. They liked to listen to our conversations and, often enough, they would just walk away once they had heard a few things.

Tutorial activities

As a cross-cultural researcher, you will be travelling to an under-developed country to do your research on HIV/AIDS. You do not share the same ethnicity as the local people, and you know that cultural sensitivity will play a crucial part in the success of your research. How will you go about this? Discuss some salient ways that you can use to gain cultural sensitivity so that you may also gain trust among the local people.

Chapter summary

In many cultures, such as the Polynesian and Micronesian, Phyllis Eide and Carol Allen (2005: 6) contend that 'the relationship is far more important than the task. People get together simply to be together and share time with one another. Clock time might be irrelevant; meetings take as long as is needed by both parties and usually begin with sharing about family and community rather than business.' This is also true for Māoris in New Zealand (see Walsh-Tapiata 2003; Pope 2008). Researchers need to 'know' about the culture. This is a process that requires a 'willingness to learn' from the researchers. It also requires more time and flexibility. As Eun-Ok Im and colleagues (2004: 895) contend, 'flexibility in time is important in cross-cultural research because time flexibility allows adequate time to establish trust, to identify reciprocal goals, to develop maps of action, and to complete the research and/or practice process'. This 'extra' time needs to be acknowledged in writing a research proposal and when apply for funding (Harris & Roberts, 2003; Walsh-Tapiata 2003).

Chih Hoong Sin (2004: 267) says that 'dedicating generous amounts of time to the "frontline" and really getting to know the [participants] is not however always practical or enthusiastically pursued by researchers'. I, however, argue that this is a crucial aspect of performing cross-cultural research. We need to learn about the cultures in which we wish to do our research. We have to get our hands dirty in order to build a good rapport and trust with our participants. There are many issues we need to consider, but most can be done sensitively. I have discussed these in this chapter. I hope that these issues allow cross-cultural researchers to have more confidence in performing their research.

SUGGESTED READING

Carter, J. (2004). Research note: Reflections on interviewing across the ethnic divide. *International Journal of Social Research Methodology* 7(4), 345–353.

Chawla, D. (2007). Subjectivity and the 'native' ethnographer: Researcher eligibility in an ethnographic study of urban Indian women in Hindu arranged marriages. *International Journal of Qualitative Methodology* **5**(4), Article 2. www/ualberta.ca/~iiqm/backissues/5_4/pdf/chawla.pdf Accessed: 2 January 2007.

Choi, J-a. (2006) Doing poststructural ethnography in the life history of dropouts in South Korea: Methodological ruminations on subjectivity, positionality, and reflexivity. *International Journal of Qualitative Studies in Education* **19**(4), 435–453.

Egharevba, I. (2001). Researching an-'other' minority ethnic community: Reflectoins of a black female researcher on the intersection of race, gender, and other power positions on the research process. *International Journal of Social Research Methodology* **4**(3), 225–241.

Sherif, B. (2001). The ambiguity of boundaries in the fieldwork experience: Establishing rapport and negotiating insider/outsider status. *Qualitative Inquiry* **7**(4), 436–447.

Sin, C. H. (2007). Ethnic-matching in qualitative research: Reversing the gaze on 'white others' and 'white' as 'other'. *Qualitative Research* **7**(4), 477–499.

Subedi, B. (2007). Recognizing respondents' ways of being and knowing: Lessons un/learned in researching Asian immigrant and Asian-American teachers. *International Journal of Qualitative Studies in Education* **20**(10), 51–71.

Walsh-Tapiata, W. (2003). A model for Maori research: *Te whakaeke i te ao rangahau o te Maori*. In R. Munford & J. Sanders (Eds.), *Making a difference in families: Research that creates change* (pp. 55–73). Sydney: Allen & Unwin.

5 Insider/Outsider perspectives and placing issues

Who can hear the voice of the colonized? Who might listen with authenticity, with sensitivity, with an open mind?

(Adler 2004: 107)

Every path I/i take is edged with thorns. On the one hand, i play into the Savior's hands by concentrating on authenticity, for my attention is numbed by it and diverted from other important issues; on the other hand, i do feel the necessity to return to my so-called roots, since they are the fount of my strength, the guiding arrow to which i constantly refer before heading for a new direction.

(Minh-Ha 2006: 249)

Rarely, do the people studied mistake the investigator for one of their own ... But if you are there for some time, as a living, reacting fellow human being, rather than a human pretending to be a disembodied fly on the wall, the people you are studying will create a space, a role for you.

(Cassell 2002: 180)

A generation ago, cross-cultural research was dominated by white researchers. Most researchers would either belong to white, middle-class backgrounds and travelled a long distance to 'study' native, or they would be local people or those who come from privileged positions such as university researchers doing a project with ethnic minority groups in their own countries. Recently, however, we have seen a growing number of scholars who carry out research among people who share their own cultural identity (see Bulmer & Solomos 2004; Ramji 2008). I am one of these new generation of researchers, as I do research with those with whom I share social, cultural and linguistic backgrounds. In current times, the increasing presence of local or native researchers in academia has brought to light debates about the insider versus outsider status of researchers.

In this chapter, I shall introduce the issue of the insider and outsider status of cross-cultural researchers. I will point out different debates centring on these two positionality binaries of cross-cultural researchers. The insider and outsider dichotomy based on cultural attributes, according to Abdi Kusow

(2003: 593), 'remains contested'. There are other issues at hand, and these include gender, social class, age and other social characteristics (see Smith 1999; Walsh-Tapiata 2003; Adler 2004: Coloma 2008; Narayan 2008; Ramji 2008; Swadener & Mutua 2008). These issues will be covered in this chapter.

A typology of cross-cultural researchers

I wish to commence the chapter with a typology of cross-cultural researchers developed by James Banks (1998). First is the 'indigenous insider'. According to Banks, the indigenous insider 'endorses the unique values, perspectives, behaviors, beliefs and knowledge of his or her indigenous community and culture' (p. 8). The indigenous researcher is seen by community members as 'a legitimate member of the community who can speak with authority about it'. This person has 'a perspective and the knowledge' which can 'promote the well-being of the community, enhance its power, and enable it to maintain cultural integrity and survive'.

The second type is the 'indigenous outsider'. Banks suggests that a researcher of this type is 'socialized within the cultural community' (p. 8). However, the indigenous outsider has assimilated into an outside culture. He or she holds values, beliefs, perspectives and knowledge which are similar to those of the outsider community. The indigenous outsider is seen by indigenous or local people as an outsider who is doing research.

The third type is the 'external insider'. This person is 'socialized within another culture' but acquires the beliefs, values, behaviours, attitudes and knowledge of the culture with which he or she is carrying out the research. Because of his or her unique experiences, for example 'personal experiences within an outside culture or community or marginalization within the culture into which he or she [is] socialized, the individual rejects many of the values, beliefs and knowledge claims of the community in which he or she is socialized'. The external insider is perceived as an 'adopted insider' by the local community where the research is being undertaken (p. 8).

The last type is the 'external outsider'. This individual is 'socialized within a community' which differs from the one in which he or she undertakes the research. The external outsider has 'a partial understanding of and little appreciation for the values, perspectives and knowledge' of the research community. With this 'lack of understanding of or empathy for' the culture or the community, the external outsider often 'misunderstands and misinterprets the behaviors within the community'. The researcher tends to distort them by comparing them with the behaviours and values of the outsiders, and may describe the research community as 'pathological or deviant'. The external outsider perceives the community that he or she studies as the 'Other' (p. 8).

The typology of cross-cultural researchers that Banks has developed is a useful means for us to categorise different types of researchers, particularly when considering who would be more suitable to conduct cross-cultural research. Among the four categories, I contend that the external outsider is the most dangerous group of researchers, who tend to claim that they are 'the best and legitimate' group of people who could do research in a local community, rather than 'researchers who live within it' (p. 8). More importantly, however, the external outsider researchers 'may violate the integrity of the communities' they study, their work 'may contribute to the disempowerment and oppression of these communities, and it may be used by policymakers to justify the marginalized positions of the indigenous people in the studied community'. The research and the policy derived from the research carried out by the external outsider 'often raise serious ethical problems about the responsibility of researchers to the communities they study' (p. 8). The precise reason that the present book was written was to prevent this type of researcher taking part in cross-cultural research. Readers may wish to read James Banks's (1998) article about examples of each type of cross-cultural researcher.

In this chapter, I shall focus largely on the first two types that Banks described, as they are more relevant to the issues that I wish to discuss. However, I also wish to point out that there have been many 'external' researchers who have good intentions and who wish to make the voices of participants in cross-cultural research heard more widely. These researchers question themselves about their legitimacy as researchers and whether they correctly interpret the people whom they research. Hence, they are cautious about how their presence and their writing represents the voices of cultural groups. I shall provide more discussion later on in the chapter (see the section 'An outsider perspective').

An insider perspective

It has been suggested that researchers who undertake cross-cultural research should be 'insiders'; meaning that only those who share social, cultural and linguistic characteristics with the research participants would be suitable to do the research (see Rakhit 1998; Smith 1999; Brayboy & Deyhle 2000; Ladson-Billings 2000; Merriam *et al.* 2001; Tillman 2002; Walsh-Tapiata 2003; Hall & Kulig 2004; Al-Makhamreh & Lewando-Hundt 2008; Bishop 2008). This is what Miri Song and David Parker (1995), as well as Hasmita Ramji (2008), refer to as 'cultural commonality'. Insider status will reduce cultural and linguistic barriers. Insider researchers claim that 'only a member of their ethnic or cultural group can really understand and accurately describe the group's culture because socialization within it gives them unique insights into it' (Banks 1998: 6). Cultural 'insiders', according to Russell Bishop (2008: 148), may be able to carry out research 'in a more sensitive and responsive manner than "outsider"' researchers. Sharan Merriam and colleagues (2001: 411) also suggest that 'being an insider means easy access, the ability to ask more meaningful questions and read non-verbal cues, and most importantly be able to project a more truthful, authentic understanding of the culture under study'. According to Roland Coloma (2008: 15), 'becoming an insider allows us to gather trust from the shared similar experiences with research participants, gain entry into spaces often inaccessible to others, sidestep cultural and linguistic barriers, and have an empathetic understanding of the communities we are working with'. Dina Birman (2006: 172) puts it succinctly: 'Cultural insiders have the additional advantage over outsiders because they have facility with the language and culture that allows them access to the cultural community, which can be extremely difficult to gain even by sensitive and knowledgeable outsiders' (see also Andersen 1993; Smith 1999; Dunbar *et al.* 2002; Walsh-Tapiata 2003; Al-Makhamreh & Lewando-Hundt 2008).

James Clifford and George Marcus (1986: 9) said long ago that 'insiders studying their own cultures offer new angles of vision and depth of understanding'. Esther Madriz's (1998) writing provides a good example of this. She contends that sharing the same race and ethnicity as the participants enhanced her rapport and hence increased the willingness of participants to respond to her research (see also Jarrett 1993; Phoenix 1994; Webster 1996; Bhopal 2001; Gunaratnam 2003; Al-Makhamreh & Lewando-Hundt 2008). Anuradha Rakhit (1998), in her research with South Asian female teachers, contends that the participants were more comfortable discussing the issues with her because of their 'shared identities'. Not only did she share with them her gender and ethnicity, but also her experience as a South Asian teacher who had to deal with racist environments in her work. Sahar Al-Makhamreh (in Al-Makhamreh & Lewando-Hundt 2008: 13) is a Jordanian researcher and did her research with social workers in Jordan.

She contends that being Jordanian improved her understanding of both the culture and the 'symbolic and concrete meanings' of the expressions and actions of the participants. It also helped her to behave according to the cultural values. She elaborates:

I was able to practice important cultural norms that put my [participants] at ease. For example, I would stand to welcome or to say goodbye to people my own age or older than me in order to show respect, I was also careful not to offer to shake hands when greeting Muslim men especially if they bent their heads and put their right hands on their hearts. This body gesture signifies a way of showing respect, but for religious reasons these men will not touch women's hands.

It is often suggested that participants tend to believe that they have common experiences and viewpoints with researchers who share the same race or ethnic background (see, for example, Beoku-Betts 1994; Ahmad *et al.* 2004; Emami & Tishelman 2004; Birman 2006). Josephine Beoku-Betts (1994: 416) is a black West African female researcher. In her study with the Gullah women (African-American women residing in the Sea Islands of South Carolina and Georgia), one participant told her that she preferred to have a black scholar, such as Beoku-Betts, carrying out research in her community because 'black scholars have a sense of soul for our people because they have lived through it'.

In the work on barriers to participation in qualitative research involving disabled refugees (Tamil, Somali, Vietnamese and Sorani-speaking Kurdish communities) conducted by Jennifer Harris and Keri Roberts (2003), all of the interviews were carried out by a team of 'first-language interviewers'. All the interviewers spoke the same language as the participants and they themselves had experienced barriers to participation in the research. They did not speak English as a first language, but they had claimed asylum in England. Three of these interviewers had also experienced impairment. This means that all the interviewers were insiders. Harris and Roberts contend that without awareness of this language barrier, it is unlikely that research would be able to incorporate the voices of those who find it difficult to participate, hence the voices of marginalised and difficult-to-access groups continue to be 'ghettoized in specialist literature' (p. 14).

It has also been theorised that research participants provide their 'best' accounts to researchers who share their social and cultural characteristics (Gwaltney 1981; Scott 1998; Adamson & Donovan 2002). In Penelope Scott's (1998: 409) study on lay beliefs and the management of diabetes among West Indians, rapport and the interpretation of data were established quickly because of their shared ethnic identity. Scott tells us, 'we traded stories about how we ended up in England, what part of Jamaica or the Caribbean we are from and generally how we coped with the cold weather and lack of sunshine'. Scott's interviews with white participants did not yield the same results; there was a lack of personal details and their accounts did not reveal the issues on which the West Indians elaborated. In his (1981) study on urban life with African Americans, John Gwaltney, an African-American researcher, revealed many complexities of urban life. He detailed in-depth experiences of black people that had not been previously told by any white researchers.

Having suggested that insider researchers are in a better position to carry out cross-cultural research, we should not treat insider status as unproblematic. Barry Troyna (1998: 101) contends that such belief is 'at best partial and, in many instances, misplaced'. This belief also runs the risk of marginalising minority issues and minority researchers within the research domains (Rhodes 1994; Carter 2004). There have also been some discussions of the difficulties faced by researchers who have the same social, cultural and linguistic backgrounds as their research participants (see for example, Beoku-Betts 1994; Song & Parker 1995; Lal 1999; Izugbara 2000; Phellas 2000; Bhopal 2001; Sherif 2001; Zinn 2001; Dunbar *et al.* 2002; Bhachu 2003; Ezeh 2003; Mand & Wilson 2006; Chawla 2007; Subedi 2007; Ramji 2008). Also, as Russel Bishop (2008: 148) suggests, insiders may be biased, and they can be 'too close to the culture to ask critical questions' (see also Hesse-Biber & Leavy 2005). Bogusia Temple and Alys Young (2008: 97) suggest that 'it is increasingly recognized that the insider/outsider boundaries cannot be as easily drawn' as in racial and ethnicity matching. France Twine (2000) points to the pitfalls of this position and argues that an insider status can be problematic and is contrary to what many researchers have suggested. And Robert Labaree (2003: 97) warns us that the advantages of an insider status 'are not absolute'. Insider researchers need to be cautious about other issues, including 'ethical and methodological dilemmas associated with entering the field, positioning and disclosure, shared relationships and disengagement'.

Peter-Jazzy Ezeh's (2003) experience with the Orring, a minority ethnic group in south-eastern Nigeria, illuminates the problems arising from being an insider. In his case, he shares nationality with his research participants but comes from a different ethnic group. Ezeh contends that 'indigenous social anthropologists investigating communities in their own country are not insulated from many of the difficulties their foreign counterparts face' (p. 191). In his work in Nigeria, initially the research went without any problems. However, as he integrated more into the community, problems arising from human relations emerged. Once, a man believed that his wife had eloped with Ezeh and started to investigate him. As a consequence, Ezeh had to exclude the man's wife from his research. Because of his lack of interest in material acquisition and the focus of his research (studying local customs and language), local people referred to him as *Olielie Grajuet*, which is literally translated as 'a mad scholar'.

The experience of Bahira Sherif (2001) also illustrates my point here. Sherif was born in Cairo to an Egyptian father and a German mother, lived in Cairo until she was nine years of age, but grew up and was educated in the United States. She returned to Egypt to do her fieldwork for her doctoral research. Sherif was really in the unique position of having immediate access to potential participants and their social network (p. 440), So she did not have to deal with problems of social acceptance and ties with the society and isolation which most outsider researchers experience. However, there was another dilemma. Sherif was not only accepted by local people, she was also 'expected to know how to behave' as an Egyptian. This placed a huge demand on her as an insider researcher. She tells us some of the difficulties that she experienced:

Given the nature of Egyptian families and Egyptians' very different conceptions of time, I was instantly faced with the problem of which world to make my priority. A visit to just one family might last from 2 p.m. to 8 p.m. or 9 p.m. On expressing my wish to leave, I would be bombarded with expressions of surprise, such as, 'But you just arrived. You can't just eat and leave'. In addition, I was completely overwhelmed by the attention and the interest that my Egyptian informants and new acquaintances were bestowing on me … I was constantly being forced to make conscious decisions about with whom I wanted to spend time and why, and which part of my increasingly complex identity I was presenting to whom.

An outsider perspective

Cross-cultural researchers have argued that being an outsider may carry some advantages (Mirza 1998; Sin 2007; Coloma 2008). Being an outsider may allow the researchers to scrutinise certain problems more closely, instead of seeing them as common phenomena or not seeing them at all (Banks 1998). As Roland Coloma (2008: 15) suggests, 'becoming an outsider also has its own usefulness, such as providing different perspectives on cultural and community norms, asking questions that require more detailed explanations, and developing other forms of interactions and spaces often relegated to non-members'.

Uvanney Maylor (1995) is an African-Caribbean woman who carried out her research with South Asian, African and Caribbean female student teachers. Different culture and ethnicity between herself and the South Asian women was not problematic in interview situations. One woman, Gita, told Maylor that it was 'easier to confide in' her as she was an outsider of her ethnic group. Gita perceived Maylor as 'someone who would not or was unlikely to judge certain aspects of her behaviour' (p. 70). Similarly, Miri Song, who is a Korean-American woman, did her research with Chinese people. She was seen as a 'safe' person by her participants as she was not the same as them, but she was not totally different (i.e. not a Western person) either (cited in Egharevba 2001: 235).

John Carter (2004) similarly contends that when the researchers do not share the same experiences as their participants, new or different perspectives may be discovered. Carter suggests: 'So taken-for-granted assumptions that remain just below the surface in interviews where the interviewer and interviewee share the same identity are likely to be made more explicit in cases where the interviewer and interviewee do *not* share the same identity' (p. 347). In his research with nurses from ethnic minorities in the UK, Carter asked the participants several questions about racism. As he is a white researcher, he thought that he would have problems getting them to discuss their experiences. However, his whiteness was not the impediment he had anticipated. In particular, the participants from an African-Caribbean background often articulated their experiences of racism 'in ways that made explicit their feelings and responses to discrimination and hostility' (p. 351). Being white is not always an obstacle. According to Rhodes (1994: 552), even when the research requires a discussion on a sensitive issue such as racism, people are prepared to talk openly about their experiences and opinions. People from ethnic minorities often say that they would not have done so with another ethnic person. In Rhodes's research, people treated him 'to information which they would have assumed was the taken for granted knowledge of an insider'. In Carter's research, he points out that 'it is the gap in experience between interviewer and interviewee that creates a space for respondents to describe and tease out meanings and assumptions that may otherwise remain unspoken' (2004: 348).

Similarly, the account of Rachel Hall (2004), in her research on the experiences of British immigration control with South Asian women in West Yorkshire, suggests that being an outsider, in her case as a white researcher doing research with non-white people, can have both positive and negative impacts on the research process. Although Hall and her participants shared the same gender, because of their different ethnicity, a white researcher is more likely to be seen as 'an outsider' by participants from ethnic minority groups. In Hall's research, there was one particular occasion that her outsider status of white British ethnicity proved to be useful in accessing the women. Hall elaborates:

Had I been a member of the South Asian community I would probably not have been granted this access. Initially this woman voiced reservations about taking part in the study, and would not give a 'yes' or 'no' answer until she had consulted her husband. At first the husband said that she should not talk with me, as they had almost sorted out her immigration status in this country, and that they did not want to jeopardize her application. After hearing this I decided to make one final attempt at securing the interview so I gave her a copy of the interview schedule with my name written on it to take home and show her husband. Fortunately (for me) when the husband read the question and more importantly my name he gave his permission to interview his wife. The interviewee later told me that to her husband my whiteness symbolized that I was neutral and had no community links. (p. 135)

Some cross-cultural researchers have questioned their legitimacy in doing research with those who are very different from them. For example, Rosaline Edwards (1990) conducted research with Afro-Caribbean women. As a white researcher, she encountered suspicion from the women and had difficulty recruiting them. And, when she interviewed the women, she was concerned about her interpretation of the lives of black women. More importantly, the racial difference between Edwards and the women disrupted the 'woman-to-woman' connection between them. Edwards tells us:

I worried that my assumptions about Black women's family lifestyles and cultural practices might be based on false understandings. I also worried (as it turns out with good reason) that Black women would not relate to me woman-to-woman, but as Black person to white person, and that this would affect the information I received from them. (p. 483)

The example of Itohan Egharevba (2001) is a good one here. Egharevba is a British-born first generation Nigerian woman. She conducted her research with a group of South Asian women, which she refers to as researching 'another "other"'. Egharevba came to do this research not solely through her own choice but through her response to an advertisement for a research studentship. At the beginning, Egharevba was very nervous about the project and was reluctant to make contact with the South Asian women. This, she suggests, was mainly due to her perceived 'outsider' status. She did not share cultural resemblance to the South Asian women and did not speak Urdu. Egharevba explains:

I believe that the absence of feelings of apprehension and trepidation related more to my background and life experiences up to that point. Being born and raised in an overwhelmingly white city in the South of England, I was used to interacting and dealing with white people, both in positions of power and as my peers … On the other hand, and in addition to feeling different from the South Asian women, I also had very limited experience of interaction with South Asian people. Therefore, in relation to ethnicity, religion, geography, culture, language and life experience, the differences between myself and the women appeared, at the time, to be more significant than those that existed between the white staff and myself. (pp. 229–230)

Additionally, ethnic communities tend to be made invisible and pathological, and very often, they are misinterpreted by white researchers. This historical account was also one of the troubles that she had when she started her research. She did not wish to further marginalise or pathologise the South Asian women. This prompted her to think seriously about whether she, as an outsider, would be the best person to do the job.

Basia Spalek (2005) is a white researcher who carried out her research with Muslim women in Birmingham. Spalek was acutely aware of her ethnicity and its impact on the data that she might have. As Gorelick (1991: 464) has said, marginalised research participants do not 'tell the truth to those in power'. So Spalek was not sure if she had gathered sufficiently accurate data. She tells us, 'I was … acutely aware of my position as "western academic" and of the negative stereotype of Muslims in western discourses. Many white, non-Muslim social commentators and journalists have propagated false images of Islam, and so the interviewers may have viewed me as a being a part of this "white, western, establishment", and so may not have fully revealed their experiences to me' (2005: 411). Because of the verbal and physical abuse that Muslim communities had suffered in the aftermath of the 11 September 2001 terrorist attacks, the women might have distrusted her interest in their lives. Although Spalek had obtained the women's accounts on worries after that date, she could not be sure how adequately and thoroughly she had done so.

Insider/Outsider boundaries: being both an insider and outsider or either?

According to Devika Chawla (2007: 2), the idea of 'an "authentic" insider is contestable'. Kirin Narayan (2008) and David Bridges (2001) argue that there should not be a dichotomy of a native (an insider) versus a non-native (outsider) researcher; that is, it is not useful to think in this way. In some situations and contexts, the researchers can be both insiders and outsiders (Merton 1972; Banks 1998; Walsh-Tapiata 2003; Adler 2004). The position and identity of the researchers may shift 'amid a field of interpenetrating communities and power relations' (Narayan 2008: 269). Ruth Behar (1993), for example, was a 'dispassionate outsider' when she observed the death of farmers in a village in Spain. However, she became an 'emotional insider' when she observed her own grandfather's death in Miami. Sofia Villenas (1996) also tells us about being both. She describes her dilemma of being between the 'colonized' and the 'colonizer' in her research with Latina mothers in North Carolina. In other words, Villenas was placed as an insider and outsider by the community and those who serve them. Davika Chawla (2007: 2) puts this clearly: 'Whether native or other, we are all "another's" in the field, because there will always be facets of ourselves that connect us with the people we study and other factors that emphasize our differences'.

Insider researchers have the privilege of knowing the life worlds of people whom they wish to learn about. But if they are 'unquestionably welcomed back into their fields', it is mere luck (Chawla 2007: 3; see also Sherif 2001; Gokah 2006; Ramji 2008). For most insider researchers, however, 'the semblance of a "complete" insider' can only be accomplished through extended periods of immersion. As Hasmita Ramji (2008: 102) puts it, 'points of connectivity' must 'be worked for'. Realistically, however, Chawla (2007: 3) warns us, 'a complete insider we might never become, as other distances persist and are often necessary to facilitate observation. Even as natives, we might find ourselves in fields of ambiguity – being and becoming insiders, outsiders, or partial insiders – positions invoked and orchestrated by our participants'.

Devika Chawla (2007) provides an account of her experiences of being both an insider and outsider in her ethnographic research on Hindu arranged marriages with Indian women in Delhi. At one point, Chawla tells us that in participating in the everyday activities of her participants, such as picking up children from schools, eating meals with family members and going shopping, it was sometimes awkward for her (p. 6). She spent many moments with Suparna at her home while Suparna was trying to complete her household chores so that she could sit down and talk to Chawla. She says, 'I have lived alone for a long time. Up to that point, my visits home were yearly and involved staying with my parents for a few weeks, or a month at best, so in some ways, even familial activities presented themselves to me with degree of unfamiliarity.'

An interesting discussion is provided by Priya Mani (2006) in her research with Indo-Canadians (children of South Asian immigrants living in Canada).

Mani is a South Asian herself, but she did not have the same religious background as her participants. Mani points out that it was crucial for the participants to know that she was not connected to their religious community (p. 3). They, however, accepted that she was also an Indo-Canadian and had a shared cultural background. Because of this 'partial outsider' status, the participants in fact appreciated that their privacy would be maintained. It was important for the participants that their involvement be kept confidential as it could affect their reputations as well as the reputation of their family within their own community. Mani contends that:

I maintained 'dual status', whereby a commonality of understanding was established based on cultural background, and yet I had access to particular components of Indo-Canadian young women and men life experiences that would not have been granted if I represented an Indo-Canadian researcher of their particular ethnic community. I was considered an insider to the norms of the South Asian community but was still perceived as an outsider to the specific cultural beliefs held by participants based on their religious background. (p. 4)

A partial insider status was also a constraint in Bahira Sherif's (2001) research. This constraint was the result of 'boundaries imposed through … personal, gendered experiences in the field' (p. 438). Due to her partial insider status, Sherif had to negotiate her gender, religion and language throughout the period she spent in her fieldwork, much more so than her American colleagues doing fieldwork in Egypt (p. 441). She was seen as being an Egyptian woman and was constrained by many rules imposed on being female in that society. She was expected to dress as upper-class Egyptian women would do. Her heavily accented Arabic was met with surprise, disappointment and amusement, for example 'you are Misrayya [Egyptian] and can't even speak Arabic!' However, her (lack of) religion has impacted on her fieldwork tremendously. When she admitted that she does not pray, her admission was 'met with expressions of extreme disapproval'. During Ramadan, she did not fast and people became appalled by her lack of religion. Sherif tells us: 'Each of the families I was studying spent hours trying to convince me that I was committing a sin, and many refused to let me participate in their evening celebrations because of my lack of practice. Any pleas on my part that I would have felt hypocritical pretending to fast fell on deaf ears. It was during Ramadan that I probably experienced the greatest feeling of alienation between myself and my informants' (p. 441).

Readers may wish to read the writings of Binaya Subedi (2006, 2007), Jung-ah Choi (2006) and Hasmita Ramji (2008). They provide vivid and valuable descriptions of being an insider and outsider in their research in

Nepal, South Korea and with British Asian women, and describe some of the benefits and difficulties they encountered in their research.

I wish to point out that even though the researcher is an insider, his or her insider status can also become an outsider within the same social groups and geographical locations (Kusow 2003). Gokah (2006) argues that our insider status and familiarity with the research setting and/or groups can also jeopardise our research process. Theophilus Gokah is Ghanaian, and in his research in Ghana, his insider status created this problem. He tells us:

My experiences in Ghana are an example of how 'familiarity' can go wrong. As a Ghanaian, my familiarity with the environment gave me the advantage of being able to identify potential respondents, but my background as a journalist made some government policy officers portray me as not only an 'outsider', but also an 'intruder', whereas in the other countries I was only seen as a doctoral student doing research. Thus, I was accorded a fairly good reception in those countries other than Ghana. (pp. 63–64)

Indigenous outsiders

Although researchers and participants may share social and cultural norms, there may also be challenges relating to class, gender and perceived outsider status (Kusow 2003; Adler 2004; Tillman 2006; Bishop 2008; see also later section in this chapter). This is what James Banks (1998) refers to as an 'indigenous outsider'. As I have discussed above, this concept refers to researchers who share the same racial group as the participants but who have a different ethnicity, or linguistic and other social and cultural backgrounds. Linda Tillman (2006: 282), for example, tells us that in her studies, her experiences were similar to those of her participants: 'I was Black, female, raised in a working-class Black neighbourhood, a first-generation college graduate, a professional, a former public school educator, and raised to be of service to the larger African-American community.' This 'indigenous insider status' permitted her to form cultural affiliations with her participants. However, her research privilege was challenged by some participants, who became suspicious of her intentions in carrying out her research and of how she would use their experiences in her reports. This made her status into an 'indigenous outsider'. She contends that 'it was not a given that my same-race/cultural affiliation would ensure that there would be no struggles with perceptions and expectations based on my outsider status'.

Similarly, Binaya Subedi (2007) is a Nepalese-born Asian. He carried out his research with other Asians, including Indians, Pakistanis and Filipinas. Although Subedi looks Asian and speaks some Hindi, he did not have any knowledge of Urdu or Filipino and did not have a deep understanding of the diverse cultures of his participants. This positions him as both indigenous and an outsider at the same time. Subedi tells us:

The term indigenous-outsider is useful in situating my identity since I self-identify as an Asian immigrant as well an Asian-American, and due to racial/immigrant affiliations I was often considered 'indigenous' by participants. Yet, I remained an 'outsider' due to language, ethnic and cultural differences when researching the teachers. (p. 67)

Abdi Kusow (2003: 594) was born in Somalia, but migrated to the United States in 1984. Because of his accent, and the fact that he is Muslim, black and was born in Africa, he became an outsider even among African Americans. When he commenced his ethnographic research with Somali immigrants in Canada for his PhD, he also discovered that he remained an outsider within the Somali community, although he was 'very much an insider to it'. Due to the politically and culturally sensitive nature of his research topic, he was seen as a kind of 'suspicious insider'. It was difficult for him to find people who were willing to discuss sensitive issues with him in the Somali immigrant community.

But this indigenous outsider status has some value. Mehreen Mirza (1998: 87) is a South Asian woman and she carried out interviews with South Asian girls and women in her research in the UK. However, she was seen as an outsider for many reasons, including coming from a different area in the UK, and being young, single and living alone. Mirza tells us that the benefit of not being counted as an insider allowed her to become more 'objective' with the information she gathered, as she did not or could not make any assumptions about what the women were telling her. She took on the role of 'the stranger within' (Collins 2008). Often, the women would say something like 'well you probably don't know this, but Asians …' or 'in our cultures …', as they assumed that Mirza was not familiar with South Asian cultures, despite the fact that she was also a South Asian woman. Mirza was seen as 'different' from the South Asian women simply because of her lack of marital status, and her appearance, demeanour and researcher status. The fact that she was carrying out research suggested that she could not be 'one of them' (Mirza 1998: 86). A similar experience was also documented by Hasmita Ramji (2008) in her research with British Asian women in London.

Similarly, in his research relating to children's rights policy in sub-Saharan Africa, Theophilus Gokah (2006: 63) came across extreme openness among the children he interviewed. This openness 'brought to the fore "insider–outsider" debates in ethnographic studies'. He says, 'for me as a social outsider, I was generally perceived as a sympathetic foreign ethnographer with an interest in children's well-being. This earned me a "stranger-value" that is reflected to a large extent in the level of openness from my informants.'

Placing and cross-cultural research

The fact that people define us in certain ways does have an effect on us, whether positive or negative. It is therefore important that researchers know who they are, before entering the field because others will define you as they see fit. (Weis 1992: 50)

Apart from an insider/outsider status (or ethnicity) that I have discussed above, there are other 'placing' issues (Mirza 1998; Adler 2004; Sin 2007) that I wish to point out in this chapter. It is suggested that the way in which researchers are 'placed' by their research participants, and vice versa, is crucial for the success of cross-cultural research (Egharevba 2001; Best 2003; Carter 2004; Sin 2007; Al-Makhamreh & Lewando-Hundt 2008; Ramji 2008). Here, I refer to the positionality of the researcher as perceived by the participants (Liamputtong 2007a). Issues of gender, class, age and other socially constructed identities have great impact on the research process in cross-cultural research (Kusow 2003; Adler 2004; Sin 2007; Subedi 2007; Al-Makhamreh & Lewando-Hundt 2008; Bishop 2008; Coloma 2008; Ramji 2008; Maylor 2009; Shockley 2009). These issues are discussed below.

Gender issues

Gender differences between the researcher and the researched play an important role in conducting research (Järviluoma *et al.* 2003). The gender of the researchers may influence the perceptions of the participants, and how they place the researchers in the research process (Pini 2005). According to Sahar Al-Makhamreh and Gillian Lewando-Hundt (2008: 11), 'cultural and social norms construct certain gender expectations that researchers can negotiate and act within'. For decades, how gender identity may shape the research encounter has been the subject of intense discussion amongst feminist researchers (see Collins 2008). Carter (2004: 346) says that 'a central strand in the debate is the tacit assumption that women are best interviewed by female interviewers'. When introducing themselves to their participants, Lariso Kosygina (2005) suggests, female researchers should do so not only as researchers but also as women. This will help them to obtain trust and more accurate information from female participants because of their shared gender identity and assumptions. Women also tend to believe that female researchers would understand their subjective experiences better than male researchers.

In her research in Jordan, Sahar Al-Makhamreh (in Al-Makhamreh & Lewando-Hundt 2008: 15–16) found that, as she was a female researcher, the participants were willing to talk openly and they also felt more comfortable discussing their personal lives with her. One woman told her that 'Of course I would prefer to talk to a woman because she would understand me. I would not be embarrassed to talk to her about how I feel.' As a Jordanian, Al-Makhamreh had to behave according to Jordanian social constructions of gender. In her attempt to negotiate access to potential participants, she adopted 'informal strategies' by using 'the informal but respectful nomenclature', such as referring to the participants as 'mother of Sahar' or 'father of Jamal' instead of their first names or formal family names. She employed fictive kinship terms so that she could establish trust. Hence, in conversation, she addressed clients, nurses, social workers or doctors as 'sister' or 'brother'. She says that this practice is commonly adopted in Arab society and is 'a way to frame interaction with a man in a non-sexual way and to indicate solidarity with a woman' (p. 18). It is also a culturally acceptable way for 'cross gender interactions' (p. 18). She would keep her distance from the patients and not get too close to them by touching or looking at them directly in the eye, as this would be culturally unacceptable. She was also very careful with her dress code and covered her arms and legs at all times.

Being a female researcher also assisted her in being able to conduct interviews in their homes. This was particularly so when the participants were young females. Al-Makhamreh contends that 'If I had been a man, meeting them in their homes would not have been readily accepted. Being a woman from the same culture helped me to know how to behave in a way that would be deemed respectful' (p. 18). As Robert Labaree (2002) has suggested, for Al-Makhamreh, sharing cultural norms and being a female researcher permitted her to have a shared understanding of the experience of women in Jordanian society. Overall, being a female from the same culture had a positive impact on her ethnographic study and allowed her to obtain rich data from her participants. She questions whether 'the same quality of data could have been collected by a male researcher' (Al-Makhamreh & Lewando-Hundt 2008: 19). However, for Al-Makhamreh, although she admits that insider status would help researchers to obtain in-depth information, when performing qualitative research in the Arab world it is crucial that researchers must focus on gender as one aspect of the socio-cultural context.

It is also valuable to discuss this gender issue from the perspective of male researchers who undertake research within societies which are segregated along gender lines. Abdi Kusow (2003) is a Somali male researcher doing his PhD research with the Somali immigrant community in Canada. He had difficulty accessing female participants and he was not able to meaningfully interact with them. In Somali communities, women and men would be separated in most public social activities and community gatherings. Even when women and men attend the same social event at the same location, they do not mix with each other. This makes interaction between men and women impossible. Kusow (2003: 597) points out: 'In such social arrangements, cultural or racial differences or similarities do not determine insider or outsider status; the social organization of gender does. What this situation suggests is that a Western, outsider, female ethnographer may have better access than would I as a native male ethnographer.'

Kusow is an insider researcher but, as I have pointed out, one of the most difficult problems he confronted during his fieldwork was how to find and interact with female participants. Kusow tells us about his dilemma:

I was able to talk to several Somali female students at the local universities, but beyond them, finding access to female participants remained a daunting experience. In the Somali social context, one cannot simply call a female participant for an appointment or go to her house without the assistance of a male relative, for one must avoid any suggestion of impropriety or other misunderstandings. If the woman is married, the situation is even more complicated. Married women cannot, at least officially, associate with men other than their husbands or relatives regardless of the circumstances. (p. 597)

Itohan Egharevba (2001: 234), who is a Nigerian-born female researcher but who did her research with South Asian women, points out that the women in her research did not feel uncomfortable talking with her despite the fact that they had no shared ethnicity, religion or professional experiences. She contends that, without doubt, it was her gender that was a crucial factor in assisting her to facilitate the relationship with her participants.

Basia Spalek (2005) is a white researcher. She interviewed Muslim women of Pakistani and Bangladeshi heritage living in the Birmingham area who wore the *hijab* (veil) about their experiences of victimisation and the management of their personal safety. Spalek acknowledges in her writing that her whiteness may have some impact on her research with Muslim women and that at times she felt uncomfortable about the differences between her own ethnicity and that of the women in her research. However, she tells us that 'I drew comfort from my position as "woman", due to feeling an intimate connection with the interviewees with respect to the issue of men' (p. 412). Much research has revealed that women often have to deal with harassment and violence committed by men (see Mooney 2000; Stanko 2002). Spalek, too, has experiences of such harassment and intimidation, and this was what she shared with the women in her study. She elaborates that 'I have ... encountered many difficult and frightening situations with men. I have been called abusive names by men, I have experienced physical and sexual intimidation, and indeed, a whole array of disturbing instances has punctuated my life. These situations have left behind strong emotions. It is these emotions that I used to help me to establish rapport with the interviewees and to uncover and record their anxiety about men.' One woman says clearly that most women, regardless of social or cultural background, would share their fears of being harmed by men:

Most women, I mean if I was walking down a dark alley and I saw a man I would constantly feel scared, I'd fear for my life. Most women feel like that. It's always in the back of your mind. Even in the daytime not necessarily in the dark so I do have that fear all of the time. (Spalek 2005: 412)

John Carter (2004) carried out his research with nurses from ethnic minority groups in the UK. As a male sociologist researching a female ethnic minority, there were some concerns about his gender and ethnicity. He elaborates: 'There is no doubt that my identity represented a highly problematic methodological issue. That is, to what extent would my identity both as a man interviewing women, and as a white person interviewing members of ethnic minority groups affect the conduct and outcome of the interviews? Given the imbalance of power between these groups at a societal level, my whiteness and masculinity were, and are, potential sources of difference that make it difficult to establish a rapport between myself and my respondents' (p. 346). However, his position as a white male meant that he was seen as an outsider by the participants and this did not seem to be an impediment to his relationship with his participants (as I have pointed out earlier).

Class issues

There are other social structures that have impact on the research process. Despite shared gender, barriers to understanding in the research process can be created because of social class differences between the researcher and the participants (Madriz 1998; Rashid 2007; Ramji 2008). This was the experience of Catherine Reissman (1991) in her research on the experience of separation and divorce with women from different social classes and ethnicity.

In her study with Latina women in New York, Esther Madriz (1998: 5) was extremely cautious about the class differences between herself as a researcher and the women of low status. Because of her middle-class background and her position as a professor at a university, she stood in stark contrast to the women who mainly worked as cleaners, street vendors and nannies. Most of the women were stay-at-home mothers. However, Madriz tried to reduce this difference by careful dressing in the manner of most Latina women, who are restrained in the way they dress (p. 5). She also referred to the women and herself by first names and used informal Spanish pronouns, and by sharing the language with the women, the gap between herself and them was markedly minimised.

Because of her higher class status, in her research with poor women in a Dhaka slum, people were suspicious of Sabina Rashid (2007). They thought she could be a police officer or a journalist who wanted to spy on them and evict them from the slum. They could not believe that a woman of higher status would be genuinely interested in the health issue of poor women. Rashid tells us: 'Over the long period of time, our status gradually changed from being complete outsiders to being what I believe was tantamount to adopted family members and guardians. We became mediators, and sympathetic listeners. However, as much as I felt we belonged, in reality, we would always be seen as the privileged but sympathetic outsiders' (p. 381).

In her research within London's Hindu Gujarati community, Hasmita Ramji (2008), who herself is Hindu, found that some participants questioned whether she was of the same or a higher caste than them. This was because caste is a crucial factor in identifying the kind of Hinduism observed by Gujaratis. Ramji contends that 'lower caste Gujaratis were somehow thought to be lesser Hindus. This is indicative of the inter-connected relationship between caste status and religion in Indian culture: a similar caste Gujarati would share a similar perception of Hinduism' (p. 106). Interestingly, many people expressed their surprise that, although Ramji was an Indian, her accent was not a London accent. London was seen as 'a natural place' for identifying Gujarati Hindu identity. Not being from London differentiated Ramji from other Gujaratis. But this was also had a positive aspect in permitting some women to talk about their lives without fear of offending others in the community. Deepika, for example, told Ramji that she was comfortable discussing her life at home and work with Ramji. She said: 'It's good you're not from London because if you had been brought up here … I'd worried that maybe you'd know all the people and places I was talking about, so I'd feel I had to be careful about what I said.'

Recent writing by Muzammil Quraishi (2008: 460–461) also points out social class status between the researcher and the researched. Although they had common religious beliefs, there were other marked differences between himself and the Muslim prisoners in the UK. For example, most prisoners in two of the prisons where he undertook his research spoke regional dialects from London and the Midlands, but Quraishi is from Manchester. Most participants had no further or higher education qualifications, but he had a law degree and was about to obtain his doctoral degree. Most of the participants from Pakistani background spoke Mirpuri and Punjabi, but he only speaks Urdu as his parents were forced to migrate from India to Pakistan during the partition in 1947. Quraishi points out that all of these social class differences made him very conscious that his social position might be too different from that of the research participants and that this might hinder the research process. However, this did not become an issue for him as most participants perceived him as being a Muslim person.

Age issues

Cross-cultural researchers have pointed to the differences in age that may have an impact on the research process. In many cultures, advanced age signifies respect. If the researcher is still young, older participants may not respect him or her, and this can jeopardise cooperation and the quality of the research findings.

Michelle Foster (1993) is an African-American researcher and undertook her life history research with black American teachers. She found that despite the fact that she shared the same ethnic identity as participants, there were other issues which affected her insider status. Age was one of these intricate issues. She was a younger woman when compared with some participants. This had an impact on the way she could access their personal narratives. Mehreen Mirza's (1998: 86) position as a young female researcher did not have any status for many participants in her research with South Asian women. She tells us: 'I was relatively young. My professional status as researcher, associated with a university, carried very little weight. I was thus perceived as "statusless"'.

In her ethnographic research on Hindu arranged marriages with Indian women in Delhi, Devika Chawla (2007: 13) talks about the 'shifting subjective experiences' that she encountered during her fieldwork. She asserts that we cannot be an absolute insider or outsider as we are always positioned by our research participants. As her research participants comprised different age groups, her experience shifted according to how she was seen by them. Chawla tells us:

With the young group, I was accorded the role of native, thus hyper-eligible. With the middle group, I was adjusted: first as an insider, and later as an outsider and stranger. With the older group, I was 'another', a comfortable stranger, and, in more ways than one, the professional stranger of ethnographic work. Ultimately, I had to experience these eligibilities to reflect on and converse with their life-histories … These eligibilities originated from my single status and not from my displaced or rooted ethnic identities. (p. 13)

Shared statuses/experiences

The way that the participants place the researchers within or outside shared status and experience is another important placing issue (see Adler 2004). In the research carried out by Itohan Egharevba (2001: 235), it was the fact that she shared a minority status with the participants that had a positive impact on the research process. Many participants told her that they would not have felt comfortable discussing some of their views and experiences with a white researcher. This was particularly when it was related to racism. One female participant talked at great length about the difficulties that she had experienced. She had not discussed this issue with any white person. When asked why, she remarked:

You know what they're like … White people (almost whispered) … They would be only too happy to hear about my worries. They'd take it as confirmation … Yes, you know, that all the negative stereotypes they have of us minorities are, right … Instead of helping me, they will be too busy reinforcing it. I have decided not to say anything to anyone. You know what they are like. (p. 236)

The participants assumed that they and Egharevba had a shared experience of racism as they both possessed minority status in England, and this affected the type of information that the participants shared with her. Egharevba concludes:

What they saw in me was another minority person who was living in a racist country, a commonality which made them feel less vulnerable than they would have felt with a white researcher. This shared experience transcended many of the apparent differences between us. (p. 239)

In her research with the British Indian Hindu community in London, Hasmita Ramji (2008: 107) suggests that many participants who have been brought up and experienced racial harassment in British society wanted to share their concerns with her in the interviews. Sunita, an accountant in Ramji's study, said this:

Whenever someone wants to have a go at you they can use the 'Paki' slur. It makes you feel like nothing ... it doesn't matter how nice a job you have or how nice a house you have because you are still just a 'Paki' to some white people ... I just feel like screaming back I'm not from Pakistan ... I am Indian!

Sunita assumed that Ramji would have the same experience as her, and she wanted to point out the commonality with her. In Ramji's case, when the participants used shared experiences of racism to identify their similarity with her, her position as Hindu/Gujarat/Indian was suspended. Ramji states: 'There was an element of commonality as experienced through shared racism which defined a British Indian cultural identity. So when racial discrimination was the subject matter, shared experience could override attributions of the researcher having a questionable Hindu identity' (p. 108).

The experience of Paul Maginn (2007: 437), in his research in three ethnically diverse areas in London, provides an interesting example of shared statuses/experiences between the researcher and the researched. Maginn tells us: 'I had anticipated that my racial identity (i.e. white) might be a problematic issue during the research process. The literature suggested that because I was white (and middle-class because of my educational background) and doing research with an emphasis on racial issues, this would reinforce the power imbalance with my informants, especially those from ethnic minority backgrounds'. But as Harrington (2003: 605) points out, 'the self is not a single homogeneous identity, but a multifaceted complex of labels and roles derived from negotiated interaction'. Maginn belongs to 'a dual racial-ethnic identity (i.e. white and Irish)'. Because of his working-class background, and having lived in Northern Ireland, he manages to 'use this "portfolio" of identities as a symbolic resource to help [him] align with others'. When he interviewed black tenants, he told them that he was familiar with 'living in a highly segregated and discriminatory environment', and learned that he was able to attract their interest and confidence. Maginn (2007: 431) says this:

When I met with people from ethnic minority backgrounds or organizations, I accentuated the fact that I was from Northern Ireland and had a clear understanding of community relations and discrimination through my lived and research experience. My strategy was to induce a sense of familiarity, similarity, and sympathy among gatekeepers and informants toward my research and me.

Having high status and association with academic institutions

Cross-cultural researchers suggest that their academic status and association with academic institutions impact on how they are placed by their research participants. In Hasmita Ramji's (2008) research, her higher educational status cultivated pride among her participants as representation of their cultural identity (being an Indian Hindu in the UK). Ramji tells us: 'It was usually made clear that I had suitable credentials to be spoken to as a Hindu Gujarati and not simply as a researcher, who could have been anyone studying in an English university and doing research on the Hindu Gujarati community in London' (p. 107). One participant said this to Ramji: 'You're doing a PhD and there can't be too many other [non-white] people doing that'.

In her work, Itohan Egharevba (2001: 232) also admits that the way in which she was placed by the South Asian women allowed her to do her research smoothly. Her associations with the Lancashire Project and the use of letter-headed paper greatly facilitated her initial access. She believes that her association 'engendered a certain level of credibility' (p. 232). She also points out that because her research position was created and financed from the recommendations of the local South Asian community, this undoubtedly enhanced her credibility as a researcher performing within the community.

Judith Berg (1999: 241), in her research of midlife Filipinas in the US, notes that the majority of the women in her study were highly educated, and hence interested in a research project which was linked with a major university. Many participants expressed pride in being included in the study. Berg gave each participant a certificate of participation, which contained the title of the study and the affiliated university. Many women said that the certificate would be prominently displayed in their homes.

This is also what I have done in my research. In my recent study of immigrant parents among Cambodian and Iraqi women in Melbourne, in which I am one of the chief investigators, we made a distinctive bilingual postcard that contained the names and logos of the two universities, and we gave these to the women as a way of reminding them about the project, as we would return to interview them at a later stage. Several Cambodian women in the study said that they were very proud of being included in our study and they displayed the postcards on their refrigerators. When their friends and families visited them, they would tell them about their participation in a project that was affiliated with two universities (field notes, 2008).

Cross-cultural researchers have also pointed to the privileged position that they hold when returning home to do their research. Roland Coloma (2008), for example, grew up and was educated in America. He returned to the Philippines to carry out his PhD. He brought with him an official document from Ohio State University in order to gain access to archive material in universities, libraries, museums and government agencies in the country. The official document signified that he was not a local student, and this provided him with access that is denied to local students in the Philippines. Coloma points out that:

> In a nation with a long history of western imperialism that spanned over three centuries of Spanish rule … and over four decades of US control … being an American provided me with privileges that were not usually afforded to locals. For instance, I gained entry into the libraries' closed reserves and received copies of out-of-print materials from staff that positively impacted my research. However, a graduate student from one of the most prestigious universities in the Philippines confided that he was never provided this type of service. 'Kano ka kasi' ('Because you're American'), he noted bluntly. (p. 16)

However, this is in contrast to the experiences of Mehreen Mirza (1998) and Rosalind Edwards (1990). Mirza, a South Asian woman, interviewed other South Asian women, and Edwards, a white woman, interviewed black women. Their association with a university prohibited them from having the credibility to gain access to their participants. For Mirza's research, the negative impact was not only created by her association with a university, but was also compounded by the fact that the South Asian women did not see the issues that she was researching as important for them. In Edwards's case, because of the negative educational experiences which black women had come across, she was placed in the position of being part of a 'white, middle-class, and oppressive institution'. This created suspicions about her motives and intentions among the women and as a result they did not wish to take part in her study.

Tutorial activities

You are a researcher who was born in and resides in England. Your social and cultural backgrounds are white, female and middle class. You will be going to do your research fieldwork with parents about infant feeding practices in Nepal. You intend to talk with both the fathers and mothers and other extended family members in some local areas in Nepal. What issues are you likely to face in doing this research? How might local people perceive you as a researcher?

Chapter summary

Acknowledging how personal biographical factors influence particular research is a vital ingredient in understanding qualitative research data. (Quraishi 2008: 459)

Robert Merton (1972: 40, original emphasis) warned us long ago, in his influential paper on the epistemological crisis 'Insiders and outsiders: A chapter in the sociology of knowledge', that '*either* the Insider or the Outsider has access to the sociological truth'. Both insider and outsider perspectives are essential in the 'process of truth seeking'. Merton puts it clearly: 'We no longer ask whether it is the Insider or the Outsider who has monopolistic or privileged access to social truth; instead, we begin to consider their distinctive and interactive roles in the process of truth seeking' (p. 36). And he emphasises the multiple roles and identities based on the race, ethnicity, gender, age, class, region and occupation of the researchers. These issues have been discussed in this chapter.

I would like to encourage readers to think about your own status carefully before the commencement of your research and continue to think about it throughout the course of your fieldwork. The insider and outsider status, as I have suggested, may shift at a particular moment of your fieldwork, and this may mean that you would need to reconsider your research process over and over again. Well, this is part of the challenge of performing qualitative cross-cultural research.

SUGGESTED READING

Banks, J. (1998). The lives and values of researchers: Implications for educating citizens in a multicultural society. *Educational Researcher* **27**(7), 4–17.

Chawla, D. (2007). Subjectivity and the 'native' ethnographer: Researcher eligibility in an ethnographic study of urban Indian women in Hindu arranged marriages. *International Journal of Qualitative Methodology* **5**(4), Article 2. www/ualberta.ca/~iiqm/backissues/5_4/pdf/chawla.pdf Accessed: 2 January 2007.

Coloma, R. S. (2008). Border crossing subjectivities and research: Through the prism of feminists of color. *Race Ethnicity & Education* **11**(1), 11–27.

Egharevba, I. (2001). Researching an-'other' minority ethnic community: Reflectoins of a black female researcher on the intersection of race, gender, and other power positions on the research process. *International Journal of Social Research Methodology* **4**(3), 225–241.

Kusow, A. M. (2003). Beyond Indigenous authenticity: Reflections on the insider/outsider debate in immigration research. *Symbolic Interaction* **26**(4), 591–599.

Maylor, U. (2009). Is it because I'm Black? A Black female research experience. *Race, Ethnicity & Education* **12**(1), 53–64.

Quraishi, M. (2008). Researching Muslim prisoners. *International Journal of Social Research Methodology* **11**(5), 453–467.

Ramji, H. (2008). Exploring commonality and difference in in-depth interviewing: A case-study of researching British Asian women. *British Journal of Sociology* **59**(1), 99–116.

Sherif, B. (2001). The ambiguity of boundaries in the fieldwork experience: Establishing rapport and negotiating insider/outsider status. *Qualitative Inquiry* **7**(4), 436–447.

Shockley, K. G. (2009). A researcher 'called' to 'taboo' places? A burgeoning research method in African-centered education. *International Journal of Qualitative Studies in Education* **22**(2), 163–176.

Subedi, B. (2007). Recognizing respondents' ways of being and knowing: Lessons un/learned in researching Asian immigrant and Asian-American teachers. *International Journal of Qualitative Studies in Education* **20**(10), 51–71.

Villenas, S. (1996). The colonizer/colonized Chicana ethnographer: Identity, marginalization, and co-option in the field. *Harvard Educational Review* **66**, 711–731.

6 Cross-cultural communication and language issues

I lack language you say
No. I lack language.
The language to clarify
my resistance to the literate …

(Cherrie Moraga, cited by Anzaldua 1983: 166)

Different languages construct different ways of seeing social life, which poses methodological and epistemological challenges for the researcher.

(Larkin *et al.* 2007: 468)

Language and communication are central to qualitative research. Language is a fundamental tool through which qualitative researchers seek to understand human behaviour, social processes and the cultural meanings that inscribe human behaviour.

(Hennink 2008: 21)

In this chapter, I shall point to the importance of language and communication in cross-cultural research. Often, researchers and the participants are from different linguistic backgrounds. But language, as Monique Hennink (2008: 22) contends, 'represents data in qualitative research and communication'. It is 'the process through which data are generated between a researcher and study participant'. Often, in carrying out cross-cultural research, the researchers are linguistically and culturally distant from their research participants (Hennink 2008). Differences in the language spoken and the meanings that are conveyed can create problems, and this has implications for the research findings. It is also an ethical issue, as misunderstanding may occur and this may result in the misinterpretation of the research findings (Irvine *et al.* 2008).

In this chapter, I shall first discuss issues pertaining to language. I then look at bicultural researchers and the need to provide training and support for them in cross-cultural research. Working with interpreters and/or translators in cross-cultural research is essential when it is not possible to work with bicultural researchers. I shall point to some limitations in working with short-term interpreters/translators as well as suggest some strategies to involve them more in a research project. I shall also introduce forward- and back-translation issues in this chapter. Last, I provide a discussion of transcription to an original language and a translation method which cross-cultural researchers could adopt in their qualitative research.

Language issues

The issue of language translation represents one of the major overarching themes in the literature on cross-cultural research. (Shklarov 2007: 529)

In qualitative research, language is crucial not only to the research process, but also to the resulting data and its interpretation. Language allows the research participants to identify meanings in the world. It permits the researchers and the participants to interact in order to produce an understanding of the social world of the participant and the interpretation of this context (Hennink 2008). Language is, therefore, a fundamental tool which allows qualitative researchers to understand human behaviour, socio-cultural processes and cultural meanings (p. 23).

In conducting qualitative cross-cultural research, the role and influence of language is more complex. Many qualitative research projects are undertaken by researchers who are not familiar with the language of the research participants. This can be seen in cross-national research, where the language of the researchers is markedly different from that of the participants and they are seen as 'outsiders'. It can also be seen in national research where the researchers investigate minority groups such as immigrants who may prefer to speak in their own language (Hennink 2008).

The most common difficulties encountered by 'outsider' cross-cultural researchers is an inability to speak the local or native language (Laverack & Brown 2003; Temple & Edwards 2002; Hall 2004). As Inez Kapborg and Carina Bertero (2002: 56) argue, it can be problematic if the researchers and the participants do not share the same language. This is because 'different languages create and express different realities, and language is a way of organising the world – one cannot understand another culture without understanding the language of the people in that culture'. Isobel Bowler (1997), in her study of sexual behaviour among ethnic minorities in the UK, suggests that at least the researchers need to obtain some simple linguistic competency. Even a basic knowledge of the main terms used within the group would assist the researchers in understanding some of the issues. More importantly, however, simple knowledge of the language of the group will make it easier for the researchers to establish a rapport with the participants.

Language differences in cross-cultural research, according to Rachel Hall (2004: 131), can be a 'potential hurdle' when the participants do not speak English as their first language (see Song & Parker 1995; Keats 2000). As Miri Song and David Parker (1995: 252) suggest, the choice of language that the researchers employ will almost certainly structure the interview process. In Hall's study, all of the participants were asked if they wished to be interviewed in the language of their choice through an interpreter, but twenty-nine out of thirty participants preferred to be interviewed in English. This was because the South Asian participants, whose first language was not English, generally spoke English very well. But as Song and Parker suggest, the participants can still 'feel more constrained and less comfortable in expressing themselves' in the interviews (p. 252). Hall (2004: 131) tells us that 'it was not uncommon for the participants to ask me to re-phrase or clarify words that I was using. On occasions, if a relative or friend was in the same room during the interview, the women would ask them to translate the English into their first language.'

I wish to bring up one important issue here. It is often assumed that when researchers carry out cross-cultural research, we must use the language of the participants so that researchers will have a fuller understanding of the issues under investigation (Lopez 2003). However, this may not be true for all cases. As I have suggested above, some participants may be very fluent in English. This is particularly so for some immigrant groups who have established themselves in a host country, like the UK, Canada, the USA, New Zealand and Australia. These people speak English very well and they may be more than happy to be interviewed in English rather than their native language.

Bicultural researchers

Typically, a bicultural (or bilingual) research assistant will be employed to work on the research project to overcome linguistic barriers in cross-cultural research (see Small *et al.* 1999a, 1999b; Brown *et al.* 2000; Kelaher & Manderson 2000; Maynard-Tucker 2000; Lindenberg *et al.* 2001; Allotey & Manderson 2003; Ahmad *et al.* 2004; Tsai *et al.* 2004; Hall & Kulig 2004; Gibson *et al.* 2005; Shklarov 2007; Hennink 2008; Davies *et al.* 2009).

Bicultural researchers share not only the language of the participants but also many social and cultural traits. They are people who are most likely to have the best of knowledge of the groups (Im *et al.* 2004; Davies *et al.* 2009). They are individuals who are able to 'convey the underlying cultural meanings of participants' words and expressions to the researchers' (Hennink 2008: 25). They play a vital role 'in the creation of knowledge and its cultural interpretation, both of which are the bedrock of qualitative research' (p. 25). In Lee and Ellenbecker's (1998) study of elderly Chinese, they worked with a bilingual (bicultural) researcher, who was able to speak both English and Chinese. Through the bicultural researcher, they were able to get more accurate information from the participants, as they could tell their experiences in their own language. The bicultural researcher could also interpret the meanings of some Chinese words which could not be translated into English exactly.

According to Svetlana Shklarov (2007: 534), because of their knowledge of the culture and their familiarity with the local language, bicultural researchers are in the best position to conduct cross-cultural research. The advantage is 'embedded' in their ability to 'identify and understand adequately the concerns'. Bicultural researchers are likely not only to be able to 'protect the participants from any possible harm (in a broad sense)' (p. 534), but they can also produce more 'honest and sound scientific results' free of any distortion that might result from language difficulties, and this can maximise the research benefits (p. 535).

Bicultural researchers, with their deeper insider's knowledge of the issues or people, are in a better position to conduct cross-cultural research than monolingual researchers working with interpreters (Tsai *et al.* 2004; Shklarov 2007: 535). Gaining knowledge of the culture under study can take a considerable amount of time for monolingual English-speaking researchers. But for bicultural researchers who commence the study within their own culture, 'these concepts might be a natural part' of their identities. And it is this natural understanding that 'secures an ideal basis for protecting the rights of research participants and avoiding any possible harm to them without leaning toward paternalistic attitudes'. However, it is also crucial to realise that the in-depth knowledge can also 'bring more doubt and become a reason for challenges' for the bicultural researchers.

Bicultural researchers have to perform a dual role in cross-cultural research. As an interpreter, Svetlana Shklarov (2007: 535) suggests, he or she is '"in the middle" of cross-language exchange' and becomes 'a single-stop "filter" of the meanings, the key tool of communication'. By taking this role, the bicultural researchers have great power, but they also carry some responsibilities. Their double role provides them with greater power than the role of translators, because they are 'associated with a perceived air of a "monopoly"' on the interpretation of their own research findings.

In their study on the prevention and treatment of tuberculosis with immigrant and aboriginal communities in Canada, Nancy Gibson and colleagues (2005) refer to bicultural researchers as 'community research associates (CAs)'. Gibson *et al.* assert that the CAs play a crucial part in their research; they link the research project with the cultural communities taking part in the study (p. 933). The CAs provide the researchers with their perspective of their own cultures and also ensure that the research will be conducted in a sensitive and respectful manner. Gibson *et al.* maintain that the CAs are essential in any cross-cultural research because of several factors. First, they are able to 'articulate the experiences of the research participants in their own language'. Second, they help to 'increase the project team's understanding of these experiences by providing the cultural lens to see beyond words'. Third, they 'acquire additional knowledge about health and illness in their communities', and last, they 'identify collective community interests beyond the research' (pp. 933–934).

However, Isobel Bowler (1997) warns us about the intrusive impact of bicultural researchers, especially when they play a crucial role in explaining the participants' expressions within a culturally sensitive area like sexuality. Svetlana Shklarov (2007: 531) points to the problem of the adequacy of cultural representations that the bicultural researchers claim. Sanja Hunt and Raj Bhopal (2004: 619) suggest that bicultural researchers do not represent the voices and concerns of 'the population from which they come' and that they are 'being biased by age, education and often gender and they produce translations that are too formal and literary for most people'. Svetlana Shklarov (2007: 531) also suggests that bicultural researchers tend to be people who are long-time immigrants, most of whom have been educated in the Western tradition. Because of this, they tend to be 'culturally distant from their non-English-speaking compatriots'.

However, the language, culture and values of some bicultural researchers who have lived in Western society for a long period of time may be 'frozen in time' (Temple & Edwards 2002). Shklarov (2007: 531) contends that these people may still hold on to the cultural meanings from when they left their countries, but the cultures and languages of their home countries have been changing. They may not know about new meanings of old words or expressions in their own countries or new words or meanings that people have constructed in their mother tongue. Therefore, in some situations, bicultural researchers may be seen as 'alien' by either the participants or both the participants and other researchers in cross-cultural communication.

Very often, bilingual researchers have to deal with 'additional ethically questionable expectations related to his or her bicultural background' (Shklarov 2007: 533). For example, Shuval (1963) undertook her research with immigrants to Israel in 1949 and 1950. The majority of the research participants were survivors of Nazi atrocities from different countries. She worked with a team of trained cross-cultural researchers, many of whom were survivors themselves. The bicultural researchers carried out interviews in the participants' native languages. Shuval tells us that 'the interviews served somewhat as a catharsis for the immigrants with the interviewer playing more the role of a therapist than a collector of social data' (p. 40). Some of the interviews lasted many hours, and the interviewers were able to provide the participants with empathy and support.

Nevertheless, Svetlana Shklarov (2007: 536) contends that the outcomes of qualitative research can be more beneficial when the bicultural researcher acts as an 'active interpreter and mediator' in cross-cultural research (see also Temple & Edwards 2002; Tsai *et al.* 2004; Hunt & Bhopal 2004; Davies *et al.* 2009). The benefits include not only that desirable outcomes can result from the research, but also that ethically justified means are taken into consideration. These benefits are the result of the responsibility which is assumed by the bicultural researcher 'in exercising particular sensitivity to those under study and to the ethical paradigms of the target culture'. In sum, Shklarov (2007: 537) contends that the bicultural researchers who act as their own translators and belong to both cultures can 'acquire a dual vision of the research context', and this dual vision can be 'represented in the dual perception of conceptual meanings, role dualism, and dual commitment to ethical paradigms'.

It is crucial that bicultural researchers undergo some training on the methodology involved in cross-cultural research. This is particularly so for the investigation of private or sensitive issues (Im *et al.* 2004; Davies et al. 2009). In their study on the experiences of HIV-positive patients, Judy Mill and Linda Ogilvie (2003) worked with bicultural researchers. As private issues such as prostitution history were included in the discussion, the bicultural researchers were invited to critically review their interview questions and styles. Similarly, in their research of paediatric palliative care with Mexican Americans and Chinese Americans, Betty Davies and colleagues (2009) provided extensive training for their bicultural researchers so that they could conduct the research ethically and were responsive to the needs of their participants and to their cultural practices.

However, working with a bicultural research project does not mean that the research will be without problems. Lynn Meadows and colleagues (2003) caution us that there are some problems in working with bicultural research assistants, and that this may make the period of the research longer than expected. See Meadows *et al.* (2003) for good examples of the problems they encountered in their research with aboriginal women in Canada.

Recruiting, training and support: bicultural researchers

Although I have proposed that bicultural researchers are more suitable for cross-cultural research, it is essential that appropriate bicultural researchers are selected. Bicultural researchers who are familiar with both the local culture and the mainstream culture (of the researchers) are crucial in cross-cultural research.

In Griselda Lopez and colleagues' (2008) study of Latino men experiencing treatment-related side effects from prostate cancer, they sought bilingual/bicultural researchers by advertising the positions. However, they found that many applicants who said that they were bilingual and/or bicultural were not able to accurately translate, or had problems translating the data 'without compromising the contextual meaning' of the responses of participants. In the end, Lopez *et al.* worked with two bilingual/bicultural staff members who had a background in prostate cancer research and its translation. Both had more than seven years of experience in translating materials. One of the bicultural researchers was a native Spanish speaker who was born and raised in Mexico but studied Spanish literature in the United States. The other one was a native English speaker who was born to immigrant parents from Mexico and Central America. Both bicultural researchers were familiar with the Spanish spoken in California; one had been living in California for eighteen years and the other was born and raised there. Both bicultural researchers had extensive training in both verbal and written translation, and both were familiar with the aims and objectives of the study.

In the Mothers in a New Country (MINC) project, where I was one of the chief investigators (Small *et al.* 1999a, 1999b), we only interviewed new mothers from immigrant backgrounds (Filipina, Turkish and Vietnamese women), and as the research was about becoming mothers and birth experiences, we needed to have female bicultural workers from these three communities. This created some problems for us as we could not specify women only interviewers because of the equal opportunity legislation enforced in Australia. So we had to indicate that because of the nature of the research, a female researcher would be more appropriate. We also had to explain this to those male workers who rang us about the nature of our study. This did not pose any discrimination issues for those few men who made enquiries. The same strategy was used with my own research project on Southeast Asian women and childbirth. I eventually employed three women, one each from Cambodian, Lao and Vietnamese communities to work with me on that project.

In Jennifer Harris and Keri Roberts's (2003: 9–10) study, the positions of bicultural researchers were advertised through refugee community groups, minority ethnic newspapers and university-based job centres. Those whom the research team already knew were informed and encouraged to apply for the posts. They particularly emphasised that applications from men and women, disabled people, and refugees and asylum seekers would be welcomed. Informal discussions with the research team prior to applying were also encouraged. Those invited for interview who required assistance with making travel arrangements were given support. One applicant was interviewed by telephone because his travel arrangements did not go as planned. In the end, through this recruitment strategy, eight bicultural researchers were successfully appointed.

It is important that the bicultural researchers are properly trained before they embark on data collection. Often, they will need to be familiar with the research project, its aims and objectives, data-collection methods and their involvement in the project. In Harris and Roberts's (2003) study with visually impaired bicultural researchers, all of them were invited to attend a two-day training course at the university. Materials used during this course were provided in Braille and on disk. All of the equipment used during the training session, including tape-recorders and microphones, was designed to take into account visual impairment and variations in dexterity. This ensured that the training venue and the hotel in which the bicultural researchers were accommodated were physically accessible. Harris and Roberts joined the bicultural researchers for an evening meal at a restaurant which met both halal and other dietary requirements.

In the MINC project, we trained our bicultural researchers prior to the fieldwork taking place. The bicultural workers were invited to take part in a week-long training session. The training included lectures on the research project, how to conduct an interview and survey, and how to recruit the participants in hospital settings. We also discussed the way we could trace the participants, as the project required several home interviews, in the event that some participants moved without informing us.

It is essential that the bicultural researchers themselves receive support from the researchers throughout the life of the project. It is likely that these bicultural researchers will encounter some barriers or difficulties when arranging, carrying out and transcribing interviews. In Harris and Roberts's study, their bicultural researchers were given support on potential barriers throughout their employment period (pp. 10–11). Telephone support was provided both before and immediately after each interview, as often the interviews covered experiences of torture. Regular contact with the bicultural interviewers was made between interviews. Their workloads were adjusted to take account of changes in both the physical and mental health status of each bicultural researcher or members of their families. Some bicultural researchers, who were refugees fleeing prosecution themselves, asked for extended leave so that they could visit their family who had been scattered in different parts of the world following their flight from persecution, and this was granted.

In the Southeast Asian (SEA) project, we provided regular support for our bicultural researchers. We had a fortnightly meeting for everyone to discuss their concerns, problematic situations and personal issues. All were able to reach me, as the chief investigator, at any time, and I provided them with my home and mobile phone numbers. Often, one or two would ring me while in the field. Sometimes, it was only a minor issue on which they wanted some reassurance and confirmation.

Translator/Interpreter perspectives

In certain situations, researchers may need to work with translators/interpreters in cross-cultural research (see Edwards 1998; Birbili 2000; Kapborg & Bertero 2002; Cortis & Kendrick 2003; Spicer 2005; Bujra 2006; Hennink 2008; Temple & Young 2008). However, there has been some debate about working through translators/interpreters (see Bujra 2006). The use of a translator/interpreter, Bogusia Temple (1997: 614) contends, is not simply a technical matter which has little influence on the outcome. Rather, 'it is of epistemological consequences as it influences what is "found"'. Working with translators/interpreters, Temple suggests, researchers have to depend on them 'not just for words but to a certain extent for perspective' (p. 608) (see Esposito 2001; Temple & Edwards 2002; Bujra 2006; Culley *et al.* 2007; Hennink 2008).

As a translator or interpreter, Joseph Kaufert and Robert Putsch (1997: 72) point out, the person is 'a gatekeeper who has the power to elicit, clarify, translate, omit, or distort messages'. Philip Larkin and colleagues (2007: 468) also contend that translators/interpreters can potentially significantly influence research by 'virtue of' their 'attempt to convey meaning from a language and culture that might be unknown to the researcher'. Bogusia Temple and Alys Young (2008: 101) state this clearly:

> The translator always makes her mark on the research, whether this is acknowledged or not, and in effect some kind of 'hybrid' role emerges in that, at the very least, the translator makes assumptions about meaning equivalence [that] makes her an analyst and cultural broker as much as a translator.

Working with a translator or an interpreter may not be as efficient as working with a bicultural worker, and some researchers have reported difficulties associated with working with interpreters/translators (Kapborg & Bertero 2002; Ryen 2002). Interpreters/translators are often used for short periods and they rarely become involved in the research (Temple 1997; Edwards 1998; Adamson & Donovan 2002; Temple 2002; Tsai et al. 2004; Hennink 2008). They therefore do not have a full understanding of the research aims and questions. Working through interpreters/translators can also be tiring for all involved. Often, people cannot continue for a very long period without a break. The interpreters/translators may become bored in the interview situation, and instead of translating the participant's responses, they may simply say 'same answer as the others'. In the interview situation, the researchers may focus only on the verbal language. But verbal exchange is only a part of a culture. Other non-verbal communication and symbols are also of significance. Hence, some important information in the interview situation might have been lost, and this could affect the quality and meaning of the data obtained (Kapborg & Bertero 2002: 55).

It is well known that concepts cannot always be translated across languages and cultures (Tsai et al. 2004: 8; see also Michaud et al. 2001; Lange 2002; Marston 2005; Bujra 2006; Hennink 2008). Because of subtle differences in meaning, translating from one language to another can be very complex and problematic (Kapborg & Bertero 2002; Bujra 2006). Because of cultural differences or non-equivalent words, some words cannot be properly translated into English. As Svetlana Shklarov (2007: 531) puts it: 'Language translation is not a simple linguistic exercise. Cultural and contextual interpretation always plays its part, because the meanings of words often carry subtle nuances and cultural connotations that have to be captured in translation.'

She also contends that a precise equivalence of expression of a concept in different languages can be difficult to obtain. Hence, a complex situation may happen. Some common Western conceptual meanings can be difficult to understand in other cultures. This is also applicable in translating cultural meanings into English. Western researchers may not be able to appreciate the complexity of concepts which are common in other cultures. Translating concepts and words then becomes, as McLaughlin and Sall (2001: 206) argue, 'a question of culture before being a question of vocabulary'.

Danielle Piette (1998) attempted to translate the Health Behaviour in School-aged Children (HBSC) survey from English to French. The word 'bullying' has no equivalent expression in French. Hence, four different expressions were adopted to convey the concept of bullying in the French context. Shklarov (2007: 531) tells us that the word 'empowerment' has no equivalent meaning in the Russian language. It is difficult to convey the same meaning as is understood in the West in Russia, and in order to translate this word meaningfully and adequately some lengthy explanations will need to be provided. Max van Manen (1990) wrote nearly two pages to explain the multidimensional meanings of the German word 'Geisteswissenschaften'. He argues that the English translation of the term 'human science', which is derived from the German, is 'not a satisfactory translation' of the term.

In a study by Philip Larkin and colleagues (2007) on the transition towards palliative care in Europe, qualitative research questions were translated into Dutch, French, Spanish and Italian. They tell us that none of the translators could find any equivalence for the concept of palliative care in their native language. This was partly due to different understandings of the concept of palliative care as a practice discipline in different European countries. Palliative care is the concept deriving from an English term, and it is not known outside medical jargon. Thus, it was unknown to the translators (p. 472).

I want to add a very recent translation issue involving Tourism Australia and Japanese tourists here, as I think it succinctly illustrates my point. Tourism Australia has recently developed a new slogan to attract more tourists to Australia. The slogan contains this catchy punchline 'So, where the bloody hell are you?' However, when it was translated into Japanese, it was nearly impossible to come up with the same catchy line. A swearword like 'bloody hell' is virtually unheard of in Japan. Additionally, the Japanese will probably see the phrase 'Where the hell are you?' as what people say in anger, not in fun. So the catchy punchline now becomes 'So, why don't you come?' (Cameron 2006: 3). I think the translation does not convey the subtle meaning as it was intended.

In qualitative research, context is extremely important, and without it misunderstanding can easily be created (Temple & Edwards 2002; Im *et al.* 2004; Larkin *et al.* 2007; Shklarov, 2007). This problem tends to occur when working with interpreters/translators. Bogusia Temple (2002: 847) points out that 'researchers often use translators and interpreters as if they were transmitters of neutral messages across languages, ignoring the linguistic imperialism central to an unquestioning use of English as a baseline language'. But as I have suggested, concepts can move problematically across cultures. We cannot assume that because an individual speaks a particular language, he or she can represent a culture. Being able to speak the language may be insufficient in cross-cultural research.

More involvement of interpreters/translators in cross-cultural research

Because of the problem of working with translators and interpreters in a short period, as outlined above, cross-cultural researchers have argued for the greater involvement of interpreters and translators in cross-cultural qualitative research (Edwards 1998; Adamson & Donovan 2002; Bradby 2002; Temple 2002; Temple & Edwards 2002; Larkin *et al.* 2007; Vinokurov *et al.* 2007; Hennink 2008). As Svetlana Shklarov (2007: 536–537) argues, translation is 'a complex and cognitive process' which can have an impact on 'the ethical standing and general outcomes of the research'. Because of the importance of the translation processes, the researchers must advocate 'a greater significance of the translator's role in research'. Temple (1997: 608), too, suggests that the views of others involved in the research, including translators and interpreters, should be seen as 'a productive methodological exercise'.

Bogusia Temple and Rosalind Edwards (2002: 3) suggest that in order to undertake sensitive and meaningful research with people who speak little or no English, the researchers must discuss important issues in their research with the interpreters and translators with whom they are working. Joy Adamson and Jenny Donovan (2002: 823) strongly advocate this, and from their experiences they suggest that it is better if researchers work with fewer interpreters/translators but more frequently. This way, each interpreter/translator has a good opportunity to become more familiar with the particular research process as well as to be more knowledgeable about the nature of the information to be collected. Therefore, it is important that the interpreters/translators must fully understand the research questions and the process of research prior to any data collection taking place. A debrief after each interview is also essential, because the researcher and interpreter/translator have an immediate opportunity to talk about the particular interview, the data collected and any observations which could be vital for the interpretation of their findings. Rosalind Edwards (1998) recommends that an interpreter/translator needs to have a clear understanding of his or her role, and hence a training or induction process is needed. In this way, the interpreter/translator will be sensitive to the research topic and objectives. Edwards suggests that the interpreters/translators should form part of the research and that they should be made more visible in research projects.

Philip Larkin and colleagues (2007: 468–469) contend that 'power dynamics' between the researchers and the interpreters/translators can have an impact on the validity of the work. Hence, they should not be ignored (Edwards 1998). Researchers must acknowledge the personal impact of the interpreter/translator on fieldwork. Failing to treat the interpreter/translator as a co-researcher or co-worker can prevent the researchers having an understanding of the research process as well as the data obtained (Temple & Edwards 2002). In their research, Larkin *et al.* (2007: 474) tell us that:

> To share ideas with people who could legitimately speak for the technicality of their language within a given culture was extremely valuable in helping us not only to feel secure in the tools for research but also to know that the translators understood the perspectives and values of the research process.

Cross-cultural researchers who work with interpreters/translators have started to examine some ways that the interpreters/translators can be made more visible within the research process (Temple & Young 2008). Edwards (1998) argues that cross-cultural researchers should treat interpreters/translators as 'key informants' rather than as 'neutral transmitters of messages'. This will open up a dialogue about possible differences in perspective. Without discussing with the interpreters/translators their perspectives of the issues, differences in understandings of words, concepts and worldviews across languages will be lost (Hennink 2008; Temple & Young 2008).

Bogusia Temple, in her (2002) research with Asian support workers, worked with two assistants (interpreters) who collected the data and undertook research on mental health issues with the Asian communities. The interpreters transcribed and translated the data. They then discussed the data with the researcher. The discussion also involved their own perspectives on the issues, the transcription process and their interpretations of the data. In their ethnographic study of how immigrant Chinese and South Asian women caregivers accessed support from community resources in Canada, Neufeld and colleagues (2002) employed the same process of having their translators collect data, transcribe it and participate in discussions about the interpretation of the results.

In Andrey Vinokurov and colleagues' (2007: 4) work, they collaborated with the translators in the research process. They tell us that:

Without developing collaborative relationships and discussing various conceptual and methodological aspects of the project, we might have been perceived as forcing our perceptions and definitions of constructs on the translators, which could then bias the results. It has been reported that translators in East European countries might be reluctant to disagree with Western researchers … To avoid this possibility, we specifically focused on developing rapport and collegial relationships with the translators, as they are the true experts in the language and culture we are study-ing. Developing and fostering collaborative relationships with the translators was essential for arriving at the final version of the translation, as well as for the overall progress of the research project. Thus, translation, as well as research, becomes a democratic, reciprocal, non-hierarchical, and cooperative process.

Bogusia Temple (1997: 613) argues that language connotes more than words. Interpreters and translators have their own views of words based on their practical encounters with the social world, and their translation of the words is influenced by these encounters. As such, there is 'no "wrong" trans-lation, just different versions with the "original" depending for its existence on the translation as much as the other way around'.

Temple provides a good example of issues relating to translation and work-ing closely with translators (pp. 615–616). I will quote her here. She shows an interview which was translated by a translator in her early thirties who was born in England after her parents had migrated from Poland. This is her translation:

Women can organise everything, but they cannot lead.

Temple, who is a bilingual researcher, went back to check the transcript and this is what she translated:

Women are allowed to organise everything but to take the lead on nothing.

Temple discussed the translation with her translator and they both agreed that the statement could be translated either way if they translated word by word. They also discussed their perspectives on the position of women in Polish soci-ety and found that their views were markedly different. The differences of the translation were due mainly to the society's perceptions and expectations of which roles which were suitable for men and for women and to the differences in definitions of the meaning of leadership. Temple contends that:

> The point is not whether any one of the translators is right and another wrong. It is that by looking at the way the interview had been translated and asking the translator why she had done it like that I realised that our views were very different. The interview meant different things to us and by discussing each other's perspectives on it we could discuss the differences. Had I not inquired I would have had to rely largely on her words. (pp. 615–616)

It was only through working closely with her translator that Temple realised the differences between their two perspectives. This case illustrates the point that I have made in this section, that the translators should be involved in the research project more than merely as interpreters or translators of information. As Larkin and colleagues (2007) suggest, they should be removed from the 'shadowy figure' in cross-cultural research, and become 'interpretive guides and co-researchers' (Hennink 2008: 31).

What about professional translators?

Rosaline Edwards (1998) and Noreen Esposito (2001) assert that when language is a concern in cross-cultural research, the use of professionally trained translators is essential. However, some writers have challenged this notion. In Jenny Tsai and colleagues' (2004) study of Chinese Americans, professional translators were employed to translate (audio-tape) all interviews in Chinese to English prior to their being transcribed. When these professional translators came across concepts which do not exist in the Chinese language, they adopted literal translations or phonetic translations. For instance, one of their translations was: 'When I had thyroid cancer, "wai dan gong" [Translation: "exercise"] was very popular … I started to do wai dan gong'. Tsai and colleague tell us: 'Wai dan gong is an exercise activity that involves low levels of body movement and promotes qi (energy in Chinese medicine) through each movement'. The word 'exercise' in English refers to vigorous activities. The choice of translation word was not completely wrong, but 'it would not fully convey the value of wai dan gong in the Chinese sociocultural context and the possible link between the interviewee's decision to do wai dan gong and his thyroid cancer' (p. 8).

Hannah Bradby (2002: 849) also points to a problem with having professional translators translate the survey she used in one of her studies relating to food choice, health and identity among Glasgow South Asian immigrants (Hindu and Urdu). She tells us:

The initial translation received from the professional translators used formal, often literary, language with the Hindi version using words of Sanskrit origin, and the Urdu version having a more Persian-influenced vocabulary and negligible English or Punjabi vocabulary. Although we had requested that both translators have a 'Pubjabi/Glaswegian' flavour, to reflect the local spoken language, this proved to be impossible since the mixing of languages would have represented a failure of the translators' skills in interpreting terms and phrases between languages.

Later on, the translators used a less literary or formal vocabulary. However, they still used 'pure Hindi' and 'pure Urdu' words. Where possible, Bradby had to replace those words with English and Punjabi words and phrases.

Bradby gives an example of the translation of marital status in Punjabi terms (p. 849). In social surveys, often the categories of married, divorced, widowed, single and having a partner but not married are used. However, the translation of 'partner' into Punjabi was problematic because marriage is a common practice in Punjabi society. In the survey, the term 'partner' was substituted by '*jeevan saathi*', which means 'lifetime companion'. However, the interviewers often replaced it with the English term 'husband' because they perceived the term '*jeevan saathi*' as 'hopelessly romantic', or carrying 'the insulting implication that the interviewee was not properly married'.

The use of professionally trained translators is also controversial in some research. In the MINC study, we interviewed new mothers from immigrant backgrounds about the sensitive issues of childbirth and mothering. Women indicated their preferences towards family members for acting as their interpreters in hospital care. They did not wish an 'outsider', an interpreter who is also a stranger to them, to interpret important issues from health care professionals. This issue has been debated among professional interpreters, who argue that family members are not eligible to interpret health information as they may not do it correctly (see Edwards 1998), or that it may put a burden on family members, who may feel uncomfortable about interpreting personal issues to health care providers (see Jack *et al.* 2001; Dunckley *et al.* 2003). But I contend that this depends on the nature of the issue and the gender of the person. In some situations, this may not be a problem, but in certain situations, such as my example above, professional interpreters may not work well for the research participants.

Jenny Tsai and colleagues (2004: 8) argue that the interpreters' and translators' perspectives, which are influenced by their culture and their own lived experiences, are not the only factors, but that their 'knowledge about the subtleties of the languages to which they translate' also has an impact on the choice of words they use. Hence, if the interpreters and translators are aware of the issues relating to the research areas, and if they consider these issues in their translation process, non-professional interpreters or translators can be as good as the professional ones (see also Temple & Edwards 2002).

Forward-translation and back-translation issues

Research on ethnic minorities requires instrumentation that is sensitive to cultural and contextual variations … Attaining cultural sensitivity in instrumentation requires translations and adaptations into languages other than English'. (Alegria *et al.* 2004: 271)

Although this book is concerned mainly with qualitative research, it is essential that I refer to the use of research tools which require a translation and back translation in cross-cultural research. I will dedicate this section solely to this issue.

Most of the validated clinical tools, such as the SF-36 Health Survey, were initially developed in the English language (Dunckley *et al.* 2003). The scope of these tools is, however, insufficient for cross-cultural assessment or for reflecting the cultural diversity of the research participants (Birbili 2000).

When research tools which are designed for English participants are simply translated into another language, it can result in measurement error, and this error may be the result of 'inadequate translation procedures, inappropriate content, insensitivity of items, and the failure of researchers to make themselves familiar with cultural norms and beliefs' (Hunt & Bhopal 2004: 618; see also Dunckley *et al.* 2003). Hence, social science researchers have developed some strategies to deal with these potential errors.

One of the most common approaches employed in cross-cultural research is forward and back translation, developed by Richard Brislin (1970, 1986). According to Sonja Hunt and Raj Bhopal (2004: 618), it has been a common practice that the instruments originally developed for English research participants are translated into the required language(s). It is assumed that 'the modes of inquiry, types of assessment, and research methods appropriate for native English speakers can be applied to other linguistic groups'. The translation of questionnaires and interview schedules was initiated in the field of cross-cultural psychology in the USA. Initially, one or several professional translators would translate the English material into the target language.

If more than one translator was involved, the translated versions would be compared. An agreement between the translators would be negotiated. The task was to reach linguistic equivalence. However, later on it became clear that the translators did not represent the group from which they came. They are biased by social class, age, gender and education, and often produce translations which are too formal and literary for most people within the group.

Traditionally, the strategy adopted in translation has been the 'back-translation method'. It involves the translation of the instrument from the original language into another language by one set of bilingual persons. The translated version is then translated back into the original language by another set of bilinguals (Brislin 1970, 1976; Vinokurov *et al.* 2007). This technique permits the researchers to be able to judge the equivalence and quality of the translation. The researchers are able to consult with the translators about possible explanations for any inconsistencies, ambiguities or discrepancies in meaning, so that the translated version of the instrument can be revised (McGorry 2000). Typically, the original-language version is used as the standard version and compared with the translated version. Therefore, the translated version is made with as little change as possible from the original piece (Brislin 1970, 1976; Baldacchino *et al.* 2002; Lange 2002; Beck *et al.* 2003; Vinokurov *et al.* 2007).

This process is also referred to as forward and back translation. Forward translation, according to Maria Dunckley and colleagues (2003: 422), pertains to 'translation of the clinical tool from the original language into the target language'. Back translation refers to 'the process of translating the tool from the target language (obtained from the initial forward translation) back into the original language'. The back translation must be carried out by different translators, who were not involved in the first step. It is often 'carried out blind, without prior sight of the original tool'. Differences between the original and back-translated versions need to be discussed by the translation team to decide on the most appropriate terms. Doris Yu and colleagues (2004) adopted this method in the translation of the Medical Outcomes Study Social Support Survey (MOS-SSS) into Chinese, and Asiye Kartala and Sühela Özsoy (2007) used it in their back translation of the Health Belief Model Scale used in diabetic patients into Turkish.

It has been argued that the current translation processes are employed to 'ensure word equivalence (such as forward-backward translation)' and that they have become 'the gold standard by which language-based academic research is judged (Larkin *et al.* 2007: 469; Usunier 1999). Nevertheless, there are some problems with the back-translation method. Larkin and colleagues

(2007: 469) point out that the process of back translation is 'inherently flawed', as it is assumed that 'research is language free and that the same meaning in the source language can be found in all target languages'. The cross-cultural translation process should acknowledge that each language is capable of creating its own meaning. It acknowledges that individuals in different cultures are 'neither bounded, integrated or organized as a whole' (Geertz 1983: 59). Cross-cultural researchers have argued that 'there is no single correct translation of a text. Meaning is constructed through a discourse between texts' (Temple & Young 2008: 94; see also Spivak 1992; Simon 1996; Temple 2006; Temple *et al.* 2006). According to Temple (1997: 610), it may be more appropriate to 'convey meaning using words' rather than 'literally translated equivalents' when instruments or accounts are translated into different languages. And 'if there is no one meaning to a text, then there can be only one translation of it'. See also the writing of Vinokurov and colleagues (2007: 5) for problems with the back-translation process.

In developing an instrument cross-culturally, Sanja Hunt and Raj Bhopal (2004: 621) suggest that researchers should 'focus upon the similarity of concepts rather than upon equivalence of items … It may not be necessary to have exact comparisons as long as the underlying purpose of the question is the same'.

An example from Hannah Bradby's (2002: 849–850) study may illustrate this point. The word 'single', meaning 'never married', was initially translated as '*kuvari*' in Punjabi. However, while it is correct that '*kuvari*' means an unmarried or single woman, it also contains a meaning which resembles 'virgin' in contemporary English. Hence, she replaced it with '*nahiñ shadi-shuda*' or 'not married'. Bradby suggests that back translation of '*nahiñ shadi-shuda*' may lead to some confusion between the option of 'unmarried' or 'cohabiting', and 'single'.

In Doris Yu and colleagues's (2004: 313–314) work, they point to difficulties which are related to cultural differences in words used in the translation of their instrument. Some words which are commonly used in one culture may not transmit similar meanings when used in the same way in another culture. In translating such words, attempts to achieve adequate literal translation may not ensure the equivalence of the meaning between the original and translated versions. For example, the original English version contains the descriptors 'private worries and fear'. Yu *et al.* contend that in its original version, the word 'private' implies 'non-disclosure or personal' (p. 313). However, this term is rarely referred to as 'the modifier for the emotional status of "worry" in the Chinese language'. The direct literal translation of this term therefore compromised the original meaning. As a result, Yu *et al.* used a phrase which would portray 'the innermost feeling for Chinese people'. Hence, the back-translated version became 'the worry and fear in your heart of hearts'.

Yu *et al.* also point to difficulties which were related to cultural experience with a concept which was etic (outsider perspective) to the Chinese culture in their study (pp. 313–314). They argue that a direct translation of some Western terms may not result in the same response from participants from a different cultural background. For instance, an original version that states 'someone who hugs you' is problematic in Chinese culture. Yu *et al.* point out that hugging is 'a commonly used body language in the Western culture. This action is, however, less likely to be done in the same manner by the more conservative Chinese people. This action carries different cultural meanings between the two cultures. Maintaining the literal meaning in translating this emic (insider perspective) item would, therefore, be inappropriate.' They consulted bilingual and bicultural individuals who have lived in Western and Chinese societies for their views. These individuals suggested 'love, care, and protection' to represent 'hugging'. The back-translated version, hence, became 'someone who gives you loving care'.

Nonetheless, Maria Birbili (2000: 4) suggests, it is essential that the translated research instrument be tested in the local culture. This is one way of eliminating translation-related problems. Additionally, when pre-testing a research instrument, as well as asking for the answers, the researchers should ask the participants for their interpretation of the meaning of each item. This will help the researchers to gain a more accurate translation of the instrument. More information about forward and back translation of survey instruments can be found in Baldacchino *et al.* (2002), Eremenco *et al.* (2005), Willgerodt *et al.* (2005) and Dean *et al.* (2007).

Some translation issues

As I have suggested previously, it is often difficult to translate cross-culturally. Some cross-cultural researchers have pointed to some salient issues in translating information from one culture to another. I wish to point to some discussions here.

Language, according to Temple and Edwards (2002: 3), is 'an important part of conceptualization … It speaks of a particular social reality that may not necessarily have a conceptual equivalence in the language into which it is to be translated'. Hence, it is more appropriate if cross-cultural researchers pay attention to 'the issue of concept equivalence so that materials have the same meaning in two or more cultures' (Irvine *et al.* 2008: 41).

Some cross-cultural researchers suggest the use of emic and etic meanings in translation (see Hunt & Bhopal 2004; Yu *et al.* 2004; Shklarov 2007). Emic meanings refer to issues which are linguistically and culturally relevant to the specific groups. Etic meanings are related to 'broader universal items' which characterise the outsider views of the Western observers. These different meanings will allow the researchers and interpreters/translators to focus on 'the similarity and contextual "fit" between the concepts expressed in different languages rather than pursuing neutral equivalency' (Shklarov 2007: 532). For example, in their research with Mexican-American and Chinese-American families in which a child had died from a life-limiting illness, Betty Davies and colleagues (2009) worked with bicultural researchers. A Latina research assistant initially translated the Spanish verb 'sobrellevar' as 'to overcome'. In the context of grief and death, the translation is inaccurate, as parents do not overcome the grief related to their child's death. Consultation with Spanish speakers indicated that despite their sadness, the word should be translated as 'to carry on', as it was a more appropriate translation in this context.

The imposition of Western framework (meanings, beliefs and worldview) on non-Western society in cross-cultural research has also been noted. This often refers to as 'a nonliteral or too precise translation, of culturally foreign, uninvited, and possibly conflicting basic perspectives' (Shklarov 2007: 534). In her work, Svetlana Shklarov had difficulty translating Western terms used in mental health into Russian:

In the West it is considered correct to refer to a person who uses mental health services as a *consumer*, whereas other words, such as *mentally ill* or *patient*, are considered less appropriate. Conversely, in the opinion of many people who have to deal with mental illness in Russia, the literal translation of the word *consumer* has a commercial connotation, which is unacceptable in their culture … Many people insisted that they could not accept the word … In the Western view, language shapes the attitudes, and thus the language that relates to human rights should be actively promoted in Russia. (p. 534, original emphasis)

This Western framework has been referred to by Joanna Overing (1987: 76) as an 'alien' framework. According to Overing, 'it is not the "word" about which we should be anxious; we should be concerned, instead, about an "alien" framework of thought which is based upon an "alien" set of universal principles about the world' (p. 76). This important issue needs to be considered in cross-cultural research, from the perspectives of both the researchers and the participants.

Issues of transcribing data in their original language

One important aspect of cross-cultural research which deserves greater attention is that of transcribing qualitative data in their original language (Irvine *et al.* 2008). Often, as Bogusia Temple (2002: 844) contends, interviews are not transcribed in their original language. As a result, 'possible differences in the meanings of words, or concepts across languages vanish into the space between spoken otherness and written sameness'. Sheila Twinn (1998) suggests that qualitative data should be transcribed in their original language in order to reduce the difficulties associated with the translation and interpretation of verbatim data. Many subtle issues have been lost in the process of translation by others than the researchers themselves.

Some qualitative studies (see Kapborg & Berterö 2002; Pitchforth & van Teijlingen 2005; Stone *et al.* 2005), which have been conducted in another language, have directly transcribed the interview data into English, instead of transcribing it in the local language and then translating it. Direct transcription into English carries the possibility that interpreter bias may be introduced (Lopez *et al.* 2008: 1730–1731). For example, Pitchforth and van Teijlingen (2005) carried out their research with Bangladeshi women with limited formal education who had recently used emergency obstetric care. They worked with a lay interpreter who carried out the interviews. The interpreter was not professionally trained, but she had research interviewing experience, a health-related postgraduate qualification and had been trained and worked full time with the research team for six months. The interviews were translated directly into English by the interpreter. For quality assurance purposes, Pitchforth and van Teijlingen arranged for an independent bilingual interpreter to transcribe four interviews into English. The review of the two transcripts revealed that the study interpreter did not translate the women's responses. Rather, she 'interpreted' the data. The level of detail which was provided by the study interpreter was also markedly different from that of the independent bilingual interpreter. She left out many details, which led to a loss of some insights into the experiences of these women. Although Pitchforth and van Teijlingen conceded that this did not greatly impact on the research in general, it could have caused some 'significant problems' with their research if they had wished to analyse issues which were not translated for them.

In their research with diabetic South Asians in the United Kingdom, Stone and colleagues (2005) used a similar method to transcribe and translate qualitative data. Interviews were carried out in a South Asian language. The transcriptionists/translators concurrently transcribed and translated the interviews. They interpreted the participants' responses as they saw appropriate. This resulted in significant problems with understanding the participants' experiences of their illnesses and the meanings they ascribed to them. In turn, this led to some problems with the interpretation of the research findings in the study.

In my own research on childbirth within the Thai ethnic community in Australia (see Liamputtong Rice & Naksook 1998; Liamputtong & Naksook 2003a, 2003b) and with Thai women in Thailand (see Liamputtong 2004, 2005, 2007b; Liamputtong et al. 2004, 2009), all interview data were transcribed in the Thai language in order to preserve the subtlety of the narratives provided by the women. I only translated the women's narratives into English if I used these in my writing. I was able to do so as I am a native Thai speaker. In my study with Southeast Asian immigrant women which include those from Laos, Cambodia and Vietnam (see Liamputtong & Watson 2002, 2006; Liamputtong 2006), my bicultural researchers transcribed and translated the interview data at the same time. This took much longer for them to do. I instructed all research assistants to translate as accurately as possible what the women said. If there were some words or concepts which were difficult to translate into English, I asked them to retain the original words and concepts but provide me with some explanation of such words/concepts. This way, I managed to interpret the women's narratives and meanings in greater depth and more accurately. In Azita Emami and Carol Tishelman's (2004) study on cancer with Iranian women in Sweden, focus group interviews were conducted in the Farsi language. Emami, who is a native Iranian woman, transcribed and analysed the data in Farsi. Four transcripts were translated into Swedish so that other members of the research team could access some of the data. The analysis done by Emami was then reviewed and discussed for verification of interpretation. In Cicely Marston's (2005) research with Mexican youth, all life histories were transcribed in Spanish and Marston analysed her data in its original language. This is similar to what I have done, but only the final quotations used in Marston's publication were translated into English. Marston contends that 'it is impossible to translate between languages "faithfully", particularly as meaning derives from context' (p. 72). In her work, she argues that her translations attempt to 'provide the best possible sense' of the participant's original speech in Spanish. Where translation was particularly problematic, clarifying notes are given. See also the work of Mitra Shavarini (2006), who used a research method she calls 'portraiture' or 'life drawings' with a young Iranian woman, and collected information in the Farsi language. Shavarini only translated the quotes that she used in her writing.

Translation method

Adequacy and accuracy of translation in cross-cultural communication is paramount for conducting research with human subjects in any methodological tradition, across all disciplines and paradigms. (Shklarov 2007: 529)

Cross-cultural researchers have come up with strategies that they can use in translating data more appropriately. Noreen Esposito (2001), for example, suggests several strategies that we may follow. These include:

- having two translators to translate the material;
- adopting a back-translation approach to convert one set of data into another language;
- using multiple focus groups for those involved to discuss the translation process;
- making use of the triangulation of participants, methods and researchers in the translation process;
- working with outside bilingual reviewers.

I wish to suggest a translation method which Griselda Lopez and colleagues (2008: 1733) have proposed, as it is a valuable strategy to follow. In this work, Brislin's (1970) steps in the forward- and back-translation method in cross-cultural research is adopted in the translation of qualitative research.

- Transcribe transcript verbatim.
- Translator reads transcript in the native language; makes notes and annotations to refer to as required.
- Translate the transcript.
- If questions or problems occur:
  - Discuss problems with the translation team.
  - Collectively make decisions about the problems and translation by the translation team.
  - Record decisions in translation log for future use.
  - Translator makes corrections accordingly.
- If no questions or problems occur:

- Proofread the translation and make sure that the translation is correct and makes sense.
- Submit the completed translation to lead translator.
- The lead translator reviews the completed translation.
- The completed translation is submitted to the research team or principal investigator.
- If further work is required, the translation is returned to the translator, and steps mentioned above are repeated.

Griselda Lopez and colleagues (2008) strongly believe that it is essential to transcribe qualitative data verbatim, in the participant's native language. The data are then translated in order to allow the true meaning of the participant's experience to be properly conveyed in the English language. Undoubtedly, the translation method that they propose permits the researchers to use qualitative data collected in the participant's local language more accurately. Lopez *et al.* contend that:

Our methodology more accurately conveys the true meaning of the participant's experience. This methodology is both more appropriate and meaningful, and opens doors to researchers who are interested in conducting research in a language other than their own, which subsequently broadens fields, while at the same time ensuring the reliability and validity of the study's data. (p. 1737)

Tutorial activities

As a doctoral student in Australia, you wish to carry out your research field-work in Thailand. You are an English-speaking person who has only simple Thai language to converse with the Thai people. How will you overcome the issue of this lack of language? You may wish to learn the Thai language before you travel to Thailand, as many others have done. However, at the beginning of your fieldwork, you may find that your Thai will not be sufficient for you to collect in-depth information from the Thai participants. What will you do to allow you to collect in-depth data? What issues will you be facing regarding data collection, data analysis and the presentation of your data?

Chapter summary

Cross-cultural qualitative research is … challenging because of difficulties of collecting reliable and valid information when conducting research in a language other than the researcher's primary language. (Lopez *et al.* 2008: 1729)

This chapter deals with language and cross-cultural communication in cross-cultural research. As I have suggested, it can be problematic when the researchers and the participants do not speak the same language. Not only may misunderstandings occur, the language can also impact on the accuracy and interpretation of the research findings. Hence, cross-cultural researchers may select to work with bicultural researchers who share similar linguistic and cultural knowledge to the participants. Under some circumstances, the researchers may need to work with interpreters or translators. Both strategies have their own benefits and limitations.

In this chapter, I have also suggested issues relating to forward and back translation of research instruments in cross-cultural research. One important issue that I have included is the transcription of research transcripts in their local language, which I believe would be more accurate than translating directly from the data. As such, I have also discussed some translation issues and a method for translating qualitative research data.

Bogusia Temple and Alys Young (2008: 97) suggest that 'the situation where the researcher is fluent in the language of communities she is working with is rare'. Not too many researchers are doing research within their own ethnic groups or countries. Due to some of the difficulties associated with language issues, sometimes researchers keep away from cross-cultural qualitative research where an interpreter/translator or bicultural research is involved (Kapborg & Bertero 2002). This is unfortunate, but still we have seen more Western researchers doing research in cross-cultural settings. Issues of cross-cultural communication become a crucial part of cross-cultural research. This has been discussed in this chapter.

SUGGESTED READING

Bujra, J. (2006). Lost in translation? The use of interpreters in fieldwork. In V. Desai & R. B. Potter (Eds.), *Doing development research* (pp. 172–179). London: Sage Publications.

Chawla, D. (2007). Subjectivity and the 'native' ethnographer: Researcher eligibility in an ethnographic study of urban Indian women in Hindu arranged marriages. *International Journal of Qualitative Methodology* **5**(4), Article 2. www/ualberta. ca/~iiqm/backissues/5_4/pdf/chawla.pdf Accessed: 2 January 2007.

Edwards, R. (1998). A critical examination of the use of interpreters in the qualitative research process. *Journal of Ethnic and Migration Studies* **24**(1), 197–208.

Hennink, M. M. (2008). Language and communication in cross-cultural qualitative research. In P. Liamputtong (Ed.), *Doing cross-cultural research: Ethical and methodological perspectives* (pp. 21–33). Dordrecht: Springer.

Larkin, P. J., Dierckx de Casterlé, B., & Schotsmans, P. (2007). Multilingual translation issues in qualitative research: Reflections on a metaphorical process. *Qualitative Health Research* **17**(4), 468–476.

Lopez, G. I., Figueroa, M., Connor, S. E., & Maliski, S. L. (2008). Translation barriers in conducting qualitative research with Spanish speakers. *Qualitative Health Research* **18**(12), 1729–1737.

Shklarov, S. (2007). Double vision uncertainty: The bilingual researcher and the ethics of cross-language research. *Qualitative Health Research* **17**(4), 529–538.

Temple, B. (2006). Being bilingual: Issues for cross language research. *Journal of Research Practice* **2**(1), Article M2. http://jrp.icaap.org/content/v2.1/temple.html Accessed: 8 March 2009.

Temple, T., & Young, A. (2008). Qualitative research and translation dilemmas. In P. Atkinson & S. Delamont (Eds.), *Representing ethnography*, Vol. 3 (pp. 90–107). London: Sage Publications.

Vinokurov, A., Geller, D., & Martin, T. L. (2007). Translation as an ecological tool for instrument development. *International Journal of Qualitative Methods* **6**(2), Article 3. 1–13. www.ualberta.ca/~iiqm/backissues/6_2/vinokurov.pdf Accessed: 20 October 2007.

7   Personal and collective testimony

In listening to the stories of indigenous storytellers, we learn new ways of being moral and political in the social world. We come together in a shared agenda, with a shared imagination and a new language, struggling together to find liberating ways of interpreting and performing in the world. In this way, does *research* cease to be a dirty word?

(Denzin et al. 2008a: 15)

By speaking collectively, women of color not only reclaim their humanity but, at the same time, empower themselves by making sense of their experience of vulnerability and subjugation.

(Madriz 2000: 843).

Based on theoretical frameworks that I discussed in Chapter 1, I now introduce some qualitative methods in this chapter and the next. I make no claim that all qualitative methods will be appropriate in cross-cultural research. This is precisely what Esther Madriz (2000: 840) has suggested: 'Some methodologies are more suitable than others for shattering a colonizing discourse in which images of research subjects as the Other are constantly reproduced' (see also Fine 1994; Denzin *et al.* 2008a; Liamputtong 2008). Thus, I will focus only on those methods that will allow cross-cultural researchers to work more sensitively with the research participants. I shall, however, provide some useful reading materials for readers to consult further at the end of the chapter.

Oral/life history, according to Valerie Yow (2005: 3), 'is the recording of personal testimony delivered in oral form' (see also Benmayor 1991; Banks-Wallace 2002). Oral/life history gives voice to the 'Other' and to know the Other (Madriz 2000: 840). There are different terminologies for oral history, including life history, life story, oral biography, personal narrative, memoir and testament (Yow 2005). Personal testimony allows the researchers to understand the meanings and interpretations of the lives of individual persons (Benmayor 1991; Banks-Wallace 2002; Yow 2005). These meanings and interpretations will 'only come to life when there are people to explain, to comment and to elaborate on them' (Yow 2005: 13). In the cotton mill village of Carrboro, North Carolina, Yow tells us that a family saved money to buy an organ for the two daughters.

If I had seen 'organ' in a list of household goods, I would have regarded this artefact as a tangible symbol of 'the arts' among working-class people. For the narrator it was the symbol of the intimate bond between her sister and her as they shared the organ in their adult lives after they married and lived in separate houses. The organ had a significance for them in a way I did not at first imagine. (p. 13)

Whereas oral/life history is based on personal testimony, the focus group method permits the possibility of hearing the multiple and collective voices of the Others 'as constructors and agents of knowledge' (Fine 1994: 75) and 'as agents of social change' (Madriz 2000: 840). At the data-gathering stage, focus groups help the researchers to hear 'the *plural voices* of the participants' (Fine 1994: 75).

Esther Madriz (2000: 842) contends that she sees the use of the focus group method 'as a form of collective testimony'. For generations, women have used these 'multivocal conversations' for exchanging with others (their mothers, sisters, and female neighbours and friends). But in a male-dominated positivist tradition, these conversations are dismissed as 'idle talk' or 'gossip'. Ironically, George Kamberelis and Greg Dimitriadis (2008: 384) contend that this 'dismissal mirrors the ways in which qualitative inquiry is periodically dismissed for being "soft", "subjective", or "non-scientific"' (see Chapter 1 in this volume).

However, these 'multivocal conversations' have been a significant means that women have used to deal with their social isolation and oppression. Therefore, 'testimonies, individual or collective, become a vehicle for capturing the socioeconomic, political, and human exchanges that women face' (Madriz 2000: 842). We can extend the experience of women to the Others; here I mean marginalised people in a cross-cultural perspective.

This chapter begins the discussion of qualitative research methods which represent the personal and collective testimonies: oral/life history and focus group methods. I shall first detail the essence of oral/life history and provide some examples of cross-cultural research which makes use of the method. I then proceed to do the same for the focus group method.

Personal testimony: oral and life history

My name is Rigoberta Menchú, I am twenty-three years old, and this is *my* testimony ... I'd like to stress that it's not only my life, it's also the testimony of my people. It's hard for me to remember everything that's happened to me in my life since there have been many very bad times but, yes, moments of joy as well. The important thing is that what has happened to me has happended to many other people too: My story is the story of all poor Guatemalans. My personal experience is the reality of a whole people. (Mehnchú 1984: 1, original emphasis)

I wasn't born and raised to be a Kyoto geisha ... I'm a fisherman's daughter from a little town called Yoroido on the Sea of Japan. In all my life, I've never told more than a handful of people anything at all about Yoroido, or about the house in which I grew up, or about my mother and father, or my older sister – and certainly not about how I became a geisha, or what it was like to be one ... After all, I did grow up in Yoroido, and no one would suggest it's a glamorous spot. Hardly anyone ever visits it. As for the people who live there, they never have occasion to leave. You're probably wondering how I came to leave it myself. That's where my story begins. (Golden 1997: 7–8)

Something else that never ever left my mind, my memory, was of a family of children being taken away and this little girl, she must have been about the same age as myself, I suppose she might have been about six, as far as I can remember back, but I can still see that little person on the back of the mission truck with a little rag hat on and she went away and we never seen her any more. She was crying, everyone was crying. Things like that never leave your memory. Sad things don't leave you. (Rintoul 1993: 3)

These three quotes represent three personal testimonies. The first one was told by Rigoberta Menchú , a young Guatemalan peasant woman who lived through an oppressive regime in her country. Her testimony is a reflection of the common experiences that many Indian communities in Latin America have been facing. Rigoberta suffered gross injustice and hardship in her early life. Her father, mother and brother were all murdered by the Guatemalan military. The second quote is from the life story of Nitta Sayuri, a geisha whose story was published in a book by Arthur Golden (1997) and was turned into a film, *Memoirs of a Geisha* (Columbia Pictures). The last one is a testimony told by an Aboriginal woman living in New South Wales, Australia and it was presented in Stuart Rintoul's book: *The Wailing: A National Black Oral History* (1993).

I present these three personal testimonies here as I believe they are good examples of representing voices in life and oral history research. Storytelling captures our imagination about the life history of individuals in which we become interested. It vividly portrays the lived experience of our research participant; a storyteller.

Oral/Life history and personal testimony

The oral collection of historical documents can be traced back to ancient times (Fontana & Prokos 2007). Three thousand years ago, the sayings of the people for the use of court historians were collected by historiographers of the Zhou dynasty in China. However, the first official record of an oral historian that we often hear about is that of the Greek historian Thucydides, centuries later. He looked for people whom he could interview and used the interview information to write his history of the Peloponnesian War (Yow 2005). Although personal testimonies have been collected since the fifth century BC, it was only after the Second World War that portable recording machines were invented, and that was the beginning of a more systematic recording of oral history, such as we see nowadays (Yow 2005).

An important development in oral/life history research is the attempt to collect the personal testimonies of oppressed groups in order to provide profound and telling stories that have been 'suppressed for too long' (Fontana & Prokos 2007: 50). For example, Govenar (2000) put together the narratives and oral histories of African-American slaves in one volume. The focus of the volume is 'upon people themselves and the ways in which they participate in the process of history through what they say and do' (Fontana & Prokos 2007: 50). See also Stewart Rintoul (1993) and Peta Stephenson (2007) for similar issues among Australian indigenous peoples.

Oral/life history only became a popular method when it was widely used in the feminist movement (Gluck 1984, 2006; Gluck & Patai 1991). Here, it was seen as a way of 'understanding and bringing forth the history of women in a culture that has traditionally relied on masculine interpretation' (Fontana & Prokos 2007: 50). Sherna Gluck (1984: 222) says this succinctly:

Refusing to be rendered historically voiceless any longer, women are creating a new history – using our own voices and experiences.

The nature of oral/life history research

Oral/life history research is an approach involving the collection of personal stories from an individual over the course of his or her life. Oral/life history is a specific method of interviewing, which requires the researcher and respondents to invest lengthy periods together in a process of the telling of and listening to life stories (Liamputtong 2009). Storytelling, JoAnne Banks-Wallace (2002), Sharlene Hesse-Biber and Patricia Leavy (2005) and Valerie

Yow (2005) suggest, is a fundamental aspect of the human experience. People convey meaning through storytelling. This means of transmitting knowledge has allowed researchers to develop techniques that provide an opportunity for individuals to express their voices.

Often, we see the terms 'life history' and 'oral history' used interchangeably, and as a single item (Bornat 2004; Yow 2005). The difference between the two terms is on emphasis and scope. An oral history emphasises a particular part of an individual's life, for example, family life or a specific function of some aspect of community life. The main focus of an oral history is on the community or on a particular historical event, juncture, period or location memorised by individuals (Candida Smith 2002). However, when an individual's entire life is the focus, it is essentially marked as a life story or life history (Atkinson 2002).

Oral/life history, Hesse-Biber and Leavy (2005) maintain, affords researchers a means of inviting their participants to tell the story of their pasts. But the individual story is often tied to historical existences, and therefore goes beyond his or her experience. It also becomes 'collective memory' (Yow 2005: 52; see also Benmayor 1991). Oral/life history, as such, 'allows for the merging of individual biography and historical processes. An individual's story is narrated through memory' (Hesse-Biber & Leavy 2005: 152). Oral/ life history is especially crucial for studying how individuals experience social changes as well as social and personal problems emerging from these changes (see Slater 2000; Al-Ali 2007; Stephenson 2007). Oral/life stories function as ideal vehicles for understanding how people perceive their lived experiences, and how they connect with others in society.

Oral/life history permits researchers to obtain in-depth information about the lives of the participants from their own perspectives. Through this method, Hesse-Biber and Leavy (2005: 151) suggest, the participants convey to the researchers 'their perspective and their voice on their own life experiences'. Researchers learn how the participants feel about things, what they consider important in their lives, how they see the relationship between different life experiences, their difficult times, and the meanings they have constructed as a member of society (Sloan 2008; Liamputtong 2009).

The value of the oral history method can be seen in the recent efforts of a team of researchers at the University of Southern Mississippi (Sloan 2008). The scope of Hurricane Katrina in August 2005 in south Mississippi was huge and affected many people. Stephen Sloan (2008: 178) asks: 'How do we begin to understand Hurricane Katrina, an event that fundamentally shook the social order?' He proposes 'a profound way to begin is to try to appreciate how the storm manifested itself for an individual, for a family, for a community – and one of the most effective and powerful ways to capture that is oral history'.

Sloan contends that the stories of individuals who have experienced the storm are critical for researchers and others to have an in-depth understanding of the true impact of Hurricane Katrina (p. 179). Many stories have been told about these individuals in the public media, but they have not been given any opportunity to tell their own story in their own words. Oral histories will permit this to happen, as it allows and encourages these people to talk about their personal experiences with Hurricane Katrina.

Oral/life history allows the researchers to access the invaluable knowledge and rich life experiences of marginalised individuals and groups which would otherwise remain hidden. In particular, the method affords a means of reaching unprivileged voices. Oral/life histories offer 'the collaborative generation of knowledge' between the participant and the researcher, and this can be an empowering experience for the researched, as they are able to gain insight into their own 'pivotal moments' in their lives (Hesse-Biber & Leavy 2005: 151).

Oral/life history, as Prue Chamberlayne and Annette King (1996: 96) suggest, enables researchers to discover both individual and collective untold stories. Thus, it offers great value 'for purposes of empowerment and identity'. Oral/life history 'gives voice to the dispossessed', and therefore it is valuable for research involving marginalised people (see Behar 1993; Auerbach 2002; Banks-Wallace 2002; Marston 2005; Stephenson 2007; Liamputtong 2007a, 2009; Beverley 2008; Bishop 2008; Chase 2008). Indeed, as Susan Chase (2008: 75) puts it, ' "giving voice" to marginalized people and "naming silenced lives" ' have been the main aims of life history research for many decades. The method is used extensively with ethnic minority groups and indigenous peoples. I shall provide some examples later on in this chapter.

Oral/life history is very useful for studying social, political and economic changes (Yow 2005; Al-Ali 2007; Stephenson 2007; Sloan 2008). In the changing world that we are witnessing at the present time, Hesse-Biber and Leavy (2005: 156–157) assert, oral history will assist us to 'understand both the shared and the personal impact of social upheaval on the individual living within it'. For instance, oral/life history would be a great method for discovering the experiences of the Iraqi people during the US-led occupation, the shift of political regime and the rebuilding of their country. How do they deal with it? How do people adjust and respond to these changes? And to what extent are their personal relationships such as courtship, marriage and family influenced by these changes? We may extend these questions to those living in many other societies where major political changes are occurring, such as Myanmar, Pakistan, Afganistan, East Timor and some war-torn countries in Africa, as well as to those who become refugees and live in resettlement countries such as Canada, France, the UK, the USA, New Zealand and Australia. I urge readers to consult a recent book, *Iraqi Women: Untold Stories from 1948 to the Present*, written by Nadje Sadig Al-Ali (2007), who employed oral history as a method for collecting testimonies from Iraqi women, and whose writing shows many of the points I have suggested in this section.

One example of the value of oral/life history in witnessing social changes in Asian societies is that in 1979 the Oral History Centre (OHC) of Singapore was established by the National Archives of Singapore 'to record the voices of people who have been eyewitnesses to events and developments that marked the growth of Singapore from a British Colony to an independent country' (Oral History Centre of Singapore 2007: ii).

Oral history and indigenous peoples

According to Roxanne Struthers and Cynthia Peden-McAlpine (2005: 1265), indigenous culture has embraced oral tradition as a means to convey and transmit information since 'time immemorial'. Oral history is essentially a way for indigenous people to tell their stories, and has long been utilised in research with indigenous populations (see Rintoul 1993; Smith 1999; Battiste 2000; Einhorn 2000; Struthers 2000; Kaomea 2004; Struthers & Eschiti 2005; Stephenson 2007; Bishop 2008).

Storytelling, or oral history, Linda Tuhiwai Smith (1999: 144–145) contends, has become an essential aspect of all indigenous research: 'Each individual story is powerful. But the point about the stories is not that they simply tell a story, or tell a story simply. These new stories contribute to a collective story in which every indigenous person has a place.'

Oral history acts as a personal testimony among indigenous peoples. An indigenous testimony, Smith (1999: 144) says, is 'a way of talking about an extremely painful event or series of events'. Testimony allows individuals to express their feelings and to relate to important events in their lives. Testimony is culturally appropriate for many indigenous participants, particularly elders.

Stuart Rintoul, in his book *The Wailing: A National Black Oral History* (1993), collected the oral histories of many Aboriginal people. Throughout Australia, Rintoul says, 'people clung to what they could of their culture and incorporated into its fabric the suffering of the missions and reserves and stations. The stories have been handed down in the homes of black Australians, told to new generations, taught in explanation of racism and mistreatment, recited with rage and dignity and sorrow' (p. 8). Rintoul further writes that the oral stories he has collected are 'memories of injustice, images of what life has been for indigenous people in Australia, an avalanche of voices, crying out in hundreds of countries across innumerable Dreamings, of great pain and small degradations, of the way society was structured ...'. See also the oral testimonies of Australian indigenous Asians in a recent book by Peta Stephenson (2007).

Oral histories have been used by many indigenous peoples as their way of transmitting the values of a culture with the hope that the new generations will value them and pass the story to the next generation. Smith (1999: 145) posits that both the story and the storyteller act 'to connect the past with the future, one generation with the other, the land with the people and the people with the story'.

Similarly, oral history has been the tradition of telling stories among native Hawaiians (Kaomea 2004) and indigenous peoples in Canada (Battiste 2000; Struthers & Peden-McAlpine 2005; Bartlett et al. 2007; Loppie 2007). In the Canadian context, Charlotte Loppie (2007: 276) contends, an oral tradition has been used to pass down the cultures and histories of indigenous peoples from generation to generation. Storytelling is also used as a teaching tool: 'Through stories, myths, and legends, elders symbolically describe socially appropriate behaviour and share knowledge, philosophy, and instruction without direct censorship'.

As a research tool, Russell Bishop (1996) contends, storytelling is a culturally appropriate means of representing the 'diversities of truth', and the storyteller, instead of the researcher, has control over the storytelling process. Māori tradition is based on an oral culture. Thus, storytelling is a way for Māori people to communicate their ideas and events (Walsh-Tapiata 2003: 63). Storytelling in Māori culture, according to Wheturangi Walsh-Tapiata, is a means which allows the Māori to voice their concerns about research that has intruded into their lives (pp. 63–64). Storytelling 'allows those who are involved in the research process to be active participants and it validates their experiences. Participants can truthfully see themselves represented in the research documentation with the use of excerpts from their stories. Such an approach also has the advantage of allowing the person who has felt silenced to have a voice.' This approach, therefore, is a 'powerful data gathering tool' for cross-cultural researchers working with Māoris.

Case studies of research using oral/life history

Using oral history as a method, Rachel Slater (2000) carried out a project to examine the experiences of urbanisation under apartheid among four black South African women. The four women had their own individual stories but also shared many experiences, and these were disclosed during the life history interview. Slater found that structural constraints shaped the economic realities of these women in extreme ways. The women also disclosed that their lives were ultimately influenced by not only the shared social reality, but also their own agency. Slater elaborated: 'Life histories enable development researchers to understand how the impact of social or economic change differs according to the unique qualities of individual men and women. This is because they allow researchers to explore the relationship between individual people's ability to take action (their agency), and the economic, social, and political structures that surround them' (p. 38).

Shane Edwards and colleagues (2005) carried out a research project to investigate the experiences and insights of Sudden Infant Death syndrome (SIDS) among Māori parents, caregivers and whânau (extended family) in New Zealand. The research team selected the method, which they called 'focus life history interviews'. This method was based on the life story framework proposed by Karen Olson and Linda Shopes (1991) and has been used successfully within the Māori context (see Anae 1998). Edwards and colleagues (2005: 97) argued that the focused life story interview method is particularly suitable for researching sensitive issues because it encourages a reflective storytelling style 'where the interviewee sets the pace and the interviewer listens, clarifies, probes and possibly brings up topics which need to be covered in the interview that have not arisen spontaneously in the course of the conversation'. The storytelling style permits 'a relaxed, almost conversational, approach to data interview'. Hence, it allows the research participants to 'feel safe and supported enough to talk through the very difficult circumstances surrounding the loss of their baby'.

Edwards *et al.* contend that storytelling and life story interviews were not only culturally appropriate, but also act as an empowering method for the participants (p. 98). One of the interviewers on the research team reflected on her experience:

Responses were often emotional expressions of appreciation and gratitude for being given the opportunity to tell their stories and most importantly to have the chance to help other whânau cope with or avoid this tragic experience. At the conclusion of each interview the sense of relief from most of the participants was so palpable I got the feeling that a major milestone had been achieved. What became abundantly clear is that this type of grief is an ongoing process, which is at times extremely difficult. This reality was made heart-wrenchingly apparent throughout the personal testimony given by each of the participants.

Importantly, most participants valued their participation in the oral history interviews. Through their narratives, the participants realised that many of the events that they were telling in the interviews, particularly those relating to schooling and whânau dynamics, 'had been all but forgotten'. The opportunity to tell their stories through a respectful stranger such as the well-trusted Mãori SIDS Parents (MSP) team, was significantly beneficial to many of the participants. Additionally, they also expressed a strong desire to help other whânau to deal with SIDS and other relevant issues (p. 99).

In their (2003) study *Te Kotahitanga: The Experiences of Year 9 and 10 Mãori Students in Mainstream Classrooms* in New Zealand, Russell Bishop and colleagues aimed to address the self-determination of Mãori secondary school students by inviting them to tell stories about factors which would limit and/or improve their educational achievement. The process of collaborative storytelling was employed to obtain a number of narratives of Mãori students' classroom experiences from five secondary schools. This approach is similar to what John Beverley (2008) has termed *testimonio*. It is the research participants (the narrators) who intend to use the researcher (an interlocutor) to bring their situations to the attention of the audiences. Through this oral history project, the students had their opportunities to share their stories of schooling with their teachers in such a way that the 'teachers who otherwise might not have had access to the narratives could reflect upon them in terms of their own experiences and understanding' (Bishop 2008: 155).

The students' stories clearly reflected the main influences on their educational achievement. They talked about 'the impacts and consequences of their living in a marginalized space. That is, they explained how they were perceived in pathological terms by their teachers and how this perception has had negative effects on their lives' (p. 155). Their stories changed the way their teachers perceived them and resulted in changing how the teachers related to and interacted with Mãori students in the classrooms. This led to the creation of a learning context wherein Mãori students' educational achievements could be improved. This was done by 'placing the self-determination of Mãori students at the centre of classroom relationships'.

Based on the suggestions of the Year 9 and Year 10 Mãori students, this research also led to the development of an 'Effective Teaching Profile'. This profile was used as a basis to form a professional development programme. When it was implemented with a group of teachers in four schools, it exhibited increased positive attendance, learning and behaviour outcomes for Māori students in these classrooms (p. 156).

Peta Stephenson collected the life stories of indigenous and Asian people in Australia as part of her PhD research in 1999 and presented their stories in her recent book *The Outsiders Within* (2007). These 'indigenous and Asians' have been seen as 'outsiders' within their own nationality – Australian. In her research, Stephenson claimed that she used 'oral testimonies' which were told by indigenous and Asians. Stephenson argued that: 'When dealing with marginalised communities and experiences, the most reliable sources are rarely books written by outsiders … they are the stories that outsiders within have to tell' (p. 13).

Storytelling, Stephenson pointed out, is 'an art form, and some of the best story-tellers are artists' (p. 13). In her research, she collected oral testimonies from many Australian artists who belong to the indigenous and Asian categories, and these included Julie Janson (a playwright of Gamilaroy descent), Gary Lee (Larrakia playwright), Trevor Jamieson (Pitjantjatjara writer and performer), Hung Le (Vietnamese-Australian comedian), Zhou Xiaoping and Shi Xiaojun (Chinese-Australian artists) and Jimmy Chi (indigenous Asian musician and writer).

These oral testimonies clearly revealed the attempts that have kept indigenous, Asian and European Australians separated. They showed the dark history of racism and discriminatory practices that have occurred in Australia. From these oral testimonies, we hear the stories of children who were taken from their parents, stories of fathers who were deported or interned, and stories of women who were sexually exploited. These stories were not only from the early days of the European presence; they continue to the present time.

These oral testimonies also revealed the ways in which indigenous and Asian Australians have tried to confront attempts from white Australians determined to exclude them and to keep them apart, and their efforts to survive. Stephenson contended that the unity of indigenous and Asians challenged the 'white narratives' of the nation 'because they foreclose on every attempt to define a homogeneous national identity conclusively' (pp. 15–16). In fact, indigenous and Asian individuals are 'living proof of failed white government attempts to guarantee racial "purity" on the Australian continent'.

Stephenson's research showed us the importance of telling stories. She contended that the oral histories of cross-cultural encounters between indigenous and Asian Australian had 'intrinsic value'. They revealed the collective experiences 'at once uniquely shaped by geography, culture, and environment and at the same time representative' (p. 209). She added that 'these stories are not only worth telling, they are also *telling*. They attest to the resourcefulness of a disempowered group, to its capacity to mobilise all the skills at the story-teller's disposal to dismantle the rhetoric of power' (p. 210).

Stephenson contended that, for the communities which she had researched, 'the story-tellers give back to the people their stories, recreating them, renewing them, keeping them alive by allowing them to evolve' (p. 13). The oral testimonies she collected were 'active, often self-consciously imaginative interpretations of what happened'. As such, the storytellers actively put their stories back in the history of communities.

Collective testimony: the focus group method

The singularity of focus groups is that they allow social scientists to observe the most important sociological process – collective human interaction. (Madriz 2000: 836)

Focus groups are a profound experience for both the researcher and the research participants that generate a unique form of data. They tell the qualitative researcher things about social life that would otherwise remain unknown. (Hesse-Biber & Leavy 2005: 197)

The focus group method, according to Esther Madriz (2000: 836), is 'a collectivist rather than an individualistic research method that focuses on the multivocality of participants' attitudes, experiences, and beliefs'. Madriz, as a Latina feminist, situates the focus group method within the 'collective testimonies and group resistance narratives' (p. 843). As a form of collective testimony, focus groups can be 'an empowering experience' for women, particularly women of colour. She contends that focus groups can be used by women 'to unveil specific and little-researched aspects of women's daily existences, their feelings, attitudes, hopes and dreams' (p. 836). Following Madriz's term 'women of colour', I suggest that this term also includes other groups of women, such as women from ethnic minority groups, indigenous women and women from non-Western societies.

Madriz contends that because the voices of women of colour have been silenced in most research projects, the focus group method will permit them to write their own culture together. Focus groups may help to expose not only the layers of oppression that have suppressed their expressions, but also facilitate the forms of resistance that they use for dealing with such oppressions in their everyday life. Madriz believes that focus groups 'can be an important element in the advancement of an agenda of social justice for women, because they can serve to expose and validate women's everyday experiences of subjugation and their individual and collective survival and resistance strategies' (p. 836). Through collective stories, focus group interviews are essentially appropriate for uncovering women's daily experiences.

The focus group method, according to Madriz, is an inquiry approach which is 'consistent with the particularities and everyday experiences of women of color' (p. 839). Traditionally, women have employed conversations with other women as a means for them to resist oppression in their everyday life. Historically and collectively, women have formed groups to discuss issues which are important to them and to become involved in political activities. For example, after slavery ended, churchwomen and teachers gathered to organise political work throughout the American South (Gikes 1994). Mexican women have been maintaining their traditional practices through getting together to talk, to make food, to arrange birthdays; all in order to keep their rich oral traditions alive (Behar 1993; Dill 1994). In 1937, Chinese women who worked in San Francisco's Chinatown organised a group to strike against the garment factory owned by the National Dollar Store (Espiritu 1997). Even nowadays, sharing with other women has been an important way for African-American, Latina and Asian-American women to deal with their marginality. These examples clearly show that the gathering and sharing of women with other women can lead to 'actions and movements for social change' (Madriz 2000: 839).

The focus group method is also particularly suitable for obtaining 'collective views' on social issues, for example a community's perceptions of drugs and alcohol, HIV risk or their experiences of crime and violence (Lloyd-Evans 2006: 153). Because individual human behaviour is affected by collective thought and behaviour, the focus group method is an essential tool for knowing 'the importance of codes of behaviour and "ways of doing" in relation to a wide range of political, social and economic activities' (p. 154). The focus group method is 'an excellent tool for highlighting the uncertainties, tensions and contradictions that must be played out before "collective decisions" are reached'. In a multicultural or development context, the method can yield information on the meanings which 'lie behind' group viewpoints, or on group processes which underscore specific positions or actions. Focus groups also offer an excellent milieu for learning about 'collective social action' and understanding group beliefs, attitudes and actions which may not be accessible to the researchers via other research means (p. 154).

According to Esther Madriz (2000: 847), for people who are part of 'communitarian cultures', such as ethnic minority women and indigenous people, 'individualistic research methods place them in artificial, unfamiliar, and even "unsafe" environments'. As Rina Benmayor (1991: 159) suggests, collective testimonies are capable of 'impacting directly on individual and collective empowerment'. Focus groups have this potential for researching women's lives. Madriz (2000: 847) points out, 'the shared dialogue, stories, and knowledge generated by the group interview have the potential to help such women to develop a sense of identity, self-validation, bonding, and commonality of experiences. Focus groups tend to create environments in which participants feel open to telling their stories and to giving their testimonies in front of other women like themselves' (see also Kamberelis & Dimitriadis 2008). Thus, the focus group method has great potential for discovering the complex layers which shape the individual and collective lived experiences of the research participants. The process of collective talk in focus groups renders it 'a culturally sensitive data gathering method' (Madriz 2000: 847; see also Chiu & Knight 1999; Berthelette *et al.* 2001; Vissandjée *et al.* 2002; Willis *et al.* 2005; Billson 2006; Buseh *et al.* 2006; Halcomb *et al.* 2007; Hennink 2007; Colucci 2007, 2008).

The collective nature of the focus group method allows the participants to take control of the discussion process. It empowers them to move the discussion towards what is important and relevant to them. The method offers 'a unique opportunity to study individuals in their social contexts, by generating high-quality interactive data, by contributing to the social construction of meaning, and by accessing the participant's shared, and often ignored, stocks of knowledge' (Madriz 2000: 847–848).

The nature and use of the focus group method

Broadly speaking, George Kamberelis and Greg Dimitriadis (2008: 375) contend that focus groups are 'collective conversations' or 'group interviews', which can be small or large, and can be directed or non-directed. According to Kamberelis and Dimitriadis, focus groups have been used by Paulo Freire (1970) in Brazil and Jonathan Kozol (1985) in New York, and were referred to as 'study circles'. Both Freire and Kozol made use of focus groups for 'imagining and enacting the emancipator political possibilities of collective work' (Kamberelis & Dimitriadis 2008: 378).

Methodologically, focus group interviews involve a group of six to eight people who come from similar social and cultural backgrounds or who have similar experiences or concerns. They gather together to discuss a specific issue with the help of a moderator in a particular setting where the participants feel comfortable enough to engage in a dynamic discussion for one or two hours (Barbour 2007; Hennink 2007; Stewart *et al.* 2007; Bryman 2008; Colucci 2008; Krueger & Casey 2009; Liamputtong 2009). Focus groups, according to Monique Hennink (2007: 6), do not aim to reach a consensus on the issues discussed. Rather, they 'encourage a range of responses which provide a greater understanding of the attitudes, behavior, opinions or perceptions of participants on the research issues'.

A successful focus group discussion relies heavily on 'the development of a permissive, non-threatening environment within the group, whereby participants feel comfortable to share their views and experiences without the fear of judgement or ridicule from others' (p. 6). Focus group discussions are more akin to natural social interaction among participants. Thus, the environment of focus groups may be more comfortable and enjoyable for the research participants (pp. 6–7; see also Krueger & Casey 2009; Liamputtong 2009).

Focus groups allow multiple lines of communication. For people who find one-on-one and face-to-face interaction 'intimidating' or 'scary', the group interview may offer them 'a safe environment where they can share ideas, beliefs, and attitudes in the company of people from the same socioeconomic, ethnic, and gender backgrounds' (Madriz 2000). Focus groups are ideal for many people from ethnic minority groups. In their study on the views of health services with Negev Bedouin Arabs, Jeffrey Borkan and colleagues (2000: 209) suggested that focus groups offer 'an enjoyable forum for interaction' among respondents and permit some data quality control because 'extreme views are often muted or marginalized by the majority'. They also offer the respondents the possibility of connecting with others and the continuous establishment of opinions during the group sessions.

Focus groups have been used to 'give a voice' to marginalised groups such as minority ethnic groups, poor women and men, or people affected by stigmatised illnesses such as HIV/AIDS. They enable researchers, policy makers and others to 'listen' to people who may have little chance otherwise to express their viewpoints about their health and other needs (Madriz 1998, 2000; Winslow *et al.* 2002; Umaña-Taylor & Bámaca 2004; Barbour 2007; Liamputtong 2007a). In early HIV/AIDS research, Joseph and colleagues (1984) used focus groups as a means of understanding gay and bisexual men who were perceived as at risk, yet whose health practices and needs were not well understood by researchers or the public. The voice of marginalised groups is essential in participatory action research (see also Chapter 8 in this volume), so focus groups are used extensively in this type of qualitative research as a basis for empowering marginalised people (Jarrett 1993; Madriz 1998, 2000; Winslow *et al.* 2002; Umaña-Taylor & Bámaca 2004; Willis *et al.* 2005; Liamputtong 2007a; Goltz 2009).

The focus group method, according to Sally Lloyd-Evans (2006: 153), is adopted widely in the field of development in a cross-cultural context, especially in eliciting community viewpoints and understanding community dynamics (see also Vissandjée *et al.* 2002; Laws *et al.* 2003; Hennink 2007; Bailey 2008; Colucci 2008). Recently, there has been a move towards more participatory research approaches which seek to 'redress issues of unequal power, positionality and Eurocentricity' which may happen when field research is undertaken in non-Western contexts. The focus group method has become 'one of the main processes for engendering public participation and facilitating the use of non-verbal techniques'. Focus groups 'offer a more effective and rapid way of engaging with community groups than other methods can' (Lloyd-Evans 2006: 153–154).

Focus groups and participatory activities in cross-cultural research

It is common that in conducting focus groups in under-developed countries other participatory activities are built into the group discussions. Focus groups offer an excellent context for more innovative participatory techniques during the group session (Lloyd-Evans 2006). Some stimulus materials such as images, display boards and music have been used to encourage discussion among the group participants. As Sally Lloyd-Evans suggests, 'visual exercises provide a focus for talking about issues and they also play a useful role in encouraging quieter members of the group to take part in the research' (p. 159). Often, it is a good strategy to encourage the participants to 'put their ideas on paper, draw images or maps, devise flow charts, respond to images, take their own photographs with disposable cameras, or use ranking exercises' (see also Kesby *et al.* 2005; Colucci 2007, 2008).

According to Erminia Colucci (2008: 243), the free listing method proposed by Russell Bernard (1995), where the participants are invited to list all elements of the topic under discussion, is often used in cross-cultural focus groups. Other participatory activities such as picture sorting can also be used in cross-cultural focus groups. Participants may also be invited to create a story around the issue under study. This strategy is particularly appropriate when the researchers aim to gain a 'real life situation' from the participants. Storytelling in focus groups can provide particularly interesting information (see Strickland 1999). Colucci (2008: 243) suggests that the inclusion of some participatory activities in focus groups is extremely useful for reducing the language barriers that some participants may encounter. This is because the participants do not have to rely on oral language to express their ideas. The participatory activities also make the experience of taking part in focus groups more enjoyable and less threatening.

Susan Bissell and colleagues (2000) carried out their research with working children in Bangladesh. At the beginning of the focus group session, they showed a documentary film which depicted such children as a means of encouraging them to discuss the issue in the focus groups. Similarly, in their research on the feeding of young children in school shelters among indigenous mothers in Mexico, Bernardo Turnbull and colleagues (2006: 507) carried out a series of workshops with the mothers. These workshops functioned very similarly to focus groups. In the workshop, the mothers were asked to discuss the nutrition of their children both at home and at the shelter. They also used 'mapping to locate food sources within their communities'. They asked the mothers to bring food from their homes and to display possible combinations on the table. The mothers were also asked to score a food matrix for nutritional value, price and acceptability.

The use of vignettes (short stories) to stimulate discussion in focus groups has also been tried. For example, Ajay Bailey (2008) used vignettes in focus groups in his research on HIV/AIDS risk assessment in Goa, India. Bailey and the research team introduced the vignettes into the discussion; they were derived from in-depth interviews which were the real experiences of migrant and mobile men. The vignettes were localized by including names such as Lingappa – a common name for rural migrant men from north Karnataka – and by situating Lingappa in a migrant area in Goa. This projective technique yielded lively discussions about Lingappa. Bailey found that men were more vocal when they had to talk about this fictitious person. The men also shared other stories of people living with HIV/AIDS or about incidents relating to HIV/AIDS. Bailey contends that the use of the fictional people and the manner in which he and the research team culturally adapted the vignettes shows that men could both identify with the characters and find other anecdotes to make sense of the situations.

Case studies of cross-cultural research using focus groups

Focus group interviews have been increasingly adopted in cross-cultural research. Jeffrey Borkan and colleagues (2000: 209) used the focus group method in their study on the perceptions of health services amongst the Negev Bedouin Arabs in Israel. They conducted twelve focus groups (158 participants) with the assistance of specially trained local moderators and observers. Each group met for three to seven sessions. The focus group method was chosen in this study because the nature of interaction in the focus group resembles the pattern of socialisation within the Bedouin. Tribal members of the same gender often meet for leisure and discussion in their tents, home or *shieg* (designated structure). The Bedouin would then be more comfortable discussing in groups than in an individual interview situation. Borkan *et al.*, however, suggested that orthodox focus groups needed to be modified to suit the local setting. They strongly argued that a direct application of Western research methods of data collection to traditional societies was 'fraught with difficulties' (p. 209). For example, drawing group members from total strangers, as suggested in orthodox focus group methods, could be problematic. They asserted that, 'in tightly knit traditional tribal societies in which social interaction and settlement patterns are strictly regulated, disclosure to strangers, and in some cases even interaction, is unacceptable, even forbidden'. Borkan *et al.* modified several aspects in their focus group research with the Bedouin in order to make it more culturally appropriate. However, in their conclusion, they contended that their study, the first of its kind with the Negev Bedouin, suggested that 'focus group method, if properly modified to cultural norms, can be a valuable research tool in traditional communities and in health service research' (p. 207).

Gisele Maynard-Tucker (2000) conducted focus groups on the knowledge of AIDS among high-risk groups, sex workers and STD patients in Antananarivo, Madagascar for the World Bank/Futures Group International in 1996. Focus group discussions with sex workers and their clients were planned for a private room in a restaurant in the red-light district. For six days, the groups were organised from noon to 2 p.m. The sex workers were informed about the research in the streets and bars the night before by a health promoter who was known to the women. Many promised to attend, but few actually turned up. Later, it became clear that these women spent all night working and then they would sleep in the morning. In the end, women were recruited from the streets and bars closer to the research venue. The choice of restaurant where the focus groups were held with the women assisted recruitment, as it was convenient for them to attend. Lunch was served after the session and it was during this lunch time that the women talked freely about their lives, expectations, difficulties and sexual behaviours. The women felt more at ease during a social gathering than in a formal focus group discussion.

In one of my own studies (Vo-Thanh-Xuan & Liamputtong 2003), my colleague and I conducted a focus group study with Vietnamese grandparents who were living in Melbourne. We aimed to raise awareness of the lived experiences of Vietnamese grandparents. In particular, we examined the changes in their relationships with their children and grandchildren that they encountered in their new homeland, and the impact of these changes on their emotional well-being. The participants in this study were Vietnamese grandparents recruited from Vietnamese senior citizens' associations in Melbourne. The resulting sample included a cross-section of people from various social and educational backgrounds, and a mixture of maternal and paternal grandfathers and grandmothers. The sample in the focus groups included thirty-six grandparents separated into four focus groups. Of the participants, 64 percent lived with their grandchildren. The earliest arrival in Australia was in 1980, and the latest in 1994.

The primary means of collecting qualitative data was through focus group interviewing. The interviews took place at their association's centre and continued to the fourth group where saturation had been reached – that is, where little additional new or relevant data could be found. In addition, all participants admitted that, to safeguard family honour, many elderly Vietnamese did not wish to participate in the interview. Although they took part in the focus group interviews, many felt that they could not discuss negative points. So three individual follow-up in-depth interviews were arranged to explore the negative points more comprehensively. They were interviewed at their homes, with each interview lasting on average an hour to an hour and a half.

To overcome communication and cultural difficulties, data were collected and analysed by James Vo-Thanh-Xuan, who is a mature male Vietnamese. Using the Vietnamese language in all stages of data collection and analysis allowed for total freedom in facilitating the focus groups' conversations. All of the elderly Vietnamese participants felt free and comfortable in expressing their feelings and illustrating their experience. These expressions might have lost their nuances if they had been analysed after being translated into English. We only made a translation when verbatim quotations were used in our report.

In our study, we found that there were changes occurring in the role of grandparenthood in the elderly immigrant Vietnamese living in Australia.

Most Vietnamese grandparents grew up in classical and traditional extended families, under one roof, based on the Confucian custom of filial piety. This moral imperative requires children to obey their parents and to take care of them during old age. After their arrival in Australia, however, they were suddenly thrust into a more complex and pressured society, one totally different from their experiences in their homeland. They encountered, right across their family, an enormous change, which rapidly took them from an extended family to a nuclear one. Many had to leave behind their long-standing customs and their traditional values and beliefs. Such enormous changes, it seems, reinforced intergenerational conflicts.

In research with Aboriginal mothers who experienced foetal alcohol syndrome/foetal alcohol effects (FAS/FAE), Amy Salmon (2007) invited the women to take part in her research and asked them to choose if they wished to be interviewed individually or in a group. All of the women selected a group interview because they felt that it would provide them with 'support, encouragement, and an increased sense of safety and trust' in a situation where the researcher was not previously known to them (p. 985). Salmon therefore undertook two group interviews with each of the women. The grouping of these women remained the same for both interviews. Although Salmon did not use the term focus groups as such, it falls within the collective testimony of focus group methodology that I am discussing in this chapter.

By participating in the group interviews, the women were able to share their individual experiences with others. Through the group discussion, the women were also able to see that their experiences were similar to, different from or related to the experiences of others in the group. As such, 'the group interviews provided a venue through which participants could give voice to collective experiences that are often privatized in health policy texts as the failings or shortcomings of individual mothers acting alone' (p. 988).

The group interview method permitted the women to build and articulate on their collective experiences as mothers. This method allowed the women to talk about their lack of knowledge (such as the intake of caffeine and aspartame) which was crucial for their ability to make informed decisions about not only their own health, but also the health of their children. The group interviews also showed that the women were 'standing alongside one another as mothers, actively seeking out information to protect and promote their children's health to incorporate consciously into their mothering practice' (p. 990).

Recently, Rajkumar and colleagues (2008) conducted focus group discussions nine months after the Asian tsunami of 26 December 2004 with two groups of fishermen, two groups of housewives, a group of village leaders and a group of young men in four affected villages of the Nagapattinam district in Tamil Nadu, India. The researchers said the tsunami wrecked many villages along the southeastern coast of India and resulted in devastating losses for many local villagers. The qualitative study aimed to explore the psychological impact of the tsunami on survivors in order to gain insights into the ethno-cultural coping mechanisms of the affected communities, as well as to evaluate resilience in the face of incomprehensible adversity. They found that despite the incomplete reconstruction of their lives, the participants used their cultural idiom to reconstruct meaning for the causes and the aftermath of the disaster. These local people revealed qualitative changes in their attitudes towards different aspects of their lives. Rajkumar *et al.* found many changes in the social structure and processes that people adopted to deal with the disaster. They also found that the survivors used their unique individual, social and spiritual coping strategies rather than seeking help from formal mental health services. The stories of these survivors confirm the belief that 'the collective response to massive trauma need not necessarily result in social collapse but also includes positive effects'. The results of their study suggested that any interventions developed to help people to cope with the disaster must be grounded within ethno-cultural beliefs and practices, and they should aim at 'strengthening prevailing community coping strategies'.

Anh Ngo and colleagues (2007) conducted focus groups in order to provide a better understanding of the environment and power structures in which sex work takes place in Vietnam. In this research, the sex workers' social and economic lives, their working environment, social relationships and presentation of self in everyday social contacts and interactions were examined. Ngo *et al.* undertook fourteen focus groups sessions with several groups of female sex workers, including street-based sex workers, waitresses, karaoke hostesses, hairdressers and massage workers. They collected the data in the cities of Da Nang and Hanoi. Through collaborative interaction in the focus groups, the participants were encouraged to speak about the context and environment of the sex work, communication patterns, the presentation of self, the expectations placed on their behaviour and the perceived stigma and attitudes of the general population towards them. The focus group discussions were conducted in private rooms in the office of a local NGO, a local health centre or in the women's homes. Each participant was given 100,000 Vietnamese dong (around US$7) for taking part in the research project.

Ngo *et al.* found that the sex workers in their study lived and worked 'within a complex system' that involved multiple relationships. The women, however, possessed limited power to protect themselves and secure payment for the services they provided. For most of the street-level sex workers, economic difficulty was a huge problem, and this also led to unsafe sexual practices. For venue-based sex workers, they had less worries about economic hardship, but they were often caught up in gambling debts. Incidents of abuse and social stigma were frequently experienced by these women. Many of them had a strong desire to leave sex work but, because of the lack of alternative employment opportunities and appropriate support, they found that they continued to be trapped in the sex industry. Ngo *et al.* pointed out that:

Women in our study face multiple barriers when they want to leave sex work. Social stigmatisation towards sex workers, the absence of alternative employment opportunities and the lack of support from the government and community hinder their reintegration into mainstream society. The rehabilitation approach to sex work, labelling women as a 'social evil' and notifying their family and home community of their arrest, does not help women leave this vocation; instead these efforts perpetuate stigma, making it more difficult for women to leave the sex industry. (p. 568)

Ngo *et al.* argued that there must be multiple attempts to improve the health and living situations of these women (pp. 568–569). Because of pervasive violence and victimisation against these women, an intervention which would increase the awareness of gender-based violence among those in power, including the police and local authorities and health service providers, is needed. Additionally, national authorities must attempt to change the 'social evil' image of these women and promote a rehabilitation approach which adopts a holistic and human-rights-based position so that these women may be less stigmatised and will have better access to health and social services.

It is crucial that community-based support systems must be developed in order to assist the women who wish to leave sex work. For example, vocational training, financial support in terms of low-interest loans and other occupational options could be considered. Ngo *et al.* concluded that, 'by capitalising on these emergent support systems, we would expect a reduction in social stigma towards F[emale] S[ex] W[orkers] along with increased numbers of women who can find another form of employment and leave the sex industry' (p. 569).

Tutorial activities

You wish to carry out research on the lived experience of being a refugee with Somali people who have been settling in your country. You wish to learn about their personal stories before they left Somalia, the transitions between Somalia and the country in which they are now living. You want to know about these issues from young people as well as older generations and you want to learn from both men and women. And you want to know, as a refugee community, how Somali people deal with the difficulties in their everyday lives. What method do you think will give you an in-depth understanding about the issues you want to learn? Discuss this.

Chapter summary

Telling and listening to stories is at the heart of social and cultural life. Much of what we understand as personhood, identity, intimacy, secrecy, experience, belief, history, and common sense turns on the exchange of stories between people. In receiving stories, we are often receiving gifts of self; it is incumbent on us as researchers to handle these gifts with respect as we pass them onward in our scholarly productions. (Narayan & George 2002: 829)

As Kirin Narayan and Kenneth George (2002: 829) write, this chapter has touched on storytelling from two angles: personal and collective stories. I have suggested that some qualitative methods will be better suited for carrying out cross-cultural research than others, and I have proposed two methods, oral/life history and focus groups, as culturally appropriate. I have suggested that stories, either personal stories as used in oral and life history or collective stories as appear in the focus group method, are powerful. They are powerful for the research participants as they are able to tell their stories in their own terms. They are powerful for the researchers as stories allow us to understand the positions of our research participants much better than any standardised predetermined methods used in positivist science. I hope that I have provided readers with some of the basic ideas of each method. Selecting which method is best suited for your cross-cultural research project is a matter of thinking carefully about what each one may offer you and then designing the research accordingly.

SUGGESTED READING

Al-Ali, N. S. (2007). *Iraqi women: Untold stories from 1948 to the present*. London: Zed Books.
Barbour, R. (2007). *Doing focus groups*. London: Sage Publications.

Behar, R. (1993). *Translating woman: Crossing the border with Esperanza's story*. Boston: Beacon Press.

Charlton, T. L., Meyers, L. E., & Sharpless, R. (Eds.) (2006). *Handbook of oral history*. Lanham, MD: AltaMira Press.

Gluck, S. B., & Patai, D. (1991). *Women's words: The feminist practice of oral history*. New York: Routledge.

Hennink, M. M. (2007). *International focus group research: A handbook for the health and social sciences*. Cambridge: Cambridge University Press.

Liamputtong, P. (2007). *Researching the vulnerable: A guide to sensitive research methods*. London: Sage Publications.

(2009). *Qualitative research methods*, 3rd edition. Melbourne: Oxford University Press.

Madriz, E. (2000). Focus groups in feminist research. In N. K. Denzin & Y. S. Lincoln (Eds.), *Handbook of qualitative research*, 2nd edition (pp. 835–850). Thousand Oaks, CA: Sage Publications.

Mehnchú, R. (1984). *I, Rigoberta Mehnchú: An Indian woman in Guatemala*, trans. A. Wright. London: Verso.

Rintoul, S. (1993). *The wailing: A national black oral history*. Port Melbourne: William Heinemann.

Stephenson, P. (2007). *The outsiders within: Telling Australia's indigenous-Asian story*. Sydney: University of New South Wales Press.

Vissandjée, B., Abdool, S. N., & Dupéré, S. (2002). Focus groups in rural Gujarat, India: A modified approach. *Qualitative Health Research* **12**(6), 826–843.

Willis, E., Pearce, M., & Jenkin, T. (2005). Adapting focus group methods to fit Aboriginal community-based research. *Qualitative Research Journal* **5**(2), 112–123.

Yow, V. R. (2005). *Recording oral history: A guide for the humanities and social sciences*, 2nd edition. Walnut Creek, CA: AltaMira Press.

8　Local knowledge, local power and collective action

What understanding begins to do is to make knowledge available for use, and that's the urgency, that's the push, that's the drive.

(Lorde 1984: 109)

CBPR [community based participatory research] also holds immense promise for insuring that research focuses on topics of deep concern to communities and is conducted in ways that can enhance validity, build community capacity, promote systems change, and work to reduce health disparities.

(Minkler & Wallerstein 2008a: 18)

This chapter continues people's testimonies in cross-cultural research. In the previous chapter, I focused on personal and collective testimonies, but this chapter will emphasise personal and collective testimonies within a collaborative effort. That is, through the combination of personal and collective testimonies, people work together with others (the researchers) to resist colonisation and find ways to improve their lives and situations. Hence, this chapter will be dedicated to the methodology of community based participatory research (CBPR), which will include discussions on CBPR, participatory action research (PAR) and the photovoice method.

In the past few decades, Nina Wallerstein and Bonnie Duran (2008: 27) contend that we have seen an emergence of a new paradigm of participatory research. This has raised many challenges to the practice of positivist science. It has also asked crucial questions about the construction and use of knowledge and the importance of the power relations which permeate the research process. More importantly, it challenges the role of the researchers in engaging with community or local people, and the capacity of the two partners to make society 'just and more equitable'.

Conducting research within this framework necessitates the use of research methodologies which 'go beyond the "mere involvement" of those whose experiences are being researched to allow for their "responsible agency in the production of knowledge"' (Salmon 2007: 983). This will significantly decrease the 'risk of co-option and exploitation of people in the realization of the plans of others' (McTaggart 1997: 28–29).

Community based participatory research (CBPR)

Community based participatory research is an emerging research approach which equally involves the community, such as community members, agency representatives and organisations, and the researchers in all facets of the research process (Israel *et al.* 2005). CBPR empowers different groups to collaborate in research in order to appreciate and address the complex social, cultural, political and structural factors impacting on the lives of individuals and their communities (Pyett *et al.* 2010). Scott Rhodes and colleagues (2008: 160) contend that CBPR ensures that: '(a) bridges are created and trust built between communities and researchers, (b) research is authentic to community experiences, (c) research questions are relevant, (d) research design and methods are culturally and educationally appropriate, (e) knowledge is incorporated into action based on community members' experiences, (f) research is translated into informed policy, and (g) infrastructure is built to promote successful implementation and longer term sustainability when appropriate'. Through CBPR, the relevance, interpretation and use of the research data can be enhanced, and the appropriate dissemination of research findings can be ensured (Israel *et al.* 2005). According to Matt Streng and colleagues (2004: 404), in the health area there has been an increasing use of this partnership approach in cross-cultural research which focuses especially on eliminating health disparities and improving the health outcomes of local people (see also Minkler & Wallerstein 2008b).

CBPR has been used in research involving indigenous groups (Pyett *et al.* 2010). In their research with indigenous people in Canada, Judith Bartlett and colleagues (2007: 2380) argue that, in contrast to other research approaches which carry an assumption that the researchers are the experts, CBPR treats local people as 'experts who bring forward indigenous knowledge and help researchers by viewing the research through a decolonizing lens'. Bartlett *et al.* suggest that this approach provides enormous benefits to local people and that these include: '(a) a team-based collaborative approach to research, (b) mutual respect and equitable participation by all involved, (c) shared ownership of the research and its outcomes, (d) reciprocal capacity building and empowerment among those involved, and ultimately, (e) safeguarding of

Indigenous knowledge, and (f) social change and transformation at personal, community, and practice (policy-making and service-provision) levels' (pp. 2380–2381). Their research provides an example of a collective decolonised approach which 'involves all who share common aspirations and goals for improving the health of Aboriginal populations'.

Similarly, the People Awakening (PA) project was constructed as a collaborative research between Alaskan Native community members and university researchers (Mohatt & Thomas 2006). Using an approach grounded within an Alaskan Native cultural worldview over a four-year period, the project was developed to examine possible protective and resilient factors among Alaskan Natives who have recovered from alcohol abuse or do not abuse alcohol. The community-focused approach adopted in this study, Gerald Mohatt and Lisa Thomas point out, 'moved away from interacting with participants as objects of representational knowledge to building equal community-investigator partnerships working together to shape and construct the research questions, methods, interpretations, and conclusions. This collaborative process imbues knowledge (or results) with the meanings ascribed to these results by the participants' (p. 97). The project was built on the framework that Paulo Friere (1970) refers to as 'conscientization', where knowledge is generated through 'a process of empowering communities' and acts as an 'emancipator' (Fals Borda 2006).

CBPR situates within the framework of participatory action research. I shall discuss this approach in the following section.

Participatory action research (PAR)

In doing research, I am educating and being educated with the people. (Freire 1982: 30)

Following the framework set out by Paulo Freire (1970), the main goal of participatory action research, as Jackie Yan-chi Kwok and Hok-Bun Ku (2008: 266) contend, is 'to lead to a more just society through transformative social change' (see also Vickers 2005; Park 2006; McIntyre 2008). Within the PAR approach, research is 'no longer seen only as a process of creating knowledge; it is simultaneously a process of education, development of consciousness, and of mobilization for action'. PAR, Peter Park (2006: 83) contends, is 'action-oriented research activity' that allows ordinary people to address common concerns which occur in their daily lives and, in the process of this participation, they also generate knowledge.

The essence of participatory research is that the project begins with the problems that people face and then they participate in the research process as fully as possible (Park 2006). The research participants are full partners in the research process and are treated as co-researchers. Together with the researchers, they became involved in the research cycle to find solutions for their problems (Park 2006; Swantz *et al.* 2006; Streck 2007; McIntyre 2008; Minkler & Wallerstein 2008b). As Alice McIntyre (2003: 48) writes:

Participatory action research (PAR) is a process whereby people reflect on particular aspects of their lives so as to engage in individual and/or collective action that leads to a useful solution which benefits the people involved.

PAR is not only simply a research methodology, but is also a social practice which assists marginalised people to acquire 'a degree of emancipation as autonomous and responsible members of society' (Park 2006: 83). To Park, PAR can be referred to as 'research of the people, by the people, and for the people'. The ultimate goal of PAR is to 'bring about changes by improving the material circumstances of affected people' (p. 84). Researchers adopting this methodological approach clearly aim to work collaboratively with people who have traditionally been oppressed and exploited. Collectively, fundamental social changes can be achieved through PAR (Brydon-Miller 2001). Ultimately, PAR, as Cornwall and Jewkes (1995: 1674) contend, is about:

Respecting and understanding the people with and for whom researchers work. It is about developing a realization that local people are knowledgeable and that they, together with researchers, can work toward analyses and solutions. It involves recognizing the rights of those whom research concerns, enabling people to set their own agenda for research and development and so giving them ownership over the process.

The history and the use of PAR

PAR arises from two research approaches, namely action research (AR) and participatory research (PR) (Khanlou & Peter 2005: 2334). PR's philosophy is grounded in the power of emancipation derived from the 'Southern tradition' of research (Wallerstein & Duran 2008). The original work was associated with oppressed peoples in less developed societies (see Fals Borda 2006; Swantz *et al.* 2006). The aim of PR is 'structural transformation' (Khanlou & Peter

2005: 2334), and its target groups include 'exploited or oppressed groups' including ethnic minority groups and indigenous peoples (Hall 1981: 7).

For more than three decades, PAR has played a significant part in the history of development in Tanzania. According to Marja-Liisa Swantz and colleagues (2006: 286), after independence Tanzania exercised 'a political programme which aimed at people's participation in their own development (*Arusha Declaration*, 1977)'. At the beginning, PAR was adopted for support-ing the national politics which was based on *ujamaa* socialism. It was used in numerous action research projects to support rural development during the radical restructuring of rural settings. This is the foundation for the present-day PAR practice which has been implemented in a different political context in that country.

Generally, PAR involves individuals, groups and communities who are vulnerable and oppressed. Therefore, it is essential that great care is taken to ensure that these vulnerable participants will benefit from the research and will not be further exploited or marginalised. The ideals of PAR are that the participants who are directly involved in the research should be benefited (Hall 1981; Israel *et al.* 2005; Khanlou & Peter 2005; Kemmis & McTaggart 2008: Kwok & Ku 2008; McIntyre 2008; Minkler & Wallerstein 2008b).

PAR commits to producing 'the political nature of knowledge' and empha-sises 'a premium on self-emancipation' (Esposito & Murphy 2000: 180). Therefore, PAR is ideally a culturally appropriate method used with and for marginalised people, and particularly those groups in cross-cultural settings. In their work on non-Western participants, Luigi Esposito and John Murphy (2000: 181) suggest that typically researchers using PAR are:

Comprised of both professionals and ordinary people, all of whom are regarded as authoritative sources of knowledge. By making minorities the authorized repre-sentatives of the knowledge produced, their experiences and concerns are brought to the forefront of the research. The resulting information is applied to resolving the problems they define collectively as significant. As a result, the integrity of distinct racial groups is not annihilated or subsumed within dominant narratives that por-tray them as peripheral members of society.

PAR allows the local people and the researchers to have their 'freedom to explore and to recreate' (Fals Borda 1991: 149). Through PAR, the par-ticipants and the researchers work collaboratively to find new knowledge and practical solutions to end their problems. It commits to 'the principle of autonomy and ownership in collective research' (dé Ishtar 2005a: 364). The indigenous self-determination PAR carried out by Zohl dé Ishtar

(2005a, 2005b, 2005c), for example, has resulted in the establishment of the Kapululangu Women's Law and Culture Centre in the Great Sandy Desert in Western Australia.

PAR, according to Kemmis and McTaggart (2003: 345), emerges deliberately as a means for resisting traditional research practices which are seen by some cultural groups as 'acts of colonization', when research aims and policy agendas are imposed on a local community and far removed from local concerns or needs (see also Freire 1982; Fals Borda 1987; Smith 1999; Tsey *et al.* 2004; Swantz *et al.* 2006; Bishop 2008; Smith 2008; Minkler & Wallerstein 2008b; see also Chapter 1 in this volume). In PAR, local people are the experts in their own lives. They should be actively involved in making decisions, planning the research, and the implementation and review of changes. As such, this research is not isolated from their everyday experiences, as is often the case with conventional research carried out solely by external researchers.

PAR is essentially an appropriate research methodology for working with indigenous people and in cross-cultural research where the researched participants are extremely oppressed by social structures and other political and economic forces. Based on the same epistemological perspective of PAR, kaupapa Māori research methodology has emerged (Denzin *et al.* 2008a; Bishop 2008; Smith 2008). Linda Tuhiwai Smith (1999: 183) asserts that kaupapa Māori research allows the researched and the researchers to be able to work together in order to set strategies for 'the priorities, policies, and practices of research for, by, and with Māoris'. Through emancipation, kaupapa Māori research permits oppressed, silenced and marginalised groups such as the Māori to have more control of their own lives and their community (Smith 2000, 2008; see also Chapter 1 in this volume).

PAR in cross-cultural research often involves innovative methods. Peter Park (2006: 84) suggests that the use of 'non-canonical approaches', such as art, photography, theatre, storytelling, music, dance and other expressive media, is essential in order to 'reveal the more submerged and difficult-to-articulate aspects of the issues involved'. As such, we have seen that PAR researchers have used community meetings and different types of community events, such as theatre, storytelling, puppets, song, drawing, painting and educational camps as means of gathering data among illiterate people (Brydon-Miller 2001; Pyett *et al.* 2010). For example, the use of drama as a method in a PAR project on AIDS education programmes in black secondary schools in KwaZulu, South Africa, was adopted by Preston-Whyte and Dalrymple (1996) and Dalrymple and Preston-Whyte (1992).

Many of these so-called 'unconventional' methods employed in PAR are essential if cross-cultural researchers wish to offer local people the chance to fully participate. Salazar (1991) argues that it is crucial for 'oppressed' people to be able to find a way to tell their stories, and this may help them to break 'a culture of silence' resulting from centuries of oppression. See also the work of Geraldine Dickson (2000), Komla Tsey and colleagues (2002, 2004), Brinton Lykes (2006), Marja-Liisa Swantz and colleagues (2006) and Jackie Yan-chi Kwok and Hok-Bun Ku (2008) for good examples of innovative methods in PAR.

Case studies of research using PAR

Participatory action research has been seen as appropriate for use in cross-cultural projects involving research with indigenous people (Dickson 2000; Dockery 2000; Tsey & Every 2000; Tandon et al. 2001; Tsey et al. 2002, 2004; Marshall & Batten 2004; Holkup et al. 2004; dé Ishtar 2005a, 2005b, 2005c; Khanlou & Peter 2005; Mosavel et al. 2005; Lykes 2006; Loppie 2007). It is argued by Anne Marshall and Suzanne Batten (2004: 3) that cross-cultural researchers need to adopt a participatory methodology which will ensure 'a more equitable relationship among parties through its partnership constructs'. This is precisely what Komla Tsey and colleagues (2002: 283) suggest in their PAR project with indigenous men in Australia:

PAR seeks explicitly to address and transform social inequalities. The approach, which integrates scientific investigation with skill development and political action, is widely acknowledged as an appropriate methodology in the context of indigenous research, not least because of its potential to empower those participating in the research.

One indigenous participant in their study, who is an educator, said it clearly:

We (indigenous people) can use research ourselves to gain accurate knowledge of our own realities, so that we are empowered to find our own solutions … Participatory action research creates opportunities for these aspirations to be met.

Komla Tsey and colleagues (2002, 2004) undertook PAR with Aboriginal men in Yarrabah, a rural Aboriginal community in north Queensland, Australia. PAR was designed to help Aboriginal men to have more control and responsibility for their health and well-being. The project was developed in response to high rates of suicide in Aboriginal men whose lives had been affected by a long history of marginalisation in Australia. The PAR project itself aimed to help the men to plan, implement and evaluate their activities.

The main activities of the Men's Health Group included 'weekly health education sessions on topics of interest to the group, counselling, men's health clinics provided by a visiting Aboriginal doctor, activities to promote social skills and bonding, such as going to restaurants for meals and visiting the cinema, hunting, fishing and camping' (Tsey *et al.* 2004: 65). Tsey *et al.* (2002: 278) contended that their research revealed 'the importance of using a reflective approach, such as PAR, to engage men's support groups to clearly define the principles and values which both define them and to which they aspire'. The results of their project also highlighted the need for 'personal development, education and employment' in attempts to make Aboriginal men take 'greater control and responsibility for their lives'.

The process of participating in the Men's Health Group was empowering for those men. As one of the members remarked:

This process has empowered participants to really develop the future of Yarrabah Men's Group, never before they had such opportunity to have input into the program and I find the process to be excellent, because what we discuss are about ourselves and the first step in man finding his rightful role we need to face our problems honestly and admit them and move forward to find solutions and these steps reveal leadership that lies in each of the men. (p. 283)

The study carried out by Zohl dé Ishtar with indigenous Australians (2005a, 2005b, 2005c, 2008) is an excellent example of PAR in cross-cultural research. She coins the methodology adopted in this study as the 'Living On the Ground' method. It is essentially based on the philosophy of PAR, but contains an element of participant observation of ethnography as well. Dé Ishtar worked with the women elders of Wirrinamu in Western Australia's Great Sandy Desert, one of the most remote Aboriginal settlements. The research was carried out for her doctoral thesis and it was a result of her involvement, as a co-ordinator, in the Kapululangu Women's Law and Culture Centre, which was created by the women elders as a way to preserve their cultural heritage for their younger generations. A *tjilimi* (women's camp) was established as a site where women's religious and cultural rites could thrive as the women elders observed, performed and relished their customs. It was a place where the women elders passed on their cultural knowledge and skills to their middle-generation daughters. Zohl dé Ishtar resided in this *tjilimi* with thirteen women for two years; participating in their daily living, gathering bush food and taking part in secret ceremonies, as well as managing the finances and administration of the centre.

As the Kapululangu was initiated by the women elders, dé Ishtar (2005a: 358) had to plan a research project that would directly engage the elders but would not be too intrusive in their lives, and which mirrored their cultural practices. She told us: 'My project needed to be flexible, responsive and responsible to the elders' needs, both immediate and longer term, and to resonate with their lives and include their realities – their concepts of the meaningful'. The outcome was therefore, 'a methodology which responded to the depth of indigenous women's knowledge and the passion of feminist commitment'. Hence, indigenous self-determination or participatory action research was chosen as a way for her to gather data in this research. Her choice of research methodology resonated with the philosophy and principles of researching the Māori people, posited by Linda Tuhiwai Smith (1999, 2008) and Russell Bishop (2008) (see also Chapter 1 in this volume).

In this research, strategies which depended on the elders' capabilities to identify their needs and to directly participate in practical activities which would lead to desirable output were developed. The women elders called this strategy 'kapululangu'. It was 'based on the notion of self-determination: the inalienable right of a people to define their own needs and to determine what actions they are going to take to fulfil those needs' (dé Ishtar 2005a: 364). Through a series of gatherings, the women talked about the problems faced by them and their families, named what they believed to be the origins of those problems, and made decisions or solutions that they believed might reduce or eradicate their problems. From these efforts, Kapululangu was born. In these gatherings, the women pinpointed several concerns about their younger generations, and these included petrol sniffing, alcoholism, teen pregnancy and domestic/family violence. Their immediate concerns were about the well-being of the children and youth. The women elders strongly believed that the trauma experienced in their community was due to the fact that people in their locality began to 'lose' their cultural life, and this was mainly because people's connection with their land declined, and they had few chances to acquire and observe their cultural rites. The women elders therefore wished to pass on their cultural knowledge to their grandchildren in order to 'bring them up properly'. To accomplish this, the children needed to be taken out camping to learn about the country, to hear the women's stories, and to learn about hunting and dancing. The children would need to be taught how to help their men in carrying out similar work with the boys and young men. The women elders decided that the Kapululangu Women's Law and Culture

Centre needed to be established, and with this they decided that a *tjilimi* must also be set up so that they and their young women could reside together, and this would enable their grandchildren to have opportunities to practise and enjoy their culture and women's *yawulyu* ('law, ritual practice').

In arguing for the essence of 'Living On the Ground' methodology, Zohl dé Ishtar maintained that: 'I sought to develop a research methodology which drew upon the women elders' knowledge and way of knowing and, fitting with indigenous process, incorporated the women elders' world-view, their cultural base and their ways of being' (p. 359). However, it was also crucial that she base her methodology on her own perspectives and the processes of knowledge which derived from her experience as a 'feminist *Kartiya* (White)'. The methodology must incorporate her ways of thinking and acting and her obligations and accountabilities to the women elders and her own cultural influences. 'Living On the Ground', dé Ishtar suggested, was 'grounded in relationship, bridged indigenous and feminist knowledge, required the researcher to be passionately involved, and produced tangible outcomes which immediately benefited the project's host' (p. 359). Moreover, 'Living On the Ground' located the researcher 'within the terrain' of indigenous people. Zohl dé Ishtar (2005a: 360) concluded that the process of this methodology could 'contribute towards culturally unburdened communications, for it is not only enlightening but it also challenges culturally-held perceptions, beliefs, and misunderstandings'.

Charlotte Loppie (2007) carried out her research to explore the perceptions of midlife health, particularly on the menopausal transition, among midlife Mi'kmaq women in Nova Scotia, Canada. She aimed to examine the issues from physical, psychological, emotional, social and spiritual perspectives. PAR, according to Loppie, is 'intimately linked to many Indigenous philosophies through the value of local participation, learning through action, collective decision making, and empowerment through group activity' (p. 278). These philosophies embody many facets, including the perspectives that Loppie wished to examine. PAR is likely to result in the promotion of self-determination among indigenous peoples through the processes of 'enhancing self-reliance, consciousness, and the creation of useful information'. The methodology was hence culturally appropriate for the women in her study.

Because of the multiple realities and unpredictable interactions between research partners, she decided to adopt an approach which would allow her to build collaboration and consensus with participating communities and participants. Loppie placed herself 'within a prevalent Indigenous epistemology by acknowledging the wisdom of elder women'. As such, in forming a partnership with the women, she invited them to participate in storytelling as a means of sharing, teaching and learning. All the participants of her study preferred group discussions as a vehicle for 'sharing their experiences' and were involved in the process of 'reciprocal learning and healing'.

This study comprised six groups, totalling forty-two Mi'kmaq women, who were from five First Nation communities in Nova Scotia. A woman from each participating community who acted as a facilitator was asked to contact and invite five or six women to take part in a group discussion about mid-life health and menopause. It was agreed by all groups that local community and health centres would be the most convenient settings for conducting the groups.

In forming the circle with the women, whose first language is Mi'kmaq, Loppie offered to have the facilitator or another woman act as an interpreter. But all of the women preferred to have the groups run in English. She also offered those women who might not feel comfortable discussing the sensitive issue of menopause in a group setting to take part in a face-to-face interview. However, all of the women suggested that they preferred and would be more comfortable doing it in the group discussion.

In running the group discussions, Loppie incorporated social activities into every group meeting (p. 280). This was based on the cultural norms of indigenous people. She said: 'This cultural custom of including opportunities to socialise provided an opportunity for me to get to know the women and for them to become more comfortable with me.' For example, her first group commenced with a lunch. Some women stayed on after the group discussion to ask questions about menopause and other health issues. Her second group started with snacks and then a visit. The social activities extended beyond the group discussion. The fifth group occupied almost a whole day because a workshop on menopause and a dinner were organised after the group discussion. Overall, the group discussion and social activities made the women feel more relaxed; they laughed frequently and this made Loppie feel very welcome. The women expressed their wishes for her to continue to develop a project which would share this information with other aboriginal women.

The process of the group discussion, Loppie contended, encouraged the women to discuss sensitive topics. It made them feel less frightened to talk about the issues as others were willing to talk, offer mutual support and confirm their perspectives. Loppie elaborated:

Within most Indigenous paradigms, knowledge is shared through stories that are intended to teach. Women shared stories of their family and community as well as their life experiences and history. In particular, sharing past experiences was particularly important, as it created an environment of safety and support. The sharing of experiences was also informative for many of the women involved, not only in terms of information about menopause but also in gauging their experience against that of other women. Listening to the stories of other women also triggered memories and responses or helped women to recall their own experiences. (p. 281)

The photovoice method

Photovoice is a method by which people can identify, represent, and enhance their community through a specific photographic technique. (Wang & Burris 1997: 369)

The photovoice process aims to use photographic images taken by persons with little money, power, or status to enhance community needs assessments, empower participants, and induce change by informing policy makers of community assent and deficits. (Strack *et al.* 2004: 49)

Within community based PAR, the method of photovoice has emerged as an innovative means of working with marginalised people in cross-cultural research. The photovoice method rejects traditional paradigms of power and the production of knowledge within the research relationship (Harrison 2002; McIntyre 2008). The researchers are more concerned about developing critical consciousness and empowerment amongst their research participants. The photovoice method thus tends to be used in collaborative and participatory research (see Wang & Burris 1997; Wang *et al.* 1996; Wang 1999, 2003; Wang *et al.* 2004; Strack *et al.* 2004; López *et al.* 2005a, 2005b; Streng *et al.* 2004; McIntyre 2008; Kwok & Ku 2008; Rhodes *et al.* 2008; Wang & Pies 2008).

Essentially, photovoice is 'an innovative participatory action research (PAR) method based on health promotion principles and the theoretical literature on education for critical consciousness, feminist theory and a non-traditional approach to documentary photography' (Wang 1999: 185). Photovoice methodology allows people to record and reflect the concerns and needs of their community by taking photographs. It also promotes critical discussion about important issues through the dialogue about photographs they have taken. Their concerns may reach policy makers through public forums and the display of their photographs. By using a camera to record their concerns and needs, it permits individuals who rarely have contact with those who make decisions over their lives to make their voices heard (Wang & Burris 1997; Wang 1999; Strack *et al.* 2004; Streng *et al.* 2004; Wang *et al.* 2004; López *et al.* 2005a, 2005b; Hargenrather *et al.* 2006; Jurkowski & Paul-Ward 2007;

Mamary *et al.* 2007; Brooks *et al.* 2008; Castleden *et al.* 2008; Kwok & Ku 2008; Rhodes *et al.* 2008; Wilkin 2008).

According to Matt Streng and colleagues (2004: 416), photovoice is a qualitative inquiry method which allows the research participants to 'record and reflect on their personal and community strengths and concerns'. The method 'promotes critical dialogue and knowledge about personal and community issues through group discussions and photographs'. It also 'provides a forum for the presentation of participants' lived experiences through the images, language, and contexts defined by participants themselves' (see also Rhodes *et al.* 2008).

Photovoice, according to Caroline Wang and Cheri Pies (2008: 184–185) is based on Paulo Freire's (1970) approach to critical education and a participatory approach to documentary photography. The educational praxis that Freire advocates emphasises that people speak from their own experience and share with others. It requires people to identify historical and social patterns which oppress their individual lives. This allows people to be able to critically examine the issues from their root causes and to find strategies to change their situations and lives. Freire stresses the power of visual images as a vehicle for assisting individuals to think critically about the forces and factors which have great impact on their lives. Photovoice emerges from this philosophy and 'builds on a commitment to social and intellectual change through community members' critical production and analysis of the visual image'.

The photovoice method is also based on feminist research (Meyer & Kroeger 2005; Wang & Pies 2008). As Wang and Pies write, 'feminist theory suggests that power accrues to those who have voice, set language, make history, and participate in decisions' (p. 185). Based on a feminist framework, photovoice practice advocates that individuals can use this approach 'to influence how their public presence is defined'. The photovoice methodology allows individuals to use 'photography as community voice to reach policymakers'. As such, the methodology moves 'beyond the personal voice to the political' (p. 185; see also McIntyre 2008; Kwok & Ku 2008; Rhodes *et al.* 2008). Helen Meyer and Steve Kroeger (2005: 187) summarise that:

Photovoice draws from documentary photography accounts, Freirean problem-posing, and feminist action research. These strands come together to create a novel methodology that supports the significance of individual's and group's experiences as a tool for understanding the social and political constructions of their lived reality.

Photovoice was originally developed by Caroline Wang and Mary Ann Burris (1997) to enable village women in China to photograph their health experiences and to transform their health outcomes. The method was used as an empowerment tool for the women, who lived in a poor mountainous and remote area in southwestern China. Through the photos and group discussions, the women explored their daily interactions. The women identified reproductive health as their main concern and this became the focus of their photovoice project.

In other projects in China, Caroline Wang and colleagues (1996) also adopted photovoice as their methodology. Women were given cameras to take photographs of their lives; they became the 'native photographers'. The photographs were then used by the women to articulate their needs from their own viewpoints. Through their participation in this photovoice project, they owned the photographs they had taken, and through dialogue, discussion and storytelling, the women were able to engage with policy makers and planners. This conferred empowerment on the Chinese women in the study.

The method of photovoice has also been referred to as participatory photography (Gotschi *et al.* 2008). It has been used widely in development research, such as in the work of Elisabeth Gotschi and colleagues (2008) with farmers in rural Mozambique. Gotschi *et al.* (2008: 220) contend that researchers must avoid carrying out research on marginalised people 'in an oppressive manner' (p. 220). This can be done by ensuring that the researchers 'make efforts towards making their research not only a self-serving exercise, but also engage in respectful and friendly relations with the participants or engage in some forms of activism'. Within this methodology, the 'problem' of the 'Other' would not occur, since 'it is the "Other" who is empowered to take pictures'. Through the photovoice method, researchers hand their power to the participants in the sense that they can tell their own stories through the photographs they take. It is the methodology that allows the photographs of the participants to 'set the agenda of the research process' (p. 216).

The practice of the photovoice method

Methodologically, photovoice requires the participants to take photographs which represent their understanding and meaning of life. The photographs are then used as the basis for discussion in later interviews, which often occur in group settings. The discussion of the photographs permits the participants to articulate their understanding and interpretations of the images they have taken. Following Wang and Burris (1994, 1997), Elizabeth

Carlson and colleagues (2006) posit that the aims of the photovoice method include:

- encouraging discussion around a topic of concern to the participants;
- creating a safe environment for discussion and reflection among the participants and the researchers;
- encouraging the participants to recognise a need for action in certain areas of their life or community;
- permitting their ideas to be disseminated to a wider community in order to facilitate changes.

According to Matt Streng and colleagues (2004: 405), the methodology of photovoice necessitates that the participants perform a few tasks, and these include:

- taking part in an informational training session, to receive a camera and determine the topic for their first photo assignment;
- taking photographs to record the realities of their experiences for each photo assignment;
- participating in group discussion sessions in order to share their photographs from each photo assignment and to examine the issues, and discuss potential strategies for change;
- organising a forum and exhibition to present their photographs and stories to local policy makers and service providers whom they have identified as potential collaborators who could influence positive changes.

Previous photovoice projects have suggested that the participants benefit personally and collectively. For example, in the Language of Light photovoice project (Wang 2003), both women and men suggested that their participation in the project promoted self-esteem, and enhanced their quality of life and status with their peers. Their participants said that they enjoyed the creative process of the method and the attention they received from the researchers, policymakers and the media. One sixty-year-old woman put up her camera and announced: 'This is history!' (Wang 2003: 187).

Collective relationships often develop through working on their photographs together with others and through the group sessions that follow. Wang (2003: 190) tells us that in her research:

Participating in this project itself enabled participants to get to know one another, build ties and friendships, and therefore bond as a peer support group for problem solving and teamwork ... this enabled homeless people to speak from their experience and talk about what mattered to them so that they could help one another survive.

In Caroline Brooks and colleagues' (2008) project, all of the women experienced positive enjoyment in many ways: 'the personal and social reflection, the creative component, the relationship building and especially the potential of the photographs to assist other women who may experience breast cancer'. One woman, Shelly, said that 'this was a wonderful, wonderful exercise'. And Dorothy said: 'I pictured right away that it [the pictures] would help others.'

Photovoice in cross-cultural research: some examples

Photovoice is a flexible method which has been employed in geographically and culturally diverse groups. Most often, the photovoice method has been used with community groups who historically have had little opportunity to influence and shape the policies that have affected them. For instance, photovoice has been used with Latino adolescents (Streng *et al.* 2004); African-American breast cancer survivors in rural North Carolina (Lopez *et al.* 2005a, 2005b); Chinese women in Yunnan Province, China (Wang & Burris 1997); ethnic adolescents in East Baltimore, Maryland (Strack *et al.* 2004); Mayan survivors of civil war in Guatemala (Lykes *et al.* 2003, 2006); gay African-American men (Mamary *et al.* 2007); indigenous people in Bolivia (Spira 2008); indigenous women in Canada (Brooks *et al.* 2008; Castleden *et al.* 2008); newly arrived female Chinese immigrants in Hong Kong (Kwok & Ku 2008); and indigenous female health workers in Melbourne, Australia (Wilkin 2008). The only two published studies that document the use of photovoice for studying HIV/AIDS issues are those of Hargenrather and colleagues (2006) and Rhodes and colleagues (2008). I shall provide some examples in greater detail here.

Ellen López and colleagues (2005a) conducted their research on quality of life among African-American breast cancer survivors in rural North Carolina using photovoice in combination with grounded theory. López *et al.* argued that because of their cultural norms and beliefs and a long history of marginalisation, African-American women have been silent about their breast cancer. It has been particularly difficult for older women to express their quality of life concerns because of their memories of their long-standing social and cultural conditions of inequality in a segregated health care system in the USA. It was felt that a research approach which was more culturally sensitive and participatory would enable these women to tell their stories about the social and cultural meanings of living in silence with breast cancer. Hence, 'The Surviving Angels–Inspirational Images Project' of rural eastern North Carolina was established. The women were given cameras so that they could take photographs, and these photographs were used to discuss and relate their experiences to others in their community. In this way, through their own eyes, the women were able to relate the realities of their lives and experiences (see also Wang and Burris 1994, 1997). Eighteen women, recruited through the North Carolina Breast Cancer Screening Program, were invited to attend a training session to learn about the project and their potential involvement in it. This training was to build rapport and trust between the researchers and the women. Breast cancer is a sensitive area and it was essential that the women would feel safe and have a chance to ask questions before agreeing to take part in the research. Thirteen women attended and agreed to take part in the project. During the training, the women learned about the ethical issues and power relationships associated with using a camera, personal safety when asking strangers if they could take their pictures and the essence of 'giving back to the community' by providing copies of photos to those being photographed (see also Wang 1999). The women practised using their cameras by taking pictures of each other and they were trained to use the acknowledgment form which they would need to use to obtain written permission before taking a person's photograph. In order to focus on particular aspects of their survivorship, the women collectively agreed that the first photo assignment would comprise at least six pictures which would represent the wishes they would have had as a survivor. It took one month for the women to complete each of their photo assignments. Then for each assignment, a three-hour photo discussion was conducted and taped, with the permission of the women. A typical photo discussion commenced with a review and discussion of the themes which emerged from the grounded theory analysis of previous sessions. This was followed by a show-and-tell activity, where each participant presented her photos and described the relevance of herself to the photo assignment. One or two photos were then chosen by the group and they were then discussed in greater depth. The following questions, adopted from the six-step inductive questioning technique **SHOWED**, were used for each photo:

- What do you **S**ee in this photograph?
- What is **H**appening in the photograph?
- How does this relate to **O**ur lives?
- **W**hy do these issues exist?
- How can we become **E**mpowered by our new social understanding?
- What can we **D**o to address these issues? (López *et al.* 2005a: 103)

At the end of each photo discussion, the women would decide about their next photo assignment and set up a date for their next discussion. At the end of the seven-month period, and after five photo discussions, no new information was being generated. This meant that their data had reached saturation and hence all the women and the researcher decided to stop taking photographs.

López *et al.* suggested that the use of photovoice was appropriate for researching socially vulnerable people such as African-American women, and topics such as breast cancer. In their paper, they concluded that the women in their study remarked that they felt they had formed a partnership with the researchers in the study, as they could make their own decision over which topics and photographs they would take and bring to their photo discussion sessions. The photographs assisted them in discussing important topics that they would not have thought they could talk about with other people. Because of this experience, the women were empowered and believed that they would be able to do anything in their lives to survive.

A photovoice method research was employed by Marie Stopes Australia (Atlas and Molloy 2005) in an innovative research project with young indigenous people in rural Victoria. Marie Stopes Australia is a non-profit organisation focusing on reproductive health in indigenous Australian communities in rural areas. In their research on developing reproductive and sexual health initiatives for indigenous communities, Marie Stopes formed a partnership with local indigenous communities in Mildura, Shepparton and Warrnambool. It aimed to allow indigenous communities to identify, control and develop their own health solutions and to build capacity for Aboriginal self-determination and community control. As such, it had to be culturally sensitive to the needs of the indigenous communities. One important aspect of their development was to empower, motivate and inspire young indigenous people to have more control of their sexual health through the photovoice project. A six-day workshop was organised. The first and second days focused on written consent, a briefing about photovoice and photographic and ethical training. These young people spent the third day taking photographs and had them developed overnight. On the fourth day, the photos were selected for discussion by the young people. Their discussions were documented. The photos were then enlarged and framed by the participants. On the fifth day, the framed photos were transported to Mildura Art Gallery. The participants categorised the themes of the photos and then positioned them in the gallery for their exhibition. On the sixth day, the opening of the local community exhibition was organised with a traditional welcome from the indigenous communities.

One photograph was called 'Unforgettable', and it was composed under the theme 'Alcohol and Drugs'. The photograph was taken by one of the indigenous youths. It showed a picture of an indigenous young woman sitting hopelessly near a bed which was surrounded by empty alcohol bottles. The story that accompanied the photographs said:

This photo is based on something that could happen if young people were to drink. They could go to bed with some stranger then him get up in the morning while you're still asleep and leave you and didn't know his name. That would make any girl feel sick in the guts. Just waking up and thinking 'Did I use a condom or could I have an STI?' Who knows? But I don't think anyone could forget what happened.

Another photograph illustrated the sign 'No Entry' commonly seen on many roads in Australia. The narrative account was expressed as:

In this picture of no entry, it makes the word no stand out when people are in a situation where they don't want to be. It might be bad if someone decides to pass this sign and find themselves in a risky situation.

This photovoice project, as Batya Atlas and Rachel Molloy (2005) suggest, has provided powerful insights into the sexual health issues important to young indigenous people in rural Victorian communities. The outcomes of this project enabled Marie Stopes Australia and the Victorian Aboriginal Community Controlled Health Organisation (VACCHO) to design sexual health initiatives culturally appropriate to the specific needs of indigenous young people and to identify important issues for discussion with decision makers, community leaders, government departments and donors.

Because of the rapid growth of the Latino population in North Carolina, in the United States, the Project Realidad Latina (Latino Reality) was initiated by Matt Streng and colleagues (2004). The project was a qualitative study and aimed to obtain insight into the experiences of migration among ten newly arrived Latino adolescents who were living in rural North Carolina. The project was a research partnership between a local high school's Latino student-led club and the School of Public Health at the University of North Carolina. The Latino adolescents were invited to engage in identifying salient topics which were impacted by their immigration experiences, both positively and negatively, and interrogating these subjects with local health and human service providers in order to develop a plan of action. Streng et al. suggested that in allowing the Latino adolescents to take an active role as co-investigators working with university researchers, they would be able to develop a more enlightened understanding of their own issues, abilities and concerns. Streng et al. pointed out that: 'This understanding was expected to generate momentum among the adolescents to organize and lead a forum with local community leaders and service providers to highlight the findings and determine next steps toward building Latino adolescents' assets and taking a community initiative to address their issues' (p. 406).

The study was placed within the framework of a community based participatory research approach and used the photovoice method as a means of collecting information from the participants. During the one-year period of the project, the Latina adolescents formed a partnership with the researchers and public health practitioners in order to develop photo assignments, took photographs which were based on the developed assignments, used the photographs for discussions and defined themes which were based on these photo-discussions.

From the adolescents' words and photographs, several issues emerged which both challenged and facilitated their adaptation and quality of life in their school and community. Conditions within the school environment hindered their achievement. The adolescents expressed their appreciation for the opportunity to attend high school and the personal development that the school provided them, but they felt that they were not given a fair opportunity to perform well at the school. This was one reason given for the fact that there were high drop-out rates among the Latino adolescents. Streng *et al.* contended that: 'When this discouraging environment is combined with other challenges such as limited English language proficiency, the devaluation of their culture, community expectations that factory-based jobs are the only appropriate employment options, and limited options for higher education, the struggle to remain in school becomes very real' (p. 412).

However, the project also indicated some themes which acted as facilitators for the adjustment process of these adolescents, including having an opportunity to share and celebrate their Latino identity with other Latinos, and to become part of a larger community through community involvement.

Streng *et al.* concluded that the use of CBPR and photovoice assisted the researchers and practitioners to establish a trusted relationship with the adolescents (pp. 404–405). The methodology also allowed the team to obtain information about 'hidden transcripts', which are referred to as 'subordinates gathering outside the gaze of power and constructing a sharply critical political and cultural discourse' (Chávez *et al.* 2008: 96). This critical discourse is likely to emerge from research using the CBPR approach and the photovoice method (Streng *et al.* 2004: 413).

Scott Rhodes and colleagues (2008) conducted a study that they called 'Visions and Voices: HIV in the 21st Century' with poor people living with HIV in the southern United States. They adopted photovoice as their method of inquiry. The participants were encouraged to examine the realities of living with HIV/AIDS through photographs and critical dialogue in order to develop a process that would allow them to reach local community leaders, policy makers and other community members. From this, it was expected that plans of action which would effect change could be developed.

The project was initiated and undertaken by a community–university partnership. The partnership included lay community members and representatives from local community-based organisations (an AIDS service organisation and community-based religious organisations); the local public health department; and the School of Medicine at Wake Forest University.

During the life of the study, the participants undertook five photo assignments. As a group, they made decisions on each photo assignment. Following Wang and Burris (1994, 1997), the aim was to 'place cameras in the hands of PLWHA [people living with HIV/AIDS], who in turn would record, discuss, and relate to others the realities of their lives through their own eyes and experiences' (p. 162). In sequential order, the photo assignments included: '(a) things that make me happy, (b) things that are important to me, (c) challenges that we face, (d) things we would change if we had superhuman powers, and (e) things that support us in our lives' (p. 162). Altogether, six photo discussions were organised; one for each photo assignment and one for a summary discussion. During the photo discussions, each participant shared up to three photographs with the group through a facilitator-led session based on the SHOWED questions (as used in the study carried out by Ellen Lopez and colleagues that I presented above). Each photo discussion lasted about one and a half to two hours and was audio-taped.

The use of CBPR and photovoice in this study enabled the researchers and other members of the research partnership to have an in-depth understanding of the reality of living with HIV/AIDS among poor people and of their priorities. Rhodes *et al.* (2008: 167) wrote: 'Unlike most other research methodologies, photovoice also promoted immediate action through the presentation of findings and facilitated discussion at the community forum. The community forum was an invaluable element of photovoice because participants not only desired their voices to be heard but, based on the findings, wanted collective action to be taken.'

Rhodes *et al.* suggested that the use of the photovoice method resulted in gaining an 'emic perspective' on the experiences of living with HIV/AIDS from poor PLWHA which might not have been accessible through the use of other methods (p. 167). The project provided poor PLWHA 'an opportunity to author individual and collective stories that represent how they experience living with HIV/AIDS and play an integral part in the formulation of actions to effect change'. In their research, photovoice was 'an empowering process' which helped to transform knowledge (themes which emerged from the data) into action. The resulting actions of this project included community-level intervention, such as a gallery exhibition, and a policy change from the no-tolerance policy into recovery supporting policies.

According to Rhodes *et al.*, photovoice is not simply just 'a basic research method' (p. 168). To them, photovoice is 'an intervention strategy that facilitates participant empowerment by creating a space for participation and control over the process and builds the capacity of participants to mobilize to explore, describe, and analyze challenges and assets and problem solve'.

Jackie Yan-chi Kwok and Hok-Bun Ku (2008) conducted a community based PAR and photovoice project with newly arrived Chinese immigrant women in Kowloon, Hong Kong. Most of the women and their children lived in extremely crowded and run-down buildings in the Sham Shui Po district. The poor living conditions had created 'environmental stress' among them. Because of their socioeconomic situation, they often had no opportunity to express their expectations relating to their living space. In order to enable the women to express their perspectives and become participants in urban planning, Kwok and Ku employed community based participatory action research, including the use of photovoice and visual simulation modelling workshops.

In the process, and in collaboration with the Girls' Clubs Association, Kwok and Ku invited the women to discuss their current living situations, articulate on their preferred housing environment and provide clear recommendations to the Hong Kong government in respect to the planning of housing and the neighbourhood. According to Wang and Burris (1997: 369), photovoice 'uses the immediacy of the visual image to furnish evidence and to promote an effective, participatory means of sharing expertise and knowledge'. Following Wang and Burris (1994, 1997), the photovoice component in this study comprised two main stages: photographs taken by the individual participants, and group discussions about the photographs they had taken. Kwok and Ku (2008: 270) contended that their photovoice project was used 'for drawing on the community's lore, observation, and stories'. They used this method in order to 'encourage the participants to become aware of, and then to comment freely upon, their living environment'. They placed marginalised women 'at the centre and treated them as experts on their own experience'. The researchers respectfully invited the women to take part in the project and share their lives with them. The researchers became 'listeners and learners', not dominant researchers. The women and their children were entrusted with the cameras. Hence, the participants became the 'research partners'. The participants took photographs of their living environment, and perspectives of their daily lives. Their photographs showed the places that they wanted and the places they liked and disliked. Kwok and Ku also created opportunities for the participants to tell their stories and make comments on the places they had photographed.

From the photographs that the participants took, three layers of meaning emerged: the physical living environment, the rhythms of everyday life, and their perspectives about themselves and their families. For instance, a woman who had recently immigrated photographed a picture of a shopping mall near her home. She articulated on her reason for taking this photograph:

After taking my son to school in the afternoon, I go to the street market because the food is cheap and fresh. Then I'll go to the shopping mall. It is new, big and beautiful, with air conditioning. I stay there until late afternoon because our home is terribly hot. (p. 270)

Kwok and Ku said that through their participation in the photovoice project, the women were able to think seriously about issues which impacted on their living conditions, to know about their rights as citizens and to learn about the problems of Hong Kong's housing policy. Through group discussion sessions, they had opportunities to listen to the stories and viewpoints of other new immigrants. Photovoice therefore became an educational process and provided empowerment for the women. This photovoice project assisted these newly arrived women to establish relationships with others, and hence strengthen their social cohesion. Once they started to know each other, they shared information and resources, and provided support for each other in their everyday life, for example by improving their children's education, applying for public housing and looking for employment. As they were no longer isolated, they started to form an informal support network. In part of their research, Kwok and Ku also organised workshops for the participants to design a model which represented the ideal places they wished to live in. The process of participating in design workshops allowed the participants to develop self-esteem and 'a strong sense of confidence and competence'. One young woman said:

I really love to come to this workshop. It's a lot of fun. In the process, I feel very happy because we can freely do what we want. Unlike our study at school, here we have to make decisions all by ourselves, and nobody condemns us. I feel I am not useless despite what my teachers tell me. (p. 279)

In their conclusion, Kwok and Ku referred to the methodology they employed in order to reach social justice:

Through participatory action research, the participants are empowered, and the researchers are inspired, to reflect critically on an understanding of urban life for the disadvantaged ... We maintain that we, as academic researchers and urban planners, should respect the views of inhabitants regarding their living space. The right of people to participate in policy decisions that affect their everyday lives is our definition of social justice. (p. 280)

Tutorial activities

You have just commenced your work as a researcher in a poor nation in Southeast Asia. You have been invited to carry out a piece of research on malaria and tuberculosis in one local area in the country. Most people in the area where you will be doing your research are poor and suffer a great deal from these illnesses. You want them to change their living situations as you know that living conditions contribute to these illnesses. How will you work with the local people in a way that they can see the benefit of changing their living situations and that they can actually change them? How will you carry out your research so that you can use the outcomes to advocate for positive change for these local people?

Chapter summary

Participatory action research or its Bengali equivalent *Gonogobeshona*, as a way of collective self-inquiry and self-development leading to holistic awareness and collective action, therefore, came to play an active part as one of the many ways in which the marginalized in society could be reached and awakened. (Guhathakurta 2008: 511)

What [visual and textual stories] *can* do is provide politically disempowered people with opportunities to author individual and collective stories that best represent how they experience their lives – individual and collective stories that carry the signature of the people who live them. (McIntyre 2003: 64)

In this chapter, I have discussed the collaborative methodology of community based and participatory action research in cross-cultural research. I argue that participatory action research provides opportunities for many marginalised individuals to be able to engage in research and find solutions which benefit not only themselves but also others in their own communities. The process of PAR is empowering. It is a crucial methodology for cross-cultural researchers who attempt to bring social justice to the society or community involved in the research.

An emerging approach within the PAR methodology is the photovoice method. Through the use of cameras, the participants are able to capture visual images which represent their lived realities. The visual stories can convey more vivid and concrete evidence to policy makers and those in authority and can influence changes in policy and practice. The process is also empowering for those who take part. A number of photovoice projects have brought about positive changes in the lives and living situations of many individuals in different parts of the world. I strongly advocate this method in cross-cultural research, particularly when we work with marginalised and vulnerable people.

SUGGESTED READING

dé Ishtar, Z. (2005). Living on the ground: The 'culture woman' and the 'missus'. *Women's Studies International Forum* **28**, 369–380.

Dickson, G. (2000). Aboriginal grandmothers' experience with health promotion and participatory action research. *Qualitative Health Research* **10**(2), 188–213.

Freire, P. (1972). *Pedagogy of the oppressed* (trans. M. B. Ramos). Harmondsworth: Penguin.

Guhathakurta, M. (2008). Theatre in participatory action research: Experiences from Bangladesh. In P. Reason & H. Bradbury (Eds.), *The Sage handbook of action research: Participative inquiry and practice,* 2nd edition (pp. 510–521). London: Sage Publications.

Israel, B. A., Eng, E., Schulz, A. J., & Parker, E. A. (2005). *Methods in community-based participatory research for health*. San Francisco: Jossey-Bass.

Kemmis, S., & McTaggart, R. (2008). Participatory action research. In N. K. Denzin & Y. S. Lincoln (Eds.), *Strategies of qualitative inquiry*, 3rd edition (pp. 271–330). Thousand Oaks, CA: Sage Publications.

Kwok, J. Y-C., & Ku, H-B. (2008). Making habitable space together with female Chinese immigrants to Hong Kong: An interdisciplinary participatory action research project. *Action Research* **6**(3), 261–283.

McIntyre, A. (2008). *Participatory action research*. Thousand Oaks, CA: Sage Publications.

Minkler, M., & Wallestein, N. (2008). *Community-based participatory research for health: From process to outcomes*, 2nd edition. San Francisco: Jossey-Bass.

Pyett, P., Waples-Crowe, P., & van der Sterren, A. (2010) Collaborative participatory research with disadvantaged communities. In P. Liamputtong (Ed.), *Research methods in health: Foundations for evidence-based practice* (pp. 345–366). Melbourne: Oxford University Press.

Reason, P., & Bradbury, H. (Eds.) (2006), *Handbook of action research: Concise paperback edition*. London: Sage Publications.

Reason, P., & Bradbury, H. (2008). *The Sage handbook of action research: Participative inquiry and practice*. Los Angeles, CA: Sage Publications.

9 Writing and disseminating in cross-cultural research

When we are dealing with marginalised or silenced voices researchers have a responsibility to challenge this silencing, or at least to provide some sort of public space for alternative and/or occluded views to be aired. As an African saying reminds us, until the hunted have their poets then songs of the hunt will always glorify the hunter, not the prey.

(Brockington & Sullivan 2003: 63–64)

In this chapter, I will discuss the way we write to represent the voices of our research participants in cross-cultural research. There are several salient issues that I believe deserve great attention from researchers. For example: How do we write our research findings in a way that what we write will not further marginalise our participants? In what language should we write the findings? Who owns the research findings? I shall also suggest ways that we can write up the findings sensitively and make use of innovative writing strategies. When we have finished our research project, it is important for us to disseminate the research findings. How do we do this in cross-cultural research so that the findings can be fed back to our participants and reach wider audiences? This will be addressed in this chapter.

Writing cross-cultural research

How do we write in a way that our writing will not further marginalise our research participants? This is a contentious issue in any sensitive research, but even more so in cross-cultural research, when we often work with very marginalised people.

Betty Davies and colleagues (2009: 12) tell us that in their research on child deaths with Mexican Americans, one father referred to the song 'México Lindo y Querido' when he was discussing the wish of his son to be buried in Mexico. The Latina research assistant explained what the song meant to the father: 'The song professes such love for Mexico that his only wish is to return at the time of his death. If he dies on foreign soil, he asks to be spared the pain by telling him it is but a dream'. For Davies *et al.*, this song helped them to understand why the man determined to bury his son far away from California. He wanted to fulfil his son's wish.

How do we write about this story? According to Bogusia Temple (1997: 608), we as researchers collect information about the lives of people. We orchestrate our interviews and then edit them to produce our reports. But for the research participants, the stories they tell us in the interviews are 'accounts of their lives, experiences and interpretations'. We must make sure that we stay closer to their lived experiences and the true meanings of their experiences. Traditional ways of writing in qualitative research may not allow us to do so, and it means that we have to write in an unconventional way. I refer to this as an innovative way of representation in cross-cultural research, which I shall discuss in more detail later on.

Cross-cultural researchers must also write responsibly. What we write must not be used to further harm our participants. As Binaya Subedi (2007: 65) argues, when it comes to writing about cultural groups, cross-cultural researchers have 'the responsibility to be accountable' to their participants and their communities. As an outsider, in her research with South Asian women in England, Itohan Egharevba (2001: 238–239) tells us that she had to be extremely sensitive about how she interpreted and presented data about 'an-"other" community in a manner which does not reinforce stereotypes and dominant structures'. This is especially crucial as she works with South Asian women who tend to be 'particularly prone to being treated as "passive victims" … and who are often blamed for their situation by institutions and services'. Linda Tuhiwai Smith (1999) was asked by the Māori mothers who participated in her research not to write their stories in ways that dominant societies could use to exploit them. These mothers also wanted Smith to observe culturally appropriate channels for her dissemination, such as speaking about her research in community meetings, rather than writing and publishing in academic journals or formal reports. For indigenous people such as the Māoris, research is a tool that they employ to 'recenter' themselves as 'ordinary'. As Fiona Cram (2009: 318) writes, in order to achieve this, researchers must ensure that their research serves the people better and it permits the stories of these people 'to be both told and heard', and this can be achieved through writing up responsibly.

Presenting findings in another language

In cross-cultural research, the researchers often collect data in one language and present their findings in another, usually in English as most of the dissemination channels such as journal articles and books are still largely accepted and published in the English language. Doing so, Maria Birbili (2000: 1) suggests, requires the researchers to make translation-related decisions which can have an impact on the quality and accuracy of the writing. Bogusia Temple and Alys Young (2008: 96) contend that how the researchers write to represent individuals who speak other languages is influenced by how they see their own social world and the world of those individuals. They argue that 'speaking for others, in any language, is always a political issue that involves the use of language to construct self and other … If researchers see themselves as active in the research process then they have a responsibility for the way that they represent others and their languages' (see also Alcoff 1991; Wilkinson & Kitzinger 1996).

Similar to the issue of translation that I discussed in Chapter 6, Birbili (2000: 2) points out that one main difficulty of cross-cultural research, where the language of the individuals participating in the study differs from that of the write-up, is how to obtain 'conceptual equivalence of comparability of meaning' (see Phillips 1960). This difficulty, for Herbert Phillips, is 'an unsolvable problem' (p. 291). This is because, Birbili (2000: 2) asserts, most languages bear some feelings, values and assumptions that the researchers, particularly as outsiders, may not be aware of. Even some apparently familiar terms or expressions which have direct lexical equivalence may carry 'emotional connotations' in one language which may not necessarily occur in another. The expression 'civil service mentality', for example, refers to the image of people who are 'very observant of their rights' in English (Moses & Ramsden 1992: 102). But Birbili (2000: 2) argues that 'it might not be easy for the English reader to pick up the full implications the term carries for a Greek unless it is accompanied by more "cultural" information on the (negative) associations and connotations that the term "civil mentality" has in a Greek context'.

It is recommended that in cases where two languages do not have direct verbal equivalence, the researchers attempt to gain comparability of meanings rather than concern about lexical comparability (p. 2). However, this process requires that the researcher not only have 'a proficient understanding of a language', but also 'an "intimate" knowledge of the culture'. This will allow the researchers to be able to interpret and translate terms in their writing to a level of accuracy acceptable to the research participants.

In qualitative inquiries, researchers present their findings in words, and this is what we refer to as direct quotation. Harry Wolcott (1994) says that the use of direct quotation is the only chance that the readers have to 'see for themselves' what the participants 'look like'. When translating the participants' words, Birbili (2000: 3) suggests that the researchers must decide whether they wish to adopt a 'literal' or 'free' translation of the text. A literal translation (meaning translating word by word) might be perceived as 'doing more justice to what participants have said and "make one's readers understand the foreign mentality better"' (Honig 1997: 17). However, this strategy can 'reduce the readability of the text, which in turn can test readers' patience and even their ability to understand "what's going on"'. If the researchers decide to adopt the 'more "elegant" free translation', they need to consider 'the implications of creating quotations that "read well"'. In translated quotations, the risk of losing information from the original is marked (Birbili 2000).

In my own work with Thai women living with HIV/AIDS in Thailand (see Liamputtong *et al.* 2009), I transcribe the interviews and analyse the data in the Thai language. When I write it up, very often I have to use the Thai terms in my explanations precisely because of the points that I have discussed above. I have difficulties in trying to translate some terms into English because I cannot find any equivalent terms which would convey the same meanings as the Thai ones. Often, too, I would retain the terms used by the women and then use English terms to loosely illustrate the meanings. The following is my example:

> The women in our study suggested that women in particular would be more stigmatised than men. Women who contract HIV and AIDS would be perceived as *pu ying mai dee*; that is being 'bad' women who liked to have sex with many men, or as *pu ying sum son* (promiscuity; sexually indulged women) who like *pai tiaw* (going to clubs and bars and drinking alcohol and having sex with men indiscriminately). Women contracted HIV from *rok mua* (promiscuous disease). As Arunee suggested, people do not see or believe that they are infected by their husbands or partners. Hence, women are blamed for having the disease and this is the reason for them keeping the illness secret. Sinjai too remarked that:
>
> People in community tend to see this disease as *rok mua*. As women, we can have only one partner or one husband. But, for those who have HIV/AIDS, people tend to see them as having too many partners and this is not good. They are seen as *pu ying mai dee*. And they will be *rang kiat* [discriminated against] more than men who have HIV/AIDS. Men who live with this disease are not seen as bad as the women are. If you are women and have HIV/AIDS, it is worse for you.

Writing differently

Many years ago, I submitted a piece of work based on my personal experience as an immigrant mother and the findings of my research with Thai immigrant women to a prestigious journal in social work (see Liamputtong 2001). Inspired by C. Wright Mills's words (1959: 216) 'you must learn to use your life experience in your intellectual work: continually to examine and interpret it', I wrote subjectively, beginning each section with poems, or some beautiful writings of well-known (and not so well-known) writers. I followed with the usual academic writing interwoven with my personal experiences. I wove my personal troubles in with those of my participants in an attempt to shed light on the lives and voices of migrant mothers who are marginalised in so many ways. At the time it was painful for me to write it, but in the end the paper speaks for me and my lived experience. This is precisely what Laurel Richardson (2000a: 930) has articulated in her alternative form of writing, that 'writing is always … situational, and that our Self is always present, no matter now much we try to suppress it … Writing from that premise frees us to write material in a variety of ways: to tell and retell.'

This new trend in representing the voices of our participants has been referred to as 'experimental writing' (Glesne 1997; Richardson 2000; Ellis 2008; Liamputtong & Rumbold 2008; Richardson & St. Pierre 2008). These new writing forms blur the boundaries between art and science (Glesne 1997). This is what Zali Gurevitch (2000: 3) refers to as 'the serious play of writing'. Writing in this way 'invites us to live through other experiences vicariously and to come away with a deeper understanding of … the human condition' (Brady 2000: 957).

There are several ways that cross-cultural researchers can write their research findings to reflect the discussion above. These types of writing have been seen as situated neatly within the cultural practices of cultural groups. Linda Tuhiwai Smith (1999), for example, suggests that poetry, fiction, non-fiction, plays and song writing are preferred by indigenous researcher/writers as they seek to write 'in ways which capture the message, nuances and flavor of indigenous lives'. In this chapter, I will provide some discussions on writing as a short story and as a poem.

Short stories

Cross-cultural researchers have used short stories to represent the voices of marginalised people. Marcelo Diversi (1998) adopts short stories to describe the lives of children who live on the streets of Campinas, Brazil. In this piece of writing, Diversi presents four short stories in order to reveal the cultural narratives shaping the everyday lives of street children and hence to allow people to have a better understanding about the lived experiences of these children. Diversi wants to 'give voice' to the street children and to provide readers with accurate representations of their lived experiences; representations which reveal 'the depth of their humanness and that transcend the limited, stereotypical image of "little criminals" prevalent in the national and local dominant narratives' (p. 132). Diversi tells us that he does not wish to represent the voice of these children from a theoretical perspective, as this will 'bury their voices beneath layers of analysis'. In order to represent the children without losing their voices, he transgresses the boundaries of conventional forms of writing in the social sciences. For this purpose, the form of a short story is chosen. Diversi writes: 'I employed short story techniques such as alternative points of view, dialogue, unfolding action, and flashback to attempt to create the tension, suspense, delay, and voice that compose a good short story and that are inseparable from lived experience' (p. 132). In arguing for using a short story to represent the voice of these street children, Diversi says clearly:

> The short story genre has the potential to render lived experience with more verisimilitude than does the traditional realist text, for it enables the reader to feel that interpretation is never finished or complete. Short stories that show, instead of tell, are less author centered, which, in turn, invites interpretation and meaning making ... This invitation is crucial to avoid authorial omnipotence ... and to avoid 'closing off or nailing down an interpretation without allowing alternative views to creep into view'. (p. 132)

In his recent investigation, Marcelo Diversi (2008) carried out his research with Latino youth on their academic experiences in the American educational system in Utah. He found it problematic to represent the voices of these young people using traditional writing formats. In the end, he chose to write his findings in short story form. Diversi believes that short stories 'provide representations that create space for more subjectivity of lived experience and interpretation by the reader' (p. 68). Short stories, to Diversi, allow social science researchers to 'create space and support representations of the Other that include voice, context, body and open-endedness of interpretation' (p. 68). In his recent piece, Diversi uses a short story to represent the voice and life of Oscar, one of the young persons who participated in his ethnographic research and with whom he interacted over a period of three years. It is a powerful short story to read, and one which I highly recommend.

Donna Goldstein (2003) undertook research with women living in urban shanty towns in Brazil amidst poverty, trauma and tragedy. The women used black humour and laughter as a means of telling their stories. The black humour and laughter used by these women, Goldstein contends, are 'windows into the sense of injustice oppressed peoples feel about their conditions ... Their laughter contains a sense of the absurdity of the world they inhabit' (pp. 12–13). The black humour and laughter emotionally unchain their frustration and marginalisation as a result of severe poverty and social despair. In this work, Goldstein writes up the women's stories, black humour and laughter as a series of humorous short stories. Presenting the women's stories this way can be dangerous, as it may create uneasy feelings among readers. However, Goldstein suggests that in order to prevent our making wrong assumptions about these poor women, readers must place the women's stories within the context of their severe poverty. Goldstein remarks:

The women I knew often joked and laughed about child death, rape, and murder in a way that made me feel and may make the reader feel ill at ease. These jokes and accompanying laughter create a seemingly paradoxical emotional aesthetic that calls for contexualization of Brazil's urban poor and feeling the sense of frustration ... that accompanies their often desperate political and economic situation. (p. 45)

Poetry

The great function of poetry is to give us back the situations of our dreams. (Gaston Bachelard, *The Poetics of Space*, cited in Brady 2008: 501)

Poetry has become one popular means of representing the voices of research participants (Dickson 2000; Richardson 2002; Kooken *et al.* 2007; Brady 2008; Marvasti 2008; Vannini & Gladue 2009). Poetry, according to Wendy Kooken and colleagues (2007: 904) is an alternative means for interpreting research findings so that 'the detached view of scientific inquiry' can be balanced with 'the emotional reaction to the content'. Poetry reveals how individuals 'make sense of and are influenced by their experiences' (p. 905). Kooken *et al.* contend that 'what may otherwise have been difficult to express may be presented in poetics and represent more than the lived experience'. This permits both the researchers and the researched to 'see and hear that which was not previously available' (p. 905). In presenting the research findings in this form, the researchers will have to work with the literary devices used in poetry, for example 'rhythms, silences, spaces, breath points, alliterations, meter, cadence, assonance, rhyme and off-rhyme' (Richardson 2000b: 12). Through these devices, the audiences/readers will be drawn into and emotionally engaged with the data. This will allow them to 'see the world in new ways' (Kooken *et al.* 2007: 905).

Poetry is an expressive means which individuals can use to examine meaning in their lives (Richardson 2002). Poetry is hence compatible with the cultural practices of African Americans. Kooken *et al.* (2007: 906) point out that 'African Americans have long used the written word to convey their innermost thoughts and their support for one another' (see Banks-Wallace 2000; Horton & Horton 2001; Armstrong 2004). Poetry for African Americans, as bell hooks (1989: 11) suggests, has been 'the place for the secret voice – for all that could not be directly stated or named – for all that would-not-be-denied expression'.

In their research relating to the breast cancer experiences of African Americans, Kooken *et al.* (2007) constructed poems from verbatim quotations in the interview transcripts as often as possible. In their paper, eleven poems were constructed to represent the women's journeys, from diagnosis to survivorship. For example, in the original transcript, one woman talked about the meaning of attractiveness for women who survived breast cancer:

You have a mind, you can think you know, you can do certain things, you have creativity, there's an uniqueness to yourself. I mean I don't consider myself what's on my chest, my chest don't think, my chest don't make choices, my chest don't believe in but standing up for decoration …

The verbatim quotation was written up as a poem, and it reads:

Attractive black women-
have a mind
and can think;
can do certain things
are creative and unique.
Breasts therefore-
cannot be attractive.

Another poem represents the long wait in a health care setting.

No News is BAD NEWS
They sit you in the room.
They wait for hours
and hours and hours
before they tell you anything.
No hurry now – I've told myself
and I done decided its BAD NEWS.

In her participatory action research with Aboriginal grandmothers, Geraldine Dickson (2000: 194) not only analyses and writes up her research findings in a conventional way (presenting themes emerging from the data), but also uses poetry to represent the voices of these marginalised grandmothers. Dickson contends that 'the poetry is mine, reflecting my musings on what I heard in the grandmothers' words and actions and what I imagined might be in their minds and thoughts but may have been left unsaid' (pp. 194–195). The following example is from Dickson's findings. When the grandmothers spoke of their well-being, self-esteem and self-respect, one woman told Dickson:

I feel good now. It seems like my health … [has] improved because that helps you when you go out and you're among … older women. You forget about … yourself. It's just like it's a new me, a new person. That's the way I feel.

It's just helped me a lot, you know. (p. 198)

In her writing, Dickson represents this narrative with the following poem:

I Feel Good Now
It doesn't take much –
A little attention and caring.
kind words, warm clasp.
That was enough for
reserve to drop
a face to open.
a smile to break.
A glow spreads on one to all.

The poem succinctly reflects the true troubled feeling of this grandmother and at the same time it is more interesting and fascinating. Dickson strongly believes that when working with people who have been oppressed and silenced for too long, attention to what is not said is essential (p. 212). Therefore, 'other opportunities need to be created that will give further voice to what is not readily expressed'. Ivan Brady (2000: 956) also suggests that by representing people's expression through poetry, researchers 'attempt to say things that might not be said as effectively or at all any other way'. And this is consistent with qualitative researchers' attempts to 'discover and examine critically all the ways a subject (including social and cultural relationships) can be represented'. In Dickson's work, poetry representation is strongly advocated.

In a PAR men's health group of Aboriginal men in northern Queensland carried out by Komla Tsey and colleagues (2002: 283), a poem entitled 'True

Friends Indeed' was written by one of the researchers as a way to capture the sentiments of the men's group leadership.

My Yabba in your times of need
We the Men's Group, are your true friends indeed.
Our aim is to heal the Inner Man,
For the sake of our family and our community
We need to make a positive stand.
In our mind, we can reverse the ripple effect of despair,
...
Cause healing is by word of mouth.
We once were peaceful warriors roaming happy and
free, we mu Gurriny Yealamucka Health Strategy Plan
to revert back to this way,
For the whole damn world to see.
...
The success of the group is testament to the power of the will,
To be part of this group is a privilege and honor,
But deep down in my heart it's a thrill.
We emphasise being a Role Model to our family and community,
Essence of our daily lives is therefore,
We as one must truly live in unity.

Having presented the ways that cross-cultural researchers may write differently, I wish to provide some warnings to readers here. This form of writing may not be considered as sociological writing (Marvasti 2004: 129, 2008). Your work may be labelled as 'sloppy sociology' (Letherby 2000: 107) or 'bad writing' (Marvasti 2008: 612). Also, how do we write up rich information for academic and professional journals with severe space limits, such as in health and medical journals? What I have proposed above may make it difficult for you to publish your work.

However, it is encouraging to see that there are many prestigious qualitative journals, which are more open-minded, and which accept academic papers written in the new form and allow for greater length. These include *Qualitative Inquiry, Symbolic Interaction, Sociological Quarterly, Qualitative Sociology, Text and Performance Quarterly, Journal of Contemporary Ethnography, International Journal of Social Research Methodology* and *Qualitative Research*. These journals regularly publish alternative forms of representation 'not because it is trendy to do so' but because 'social scientists have far too long ignored these important forms of [research] representation and interpretation' (Norman Denzin, personal communication, cited in

Brady 2000: 962). I suggest that if you are concerned about your academic future, you may write your work in a conventional academic form. But for many cross-cultural researchers, you must try out different ways of writing because it is a powerful means of expanding your interpretive skills, raising your consciousness and bringing a fresh and more interesting perspective to your research. This way, you may bring to the fore the many silent voices of your research participants, the Others, for whom you try to provide a better world in your research agenda.

I have been doing this in my own writings. My first book on cross-cultural childbirth, which was targeted at health professionals in birthing services, began with the women's stories, followed by themes emerging from the stories and some practical suggestions and resources (see Liamputtong Rice 1993). Comments that I received from readers about this book were that it was like reading a novel. The book was entertaining, yet the stories were serious enough to make the readers think about caring for women from different ethnic backgrounds. Of course, the book may be seen by some academic colleagues as a piece of 'sloppy sociology/anthropology' work as I did not discuss, nor propose, any theoretical discovery. But the book has been adopted widely in Australian hospitals and community health centres. Even now, I still hear good comments from people about its usefulness.

Ownership of research findings and writing sensitively

Often, individuals and communities involved in the research project would question the ownership of research findings when the project is completed (Trimble & Fisher 2006a). People wish to know if they or their communities have the final say on how the data will be used, and how it will be written up. Joseph Trimble and Celia Fisher say that people from minority groups who take part in research have good reason to become suspicious about the way their stories and lived experiences are written and disseminated, as often the findings are 'twisted and distorted to the extent that the "true and authentic" information is obscured through interpretation' (p. xxi; see also Norton & Manson 1996; see also Chapter 1 in this volume). The way that ethnic minority and cultural groups are represented in research findings has been of great concern among community representatives and research scholars in cross-cultural research. All too often, 'problems associated with the "mistranslation" of research outcomes' abound. This is particularly so in positivist science that utilises measurements to categorise individuals into groups such as ethnic and racial identification, socioeconomic status and levels of acculturation. This categorisation situates the participants within 'artificially constructed subgroups ostensibly for purposes of analysis and teasing out of differences among groupings'. See also my discussions regarding this issue in Chapter 1.

I wish to present an interesting example regarding how researchers may be able to write their data up. In her research with young Indo-Canadians, Priya Mani (2006) tells us that the participants questioned her about the ownership of the research. Also, a common question that the young Indo-Canadian people asked was how the results of their interviews would be written and disseminated. Through their academic work, these young people have read many qualitative research findings. They did not wish her to use very specific quotes from their interviews to illustrate emergent themes because they were afraid that their sense of privacy might be compromised. They felt that others in their ethnic community would be able to identify them because of the familiarity with the speech patterns that they have established over time.

The following is what Mani (2006: 8) did in order to protect the participants in her study:

I distilled the representations of the participants' thoughts and ideas to protect their confidentiality, and their personal requests to not use numerous specific quotes to represent their experiences were respected ... Instead, I distilled participants' statements. The process of distilling the data into flow charts and then writing a depiction of the flow chart maintained consistency of the findings and prevented identification of an individual.

But Mani also admits that it limited the way she could portray the richness and contextual nature of their experiences (p. 8). Because she could not include many specific quotes, it became difficult for her to portray the meanings and contexts of what was said in the interviews. Eventually, after some negotiations, she and the participants agreed that she could write some generalised quotes which were used by most of the young women and men to illustrate important ideas. Mani had to 'make a mental shift from scholarly feminist research, which would encourage participants to have a "voice"', and accept that the young people in her study 'wanted to be heard but not seen' (p. 12). She writes:

I made choices that allowed me to represent the findings in a manner that was congruent with how the participants wished to be portrayed and represented their worldview of what 'research' is to them. It became important for me to integrate the core values of the participants into consideration of the research design and to find creative solutions to address struggles that the participants and researcher experienced. (p. 12)

Sharing knowledge

Sharing the findings with the participants and their communities, suggest Phyllis Eide and Carol Allen (2005: 8), allows cross-cultural researchers to 'complete the research process in a way that can continue to build trust and knowledge'. This is particularly crucial for cultural groups who have been asked to take part in the research projects but who never have any opportunity to share the research findings. Worse, they can be misinterpreted by the researchers.

As we have seen, one of the major criticisms of research among indigenous communities is that, all too often, the researchers do not share the results with the communities from which they have collected their information (Mohatt & Thomas 2006; Cram 2009). Linda Tuhiwai Smith (1999) contends that one important task of indigenous projects is 'sharing knowledge'. She means that cross-cultural researchers must disseminate their research results to wider audiences, but particularly to the community in which the researchers have carried out their inquiries. It is a moral obligation for all researchers that we disseminate our findings so that the knowledge we have gained can be used to benefit the participants and their communities (Mutu 1998; Cram 2009). Margaret Mutu (1998: 51) says it clearly:

Shared knowledge ... is one of the key tools for empowering the people and providing controls to prevent the misuse and abuse of power ... [T]he results of research are of little use to the people if they are not then made available to form part of the knowledge base of the people and to help them make decisions.

In her research with native Hawaiians, Julie Kaomea (2004: 32) tells us that she immediately took her research findings back to the Hawaiian community. Through formal and informal presentations, she shared the knowledge that she had gained from her research with different Hawaiian groups, including university students, immersion classroom teachers, native elders and sovereignty activists. Through the process of sharing knowledge, she learned to present her research in a culturally appropriate way and in a language suitable for a specific group or audience.

Kaomea uses the term 'sharing knowledge' deliberately (pp. 32–33). She does not wish only to share 'the surface "information" or the "in a nutshell" findings' of her research, but also to diligently share 'the critical theories and analyses' which would inform her study with the Hawaiian community. She writes:

In doing so, I aimed to demystify the way in which academic knowledge is constructed and represented. Through this process, I was able to introduce members of the Hawaiian community who may have had little formal schooling to a wider world, a world that includes other indigenous people who have experienced similar oppression, share in similar struggles, and voice their concerns in similar ways.

Sharing of knowledge has been done in different ways. Janine Jurkowski and Amy Paul-Ward (2007: 363), in their photovoice project with Latinos with intellectual disabilities, made a scrapbook of photos which was accompanied by matched verbatim quotes from the interviews with pictures of each of the participants. The Latino participants proudly showed their scrapbook around the agency where they receive care, and talked about their photographs with friends and staff. In addition to a formal report, Jurkowski and Paul-Ward wrote a second report of their results which was appropriate for people with low literacy so that their participants were able to share the research findings.

In the People Awakening (PA) project with Alaskan Natives, Gerald Mohatt and Lisa Thomas (2006: 107–108) prepared a CD-ROM and a booklet of excerpts of the life histories to send to each participant and each tribal corporation. The booklet has short excerpts of the life histories, and each one that was included was approved by the participant. Mohatt and Thomas wanted to develop a final report in a form that went beyond a written format and which would provide a tool for the individuals in Alaskan Native communities.

Dissemination of research findings

It is also a moral obligation for cross-cultural researchers to disseminate their findings to wider audiences. This includes not only disseminating our research findings to the participants, but also to others who have the authority or power to change policies and practices. Only then can our findings be used in more meaningful ways, such as in the development of culturally sensitive policies or interventions for our research participants. This way, our participants will receive something in return for taking part in our research. I am a strong believer in this moral task.

According to Gerald Mohatt and Lisa Thomas (2006: 107), cross-cultural researchers have responsibility for the dissemination of their research results not just in peer reviewed journals but also in other channels that their participants will be able to access and use. Often, the accepted route of dissemination for most academic research is through peer reviewed journals. However, we will find that this route excludes our research participants as most do not have access to journals. We need to find ways that they will have access to their valuable contributions.

The People Awakening project that Gerald Mohatt and Lisa Thomas (2006: 107) carried out was 'ethically bound' to their participants in that they had to share their data and findings with the Alaskan Native community. This belief was shared and committed to by the research team. Information resulting from the project was disseminated with the Alaskan Native communities across the state in various ways. For example, they published an annual newsletter that contained information about the progress of the project, the research team, the non-identifying participants and emerging trends from the data. These newsletters were sent to individuals within the Native community and service providers across the state of Alaska. A number of the research team members gave oral presentations to the communities, Native organisations, health agencies and corporations.

In my own research with ethnic communities in Australia, I not only write up my results and publish in refereed journals, but also write up reports and send them out to health providers. For example, when I disseminated the findings of my work regarding childbirth issues among Southeast Asian immigrant women, I organised seminars within the community and orally presented the findings to community members and policy makers. I invited many of the women in the project to attend. Lunch and refreshments were prepared for those who came. With one of the projects, I launched the final report, which was written as a novel-like book, and I invited many of the women who had told me their stories. Many of them turned up. It was a very nice event. On the day, the women brought their children along. The children were running everywhere in the garden setting where I chose to have the launch. I invited a local member of the Victorian Government to launch the booklet, and this made my participants feel proud of their contributions to my book.

Disseminating differently

Sharing is a responsibility of research. The technical term for this is the dissemination of results, usually very boring to non-researchers, very technical and very cold. For indigenous researchers sharing is about demystifying knowledge and information and speaking in plain terms to the community (Smith 1999: 161).

As with the writing up of research findings, there are innovative means cross-cultural researchers may adopt to disseminate their findings. As Linda Tuhiwai Smith says above, traditional disseminating methods may not suit our research participants and they are not too exciting. Here, I shall present several means that we can use.

Theatrical performance

Performance, Stacey Holman Jones (2008: 225) suggests, 'has long been a site and means for negotiating social, cultural, and political dialogue'. Theatrical performance is based on the 'principles and traditions of Forum Theatre', which was developed by Augusto Boal (1979, 2000), what he called *Teatro do Oprimido* (Theatre of the Oppressed). It is grounded in the liberation impulses of Paulo Freire (1972). The theatre was used by Boal to 'blur the line' between the off-stage audience and the on-stage actors. The Theatre of the Oppressed, George Kamberelis and Greg Dimitriadis (2008: 380) contend, is 'a public, improvisational, and highly interactive form of theatre with strong transformative and pedagogical impulses and potential'.

Theatrical performance is often used as a form of 'political analysis, catharsis, and group healing by indigenous peoples who have experienced ethnic, cultural, and social displacement; grinding poverty; and horrendous acts of violence' (Tedlock 2008: 155). In his recent writing on theatrical performance, Norman Denzin (2008: 458) refers to it as performance ethnography and suggests that theatrical performance can be conceived as 'a pedagogy of freedom'. As he puts it, 'performance texts provide the grounds for liberation practice by opening up concrete situations that are being transformed through acts of resistance'. As such, the theatrical performance 'advances the causes of liberation'.

Performances shun written words but show research findings as stage performances (Saldaña 2005). Theatrical performance, to Joni Jones (2002), is 'a form of cultural exchange', and to Jim Mienczakowsi (1997, 2001, 2008), Linda Park-Fuller (2003), Barbara Tedlock (2008) and Johnny Saldaña (2005), it is a theatre form which promotes emancipation. In theatrical performance, Bryant Alexander (2008: 76) suggests, theatre is used to 'illuminate cultural politics and to instill understanding with the potential to invoke change and have a positive effect on the lived conditions of self and others'.

The following example, *Performing Street Vendors*, provides a remarkable example of theatrical performance taken from Alexander's work (pp. 78–79). It is an example that, I believe, vividly shows audiences the many difficulties faced by migrant street vendors who are extremely marginalised in US society.

A group of students (three men and two women) perform a play focusing on the lived experiences of migrant roadside vendors. In the Los Angeles area, there are many immigrant Mexican street vendors, both women and men, who hang around the entrances and exits of major interstates and highways, trying to sell anything they can, such as bagged oranges, cherries, peanuts, flowers, handmade cultural artefacts and clothing.

The performance of these students brings the voices of these marginalised street vendors into a public place. Alexander tells us that the student performance 'serves as product and process, a performative representation of their knowing, a starting point of their understanding, and a method of engaging others in the issues that undergird cultural experience' (pp. 78–79). This piece of theatrical performance assists in developing 'a critical site, an instance in which embodied experience meets social and theoretical knowing to establish a critical dialogue between researcher-performers and observers'.

Theatrical performance, Alexander asserts, is 'a moral discourse' because it attempts to reduce gaps between what we know and what we do not know. It explores and interprets the lived experiences of research participants, and connects social and geographical distance through 'vivid description, narration, and embodiment'. This helps readers/audiences to see possible realities through the 'visualization of experience'. Alexander's conclusion speaks clearly for the suitability of theatrical performance in the representation of the voices of marginalised and vulnerable people:

[Theatrical performance] can help us to understand the lived cultural experiences of others, but it also can help us to claim the joint culpability of history's legacy. It can then help us to strategize possibility, ways in which collective social action might lead to a more compatible human condition. (p. 106)

There have been other theatrical performances which have been used to disseminate research findings in cross-cultural research. See, for example, Sna Jtz'ibajom (1996) about two brothers who killed their sister because of a dispute over land, Carolyn Nordstrum (1997) about the impact of violence and victimisation on women in Mozambique, and Dudley Cocke and colleagues (2002) about the physical and spiritual care of the Zuni people of Salt Lake. Johnny Saldaña's book, *Ethnodrama: An Anthology of Reality Theatre*

(2005) is an excellent resource for readers who are interested in using drama and theatre as a means for disseminating their research findings.

Applied theatre

Applied theatre has been used as a means of disseminating research findings back to research participants and audiences. According to Maria Stuttaford and colleagues (2006: 32–33), applied theatre refers to theatre which is 'created for a specific need' and is 'motivated by a desire to generate social change' (p. 32). Usually, it is performed in non-theatre spaces. The drive for applied theatre is to invent theatre for individuals who might not be able to attend mainstream theatres or art centres. It is performed in various settings; from formal settings such as schools, hospitals and prisons to informal spaces such as community centres in deprived urban areas and rural communities. Applied theatre, according to Stuttaford *et al.*, 'has no borders and finds its forms in the existing cultural expression of the communities that create it. This offers the means for creating an analysis of the economic, cultural and social conditions, particularly of the very poor' (p. 33).

Applied theatre offers many advantages for disseminating research findings. The live performance of the findings makes the experiences of research participants concrete/vivid/real, rather than abstract (Paget 2008). Applied theatre requires audiences to engage with the research material, and thus 'there is greater potential for transforming social understanding than with textual presentation' (Stuttaford *et al.* 2006: 33). Applied theatre is often 'created through composites as focal points for audience members to discuss their own experiences of topics and is often used to gain access to the "closed world" of the participants' (p. 33). Applied theatre is therefore 'a means to give insight into the lives of those who have become marginalised and disempowered' because of their social structure and health issues (Mienczakowski 1997: 163).

One valuable benefit of applied theatre is its application for seeking the validity of the findings by bringing and presenting the research material to the participants. This will help to prevent any bias which may occur in the interpretation and representation, and enhance the credibility of the findings. It is also a gesture from the researchers that shows to the participants that their contribution is valued (Stuttaford *et al.* 2006).

As with theoretical performance, applied theatre is based on the traditions of Forum Theatre invented by Augusto Boal (1979, 2000). His interventionist theatre has 'gained international recognition as a theoretical model of revolutionary theatre' (Stuttaford *et al.* 2006: 35). The audiences in Boal's theatre are referred to as 'spect-actors' (Boal 1992: 28). He suggests that:

In Forum Theatre at no time should an idea be imposed. Forum Theatre does not preach, it is not dogmatic, it does not seek to manipulate people. At best, it liberates the spect-actors. At best, it stimulates them. At best, it transforms them into actors. Actor – he or she who acts.

In Forum Theatre, community members make decisions about what they see as important issues. Either individuals from the community, or actors from Boal's company, then act to dramatise the issue decided on. A facilitator, called a 'joker', encourages the 'spectators' to play their parts in the action; that is to become 'spect-actors'.

There have been several cross-cultural researchers who selected this type of strategy to disseminate their research findings. For example, Helen Liebling (2004) used applied theatre as a means of reporting her research with Ugandan women about their lived experiences of violence, rape and torture during the civil war in their country. A community-based drama group was set up and presented the research findings at a local community workshop.

In their health research in South Africa, as part of the Southern Africa Stroke Prevention Initiative (SASPI), Maria Stuttaford and colleagues (2006) adopted applied theatre as a venue for them to disseminate their findings to the participants. SASPI aimed to examine the prevalence of strokes in various social contexts. The findings from this multidisciplinary project were complex, and the research team members believed that it was essential for them to communicate the findings back to their participants. They also attempted to check the validity of their data by presenting the research material to the participants.

Hence, they used applied theatre, which they called *Xiseveseve* ('Coming Together to Share'), to disseminate their results, which included the social contexts of health, plural understandings of health, illness and stroke, and health-seeking behaviour. *Xiseveseve* was performed six times to different groups. The size of these groups varied from 30 to 100 people. The performances were carried out on the grass mats depicting a 'stage', under a tree, and used minimal props. For example, different coloured cloth was used to wrap around the shoulders of the performer to depict the change in roles.

In the performance, the actor was the afflicted; a man who fell down while working in his fields and experienced stroke-like symptoms. The researchers invited the audiences to act as the extended family of the actor and to provide their advice regarding their decision about where to take the afflicted man for care. They were also asked to take part in discussions about what might have caused his situation to happen.

The script was flexible so that it could be responsive to the decision made by the extended family. The acts they had planned beforehand did not always happen in the same order. Often, the spect-actors would decide what the afflicted should do. For instance, the joker would turn to the spect-actors and say: 'My family, what shall we do?' The spect-actors would then collectively make a decision.

The spect-actors were asked about the accuracy of the portrayals of family decision making and plural healing that were enacted. They were also consulted about possible future directions for similar research. On reflection, one of the fieldworkers on the project said that:

This was a different form of feedback not like a conventional presentation. People found it interesting and they became part of the story with their views and were involved.

Readers may wish to read the forum theatre performance called *Alor Shondhaney* ('In Quest for Light'), which was performed by troubled youth groups in Bangladesh and was written by Meghna Guhathakurta (2008).

Photovoice exhibition

In Chapter 8, I discussed the use of the photovoice method as a culturally appropriate means of collecting data from participants in cross-cultural research. A common way in which the researchers disseminate their findings from their photovoice projects is to organise exhibitions of the photographs from their research that the participants have taken. According to Janine Jurkowski and Amy Paul-Ward (2007: 363), photovoice allows 'a sense of ownership' among the research participants.

As I have suggested in Chapter 8, the photovoice method was used by Marie Stopes Australia (Atlas & Molloy 2005) in a research project with young indigenous people in rural Victoria, Australia. The photographs were displayed at the Mildura Art Gallery. The opening of the local community exhibition was organised with a traditional welcome from the indigenous communities.

In their project Realidad Latina, Matt Streng and colleagues (2004) carried out a photovoice project to gain insight into the immigration experiences of ten newly arrived Latino young people living in rural North Carolina. The participants organised a community forum and a photovoice exhibition to display and describe their photographs to their parents, local community leaders, teachers, counsellors, school administrators, policymakers and service providers. Forty people attended the exhibition.

Streng *et al.* say that the community forum and photograph exhibition allowed the participants to 'raise awareness of their themes' among others who have influence over their lives and school performances (pp. 411–412). They displayed their photographs, themes and verbatim examples on blackboards. They also gave a slide presentation which described the project, its purpose, the photo-assignments, the emerging themes and their interpretations with examples to the attendees. Streng *et al.* contend that:

> The photograph exhibition was an important component of the project because it increased awareness among attendees of the themes represented in participants' photographs, quotations, and discussions. Attendees of the exhibition expressed thoughts that were directed at making changes within the high school and local community … The findings gave a platform for this marginalized group of Latino adolescents to express their concerns and push for change. Because every aspect of Realidad Latina was driven by photographs, quotations, and themes generated by the participants, their issues and assets could not be disqualified by the principal and other teachers. (p. 413)

Scott Rhodes and colleagues (2008), in their Visions and Voices: HIV in the 21st Century study with PLWHA in the US South, used the photovoice method as their main data collection tool. At the end of the project, they organised a community forum to disseminate their findings to influential advocates. The community forum gave the participants an opportunity to tell influential advocates about important issues which have impacted on their lives and well-being. These influential advocates include local community members and leaders and policy makers.

North Carolina has a strong arts community. It was decided by the photovoice participants and the forum attendees that a gallery exhibition should be organised to raise awareness of HIV/AIDS in the community. The research team then created a portable gallery exhibition of photovoice photographs which were framed with corresponding quotations. The gallery was opened on World AIDS Day 2004 (1 December) at a local art gallery. After its opening, four newspapers interviewed some of the participants and published stories which were shown in the exhibition. Two news segments on the study were broadcast by a local television station. It was shown during the early evening news time and included one of the participants whose photographs were shown at the exhibition. Rhodes *et al.* tell us that:

Unlike most other research methodologies, photovoice also promoted immediate action through the presentation of findings and facilitated discussion at the community forum. The community forum was an invaluable element of photovoice because participants not only desired their voices to be heard but, based on the findings, wanted collective action to be taken. (p. 167)

Based on the work of my honours student, Alice Wilkin, we used the photovoice method to work with female health workers who were from the Australian indigenous communities in Melbourne (Wilkin & Liamputtong 2009). We worked with six women on this project. The women took photographs which depicted the realities of their private and working lives. We originally planned to have the photographs displayed at the La Trobe University Art Gallery in late 2008 and we intended to invite influential people within the university and those from indigenous communities. However, due to many unforeseen reasons, we had to abandon this plan. We then decided that we would use a seminar programme within the university as a venue for us to disseminate our findings. At the time of writing, we are making concrete plans which we believe will work well. We will invite the participants and others who play important roles in the health and welfare of the indigenous people. We will also invite many students and staff within our university. We plan to place the details of our seminar on the university's weekly news and on the school's website. We will send an email to many people whom we believe would be interested in our work. We will also place an advertisement for our seminar at different indigenous health and welfare centres, community health centres and hospitals around Melbourne. On the day, we plan to display the photographs as taken by the women in the seminar room, and present our work using a PowerPoint presentation. We will also prepare indigenous tucker (food) instead of sandwiches on the day so that the atmosphere of the day will merge with the theme of the day. We hope that through our dissemination attempts, important information from our research findings will reach many people. We will also ensure that the presentation will provide the women with empowerment, as their photographs and their stories will be shared by others who have impacted on their private and working lives.

Tutorial activities

(1) By now, you have carried out your research using one of the methods discussed in this book. You wish to write it up in a way that your research participants can understand and feel proud of their contribution. How would you go about this? Discuss in detail the writing format and some salient issues that you might confront.

(2) You know that you must disseminate your research findings to a wider audience. You also want to make sure that the information you present will have a good impact on that audience. What would be your disseminating strategies? Provide at least two strategies.

Chapter summary

The interpretive practice of making sense of one's findings is both artistic and political ... There is no single interpretive truth ... there are multiple interpretive communities, each with its own criteria for evaluating interpretations. (Denzin & Lincoln 2008: 35)

In this chapter, I have discussed ways that cross-cultural researchers can write up their findings to represent their participants in a way which will not harm them, and the language issue when we report our findings. I have offered some different ways for researchers to consider. In cross-cultural research, there is a question about who owns the research findings. Hence, sharing new knowledge with the research participants is an essential aspect that cross-cultural researchers must consider. A crucial aspect of any piece of research is the dissemination of research findings. I have argued that it is our moral obligation and responsibility that the data we have collected from our participants must be disseminated as widely as possible. It is only through dissemination that the findings may be used to give some positive outcomes to our participants. I have suggested that we need to bring the results back to our participants as well as presenting them to influential people. Innovative means of disseminating research findings have also formed part of this chapter.

SUGGESTED READING

Alexander, B. K. (2008). Performance ethnography: The reenacting and inciting of culture. In N. K. Denzin, and Y. S. Lincoln (Eds.), *Strategies of qualitative inquiry*, 3rd edition (pp. 75–118). Thousand Oaks, CA: Sage Publications.

Diversi, M. (1998). Glimpses of street life: Representing lived experience through short stories. *Qualitative Inquiry* **4**(2), 131–147.

(2008). Young and strapped in America: Learning through a short story about a Latino youth finding meaning in Tupac's rap. In P. Liamputtong & J. Rumbold (Eds.), *Knowing differently: Arts-based and collaborative research methods* (pp. 67–80). New York: Nova Science Publishers.

Guhathakurta, M. (2008). Theatre in participatory action research: Experiences from Bangladesh. In P. Reason & H. Bradbury (Eds.), *The Sage handbook of action research: Participative inquiry and practice,* 2nd edition (pp. 510–521). London: Sage Publications.

Kooken, W. C., Haase, J. E., & Russell, K. M. (2007). 'I've been through something': Poetic explorations of African American women's cancer survivorship. *Western Journal of Nursing Research* **29**(7), 896–919.

Lather, P., & Smithies, C. (1997). *Troubling the angels: Women living with HIV/AIDS.* Boulder, CO: Westview.

Saldaña, J. (Ed.) (2005). *Ethnodrama: An anthology of reality theatre.* Walnut Creek, CA: AltaMira Press.

Stuttaford, M., Bryanston, C., Hundt, G. L., Connor, M., Thorogood, M., & Tollman, S. (2006). Use of applied theatre in health research dissemination and data validation: A pilot study from South Africa. *Health: An Interdisciplinary Journal for the Social Study of Health, Illness and Medicine* **10**(1), 31–45.

Vannini, A., & Gladue, C. (2009). Moccasin on one foot, high heel on the other: Life story reflections of Coreen Gladue. *Qualitative Inquiry* **15**(4), 675–720.

In closing ...

Ignorance is the oppressor
Knowledge is the liberator
Know your limitations
Know your vision
To be the master of your destiny.

(Walsh-Tapiata 2003: 72)

There is hope, however timid, on the street corners, a hope in each and everyone of us ... Hope is an ontological need.

(Freire 1992/1999: 8).

So we have now come to the end of this volume. As I have said in the Preface, what I write in this book may not make everyone happy because there is no way that I can cover every angle of performing cross-cultural research in one volume. I have also deliberately excluded specific qualitative methods because I believe that they do not do justice to sensitive cross-cultural research. You can blame me if you like.

Throughout the book, however, I have advocated the performance of cross-cultural research more ethically, sensibly and responsibly. I have pointed to many challenges that cross-cultural researchers may have to deal with in their research. I have suggested culturally sensitive and appropriate research methods that would work well with cultural groups. I have offered many thought-provoking angles which I am sure will be of value to many new and experienced researchers who wish to perform cross-cultural research. If you have stayed with me throughout the book, I am sure that you will be able to perform your cross-cultural research responsibly and successfully. This is your reward.

Pierre Bourdieu (1977) tells us that, as researchers, we need to stand back and look closely at the relationships of our methodology and the data we collect and represent because this will allow us to undertake good research which will be beneficial to those we work with in our research endeavours.

If you follow this text, from the first chapter to the end, you will be able to see a close relationship between the methodologies, the practices and the end results. You will see the reasons for my advocating qualitative inquiry in this book. You will see the theoretical frameworks which link with the qualitative methods that I have included in the volume. You will see that the theories and methods that I suggest then dictate the processes that cross-cultural researchers must perform in order to ensure that their research is ethically, sensitively and responsibly undertaken. And, based on the advocated theories and methods, you will see what we must do to represent the many silent voices of our participants in our research projects. I hope that you will be able to adopt the processes that I have outlined in this book to your work.

One positive feedback which I received from reviewers was that the book makes use of widely diverse cultural examples. Throughout the volume, I have deliberately referred to the excellent work of many cross-cultural researchers who have paved the way for us in different social and cultural settings. I strongly believe that, through the experiences of earlier cross-cultural researchers, we may learn about how research can be done ethically, sensibly and responsibly. I hope that my discussions in this book will be a learning experience for all novice and even experienced researchers who would like to embark on cross-cultural research. Good luck with your project, too. Once you have carried out your cross-cultural research, you must write. Your writing will then become a learning experience that future cross-cultural researchers may follow.

Cross-cultural research will continue to be at the forefront of debate among qualitative researchers. Although more social science researchers have started to work in collaboration with cultural groups, including ethnic minorities and indigenous peoples, I contend that there is much more to be done when it comes to performing research within a cross-cultural context. As I suggested in Chapter 1, too much damage has been done to local, native peoples by researchers. It is time for researchers to perform their research in a way that they will not repeat the history of treating local people badly. I believe cross-cultural qualitative researchers can take a lead in this, and I hope that, for you and me, our paths will cross in our cross-cultural research in the future. I would like to close this book with the beautiful writing of James Banks (1998: 4):

I now believe that the biographical journeys of researchers greatly influence their values, their research questions, and the knowledge they construct. The knowledge they construct mirrors their life experiences and their values.

References

Abel, S., Park, J., Tipene-Leach, D., Finau, S., & Lennan, M. (2001). Infant care practices in New Zealand: A cross-cultural qualitative study. *Social Science & Medicine* **53**, 1135–1148.

Abu-Lughod, L. (1988). Fieldwork of a dutiful daughter. In S. Altorki & C. F. El-Solh (Eds.), *Arab women in the field: Studying your own society* (pp. 139–161). Syracuse, NY: Syracuse University Press.

Adams, V., Miller, S., Craig, S., Sonam, Nyima, Droyoung, Le, P. V., & Varner, M. (2007). Informed consent in cross-cultural perspective: Clinical research in the Tibetan Autonomous Region, PRC. *Culture, Medicine & Psychiatry* **31**, 445–472.

Adamson, J., & Donovan, J. L. (2002). Research in black and white. *Qualitative Health Research* **12**(6), 816–825.

Adler, S. M. (2004). Multiple layers of a researcher's identity: Uncovering Asian American voices. In K. Mutua & B. B. Swadener (Eds.), Decolonizing research in cross-cultural contexts: Critical personal narratives (pp. 107–121). Albany: State University of New York (SUNY) Press.

Ahmed, F., Shik, A., Vanza, R., Cheung, A., George, U., & Stewart, D. E. (2004). Voices of South Asian women: Immigration and mental health. *Women & Health* **40**(4), 113–130.

Al-Ali, N. S. (2007). *Iraqi women: Untold stories from 1948 to the present*. London: Zed Books.

Alcoff, L. (1991). The problem of speaking for others. *Cultural Critique* **20**, 5–32.

Alegria, M., Vila, D., Woo, M., Canino, G., Takeuchi, D., Vera, M., Feb, V., Guarnaccia, P., Aguilar-Gaxiola, S., & Shrout, P. (2004). Cultural relevance and equivalence in the NLSS instrument: Integrating etic and emic in the development of cross-cultural measures for a psychiatric epidemiology and services study of Latinos. *International Journal of Methods in Psychiatric Research* **13**(4), 270–288.

Alexander, B. K. (2000). Skin flint (or the garbage man's kid): A generative autobiographical performance based on Tami Spry's Tattoo stories. *Text and Performance Quarterly* **20**(1), 97–114.

(2008). Performance ethnography: The reenacting and inciting of culture. In N. K. Denzin, and Y. S. Lincoln (Eds.), *Strategies of qualitative inquiry*, 3rd edition (pp. 75–118). Thousand Oaks, CA: Sage Publications.

Al-Makhamreh, S. S., & Lewando-Hundt, G. (2008). Researching 'at home' as an insider/outsider. *Qualitative Social Work* **7**(1), 9–23.

Anae, M. (1998). Fofoa-I-voa-'ese: The identity of NZ-born Samoans. Unpublished PhD thesis, University of Auckland, Auckland, New Zealand.

Andersen, M. (1993). Studying across difference: Race, class, and gender in qualitative research. In J. H. Stanfield II & R. M. Dennis (Eds.), *Race and ethnicity in research methods* (pp. 39–52). Newbury Park, CA: Sage Publications.

Angell, M. (1997). Editorial: The ethics of clinical research in the third world. *New England Journal of Medicine* **337**(12), 847–850.

Anzaldua, G. (1983). Speaking tongues: A letter to 3rd World women writers. In C. Moraga & G. Anzaldua (Eds.), *This bridge called my back: Writings by radical women of color* (pp. 165–174). New York: Kitchen Table: Women of Color Press.

Armstrong, E. (2004). A mental and moral feast: Reading, writing, and sentimentality in Black Philadelphia. *Journal of Women's History* **16**, 78–102.

Ash, A., & Rampersad, A. (1993). *Days of grace: A memoir*. New York: Ballantine Books.

Aspin, C., & Hutchings, J. (2007). Reclaiming the past to inform the future: Contemporary views of Maori sexuality. *Culture, Health & Sexuality* **9**(4), 415–427.

Atkinson, R. (2002). The life story interview. In J. F. Gubrium & J. A. Holstein (Eds.), *Handbook of interview research: Context and method* (pp. 121–140). Thousand Oaks, CA: Sage Publications.

Atlas, B., & Molloy, R. (2005). *Photo Voice*. Paper presented at the Melbourne Interest Group in International Health, The University of Melbourne, Melbourne, 9 August.

Auerbach, S. (2002). 'Why do they give the good classes to some and not to others': Latino parent narratives of struggles in a college access program. *Teachers College Record* **104**, 1369–1392.

Bailey, A. (2008). Let's tell you a story: Use of vignettes in focus group discussions on HIV/AIDS among migrant and mobile men in Goa, India. In P. Liamputtong (Ed.), *Doing cross-cultural research: Ethical and methodological perspectives* (pp. 253–264). Dordrecht: Springer.

Baldacchino, D. R., Bowman, G. S., & Buhagiar, A. (2002). Reliability testing of the hospital anxiety and depression (HAD) scale in the English, Maltese and back-translation versions. *International Journal of Nursing Studies* **39**(2), 207–214.

Banks, J. (1998). The lives and values of researchers: Implications for educating citizens in a multicultural society. *Educational Researcher* **27**(7), 4–17.

Banks-Wallace, J. (2000). Womanist ways of knowing: Theoretical considerations for research with African American women. *Advances in Nursing Science* **22**(3), 33–45.

   (2002). Talk that talk: Storytelling and analysis rooted in African American oral tradition. *Qualitative Health Research* **12**(3), 410–426.

Barata, P. C., Gucciardi, E., Ahmad, F., & Stewart, D. E. (2006). Cross-cultural perspectives on research participation and informed consent. *Social Science & Medicine* **62**(2), 479–490.

Barbour, R. (2007). *Doing focus groups*. London: Sage Publications.

Barnes, H. M. (2000). Kaupapa Maori: Explaining the ordinary. *Pacific Health Dialogue* **7**, 13–16.

Barrett, M. (1992). Words and things: Materialism and method. In M. Barrett & A. Phillips (Eds.), *Destabilizing theory: Contemporary feminist debates* (pp. 201–219). Cambridge: Polity Press.

Bartlett, J. G., Iwasaki, Y., Gottlieb, B., Hall, D., & Mannell, R. (2007). Framework for Aboriginal-guided decolonizing research involving Métis and First Nations persons with diabetes. *Social Science & Medicine* **65**(11), 2371–2382.

Battiste, M. (2000). *Reclaiming indigenous voice and vision.* Vancouver, BC: University of British Columbia Press.

(2008). Research ethics for protecting indigenous knowledge and heritage. In N. K. Denzin, Y. S. Lincoln, & L. T. Smith (Eds.), *Handbook of critical and indigenous methodologies* (pp. 497–509). Thousand Oaks, CA: Sage Publications.

Baylis, F., Downie, J., & Sherwin, S. (1998). Reframing research involving humans. In S. Sherwin (Ed.), *The politics of women's health* (pp. 234–260). Philadelphia: Temple University Press.

Beauchamp, T. L., Jennings, B., Kinney, E. D., & Levine, R. J. (2002). Pharmaceutical research involving the homeless. *Journal of Medicine and Philosophy* **27**(5), 547–564.

Beauvais, F. (2006) Changing models of research ethics in prevention research within ethnic communities. In J. E. Trimble & C. B. Fisher (Eds.), *The handbook of ethical research with ethnocultural populations and communities* (pp. 241–255). Thousand Oaks, CA: Sage Publications.

Beck. C. T., Bernal, H., & Froman, R. D. (2003). Methods to document semantic equivalence of a translated scale. *Research in Nursing & Health* **26**, 64–73.

Behar, R. (1993). *Translating woman: Crossing the border with Esperanza's story.* Boston: Beacon Press.

Benatar, S. R., & Singer, P. A. (2000). A new look at international research ethics. *British Medical Journal* **321** (30 September), 824–826.

Bender, D. E., Harbour, C., Thorp, J., & Morris, P. (2001). 'Tell me what you mean by "si"': Perceptions of quality of prenatal care among immigrant Latina women. *Qualitative Health Research* **11**(6), 780–794.

Benitez, O., Devaus, D., & Dausset, J. (2002). Audiovisual documentation of oral consent: A new method of informed consent for illiterate populations. *The Lancet* **359**(9315), 1406–1407.

Benmayor, R. (1991). Testimony, action research, and empowerment: Puerto Rican women and popular education. In S. B. Gluck & D. Patai (Eds.), *Women's words: The feminist practice of oral history* (pp. 159–174). New York: Routledge.

Beoku-Betts, J. (1994). When black is not enough: Doing field research among Gullah women. *NWSA Journal* **6**(3), 413–433.

Berg, J. A. (1999). Gaining access to underresearched populations in women's health research. *Health Care for Women International* **20**, 237–243.

Bernard, H. R. (1995). *Research methods in anthropology: Qualitative and quantitative approaches*, 2nd edition. Walnut Creek, CA: Altamira Press.

Berthelette, G., Raftis, Y., & Henderson, G. (2001). A culturally appropriate format for a focus group? *Aboriginal Nurse* **16**, 17–18.

Best, A. L. (2003). Doing race in the context of feminist interviewing: Constructing whiteness through talk. *Qualitative Inquiry* **9**(6), 895–914.

Best, D. L. (2001). Gender concepts: Convergence in cross-cultural research and methodologies. *Cross Cultural Research* **35**(1), 23–43.

Beverley, J. (2008). Testimonio, subalternity, and narrative authority. In N. K. Denzin & Y. S. Lincoln (Eds.), *Strategies of qualitative research*, 3rd edition (pp. 257–270). Thousand Oaks, CA: Sage Publications.

Beyrer, C., & Kass, N. E. (2002). Human rights, politics and reviews of research ethics. *Lancet* **359**(9328), 246–251.

Bhachu, P. (2003). *Dangerous designs: Asian women fashion the diaspora economies.* London: Routledge.

Bhopal, K. (1997). *Gender, 'race' and patriarchy: A study of South Asian women.* Aldershot: Ashgate.

(2001). Researching South Asian women: Issues of sameness and difference in the research process. *Journal of Gender Studies* **10**(3), 279–286.

Billson, J. M. (2006). *Conducting focus group research across cultures: Consistency and comparability.* UK: ESRC Research Group on Wellbeing in Developing Countries.

Birbili, M. (2000). Translating from one language to another. *Social Research Update* **31**. www.soc.surrey.ac.uk/sru/SRU31.html Accessed: 6 December 2005.

Birman, D. (2006) Ethical issues in research with immigrants and refugees. In J. E. Trimble & C. B. Fisher (Eds.), *The handbook of ethical research with ethnocultural populations & communities* (pp. 155–177). Thousand Oaks, CA: Sage Publications.

Bishop, R. (1996). *Collaborative research stories.* Palmerston North, NZ: Dunmore Press.

(2008). Freeing ourselves from neocolonial domination in research: A kaupapa Māori approach to creating knowledge. In N. K. Denzin & Y. S. Lincoln (Eds.), *The landscape of qualitative research*, 3rd edition (pp. 145–183). Thousand Oaks, CA: Sage Publications.

Bishop, R., Berryman, M., & Richardson, C. (2003). *Te kotahitanga: The experiences of year 9 and 10 Māori students in mainstream classrooms.* Wellington, NZ: Ministry of Education.

Bissell, S., Manderson, L., & Allotey, P. (2000). In focus: Film, focus groups, and working children in Bangladesh. *Visual Anthropology* **13**(2), 169–184.

Boal, A. (1979). *Theatre of the oppressed.* London: Pluto Press.

(1992). *Games for actors and non-actors*, London: Routledge.

(2000). *Theatre of the oppressed*, London: Pluto Press.

Booth, S., (1999). Researching health and homelessness: Methodological challenges for researchers working with a vulnerable, hard-to-reach, transient population. *Australian Journal of Primary Health* **5**(3), 76–81.

Borkan, J. M., Morad, M., & Shvarts, S. (2000). Universal health care? The views of Negev Bedouin Arabs on health services. *Health Policy and Planning* **15**(2), 207–216.

Bornat, J. (2004). Oral history. In C. Seale, G. Gobo, J. F. Gubrium, & D. Silverman (Eds.), *Qualitative research practice* (pp. 34–47). London: Sage Publications.

Bourdieu, P . (1977). *Outline of a theory of practice.* Cambridge: Cambridge University Press.

Bourgois, P. (1995). *In search of respect: Selling crack in El Barrio.* Cambridge: Cambridge University Press.

Bowler, I. (1997). Problems with interviewing: Experiences with service providers. In G. Miller & R. Dingwell (Eds.), *Context and method in qualitative research* (pp. 66–76). London: Sage Publications.

Bradburd, D. (1998). *Being there: The necessity of fieldwork.* Washington DC: Smithsonian Institute Press.

Bradby, H. (2002). Translating culture and language: A research note on multilingual settings. *Sociology of Health & Illness* **24**(6), 842–855.

Bradby, H., Varyani, M., Oglethorpe, R., Raine, W., White, I., & Helen, M. (2007). British Asian families and the use of child and adolescent mental health services: A qualitative study of a hard to reach group. *Social Science & Medicine* **65**(12), 2413–2424.

Brady, I. (2000). Anthropological poetics. In N. K. Denzin & Y. S. Lincoln (Eds.), *Handbook of qualitative research*, 2nd edition (pp. 949–979). Thousand Oaks, CA: Sage Publications.

(2008). Poetics for a planet: Discourse on some problems of being-in-place. In N. K. Denzin & Y. S. Lincoln (Eds.), *Collecting and interpreting qualitative materials*, 3rd edition (pp. 501–564). Thousand Oaks, CA: Sage Publications.

Brah, A. (2002). Difference, diversity, and differentiation. In J. Donald & A. Rattansi (Eds.), *Race, culture, and difference* (pp. 126–145). London: Sage Publications.

Brah, A., & Shaw, S. (1992). *Working choices: South Asian young Muslim women in the labour market.* (Research paper No 91). London: London Department of Employment.

Brant Castellano, M. (2004). Ethics of aboriginal research. *Journal of Aboriginal Health* **1**(1), 98–114.

Brayboy, B. M., & Deyhle, D. (2000). Insider-outsider: Researchers in American Indian communities. *Theory into Practice* **39**(3), 163–169.

Bridges, D. (2001). The ethics of outsider research. *Journal of Philosophy of Education* **35**(3), 371–386.

Brislin, R. W. (1970). Back-translation for cross-cultural research. *Journal of Cross-Cultural Psychology* **1**(3), 186–216.

(1976). Comparative research methodology: Cross-cultural studies. *International Journal of Psychology* **11**, 215–229.

(1986). The wording and translation of research instruments. In W. J. Lonner & J. W. Berry (Eds.), *Field methods in cross-cultural research* (pp. 137–164). Beverly Hills, CA: Sage Publications.

Brockington, D., & Sullivan, S. (2003). Qualitative research. In R. Scheyvens & D. Storey (Eds.), *Development fieldwork: A practical guide* (pp. 57–74). London: Sage Publications.

Brooks, C., Poudrier, J., & Thomas-MacLean, R. (2008). Creating collaborative visions with Aboriginal women: A photovoice project. In P. Liamputtong (Ed.), *Doing cross-cultural research: Ethical and methodological perspectives* (pp. 193–212). Dordrecht: Springer.

Brown, B. A., Long, H. L., Weitz, T. A., & Milliken, N. (2000). Challenges of recruitment: Focus groups with research study recruiters. *Women & Health* **31**(2/3), 153–166.

Brydon, L. (2006). Ethical practices in doing development research. In V. Desai & R. B. Potter (Eds.), *Doing development research* (pp. 25–33). London: Sage Publications.

Brydon-Miller, M. (1993). Breaking down barriers: Accessibility self-advocacy in the disabled community. In P. Park, M. Brydon-Miller, B. Ha, & T. Jackson (Eds.), *Voices of change: Participatory research in the United States and Canada* (pp. 125–143). Westport, CT: Bergin & Garvey.

(2001). Education, research, and action: Theory and methods of participatory action research. In D. L. Tolman & M. Brydon-Miller (Eds.), *From subjects to subjectivities: A handbook of interpretive and participatory methods* (pp. 76–89). New York: New York University Press.

Bryman, A. (2008). *Social research methods*, 3rd edition. Oxford: Oxford University Press.

Bujra, J. (2006). Lost in translation? The use of interpreters in fieldwork. In V. Desai & R. B. Potter (Eds.), *Doing development research* (pp. 172–179). London: Sage Publications.

Bulmer, M., & Solomos, J. (Eds.) (2004). *Researching race and racism.* London: Routledge.

Busch-Rossnagel, N. (2006). First, do no harm: Culturally centered measurement for early intervention. In J. E. Trimble & C. B. Fisher (Eds.), *The handbook of ethical research with ethnocultural populations and communities* (pp. 51–64). Thousand Oaks, CA: Sage Publications.

Buseh, A., Stevens, P. E., McManus, P., Jim, R., Morgan, S., & Millon-Underwood, S. (2006). Challenges and opportunities for HIV prevention and care: Insights from focus groups of HIV-infected African American men. *Journal of the Association of Nurses in AIDS Care* **17**(4), 3–15.

Cameron, D. (2006). What the bloody hell does it mean? Slogan baffles Japan. *The Age*, 28 March, p. 3.

Candida Smith, R. (2002). Analytic strategies for oral history interviews. In J. Gubrium & J. Holstein (Eds.), *Handbook of interviews research: Context & method* (pp. 711–733). Thousand Oaks, CA: Sage Publications.

Carlson, E. D., Engegretson, J., & Chamberlain, R. M. (2006). Photovoice as a social process of critical consciousness. *Qualitative Health Research* **16**(6), 836–852.

Carpenter, C., & Suto, M. (2008). *Qualitative research for occupational and physical therapists: A practical guide*. Oxford: Blackwell Publishing.

Carpenter, V. M., & McMurchy-Pilkington, C. (2008). Cross-cultural researching: Māori and pākehā in te whakapakari. *Qualitative Research* **8**(2), 179–196.

Carter, J. (2004). Research note: Reflections on interviewing across the ethnic divide. *International Journal of Social Research Methodology* **7**(4), 345–353.

Carter, M. (2003). Telling tales out of school: What's the fate of a black story in a white world of white stories? In G. Lopez & L. Parker (Eds.), *Research (im-)positions: interrogating racism in qualitative research methodology*. New York: Peter Lang.

Cassell, J . (2002). Perturbing the system: 'Hard science', 'soft science', and social science, the anxiety of madness and method. *Human Organization* **61**(2), 177–185.

Castleden, H., Garvin, T., & Huu-ay-aht First Nation (2008). Modifying photovoice for community-based participatory indigenous research. *Social Science & Medicine* **66**(6), 1393–1405.

Castro, F. G., Rios, R., & Montoya, H. (2006). Ethical community-based research with Hispanic or Latina(o) populations. In J. E. Trimble & C. B. Fisher (Eds.), *The handbook of ethical research with ethnocultural populations and communities* (pp. 137–153). Thousand Oaks, CA: Sage Publications.

Caufield, C. (2006). Challenges for a North American doing research with traditional indigenous Guatemalan midwives. *International Journal of Qualitative Methodology* **5**(4), Article 4. www.ualberta.ca/~iiqm/backissues/5_4/pdf/caufield.pdf Accessed: 10 January 2007.

Chamberlayne, P., & King, A. (1996). Biographical approaches in comparative work: The 'Culture of Care' Project. In L. Hantrais & S. Mangen (Eds.), *Cross-national research methods in the social sciences* (pp. 95–104). London: Pinter.

Charlton, T. L., Meyers, L. E., & Sharpless, R. (Eds.) (2006). *Handbook of oral history*. Lanham, MD: AltaMira Press.

Chase, S. E. (2008). Narrative inquiry: Multiple lenses, approaches, voices. In N. K. Denzin & Y. S. Lincoln (Eds.), *Collecting and interpreting qualitative materials*, 3rd edition (pp. 57–94). Thousand Oaks, CA: Sage Publications.

Chávez, V., Duran, B., Baker, Q. E., Avila, M. M., & Wallerstein, N. (2008). The dance of race and privilege in CBPR. In M. Minkler & N. Wallestein (Eds.), *Community-based participatory research for health: From process to outcomes*, 2nd edition (pp. 91–105). San Francisco: Jossey-Bass.

Chawla, D. (2007). Subjectivity and the 'native' ethnographer: Researcher eligibility in an ethnographic study of urban Indian women in Hindu arranged marriages. *International Journal of Qualitative Methodology* **5**(4), Article 2. www/ualberta. ca/~iiqm/backissues/5_4/pdf/chawla.pdf Accessed: 2 January 2007.

Chilisa, B. (2009). Indigenous African-centered ethics: Contesting and complementing dominant models. In D. M. Martens & P. E. Ginsberg (Eds.), *The handbook of social research ethics* (pp. 407–425). Thousand Oaks, CA: Sage Publications.

Chin, J. L., Mio, J. S., & Iwamasa, G. Y. (2006). Ethical conduct of research with Asian and Pacific Islander American populations. In J. E. Trimble & C. B. Fisher (Eds.), *The handbook of ethical research with ethnocultural populations and communities* (pp. 67–75). Thousand Oaks, CA: Sage Publications.

Chiu, L.-F., & Knight, D. (1999). How useful are focus groups for obtaining the views of minority groups? In R. Barbour & J. Kitzinger (Eds.), *Developing focus group research: Politics, theory, and practice* (pp. 99–112). London: Sage Publications.

Choi, J-a. (2006) Doing poststructural ethnography in the life history of dropouts in South Korea: Methodological ruminations on subjectivity, positionality, and reflexivity. *International Journal of Qualitative Studies in Education* **19**(4), 435–453.

Chow, R. (1993). *Writing diaspora: Tactics of intervention in contemporary cultural studies.* Bloomington: Indiana University Press.

Chris, J., & Escandon-Dominguez, S. (2003). Identifying and recruiting Mexican-American partners and sustaining community partnerships. *Journal of Transcultural Nursing* **14**(3), 255–271.

Christians, C. G. (2008). Ethics and politics in qualitative research. In N. K. Denzin & Y. S. Lincoln (Eds.), *The landscape of qualitative research,* 3rd edition (pp. 185–220). Thousand Oaks, CA: Sage Publications.

Chung, R. C.-Y., & Bemak, F. (1997). Methodological issues and recommendations on research with at-risk youth across cultures: A case study. *Childhood* **4**(4), 465–475.

Clifford, J., & Marcus, G. (1986). *Writing culture.* Berkeley, CA: University of California Press.

Cocke, D., Porterfield, D., & Wemytewa, E. (2002). *Journeys home: Revealing a Zuni-Appalachia collaboration.* Zuni, NM: Zuni Ashiwi Publishing.

Coffey, A. (2002). Sex in the field: Intimacy and intimidation. In T. Welland & L. Pugsley (Eds.), *Ethical dilemmas in qualitative research* (pp. 57–74). London: Ashgate.

Collins, P. H. (2008). *Black feminist thought: Knowledge, consciousness, and the politics of empowerment.* London: Routledge.

Coloma, R. S. (2008). Border crossing subjectivities and research: Through the prism of feminists of color. *Race Ethnicity and Education* **11**(1), 11–27.

Colucci, E. (2007). 'Focus groups can be fun': The use of activity-oriented questions in focus group discussions. *Qualitative Health Journal* **17**(10), 1422–1433.

   (2008). On the use of focus groups in cross-cultural research. In P. Liamputtong (Ed.), *Doing cross-cultural research: Ethical and methodological perspectives* (pp. 233–252). Dordrecht: Springer.

Connor, E. M., Sperling, R. S., Gelber, R., Kiselev, P., Scott, G., O'Sullivan, M. J., VanDyke, R., Bey, M., Shearer, W., Jacobson, R. L., *et al.* (1994). Reduction of maternal-infant transmission of Human Immunodeficiency Virus Type 1 with zidovudine treatment. *New England Journal of Medicine* **331**(18), 1173–1180.

Conrad, D., & Campbell, G. (2008). Participatory research – An empowering methodology with marginalized populations. In P. Liamputtong & J. Rumbold (Eds.), *Knowing differently: Arts-based and collaborative research methods* (pp. 247–263). New York: Nova Science Publishers.

Corbie-Smith, G., Thomas, S. B., & St. George, D. M. M. (2002). Distrust, race, and research. *Archives of Internal Medicine* **162**, 2458–2463.

Cornwall, A., & Jewkes, R. (1995). What is participatory research? *Social Science & Medicine* **41**(2), 1667–1676.

Corti, L., & Thompson, P. (2004). Secondary analysis of archived data. In C. Seale, G. Gobo, J. F. Gubrium, & D. Silverman (Eds.), *Qualitative research practice* (pp. 327–343). London: Sage Publications.

Cortis, J. D., & Kendrick, K. (2003). Nursing ethics, caring and culture. *Nursing Ethics: An International Journal for Health Care Professionals* **10**(1), 77–88.

Cram, F. (2001). The validity and integrity of Maori research. In M. Tolich (Ed.), *Research ethics in Aotearoa New Zealand* (pp. 35–51). Auckland: Pearson Education.

(2009). Maintaining indigenous voices. In D. M. Martens & P. E. Ginsberg (Eds.), *The handbook of social research ethics* (pp. 308–322). Thousand Oaks, CA: Sage Publications.

Crigger, N. J., Holcomb, L., & Weiss, J. (2001). Fundamentalism, multiculturalism, and problems conducting research with populations in developing nations. *Nursing Ethics* **8**(5), 459–469.

Crowley, J. E. (2007). Friend or foe? Self-expansion, stigmatized groups, and the researcher-participant relationship. *Journal of Contemporary Ethnography* **36**(6): 603–630.

Culhane, D. (2004). Domesticated time and restricted space: University and community women in Downtown Eastside Vancouver. *BC Studies* **140**, 91–107.

Culley, L., Hudson, N., & Rapport, F. (2007). Using focus groups with minority ethnic communities: Researching infertility in British South Asian communities. *Qualitative Health Research* **17**(1), 102–112.

Dalrymple, L., & Preston-Whyte, E. M. (1992). A drama approach to AIDS education: An experiment in 'action research'. *AIDS Bulletin* **1**(1), 9–11.

Darou, W. G., Hum, A., & Kurtness, J. (1993). An investigation of the impact of psychosocial research on a native population. *Professional Psychology: Research and Practice* **24**(3), 325–329.

Davies, B., Larson, J., Contro, N., Reyes-Hailey, C., Ablin, A. R., Chesla, C. A., Sourkes, B., & Cohen, H. (2009). Conducting a qualitative culture study of pediatric palliative care. *Qualitative Health Research* **19**(1), 5–16.

Dawson, L., & Kass, N. E. (2005). Views of US researchers about informed consent in international collaborative research. *Social Science & Medicine* **61**(6), 1211–1222.

dé Ishtar, Z. (2005a). Striving for a common language: A white feminist parallel to indigenous ways of knowing and researching. *Women's Studies International Forum* **28**, 357–368.

(2005b). Living on the ground: The 'culture woman' and the 'missus'. *Women's Studies International Forum* **28**, 369–380.

(2005c). *Holding yawulyu: White culture and black women's law.* North Melbourne: Spinifex Press.

(2008). 'Living on the ground': Research which sustains living culture. In P. Liamputtong (Ed.), *Doing cross-cultural research: Ethical and methodological perspectives* (pp. 161–174). Dordrecht: Springer.

De Zulueta, P. (2001). Randomised placebo-controlled trails and HIV-infected pregnant women in developing countries. Ethical imperialism or unethical exploitation? *Bioethics* **15**(4), 289–311.

Dean, E., Caspar, R., McAninchey, G., Reed, L., & Quiroz, R. (2007). Developing a low-cost technique for parallel cross-cultural instrument development: The question appraisal system (QAS-04). *International Journal of Social Research Methodology* **10**(3), 227–241.

Denzin, N. K. (2003). *Performance ethnography: Critical pedagogy and the politics of culture.* Thousand Oaks, CA: Sage Publications.

(2008). Emancipatory discourses and the ethics and politics of interpretation. In N. K. Denzin & Y. S. Lincoln (Eds.), *Collecting and interpreting qualitative materials*, 3rd edition (pp. 435–471). Thousand Oaks, CA: Sage Publications.

Denzin, N. K., & Lincoln, Y. S. (2008). Introduction: The discipline and practice of qualitative research. In N. K. Denzin & Y. S. Lincoln (Eds.), *Strategies of qualitative inquiry,* 3rd edition (pp. 1–44). Thousand Oaks, CA: Sage Publications.

Denzin, N. K., Lincoln, Y. S., & Smith, L. T. (2008a). Introduction: Critical methodologies and indigenous inquiry. In N. K. Denzin, Y. S. Lincoln, & L. T. Smith (Eds.), *Handbook of critical and indigenous methodologies* (pp. 1–20). Thousand Oaks, CA: Sage Publications.

(2008b). (Eds.) *Handbook of critical and indigenous methodologies.* Thousand Oaks, CA: Sage Publications.

Devine, F., & Heath, S. (1999). *Sociological research methods in context.* Basingstoke: Macmillan.

Dew, K. (2007). A health researcher's guide to qualitative methodologies. *Australian and New Zealand Journal of Public Health* **31**(5), 433–437.

Dickson, G. (2000). Aboriginal grandmothers' experience with health promotion and participatory action research. *Qualitative Health Research* **10**(2), 188–213.

Dickson-Swift, V., James, E., & Liamputtong, P. (2008). *Undertaking sensitive research in the health and social sciences: Managing boundaries, emotions, and risks.* Cambridge: Cambridge University Press.

Dill, B. T. (1994). Fictive kin, paper sons, and compadrazgo: Women of color and the struggle for family survival. In M. B. Zinn & B. T. Dill (Eds.), *Women of color in U. S. society* (pp. 149–169). Philadelphia: Temple University Press.

Dillard, C. B. (2008). When the ground is black, the ground is fertile: Exploring endarkened feminist epistemology and healing methodologies in the spirit. In N. K. Denzin, Y. S. Lincoln, & L. T. Smith (Eds.), *Handbook of critical and indigenous methodologies* (pp. 277–292). Thousand Oaks, CA: Sage Publications.

Diversi, M. (1998). Glimpses of street life: Representing lived experience through short stories. *Qualitative Inquiry* **4**(2), 131–147.

(2008). Young and strapped in America: Learning through a short story about a Latino youth finding meaning in Tupac's rap. In P. Liamputtong & J. Rumbold (Eds.), *Knowing differently: Arts-based and collaborative research methods* (pp. 67–80). New York: Nova Science Publishers.

Dockery, G. (2000). Participatory research: Whose roles, whose responsibilities? In C. Truman, D. M. Mertens, & B. Humphries (Eds.), *Research and inequality* (pp. 95–100). London: UCL Press.

Douglas, J. (1998). Developing appropriate research methodologies with black and minority ethnic communities. Part I: Reflections on the research process. *Health Education Journal* **57**, 329–338.

Dunbar, C. (2001). *Does anyone know we're here: Alternative schooling for African-American youth*. New York: Peter Lang.

Dunbar, C., Rodriques, D., & Parker, L. (2002). Race, subjectivity, and the interview process. In J. F. Gubrium & J. A. Holstein (Eds.), *Handbook of interview research: Content and method* (pp. 279–298). Thousand Oaks, CA: Sage Publications.

Dunckley, M., Hughes, R., Addington-Hall, J. M., & Higgingon, I. J. (2003). Translating clinical tools in nursing practice. *Journal of Advanced Nursing* **44**(4), 420–426.

Duran, B., & Duran, E. (2000). Applied post-colonial clinical and research strategies. In M. Battiste (Ed.), *Reclaiming indigenous voice and vision* (pp. 57–100). Vancouver, BC: University of British Columbia Press.

Edwards, R. (1990). Connecting method and epistemology: A white woman interviewing black women. *Women's Studies International Forum* **13**, 477–490.

(1998). A critical examination of the use of interpreters in the qualitative research process. *Journal of Ethnic and Migration Studies* **24**(1), 197–208.

Edwards, R. W., Jumper-Thurman, P., Plested, B. A., Oetting, E. R., & Swanson, L. (2000). Community readiness: Research to practice. *Journal of Community Psychology* **28**(3), 291–307.

Edwards, S., McManus, V., & McCreanor, T. (2005). Collaborative research with Māori on sensitive issues: The applications of tikanga and kaupapa in research on Māori Sudden Infant Death Syndrome. *Social Policy Journal of New Zealand* **25**, 88–104.

Egharevba, I. (2001). Researching an-'other' minority ethnic community: Reflectoins of a black female researcher on the intersection of race, gender, and other power positions on the research process. *International Journal of Social Research Methodology* **4**(3), 225–241.

Eide, P., & Allen, C. B. (2005). Recruiting transcultural qualitative research participants: A conceptual model. *International Journal of Qualitative Methods* **4**(2), Article 4. www.ualberta.ca/~ijqm/backissues/4_2/pdf/eide.pdf Accessed: 9 October 2005.

Einhorn, I. J. (2000). *The Native American oral tradition: Voices of the spirit and soul*. Westport, CT: Praeger.

Ellis, C. (2008). *Revision: Autoethnographic reflections on life and work (writing lives)*. Walnut Creek, CA: Left Coast Press.

Emami, A., & Tishelman, C. (2004). Reflections on cancer in the context of women's health: Focus group discussions with Iranian immigrant women in Sweden. *Women & Health* **39**(4), 75–95.

Emanuel, E. J., Wendler, D., & Grady, C. (2000). What makes clinical research ethical? *Journal of the American Medical Association* **283**(20), 2701–2711.

Eremenco, S. L., Cella, D., & Arnold, B. J. (2005). A comprehensive method for the translation and cross-cultural validation of health status questionnaires. *Evaluation & The Health Professions* **28**(2), 212–232.

Espiritu, Y. L. (1997). *Asian American women and men: Labor, laws, and love.* Thousand Oaks, CA: Sage Publications.

Esposito, L., & Murphy, J. W. (2000). Another step in the study of race relations. *Sociological Quarterly* **41**(2), 171–187.

Esposito, N. (2001). From meaning to meaning: The influence of translation techniques on non-English focus group research. *Qualitative Health Research* **11**(4), 568–579.

Ezeh, P-J. (2003). Integration and its challenges in participant observation. *Qualitative Research* **3**(2), 191–205.

Fals Borda, O. (1987). The application of participatory action research in Latin America. *International Sociology* **2**, 329–347.

   (1991). Remaking knowledge. In O. Fals Borda & M. A. Rahman (Eds.), *Action and knowledge: Breaking the monopoly with participatory action research* (pp. 349–356). London: Intermediate Technology Publications.

   (2006). Participatory (action) research in social theory: Origins and challenges. In P. Reason & H. Bradbury (Eds.), *Handbook of action research: Concise paperback edition* (pp. 27–37). London: Sage Publications.

Ferdinand, K. C. (1997). Lessons learned from the Healthy Heart Community Prevention Project in reaching the African American population. *Journal of Health Care for the Poor and Underserved* **8**, 366–371.

Fine, M. (1994). Working the hyphens: Reinventing self and other in qualitative research. In N. K. Denzin & Y. S. Lincoln (Eds.), *Handbook of qualitative research* (pp. 70–82). Thousand Oaks, CA: Sage Publications.

Fisher, C. B. (2004). Ethics in drug abuse and related HIV risk research. *Applied Developmental Science* **8**, 90–102.

Fisher, C. B., & Ball, T. J. (2002). The Indian family wellness project: An application of the tribal participatory research model. *Prevention Science* **3**(3), 235–240.

Fisher, C. B., and Ragsdale, K. (2006). Goodness-of-fit ethics for multicultural research. In J. E. Trimble, and C. B. Fisher (Eds.), *Handbook of ethical research with ethnocultural populations and communities* (pp. 3–25). Thousand Oaks, CA: Sage Publications.

Fisher, C. B., & Wallace, S. A. (2000). Through the community looking glass: Re-evaluating the ethical and policy implications of research on adolescent risk and psychopathology. *Ethics & Behavior* **10**, 99–118.

Flory, J., & Emanuel, E. (2004). Interventions to improve research participants' understanding in informed consent for research: A systematic review. *Journal of the American Medical Association* **292**(13), 1593–1601.

Fluehr-Lobban, C. (1994). Informed consent in anthropological research: We are not exempt. *Human Organization* **53**(1), 1–10.

   (1998). Ethics. In H. R. Bernard (Ed.), *Handbook of methods in cultural anthropology* (pp. 173–202). Walnut Creek, CA: AltaMira Press.

   (2003). *Ethics and the profession of anthropology,* 2nd edition. Walnut Creek, CA: AltaMira Press.

Fontana, A., & Frey, J. H. (2005). The interview: From neutral stance to political involvement. In N. K. Denzin & Y. S. Lincoln (Eds.), *The Sage handbook of qualitative research,* 3rd edition (pp. 695–727). Thousand Oaks, CA: Sage Publications.

Fontana, A., & Prokos, A. H. (2007). *The interview: From formal to postmodern.* Walnut Creek, CA: Left Coast Press.

Fontes, L. A. (1998). Ethics in family violence research: Cross-cultural issues. *Family Relations* **47**(1), 53–61.

Foster, M. (1993). Educating for competence in community and culture: Exploring the views of exemplary African American teachers. *Urban Education* **27**(4), 370–394.

Freedman, T. G. (1998). 'Why don't they come to Pike Street and ask us?': Black American women's health concerns. *Social Science & Medicine* **47**(7), 941–947.

Freimuth, V., Quinn, S. G., Thomas, S. B., Cole, G., Zook, E., & Duncan, T. (2001). African American views on research and the Tuskegee syphilis study. *Social Science & Medicine* **52**(2), 797–808.

Freire, P. (1970). *Pedagogy of the oppressed.* New York: Continuum.

(1972). *Pedagogy of the oppressed* (trans. M. B. Ramos). Harmondsworth: Penguin.

(1982). Creating alternative research methods: Learning to do it by doing it. In B. L. Hall, A. Gillette, & R. Tandon (Eds.), *Creating knowledge: A monopoly? Participatory research in development* (pp. 29–37). New Delhi: Society for Participatory Research in Asia.

(1999). *Pedagogy of hope.* New York: Continuum (originally published 1992).

Gamble, V. (1997). Under the shadow of Tuskegee: African Americans and health care. *American Journal of Public Health* **87**, 1773–1778.

Gandhi, L. (1998). *Postcolonial theory: A critical introduction.* New York: Columbia University Press.

Geertz, C. (1983). *Local knowledge.* New York: Basic Books.

Gibbs, A. (2001). Social work and empowerment-based research: Possibilities, process, and questions. *Australian Social Work* **54**, 29–40.

Gibson, N., Cave, A., Doering, D., Ortiz, L., & Harms, P. (2005). Socio-cultural factors influencing prevention and treatment of tuberculosis in immigrant and aboriginal communities in Canada. *Social Science & Medicine* **61**(5), 931–942.

Gikes, C. T. (1994). 'If it wasn't for the women …': African American women, community work, and social change. In M. B. Zinn & B. T. Dill (Eds.), *Women of color in U. S. society* (pp. 229–246). Philadelphia: Temple University Press.

Gilligan, C. (1982). *In a different voice: Psychological theory and women's development.* Cambridge, MA: Harvard University Press.

(2003). *The birth of pleasure: A new map of love.* New York: Vintage.

Giuliano, A. R., Mokuau, N., Hughes, C., Tortolero-Luna, G., Risendal, B., Ho, R. C. S., McCaskill-Stevens, W., & Prewitt, T. E. (2000). Participation of minorities in cancer research: The influence of structural, cultural, and linguistic factors. *Annals of Epidemiology* **10**(8 Supp), S22–34.

Glantz, N. M., Halperin, D. C., & Hunt, L. M. (1998). Studying domestic violence in Chiapas, Mexico. *Qualitative Health Research* **8**(3), 377–392.

Glesne, C. E. (1997). That rare feeling: Re-presenting research through poetic transcription. *Qualitative Inquiry* **3**(2), 202–221.

Glesne, C. E., & Peshkin, A. (1991). *Become qualitative researchers: An introduction.* New York: Routledge.

Gluck, S. B. (1984). What's so special about women?: Women's oral history. In D. Dunaway & W. K. Baum (Eds.), *Oral history: An interdisciplinary anthology* (pp. 221–237). Nashville, TN: American Association for State and Local History.

(2006). Women's oral history: Is it so special? In T. L. Charlton, L. E. Meyers, & R. Sharpless (Eds.), *Handbook of oral history* (pp. 357–383). Lanham, MD: AltaMira Press.

Gluck, S. B., & Patai, D. (1991). *Women's words: The feminist practice of oral history*. New York: Routledge.

Gokah, T. (2006). The naïve researcher: Doing social research in Africa. *International Journal of Social Research Methodology* **9**(1), 61–73.

Golden, A. (1997). *Memoirs of a geisha*. London: Vintage.

Goldstein, D. M. (2003). *Laughter out of place: Race, class, violence, and sexuality in a Rio Shantytown*. Berkeley, CA: University of California Press.

Goldzieher, J. W., Moses, L., Averkin, E., Scheel, C., & Taber, B. (1971a). A placebo-controlled double-blind crossover investigation of the side effects attributed to oral contraceptives. *Fertility and Sterility* **22**(9), 609–623.

(1971b). Nervousness and depression attributed to oral contraceptives: A double-blind, placebo-controlled study. *American Journal of Obstetrics and Gynecology* **22**, 1013–1020.

Goltz, D. (2009). Investigating queer future meanings: Destructive perceptions of 'the harder path'. *Qualitative Inquiry* **15**(3), 561–586.

Goodenough, W. H. (1980). Ethnographic field techniques. In H. C. Triandis & J. W. Berry (Eds.), *Handbook of cross-cultural psychology*, Vol. 2: *Methodology* (pp. 39–55). Boston: Allyn & Bacon.

Goodman, J. H. (2004). Coping with trauma and hardship among unaccompanied refugee youths from Sudan. *Qualitative Health Research* **14**(9), 1177–1196.

Gorelick, S. (1991). Contradictions of feminist methodology. *Gender & Society* **5**(4), 459–477.

Gostin, L. O. (1995). Informed consent, cultural sensitivity, and respect for persons. *Journal of the American Medical Association* **274**, 844–845.

Gotschi, E., Freyer, B., & Delve, R. (2008). Participatory photography in cross-cultural reserach: A case study of investigating farmer groups in rural Mozambique. In P. Liamputtong (Ed.), *Doing cross-cultural research: Ethical and methodological perspectives* (pp. 213–231). Dordrecht: Springer.

Govenar, A. (2000). *African American frontiers*. Santa Barbara, CA: ABC-CLIO.

Gray, F. D. 1998, *The Tuskegee syphilis study: The real story and beyond*. Montgomery, AL: New South Books.

Greig, A., Taylor, J., & MacKay, T. (2007). *Doing research with children*, 2nd edition. Thousand Oaks, CA: Sage Publications.

Groger, L., Mayberry, P., & Straker, J. (1999). What we didn't learn because of who would not talk to us. *Qualitative Health Research* **9**(6), 829–835.

Guhathakurta, M. (2008). Theatre in participatory action research: Experiences from Bangladesh. In P. Reason & H. Bradbury (Eds.), *The Sage handbook of action research: Participative inquiry and practice*, 2nd edition (pp. 510–521). London: Sage Publications.

Gunaratnam, Y. (2003). *Researching race and ethnicity: Methods, knowledge, and power*. London: Sage Publications.

Gurevitch, Z. (2000). The serious play of writing. *Qualitative Inquiry* **6**(1), 3–8.

Guthrie, R. V. (1998). *Even the rat was white: A historical view of psychology*. Boston: Allyn & Bacon.

Gutierrez, G. (2003). *We drink from our own wells: The spiritual journey of a people.* Maryknoll, NY: Orbis.

Gwaltney, J. L. (1981). Common sense and science: Urban core black observations. In D. L. Messerschmidt (Ed.), *Anthropological at home in North America: Methods and issues in the study of one's own society* (pp. 46–61). Cambridge: Cambridge University Press.

Habashi, J. (2005). Creating indigenous discourse: History, power, and imperialism in academia, Palestinian case. *Qualitative Inquiry* **11**(5), 771–788.

Halcomb, E. J., Gholizadeh, L., DiGiacomo, M., Phillips, J., & Davidson, P. M. (2007). Literature review: Considerations in undertaking focus group research with culturally and linguistically diverse groups. *Journal of Clinical Nursing* **16**(6), 1000–1011.

Hall, B. L. (1981). Participatory research, popular knowledge, and power: A personal reflection. *Convergence* **14**(3), 6–17.

Hall, B. L., & Kulig, J. C. (2004). Kanadier Mennonites: A case study examining research challenges among religious groups. *Qualitative Health Research* **14**(3), 359–368.

Hall, R. A. (2004). Inside out: Some notes on carrying out feminist research in cross-cultural interviews with South Asian women immigrant applicants. *International Journal of Social Research Methodology* **7**(2), 127–141.

Hallowell, N., Lawton, J., & Gregory, S. (2005). *Reflections on research: The realities of doing research in the social sciences.* Maidenhead: Open University Press.

Hamilton, J. (1996). Women and health policy: On the inclusion of females in clinical trials. In C. Sargent & C. Brettell (Eds.), *Gender and health: An international perspective* (pp. 292–325). Upper Saddle River, NJ: Prentice Hall.

Hammersley, M. (1992). *What's wrong with ethnography?* London: Routledge.

Hancock, L. (2001). *Community, crime, and disorder: Safety and regeneration in urban neighbourhoods.* London: Palgrave.

Hanh, T. N. (1998). *Teaching on love.* Berkeley, CA: Parallax Press.

Hargenrather, K. C., Rhodes, S. D., & Clark, G. (2006). Windows to work: Exploring employment-seeking behaviors of persons with HIV/AIDS through photovoice. *AIDS Education and Prevention* **18**(3), 243–258.

Harrington, B. (2003). The social psychology of access in ethnographic research. *Journal of Contemporary Ethnography* **32**(5), 592–625.

Harris, J., & Roberts, K. (2003). Challenging barriers to participation in qualitative research: Involving disabled refugees. *International Journal of Qualitative Methods* **2**(2), Article 2. Available at: www.ualberta.ca/~iiqm/backissues/2_2/pdf/harrisetal.pdf Accessed: 4 December 2003.

Harrison, B. (2002). Seeing health and illness worlds – using visual methodologies in a sociology of health and illness: A methodological review. *Sociology of Health and Illness* **24**(6), 856–872.

Heintzelman, C. (1996). Human subjects and informed consent: The legacy of the Tuskegee syphilis study. *Scholars: Research, Teaching and Public Service* Fall, 23–29.

Hennings, J., Williams, J., & Haque, B. N. (1996). Exploring the health needs of Bangladeshi women: A case study in using qualitative research methods. *Health Education Journal* **55**, 11–23.

Hennink, M. M. (2007). *International focus group research: A handbook for the health and social sciences.* Cambridge: Cambridge University Press.

(2008). Language and communication in cross-cultural qualitative research. In P. Liamputtong (Ed.), *Doing cross-cultural research: Ethical and methodological perspectives* (pp. 21–33). Dordrecht: Springer.

Hermes, M. (1998). Research methods as a situated response: Towards a First Nations' methodology. *Qualitative Studies in Education* **11**(1), 155–168.

Hill, D., & King, J. E. (2005) Appendix C. Glossary of Terms. In J. E. King (Ed.), *Black education: A transformative research and action agenda for the new century.* Mahwah, NJ: Lawrence Erlbaum.

Hess, R. F. (2006). Postabortion research: Methodological and ethical issues. *Qualitative Health Research* **16**(4), 580–587.

Hesse-Biber, S. N., & Leavy, P. (2005). *The practice of qualitative research.* Thousand Oaks, CA: Sage Publications.

Hoeyer, K., Dahlager, L., & Lynöe, N. (2005). Conflicting notions of research ethics: The mutually challenging traditions of social scientists and medical researchers. *Social Science & Medicine* **61**, 1741–1749.

Holkup, P. A., Tripp-Reimer, T., Salois, E. M., & Weinert, C. (2004). Community-based participatory research: An approach to intervention research with a Native American community. *Advances in Nursing Science* **27**(3), 162–175.

Holman Jones, S. (2008). Autoethnography: Making the personal political. In N. K. Denzin, and Y. S. Lincoln (Eds.), *Collecting and interpreting qualitative materials,* 3rd edition (pp. 205–245). Thousand Oaks, CA: Sage Publications.

Holt, C. L., & McClure, S. M. (2006). Perceptions of the religion-health connection among African American church members. *Qualitative Health Research* **16**(2), 268–281.

Honig, H. (1997). Positions, power, and practice: Functionalist approaches and translation quality assessment. *Current Issues in Language and Society* **4**(1), 6–34.

hooks, b. (1989). *Talking back – Thinking feminist, thinking black.* Boston: South End Press.

(2000). *All about love: New visions.* New York: Morrow.

Horton, J., & Horton, L. (2001). *Hard road to freedom – The story of African America.* New Brunswick, NJ: Rutgers University Press.

Hunt, S. M., & Bhopal, R. (2004). Self report in clinical and epidemiological studies with non-English speakers: The challenge of language and culture. *Journal of Epidemiology & Community Health* **58**(7), 618–622.

Husaini, B. A., Sherkat, D. E., Bragg, R. *et al.* (2001). Predictors of breast cancer screening in a panel study of African American women. *Women Health* **34**(3), 35–51.

Im, E.-O., Page, R., Lin, L.-C., Tsai, H.-M., & Cheng, C.-Y. (2004). Rigor in cross-cultural nursing research. *International Journal of Nursing Studies* **41**, 891–899.

Irvine, F., Roberts, G., & Bradbury-Jones, C. (2008). The researcher as insider versus the researcher as outsider: Enhancing rigour through language and cultural sensitivity. In P. Liamputtong (Ed.), *Doing cross-cultural research: Ethical and methodological perspectives* (pp. 35–48). Dordrecht: Springer.

Israel, B. A., Eng, E., Schulz, A. J., & Parker, E. A. (2005). *Methods in community-based participatory research for health.* San Francisco: Jossey-Bass.

Israel, M., & Hay, I. (2006). *Research ethics for social scientists: Between ethical conduct and regulatory compliance.* London: Sage Publications.

Iwamasa, G. Y., & Sorocco, K. H. (2002). Aging and Asian Americans: Developing appropriate research methodology. In G. C. N. Hall & S. Okazaki (Eds.), *Asian American psychology: The science of lives in context* (pp. 105–130). Washington, DC: APA.

Iwasaki, Y., Bartlett, J., & O'Neil, J. (2005). Coping with stress among Aboriginal women and men with diabetes in Winnipeg, Manitoba. *Social Science & Medicine* **60**(5), 977–988.

Izugbara, C. O. (2000). Observations bearing on fieldworkers manners and conduct. *Indigenous Knowledge and Development Monitor* **8**(3), 19.

Jack C. M., Penny L., & Nazar W. (2001). Effective palliative care for minority ethnic groups: The role of a liaison worker. *International Journal of Palliative Nursing* **7**, 375–380.

Jackson, M. S., & Mead Niblo, D. (2003). The role of qualitative methodology in cross-cultural research. *Qualitative Research Journal* **3**(1), 18–27.

Jackson, P. (2000). Methodology out of context: Getting Zimbabwean entrepreneurs to participate in research. *International Journal of Social Research Methodology* **3**(4), 347–359.

Jacobs, B. (1998). Researching crack dealers: Dilemmas and contradictions. In J. Ferrell & M. Hamm (Eds.), *Ethnography at the edge: Crime, deviance, and field research* (pp. 160–177). Boston: Northeastern University Press.

Jankie, D. (2004). 'Tell me who you are': Problematizing the construction and positionalities of 'insider'/'outsider' of a 'native' ethnographer in a postcolonial context. In K. Mutua & B. B. Swadener (Eds.), *Decolonizing research in cross-cultural contexts: Critical personal narratives* (pp. 87–105). Albany: State University of New York (SUNY) Press.

Jarrett, R. L. (1993). Focus group interviewing with low-income minority populations: A research experience. In D. L. Morgan (Ed.), *Successful focus groups: Advancing the state of the art* (pp. 184–201). Newbury Park, CA: Sage Publications.

Järviluoma, H., Moisala, P., & Vilkko, A. (2003). *Gender and qualitative methods.* London: Sage Publications.

Jeffries, S. K., Choi, W., Butler, J., Harris, K. J., & Ahluwalia, J. S. (2005). Strategies for recruiting African-American residents of public housing developments into a randomized controlled trial. *Ethnicity & Disease* **15**(4), 806–807.

Jezewski, M. (1990). Culture brokering in migrant farmworker health care. *Western Journal of Nursing Research* **12**(4), 497–513.

(1993). Culture brokering as a model for advocacy. *Nursing and Health Care* **14**(2), 78–89.

Johnson, V., & Thomas, D. (2008). Smoking behaviours in a remote Australian indigenous community: The influence of family and other factors. *Social Science & Medicine* **67**(11), 1708–1716.

Jones, J. H. (1993). *Bad blood: The Tuskegee syphilis experiment.* New York: Free Press.

Jones, J. L. (2002). Performance ethnography: The role of embodiment in cultural authenticity. *Theatre Topics* **12**(1), 1–15.

Joseph, J. G., Emmons, C. A., Kessler, R. C., Wortman, C. B., & O'Brien, K. (1984). Coping with the threat of AIDS: An approach to psychosocial assessment. *American Journal of Psychology* **39**(11), 1297–1302.

Jtz'ibajom, S. (1996). *Xcha'kuxesel ak'ob elav ta slumal batz'i viniketik ta Chyapa. Renacimiento del teatro Maya en Chiapas,* 2 vols. San Cristóbal, Mexico: La Casa del Escritor.

Jurkowski, J., & Paul-Ward, A. (2007). Photovoice with vulnerable populations: Addressing disparities in health promotion among people with intellectual disabilities. *Health Promotion Practice* **8**(4), 358–365.

Kamberelis, G., & Dimitriadis, G. (2008). Focus groups: Strategic articulations of pedagogy, politics, and inquiry. In N. K. Denzin & Y. S. Lincoln (Eds.), *Collecting and interpreting qualitative materials,* 3rd edition (pp. 375–402). Thousand Oaks, CA: Sage Publications.

Kaomea, J. (2004). Dilemmas in an indigenous academic: A Native Hawaiian story. In K. Mutua & B. B. Swadener (Eds.), *Decolonizing research in cross-cultural contexts: Critical personal narratives* (pp. 27–44). Albany: State University of New York (SUNY) Press.

(2005). Reflections on an 'always already' failing Native Hawaiian mother: Deconstructing colonial discourses on indigenous childrearing and early childhood education. *Hulili: Multidisciplinary Research on Hawaiian Well-Being* **2**(1), 67–85.

Kapborg, I., & Bertero, C. (2002). Using an interpreter in qualitative interviews: Does it threaten validity? *Nursing Inquiry* **9**(1), 52–56.

Kartala, A., & Özsoy, S. A. (2007). Validity and reliability study of the Turkish version of Health Belief Model Scale in diabetic patients. *International Journal of Nursing Studies* **44**, 1447–1458

Kaufert, J. M., & Putsch, R. W. (1997). Communication through interpreters in healthcare: Ethical dilemmas arising from differences in class, culture, language, and power. *Journal of Clinical Ethics* **8**(1), 71–87.

Keats, D. (2000). *Interviewing.* Buckingham: Open University Press.

Kelaher, M., & Manderson, L. (2000). Migration and mainstreaming: Matching health servies to immigrants' needs in Australia. *Health Policy* **54**, 1–11.

Kemmis, S., & McTaggart, R. (2003). Participatory action research. In N. K. Denzin & Y. S. Lincoln (Eds.), *Strategies of qualitative inquiry,* 2nd edition (pp. 336–396). Thousand Oaks, CA: Sage Publications.

(2008). Participatory action research. In N. K. Denzin & Y. S. Lincoln (Eds.), *Strategies of qualitative inquiry,* 3rd edition (pp. 271–330). Thousand Oaks, CA: Sage Publications.

Kesby, M., Kindon, S., & Pain, R. (2005). Participatory approaches and diagramming techniques. In R. Flowerdew & D. Martin (Eds.), *Methods in human geography: A guide for students doing a research project* (pp. 144–165). Harlow: Pearson.

Key, S. W., & Marble, M. (1996). Trip to beauty parlor means more than a hair cut. *Cancer Weekly Plus*, 7–8.

Khanlou, N., & Peter, E. (2005). Participatory action research: Considerations for ethical review. *Social Science & Medicine* **60**(10), 2333–2340.

King, J. E. (2005). *Black education: A transformative research and action agenda for the new century.* Mahwah, NJ: Lawrence Erlbaum.

King, M. L. (1994). *Letter from the Birmingham jail.* San Franciso: HarperSanFrancisco.

Kissell, J. (2008). The 'vulnerability' quagmire in international research. In D. N. Weisstub & G. D. Pintos (Eds.), *Autonomy and human rights in health care* (pp. 331–340). Dordrecht: Springer.

Kong, B. W. (1997). Community-based hypertension control programs that work. *Journal of Health Care for the Poor and Underserved* **8**, 409–415.

Kooken, W. C., Haase, J. E., & Russell, K. M. (2007). 'I've been through something': Poetic explorations of African American women's cancer survivorship. *Western Journal of Nursing Research* **29**(7), 896–919.

Kosygina, L. (2005). Doing gender in research: Reflection on experience in field. *The Qualitative Report* **10**(1), 87–95.

Kozol, J. (1985). *Illiterate America*. New York: Random House.

Kressin, N. R., Meterko, M., & Wilson, N. J. (2000). Racial disparities in participation in biomedical research. *Journal of the National Medical Association* **92**(2), 62–69.

Krueger, R. A., & Casey, M. A. (2009). *Focus groups: A practical guide for applied research*, 4th edition. Thousand Oaks, CA: Sage Publications.

Kusow, A. M. (2003). Beyond indigenous authenticity: Reflections on the insider/outsider debate in immigration research. *Symbolic Interaction* **26**(4), 591–599.

Kwok, J. Y.-C., & Ku, H.-B. (2008). Making habitable space together with female Chinese immigrants to Hong Kong: An interdisciplinary participatory action research project. *Action Research* **6**(3), 261–283.

Labaree, R. (2002). The risk of 'going observationalist': Negotiating the hidden dilemmas of being an insider participant observer. *Qualitative Research* **2**(1), 97–122.

Ladson-Billings, G. (2000). Racialized discourses and ethnic epiostemologies. In D. K. Denzin and Y. S. Lincoln (Eds.), *Handbook of qualitative research,* 2nd edition (pp. 257–278). Thousand Oaks, CA: Sage Publications.

Lal, J. (1999). Situating locations: The politics of self, identity and 'other' in living and writing the text. In S. N. Hesse-Biber, C. Gilmartin & R. Lydenberg (Eds.), *Feminist approaches to theory and methodology: An interdisciplinary reader* (pp. 100–137). New York: Oxford University Press.

Landrine, H., Klonoff, E., & Brown-Collins, A. (1995). Cultural diversity and methodology in feminist psychology: Critique, proposal, empirical example. In H. Landrine (Ed.), *Bringing cultural diversity to feminist psychology* (pp. 55–75). Washington DC: American Psychological Association.

Lange, J. W. (2002). Methodological concerns for non-Hispanic investigators conducting research with Hispanic Americans. *Research in Nursing & Health* **25**, 411–419.

Langford, D. R. (2000). Developing a safely protocol in qualitative research involving battered women. *Qualitative Health Research* **10**(1), 133–142.

Larkin, P. J., Dierckx de Casterlé, B., & Schotsmans, P. (2007). Multilingual translation issues in qualitative research: Reflections on a metaphorical process. *Qualitative Health Research* **17**(4), 468–476.

Lather, P., & Smithies, C. (1997). *Troubling the angels: Women living with HIV/AIDS*. Boulder, CO: Westview.

Laverack, G. R., & Brown, K. M. (2003). Qualitative research in a cross-cultural context: Fijian experiences. *Qualitative Health Research* **13**(3), 333–342.

Laws, S., Harper, C., & Marcus, R. (2003). *Research for development*. London: Sage Publications.

Leaning, J. (2001). Ethics of research in refugee populations. *The Lancet* **357**(9266), 1432–1433.

Lee, A. A., & Ellenbecker, C. H. (1998). The perceived life stressors among elderly Chinese immigrants: Are they different from those of other elderly Americans? *Clinical Excellence for Nurse Practitioners* **2**, 96–101.

Lee-Treweek, G., & Linkogle, S. (2000). Overview. In G. Lee-Treweek & S. Linkogle (Eds.), *Danger in the field: Risk and ethics in social research* (pp. 1–7). London: Routledge.

Leflar, R. B. (1997). The cautious acceptance of informed consent in Japan. *Medical Law* **16**, 705–720.

Leipert, B., & Reutter, L. (2005). Developing resilience: How women maintain their health in northern geographically isolated settings. *Qualitative Health Research* **15**(1), 49–65.

Leslie, H., & Story, D. (2003). Practical issues. In R. Scheyvens & D. Storey (Eds.), *Development fieldwork: A practical guide* (pp. 77–95). London: Sage Publications.

Letherby, G. (2000). Dangerous liaisons: Auto/biography in research and research writing. In G. Lee-Treweek & S. Linkogle (Eds.), *Danger in the field: Risk and ethics in social research* (pp. 91–113). London: Routledge.

Levine, C. (1998). Placebos and HIV: Lessons learned. *Hastings Center Report* **28**(6), 43–48.

Levkoff, S., & Sanchez, H. (2003). Lessons learned about minority recruitment and retention from the Centers on Minority Aging and Health Promotion. *Gerontologist* **43**(1), 18–26.

Liamputtong, P. (2001). Motherhood and the challenge of immigrant mothers: A personal reflection. *Families in Society: The Journal of Contemporary Human Services* **82**(2), 195–201.

(2004). *Yu duan* practices as embodying tradition, modernity, and social change in Chiang Mai, Northern Thailand. *Women & Health* **40**(1), 79–99.

(2005). Birth and social class: Northern Thai women's lived experiences of caesarean and vaginal birth. *Sociology of Health & Illness* **27**(1), 243–270.

(2006). Motherhood and 'moral career': Discourses of good motherhood among Southeast Asian immigrant women in Australia. *Qualitative Sociology* **29**(1), 25–53.

(2007a). *Researching the vulnerable: A guide to sensitive research methods*. London: Sage Publications.

(2007b). *The journey of becoming a mother amongst women in northern Thailand*. Lanham, MD: Lexington Books.

(2008). Doing research in a cross-cultural context: Methodological and ethical challenges. In P. Liamputtong (Ed.), *Doing cross-cultural research: Ethical and methodological perspectives* (pp. 3–20). Dordrecht: Springer.

(2009). *Qualitative research methods,* 3rd edition. Melbourne: Oxford University Press.

(2010). The science of words and the science of numbers: Research methods as foundations for evidence-based practice in health. In P. Liamputtong (Ed.), *Research methods in health: Foundations for evidence-based practice* (pp. 3–26). Melbourne: Oxford University Press.

Liamputtong, P., & Dwyer, J. (2003). Women and health: An ongoing agenda. In P. Liamputtong & H. Gardner (Eds.), *Health, social change, and communities* (pp. 119–140). Melbourne: Oxford University Press.

Liamputtong, P., Haritavorn, N., & Kiatying-Angsulee, N. (2009). HIV and AIDS, stigma and AIDS support groups: Perspectives from women living with HIV and AIDS in central Thailand. *Social Science & Medicine*, special issue: 'Women, Motherhood and HIV Care in Resource Poor Settings', **69**(6), 862–868.

Liamputtong, P., & Naksook, C. (2003a). Life as mothers in a new land: The experience of motherhood among Thai women in Melbourne. *Health Care for Women International* **24**(7), 650–668.

(2003b). Perceptions and experiences of motherhood, health, and the husband's role among Thai women in Australia. *Midwifery* **19**(1), 27–36.

Liamputtong, P., & Rumbold, J. (Eds.) (2008). *Knowing differently: Arts-based and collaborative research methods*. New York: Nova Science Publishers.

Liamputtong, P., & Watson, L. (2002). The voices and concerns about prenatal testing of Cambodian, Lao, and Vietnamese women in Australia. *Midwifery* **18**(4), 304–313.

(2006). The meanings and experiences of cesarean birth amongst Cambodian, Lao, and Vietnamese immigrant women in Australia. *Women & Health* **43**(3), 63–81.

Liamputtong, P., Yimyam, S., Parisunyakul, S., Baosoung, C., & Sansiriphun, N. (2004). When I become a mother!: Discourses of motherhood among Thai women in northern Thailand. *Women's Studies International Forum* **27**(5–6), 589–601.

Liamputtong Rice, P. (1993). *My forty days: A cross-cultural resource book for health professionals in birthing services*. Melbourne: The Vietnamese Ante/Postnatal Support Project.

(1996). Health research and ethnic communities: Reflection on practice. In D. Colquhoun & A. Kellehear (Eds.), *Health research in practice*, Vol. 2: *Personal experiences, public issues* (pp. 50–61). London: Chapman & Hall.

(1999). *Asian mothers, western birth*. Melbourne: Ausmed Publications.

(2000). *Hmong women and reproduction*. Westport, CT: Bergin & Garvey.

Liamputtong Rice, P., Ly, B., & Lumley, J. (1994). Childbirth and soul loss: The case of a Hmong woman. *Medical Journal of Australia* **160**(9), 577–578.

Liamputtong Rice, P., & Naksook, C. (1998). Caesarean or vaginal birth?: Perceptions and experience of Thai women in Australian hospitals. *Australian and New Zealand Journal of Public Health* **22**(5), 604–608.

Liebling, H. (2004). *Ugandan women's experiences of violence, rape, and torture during civil war years in Luwero District: Implications for health policy, welfare, and human rights*. Centre for Social Justice Annual Conference: Getting the message across: Social justice in the real world, 28 April, Coventry.

Lindenberg, C., Solorzano, R., Vilaro, F., & Westerbrook, L. (2001). Challenges and strategies for conducting intervention research with culturally diverse populations. *Journal of Transcultural Nursing* **12**(2), 132–139.

Linkogle, S. (2000). Relajo: Danger in a crowd. In G. Lee-Treweek & S. Linkogle (Eds.), *Danger in the field: Risk and ethics in social research* (pp. 132–146). London: Routledge.

Linnan, L. A., Ferguson, Y. O., Wasilewski, Y., Lee, A. M., Yang, J., Solomon, F., & Katz, M. (2005). Using community-based participatory research methods to reach women with health messages: Results from the North Carolina BEAUTY and Health Pilot Project. *Health Promotion Practice* **6**(2), 164–173.

Lipson, J., & Meleis, A. (1989). Methodological issues in research with immigrants. *Medical Anthropology* **12**(1), 103–115.

Littlewood, J., & Harrow, J. (1999). 'Drawing the veil?': Some reflections on joint research supervision of women students in Saudi Arabia. *International Journal of Social Research Methodology* **2**(3), 231–245.

Lloyd-Evans, S. (2006). Focus groups. In V. Desai & R. B. Potter (Eds.), *Doing development research* (pp. 153–162). London: Sage Publications.

Lomawaima, K. T. (2000). Tribal sovereigns: Reframing research in American Indian education. *Harvard Educational Review* **70**(1), 1–21.

Lopez, E. D. S., Eng, E., Randall-David, E., & Robinson, N. (2005a). Quality-of-life concerns of African American breast cancer survivors within rural North Carolina: Blending the techniques of photovoice and grounded theory. *Qualitative Health Research* **15**(1), 99–114.

Lopez, E. D.S., Eng, E., Robinson, N., & Wang, C. C. (2005b). Photovoice as a community-based participatory research method: A case study with African American breast cancer survivors in rural Eastern North Carolina. In B. Israel, E. Eng, A. J. Schulz, E. Parker and D. Satcher (Eds.), *Methods for conducting community-based participatory research for health*. San Francisco, CA: Jossey-Bass.

Lopez, G. I., Figueroa, M., Connor, S. E., & Maliski, S. L. (2008). Translation barriers in conducting qualitative research with Spanish speakers. *Qualitative Health Research* **18**(12), 1729–1737.

Lopez, V. (2003). Clinical teachers as caring mothers from the perspectives of Jordanian nursing students. *International Journal of Nursing Studies* **40**(1), 51–60.

Loppie, C. (2007). Learning from the grandmothers: Incorporating indigenous principles into qualitative research. *Qualitative Health Research* **17**(2), 276–284.

Lorde, A. (1984). *Sister outsider*. Trumansburg, NY: Crossing Press.

Loue, S., Okello, D., & Kawuma, M. (1996). Research bioethics in the Ugandan context: A program summary. *Journal of Law and Medical Ethics* **24**, 47–53.

Lu, Y., Trout, S. K. Lu, K., & Creswell, J. W. (2005). The needs of AIDS-infected individuals in rural China. *Qualitative Health Research* **15**(9), 1149–1163.

Lurie, P., & Wolfe, S. M. (1997). Unethical trials of interventions to reduce perinatal transmission of the human immunodeficiency virus in developing countries. *New England Journal of Medicine* **337**(12), 853–856.

Lykes, M. B., in collaboration with the Association of Maya Ixil Women – New Dawn, Chajul, Guatemala (2006). Creative arts and photography in participatory action research in Guatemala. In P. Reason & H. Bradbury (Eds.), *Handbook of action research: Concise paperback edition* (pp. 269–278). London: Sage Publications.

Lykes, M. B., Blanche, M. T., & Hamber, B. (2003). Narrating survival and change in Guatemala and South Africa: The politics of representation and a liberatory community psychology. *American Journal of Community Psychology* **31**, 79–90.

Macklin, R. (2000). Informed consent for research: International perspectives. *Journal of the American Medical Women's Association* **55**, 290–293.

(2004). *Double standards in medical research in developing countries*. New York: Cambridge University Press.

Madge, C. (1997). The ethics of research in the 'Third World'. In E. Robson & K. Willis (Eds.), *Postgraduate fieldwork in developing areas: A rough guide* (pp. 113–124). London: Monograph No. 9, Developing Areas Research Group, Royal Geographical Society, and Institute of British Geographers.

Madriz, E. (1998). Using focus groups with lower socioeconomic status Latina women. *Qualitative Health Research* **4**, 114–128.

(2000). Focus groups in feminist research. In N. K. Denzin & Y. S. Lincoln (Eds.), *Handbook of qualitative research*, 2nd edition (pp. 835–850). Thousand Oaks, CA: Sage Publications.

Maginn, P. (2007). Negotiating and securing access: Reflections from a study into urban regeneration and community participation in ethnically diverse neighborhoods in London, England. *Field Methods* **19**(4), 425–440.

Mamary, E., McCright, J., & Roe, K. (2007). Our lives: An examination of sexual health issues using photovoice by non-gay identified African American men who have sex with men. *Culture, Health & Sexuality* **9**(4), 359–370.

Mand, K., & Wilson, S. (2006). *Ambivalent positions: Ethnicity and working in our own communities.* Paper presented at 'Multicultural Britain: From Anti-Racism to Identity Politics to …?' conference, University of Surrey, 14–15 June.

Mangen, S. (1999). Qualitative research methods in cross-national settings. *International Journal of Social Research Methodology* **2**(2), 109–124.

Mani, P. S. (2006). Methodological dilemmas experienced in researching Indo-Canadian young adults' decision-making process to study the sciences. *International Journal of Qualitative Methods,* **5**(2). www.ualberta.ca/~iiqm/backissue/5_2/pdf/mani.pdf Accessed: 5 September 2006.

Marshall, A., & Batten, S. (2004). Researching across cultures: Issues of ethics and power. *Forum: Qualitative Social Research* **5**(3), Article 39. www.qualitative-research.net/fqs-texte/3–04/04–3–39-e.htm Accessed: 14 October 2005.

Marston, C. (2005). What is heterosexual coercion? Interpreting narratives from young people in Mexico City. *Sociology of Health & Illness* **27**(1), 68–91.

Martinez-Ebers, V. (1997). Using monetary incentives with hard-to-reach populations in panel surveys. *International Journal of Public Opinion Research* **9**(1), 77–87.

Marvasti, A. B. (2004). *Qualitative research in sociology.* London: Sage Publications.

(2008). Writing and presenting social research. In P. Alasuutari, L. Bickman, & J. Brannen (Eds.), *The Sage handbook of social research methods* (pp. 602–616). London: Sage Publications.

Maylor, U. (1995). The experiences of African, Caribbean, and South Asian women in initial teacher education. Unpublished PhD thesis, Open University, Buckingham.

(2009). Is it because I'm Black? A Black female research experience. *Race, Ethnicity & Education* **12**(1), 53–64.

Maynard-Tucker, G. (2000). Conducting focus groups in developing countries: Skill training for local bilingual facilitators. *Qualitative Health Research* **10**(3), 396–410.

McCall, J. C. (2000). *Dancing histories – Heuristic ethnography with the Ohafia Igbo.* Ann Arbor: University of Michigan Press.

McCreanor, T., Tipene-Leach, D., & Abel, S. (2004). The SIDS Careworkers Study: Perceptions of the experience of Māori SIDS families. *Social Policy Journal of New Zealand* **23**, 154–166.

McDonald, G. (2000). Cross-cultural methodological issues in ethical research. *Journal of Business Ethics* **27**(1/2), 89–104.

McGorry, S. Y. (2000). Measurement in cross-cultural environment: Survey translation issues. *Qualitative Market Research: An International Journal* **2**, 74–81.

McIntyre, A. (2003). Through the eyes of women: Photovoice and participatory research as tools for reimagining place. *Gender, Place & Culture* **10**, 47–66.

(2008). *Participatory action research.* Thousand Oaks, CA: Sage Publications.

McLaughlin, F., & Sall, T. S. (2001). The give and take of fieldwork: Noun classes and other concerns in Fatick, Senegal. In P. Newman & M. Ratliff (Eds.), *Linguistic fieldwork* (pp. 189–210). Cambridge: Cambridge University Press.

McMillan, B., Green, J. M., Woolridge, M. W., Dyson, L., Renfrew, M. J., & Clarke, G. P. (2009). Studying the infant feeding intentions of pregnant women experiencing material deprivation: Methodology of the Looking at Infant Feeding Today (LIFT) study. *Social Science & Medicine* **68**(5), 845–849.

McTaggart, R. (Ed.) (1997). *Participatory action research: International contexts and consequences.* Albany, NY: State University of New York (SUNY) Press.

Meadows, L. M., Lagendyk, L. E., Thurston, W. E., & Eisener, A. C. (2003). Balancing culture, ethics, and methods in qualitative health research with aboriginal peoples. *International Journal of Qualitative Methods* **2**(4), Article 1. www.ualberta.ca/~iiqm/backissues/2_4/pdf/meadows.pdf Accessed: 9 October 2005.

Meadows, L. M., Thurston, W. E., & Melton, C. (2001). Immigrant women's health. *Social Science & Medicine* **52**, 1451–1458.

Mehnchú, R. (1984). *I, Rigoberta Mehnchú: An Indian woman in Guatemala,* trans. A. Wright. London: Verso.

Melrose, M. (2002). Labour pains: Some considerations on the difficulties of researching juvenile prostitution. *International Journal of Social Research Methodology* **5**(4), 333–351.

Merriam, S. B., Johnson-Bailey, J., Lee, M.-Y., Kee, Y., Ntseane, G., & Muhamad, M. (2001). Power and positionality: Negotiating insider/outsider status within and across cultures. *International Journal of Lifelong Education* **20**(5), 405–416.

Merton, R. K. (1972). Insiders and outsiders: A chapter in the sociology of knowledge. *American Journal of Sociology* **78**(1), 9–47.

Meyer, H., & Kroeger, S. (2005). Photovoice as an educational action research tool. *Qualitative Research Journal* **5**(2), 185–194.

Michaud, P.-A., Blum, R. W., & Slap, G. B. (2001). Cross-cultural surveys of adolescent health and behavior: Progress and problems. *Social Science & Medicine* **53**(9), 1237–1246.

Mienczakowski, J. (1997). Theatre for change. *Research in Drama Education* **2**(2), 159–172.

(2001). Ethnodrama: Performed research. In P. Atkinson, A. Coffey, S. Delamont, J. Lofland, & L. Lofland (Eds.), *Handbook of ethnography* (pp. 468–476). London: Sage Publications.

(2008). The theater of ethnography: The reconstruction of ethnography into theater with emancipatory potential. In P. Atkinson & S. Delamont (Eds.), *Representing ethnography,* Vol. 4 (pp. 32–47). London: Sage Publications.

Mill, J. E., & Ogilvie, L. D. (2003). Establishing methodological rigour in international qualitative nursing research: A case study from Ghana. *Journal of Advanced Nursing* **41**(1), 80–87.

Miller, T., & Boulton, M. (2007). Changing constructions of informed consent: Qualitative research and complex social worlds. *Social Science & Medicine* **65**(11), 2199–2211.

Mills, C. W. (1959). *The sociological imagination.* Harmondsworth: Penguin.

Mills, E., Wilson, K., Rachlis, B., Griffith, L., Wu, P., Guyatt, G., & Cooper, C. (2006). Barriers to participation in HIV drug trials: A systematic review. *Lancet Infectious Disease* **6**(1), 32–38.

Minh-Ha, T. T. (1989). *Woman, native, other: Writing postcoloniality and feminism.* Bloomington: Indiana University Press.

(2006). Writing postcoloniality and feminism. In B. Ashcroft, G. Griffiths, & H. Tiffin (Eds.), *The post-colonial studies reader,* 2nd edition (pp. 246–249). London: Routledge.

Minkler, M., & Wallestein, N. (2008a). Introduction to CBPR: New issues and emphases. In M. Minkler & N. Wallestein (Eds.), *Community-based participatory research for health: From process to outcomes,* 2nd edition (pp. 5–23). San Francisco: Jossey-Bass.

(2008b). *Community-based participatory research for health: From process to outcomes*, 2nd edition. San Francisco: Jossey-Bass.

Mirza, M. (1998). 'Same voices, same lives': Revisiting black feminist standpoint epistemology. In P. Connolly & B. Troyna (Eds.), *Researching racism in education: Politics, theory, and practice* (pp. 79–94). Buckingham: Open University Press.

Mitchell, E. A., Scragg, R., Stewart, A. W., Becroft, D. M. O., Taylir, B. J., & Ford, R. P. K. (1991). Results from the first year of the New Zealand Cot Death Study. *New Zealand Medical Journal* **104**, 71–76.

Mkabela, Q. (2005). Using the Afrocentric method in researching indigenous African culture. *The Qualitative Report* **10**(1), 178–189.

Mohatt, G. V., & Thomas, L. R. (2006). 'I wonder, why would you do it that way?': Ethical dilemmas in doing participatory research with Alaska Native communities. In J. E. Trimble & C. B. Fisher (Eds.), *The handbook of ethical research with ethnocultural populations and communities* (pp. 67–75). Thousand Oaks, CA: Sage Publications.

Molyneux, C. S., Peshu, N. & Marsh, K. (2004). Understanding of informed consent in a low-income setting: Three case studies from the Kenyan coast. *Social Science & Medicine* **59**(12), 2547–2559.

Molyneux, C. S., Wassenaar, D. R., Peshu, N., & Marsh, K. (2005). 'Even if they ask you to stand by a tree all day, you will have to do it (laughter)…!': Community voices on the notion and practice of informed consent for biomedical research in developing countries. *Social Science & Medicine* **61**(2), 443–454.

Molzahn, A. E., Starzomski, R., McDonald, M., & O'Laughlin, C. (2005). Chinese Canadian beliefs toward organ donation. *Qualitative Health Research* **15**(2), 82–98.

Mooney, J. (2000). *Gender, violence, and the social order*. London: Palgrave.

Morris, E. W. (2007). Researching race: Identifying a social construction through qualitative methods and an interactionist perspective. *Symbolic Interaction* **30**(3), 409–425.

Morse, J. (2007). Ethics in action: Ethical principles for doing qualitative health research. *Qualitative Health Research* **17**(8), 1003–1005.

Mosavel, M., Simon, C., van Stage, D., & Buchbinder, M. (2005). Community-based participatory research (CBPR) in South Africa: Engaging multiple constituents to shape the research question. *Social Science & Medicine* **61**, 2577–2587.

Moses, I., & Ramsden, P. (1992). Academic values and practice in new universities. *Higher Education Research and Development* **11**(2), 101–118.

Mouton, C. P., Harris, S., Rovi, S., Solorzano, P., & Johnson, M. S. (1997). Barriers to black women's participation in cancer clinical trials. *Journal of the National Medical Association* **89**(11), 721–727.

Mulder, S. S., Rance, S., Suarez, M. S., & Condori, M. C. (2000). Unethical ethics? Reflections on intercultural research practices. *Reproductive Health Matters* **8**, 104–112.

Munhall, P. L. (2006). The landscape of qualitative research in nursing. In P. L. Munhall (Ed.), *Nursing research: A qualitative perspective,* 4th edition (pp. 131–144). Sudbury, MA: Jones and Bartlett Publishers.

Mutu, M. (1998). Barriers to research: The constraints of imposed framework. In Te Pŭmanawa Hauora (Ed.), *Proceedings of Te Oru Rangahau Māori Research and Development Conference* (pp. 51–61). Palmerston North, Massey University, Auckland, New Zealand.

Mutua, K., & Swadener, B. B. (Eds.) (2004). *Decolonizing research in cross-cultural contexts: Critical personal narratives*. Albany, NY: State University of New York (SUNY) Press.

Narayan, K. (2008). How native is the 'native' anthropologist? In P. Atkinson & S. Delamont (Eds.), *Representing ethnography,* Vol. 3 (pp. 269–289). London: Sage Publications.

Narayan, K., & George, K. (2002). Personal and folk narrative as cultural representation. In J. F. Gubrium & J. A. Holstein (Eds.), *Handbook of interview research: Context and method* (pp. 815–831). Thousand Oaks, CA: Sage Publications.

Neufeld, A., Harrison, M. J., Stewart, M. S., Hughes, K. D., & Spitzer, D. (2002). Immigrant women: Making connections to community resources for support in family caregivers. *Qualitative Health Research* **12**, 751–768.

Ngamvithayapong-Yanai, J., Winkvist, A., Luangjina, S., & Diwan. V. (2005). 'If we have to die, we just die': Challenges and opportunities for tuberculosis and HIV/AIDS prevention and care in northern Thailand. *Qualitative Health Research* **15**(9), 1164–1179.

Ngo, A. D., McCurdy, S. A., Ross, M. W., Markham, C., Ratliff, E. A., & Pham, H. T. B. (2007). The lives of female sex workers in Vietnam: Findings from a qualitative study. *Culture, Health & Sexuality* **9**(6), 555–570.

Nordstrum, C. (1997). *A different kind of war story.* Philadelphia: University of Pennsylvania Press.

Norton, I. M., & Manson, S. M. (1996). Research in American Indian and Alaska Native communities: Navigating the cultural universe of values and process. *Journal of Consulting and Clinical Psychology* **64**, 856–860.

O'Neil, J. D. (1986). The politics of health in the fourth world: A northern Canadian example. *Human Organization* **45**, 119–128.

Olson, K., & Shopes, L. (1991). Crossing boundaries, building bridges: Doing oral history among working class women and men. In S. Gluck & D, Patai (Eds.), *Women's words: The feminist practice of oral history* (pp. 189–204). New York: Routledge.

Onwumere, J., Holttum, S., & Hirst, F. (2002). Determinants of quality of life in Black African women with HIV living in London. *Psychology, Health and Medicine* **7**(1), 61–74.

Oral History Centre (OHC) (2007). *Memories and reflections, the Singapore experience: Documenting a nation's history through oral history.* Singapore: Oral History Centre, National Archives of Singapore.

Orentlicher, D. (2002). Universality and its limits: When research ethics can reflect local circumstances. *Journal of Law, Medicine & Ethics* **30**(3), 403–410.

Overing, J. (1987). Translation as a creative process: The power of the name. In L. Holly (Ed.), *Comparative anthropology* (pp. 70–87). Oxford: Basil Blackwell.

Padgett, D. K. (2008). *Qualitative methods in social work research,* 2nd edition. Thousand Oaks, CA: Sage Publications.

Paget, M. A. (2008). Performing the text. In P. Atkinson & S. Delamont (Eds.), *Representing ethnography,* Vol. 4 (pp. 266–281). London: Sage Publications.

Papadopoulos, I., & Lees, S. (2002). Developing culturally competent researchers. *Journal of Advanced Nursing* **37**(3), 258–264.

Paradis, E. K. 2000. Feminist and community psychology ethics in research with homeless women. *American Journal of Community Psychology* **28**(6), 839–858.

Park, P. (2006). Knowledge and participatory research. In P. Reason & H. Bradbury (Eds.), *Handbook of action research: Concise paperback edition* (pp. 83–93). London: Sage Publications.

Parker, M. (2007). Ethnography/ethics. *Social Science & Medicine* **65**(11), 2248–2259.

Park-Fuller, L. (2003). A clean breast of it. In L. C. Miller, J. Taylor, & M. H. Carver (Eds.), *Voices made flesh: Performing women's autobiography* (pp. 215–236). Madison, WI: University of Wisconsin Press.

Pauw, I., & Brener, L. (2003). 'You are just whores – you can't be raped': Barriers to safer sex practices among women street sex workers in Cape Town. *Culture, Health & Sexuality* **5**(6), 465–481.

Pearpoint, J. (1989). All welcome! Everyone belongs: Leadership from voices seldom heard. *International Review of Education* **35**(4), 491–503.

Pelias, R. J. (2004). *A methodology of the heart.* Walnut Creek, CA: AltaMira Press.

Peritore, P. (1990). Reflections on dangerous fieldwork. *American Sociologist* **21**(4), 359–372.

Phellas, C. N. (2000). Cultural and sexual identities in in-depth interviewing. In C. Truman, D. M. Mertens, & B. Humphries (Eds.), *Research and inequality* (pp. 52–64). London: UCL Press.

Phillips, H. P. (1960). Problems of translation and meaning in field work. In R. N. Adams and J. J. Preiss (Eds.), *Human organisation research: Field relations and techniques* (pp. 290–307). Homewood, IL: Dorsey Press Inc.

Phoenix, A. (1994). Practicing feminist research: The intersection of gender and 'race' in the research process. In M. Maynard & J. Purvis (Eds.), *Researching women's lives from a feminist perspective* (pp. 49–71). London: Taylor & Francis.

    (1995). Practising feminist research: The intersection of gender and race. In M. Maynard & J. Purvis (Eds.), *Researching women's lives from a feminist perspective* (pp. 49–71). London: Taylor & Francis.

Piette, D. (1998). Les problèmes de la comparaison international d'indicateurs de santé chez les adolescents. In C. Dressen, C. Chan Chee, & M. C. Lamarre (Eds.), *Séminaire international sur les indicateurs de santé chez les adolescents* (pp. 32–40). Paris: CFES.

Pihama, L., Cram, F., & Walker, S. (2002). Creating a methodological space: A literature review of kaupapa Māori research. *Canadian Journal of Native Education* **26**(1), 30–43.

Pini, B. (2005). Interviewing men: Gender and the collection and interpretation of qualitative data. *Journal of Sociology* **41**(2), 201–216.

Piquemal, N. (2001). Free and informed consent in research involving Native American communities. *American Indian Culture and Research Journal* **25**(1), 65–79.

Pitchforth, E., & van Teijlingen, E. (2005). International public health research involving interpreters: A case study from Bangladesh. *BMC Public Health* **5**, 71–78.

Ponce, C., & Comer, B. (2003). *Is acculturation in Hispanic health research a flawed concept?* Working Paper No. 60. East Lansing: Julian Samora Research Institute, Michigan State University.

Pope, C. (2008). Kaupapa Māori research, supervision and uncertainty: 'What's a Pākehā fella to do?'. In P. Liamputtong (Ed.), *Doing cross-cultural research: Ethical and methodological perspective* (pp. 61–71). Dordrecht: Springer.

Poulin, M. (2007). Sex, money, and premarital partnerships in southern Malawi. *Social Science & Medicine* **65**, 2387–2393.

Powick, K. (2003). *Maori research ethics.* Hamilton: Wilf Malcolm Institute of Educational Research, University of Waikato, New Zealand.

Preloran, H. M., Browner, C. H., & Lieber, E. (2001). Strategies for motivating Latino couples' participation in qualitative health research and their effects on sample construction. *American Journal of Public Health* **91**(11), 1832–1841.

Preston-Whyte, E., & Dalrymple, L. (1996). Participation and action: Reflections on community-based AIDS. In K. de Koning & M. Martin (Eds.), *Participatory research in health: Issues and experiences* (pp. 108–118). London: Zed Books.

Prior, D. (2007). Decolonising research: A shift toward reconciliation. *Nursing Inquiry* **14**(2), 162–168.

Pyett, P., Waples-Crowe, P., & van der Sterren, A. (2010) Collaborative participatory research with disadvantaged communities. In P. Liamputtong (Ed.), *Research methods in health: Foundations for evidence-based practice* (pp. 345–366). Melbourne: Oxford University Press.

Quraishi, M. (2008). Researching Muslim prisoners. *International Journal of Social Research Methodology* **11**(5), 453–467.

Rajkumar, A. P., Premkumar, T. S., & Tharyan, P. (2008). Coping with the Asian tsunami: Perspectives from Tamil Nadu, India on the determinants of resilience in the face of adversity. *Social Science & Medicine* **67**(5), 844–853.

Rakhit, A. (1998). Silenced voices: Life history as an approach to the study of South Asian women teachers. In P. Connolly & B. Troyna (Eds.), *Researching racism in education: Politics, theory, and practice* (pp. 55–66). Buckingham: Open University Press.

Ramji, H. (2008). Exploring commonality and difference in in-depth interviewing: A case-study of researching British Asian women. *British Journal of Sociology* **59**(1), 99–116.

Rashid, S. F. (2007). Accessing married adolescent women: The realities of ethnographic research in an urban slum environment in Dhaka, Bangladesh. *Field Methods* **19**(4), 369–383.

Rawson, H. (2007). What shapes the sexual behavior of Vietnamese Australian young women living in Australia? Unpublished PhD thesis, School of Public Health, La Trobe University, Melbourne, Australia.

Rawson, H., & Liamputtong, P. (2009). Influence of traditional Vietnamese culture on the utilisation of mainstream health services for sexual health issues by second-generation Vietnamese Australian young women. *Sexual Health* **6**, 75–81.

Reason, P., & Bradbury, H. (2006a). Introduction: Inquiry and participation in search of a world worthy of human aspiration. In P. Reason & H. Bradbury (Eds.), *Handbook of action research: Concise paperback edition* (pp. 1–14). London: Sage Publications.

(2006b) (Eds.), *Handbook of action research: Concise paperback edition*. London: Sage Publications.

(2008). *The Sage handbook of action research: Participative inquiry and practice*. Los Angeles, CA: Sage Publications.

Redmond, M. (2003). Cultural and ethical challenges in cross-national research: Reflections on a European Union study on child and youth migration. *International Journal of Qualitative Methods* **2**(4), Article 2. www.ualberta.ca/~ijqm/backissues/2_4/pdf/redmond.pdf Accessed: 9 October 2005.

Reissman, C. K. (1991). When gender is not enough: Women interviewing women. In S. A. Farrell & J. Lorber (Eds.), *The social construction of gender* (pp. 217–236). Thousand Oaks, CA: Sage Publictions.

Reverby, S. M. (2008). 'Special treatment': BiDil, Tuskegee, and the logic of race. *Journal of Law, Medicine & Ethics* **36**(3), 478–484.

Rhodes, P. (1994). Race of interviewer effects: A brief comment. *Sociology* **28**, 547–558.

Rhodes, S. D., Hergenrather, K. C., Wilkin, A. M., & Jolly, C. (2008). Visions and voices: Indigent persons living with HIV in the southern United States use photovoice to create knowledge, develop partnerships, and take action. *Health Promotion Practice* **9**(2), 159–169.

Richardson, L. (2000a). Writing: A method of inquiry. In N. K. Denzin & Y. S. Lincoln (Eds.), *Handbook of qualitative research*, 2nd edition (pp. 923–948). Thousand Oaks, CA: Sage Publications.

(2000b). New writing practice in qualitative research. *Sociology of Sport Journal* **17**, 5–20.

(2002). Poetic representation of interviews. In J. Gubrium & J. Holstein (Eds.), *Handbook of interview research: Context & method* (pp. 877–891). Thousand Oaks, CA: Sage Publications.

Richardson, L., & St. Pierre, E. A. (2008). Writing: A method of inquiry. In N. K. Denzin & Y. S. Lincoln (Eds.), *Collecting and interpreting qualitative materials,* 3rd edition (pp. 473–499) Thousand Oaks, CA: Sage Publications.

Rickard, W. (2003). Collaborative with sex workers in oral history. *Oral History Review* **30**(1), 47–59.

Rigney, L. (1999). Internationalization of an indigenous anticolonial cultural critique of research methodologies: A guide to indigenist research methodology and its principles. *Wicazo SA Journal of Native American Studies Review* **14**(2), 109–121.

Rintoul, S. (1993). *The wailing: A national black oral history*. Port Melbourne: William Heinemann.

Robinson, J. M., & Trochim, W. M. K. (2007). An examination of community members', researchers' and health professionals' perceptions of barriers to minority participation in medical research: An application of Concept Mapping. *Ethnicity & Health* **12**(5), 521–539.

Rock, M. (2003). Sweet blood and social suffering: Rethinking cause-effect relationships in diabetes, distress, and duress. *Medical Anthropology* **22**, 131–174.

Rodríguez, M. D., Rodríguez, J., & Davis, M. (2006). Recruitment of first-generation Latinos in a rural community: The essential nature of personal contact. *Family Process* **45**(1), 87–100.

Romero-Daza, N., Weeks, M., & Singer, M. (2003). 'Nobody gives a damn if I live or die': Violence, drugs, and street-level prostitution in inner-city Hartford, Connecticut. *Medical Anthropology* **22**, 233–259.

Ross-Owens, G. (2003). What! Me a spy? Intrigue and reflexivity in Zanzibar. *Ethnography* **4**(**1**), 122–144.

Russon, C. (1995). The influence of culture on evaluation. *Evaluation Journal of Australasia* **7**(1), 44–49.

Ruzek, S. B. (1978). *The women's health movement: Feminist alternatives to medical control.* New York: Praeger Publishers.

Ryen, A. 2002. 'Cross-Cultural Interviewing'. In J. F. Gubrium, and J. A. Holstein (Eds.), *Handbook of Interview Research: Context & method* (pp. 335–354). Thousand Oaks, CA: Sage Publications.

Sadler, G. R., Thomas, A. G., Gebrekristos, B., Dhanjal, S. K., & Mugo, J. (2000). Black cosmetologists promoting health program: Pilot study outcomes. *Journal of Cancer Education* **15**, 33–37.

Said, E. (1995). Secular interpretation, the geographical element, and the methodology of imperialism. In G. Prakash (Ed.), *After colonialism: Imperial histories and postcolonial displacements* (pp. 21–39). Princeton: Princeton University Press.

Salazar, M. C. (1991). Young laborers in Bogota: Breaking authoritarian ramparts. In O. Fals-Borda & M. A. Rahman (Eds.), *Action and knowledge: Breaking the monopoly with participatory action-research* (pp. 54–63). New York: Apex Press.

Saldaña, J. (Ed.) (2005). *Ethnodrama: An anthology of reality theatre.* Walnut Creek, CA: AltaMira Press.

Salmon, A. (2007). Walking the talk: How participatory interview methods can democratize research. *Qualitative Health Research* **17**(7), 982–993.

Sampson, H., & Thomas, M. (2003). Risk and responsibility. *Qualitative Research* **3**(2), 165–189.

Sandoval, C. (2000). *Methodology of the oppressed: Theory out of bounds.* Minneapolis: University of Minnesota Press.

Schensul, J. J., & Le Compte, M. (1999). *The ethnographic tool kit,* Vol. 1. Walnut Creek, CA: AltaMira Press.

Scheyvens, R., Nowak, B., & Scheyvens, H. (2003). Ethical issues. In R. Scheyvens & D. Storey (Eds.), *Development fieldwork: A practical guide* (pp. 139–166). London: Sage Publications.

Schoenberg, N. E., Hopenhayn, C., Christian, A., Knight, E. A., & Rubio, A. (2005). An in-depth and updated perspective on determinants of cervical cancer screening among central Appalachian women. *Women & Health* **42**(2): 89–105.

Schwandt, T. A. (2000). Three epistemological stances for qualitative inquiry: Interpretivism, hermeneutics, and social constructionism. In N. K. Denzin & Y. S. Lincoln (Eds.), *Handbook of qualitative research,* 2nd edition (pp. 189–213). Newbury Park, CA: Sage Publications.

Scott, P. (1998). Lay beliefs and the management of disease amongst West Indians with diabetes. *Health and Social Care in the Community* **6**, 407–419.

Scragg, R., Mitchell, E. A., Taylor, B. J., Stewart, A. W., Ford, R. P. K., Thompson, J. M. D., Allen, E. M., & Becroft, D. M. O. (1993). Bed sharing, smoking, and alcohol in the Sudden Infant Death Syndrome. *British Medical Journal* **307**, 1312–1318.

Scragg, R., Stewart, A. W., Mitchell, E. A., Ford, R. P. K., & Thomspon, J. M. D. (1995). Public health policy on bed sharing and smoking in the Sudden Infant Death Syndrome. *New Zealand Medical Journal* **198**, 218–222.

Seaman, B. (1972). *Free and female.* New York: Fawcett.

Sechrest, L., Fay, T. L., & Zaidi, S. M. H. (1972). Problem of translation in cross-cultural research. *Journal of Cross-Cultural Psychology* **3**(1), 41–56.

Sengupta, S., Strauss, R. P., DeVeillis, R., Crouse-Quinn, S., Deveillis, B., & Ware, W. B. (2000). Factors affecting African American participation in AIDS research. *Journal of Acquired Immune Deficiency Syndromes* **24**, 275–284.

Shaffir, W. B., & Stebbins, R. A. (Eds.) (1991). *Experiencing fieldwork: An inside view of qualitative research.* Newbury Park, CA: Sage Publications.

Shah, S. (2006). *The body hunters: Testing new drugs on the world's poorest patients.* New York: New Press.

Shahidian, H. (2001). 'To be recorded in history': Researching Iranian underground political activists in exile. *Qualitative Sociology* **24**(1), 55–81.

Shavarini, M. K. (2006). The role of higher education in the life of a young Iranian woman. *Women's Studies International Forum* **29**, 42–53.

Shavers, V. L., Lynch, C. F., & Burmeister, L. F. (2002). Racial differences in factors that influence the willingness to participate in medical research studies. *Annals of Epidemiology* **12**, 248–256.

Shelton, A. (1995). The man at the end of the machine. *Symbolic Interaction* **18**, 505–518.

Shelton, A. J., & Rianon, N. J. (2004). Recruiting participants for a community of Bangladeshi immigrants for a study of spousal abuse: An appropriate cultural approach. *Qualitative Health Research* **14**(3), 369–380.

Sherif, B. (2001). The ambiguity of boundaries in the fieldwork experience: Establishing rapport and negotiating insider/outsider status. *Qualitative Inquiry* **7**(4), 436–447.

Shin, K. R., Cho, M. O., & Kim, J. S. (2005). The meaning of death as experienced by elderly women of a Korean clan. *Qualitative Health Research* **15**(1), 5–18.

Shklarov, S. (2007). Double vision uncertainty: The bilingual researcher and the ethics of cross-language research. *Qualitative Health Research* **17**(4), 529–538.

Shockley, K. G. (2009). A researcher 'called' to 'taboo' places?: A burgeoning research method in African-centered education. *International Journal of Qualitative Studies in Education* **22**(2), 163–176.

Shuval, J. T. (1963). *Immigrants: On the threshold*. New York: Atherton.

Siddle Walker, V. (2003). The architects of black schooling in the segregated South: The case of one principal leader, *Journal of Curriculum and Supervision* **19**(1), 54–72.

Sieber, J. E. (1992). *Planning ethically responsible research: A guide for students and internal review boards*. Newbury Park, CA: Sage Publications.

Simmons, J., & Koester, K. (2003). Hidden injuries of research on social suffering among drug users. *Practicing Anthropology* **25**, 53–57.

Simon, S. (1996). *Gender in translation: Cultural identity and the politics of transmission*. London: Routledge.

Sin, C. H. (2004). Sampling minority ethnic older people in Britain. *Ageing & Society* **24**, 257–277.

(2005). Seeking informed consent: Reflections on research practice. *Sociology* **39**(2), 277–294.

(2007). Ethnic-matching in qualitative research: Reversing the gaze on 'white others' and 'white' as 'other'. *Qualitative Research* **7**(4), 477–499.

Singer, M., & Easton, D. (2006). Ethnographic research on drugs and HIV/AIDS in ethnocultural communities. In J. E. Trimble & C. B. Fisher (Eds.), *The handbook of ethical research with ethnocultural populations and communities* (pp. 257–278). Thousand Oaks, CA: Sage Publications.

Sixsmith, J., Boneham, M., & Goldring, J. (2003). Accessing the community: Gaining insider perspectives from the outside. *Qualitative Health Research* **13**(4), 578–589.

Skaff, M. M., Chesla, C. A., Mycue, V., & Fisher, L. (2002). Lessons in cultural competence: Adapting research methodology for Latino participants. *Journal of Community Psychology* **30**(3), 305–323.

Slater, R. (2000). Using life histories to explore change: Women's urban struggles in Cape Town, South Africa. *Gender and Development* **8**(2), 38–46.

Sloan, S. (2008). Oral history and Hurricane Katrina: Reflections on shouts and silences. *Oral History Review* **35**(2), 176–186.

Small, R., Yelland, J., Lumley, J., & Liamputtong Rice, P. (1999a). Cross-cultural research: Trying to do it better, 1. Issues in study design. *Australian and New Zealand Journal of Public Health* **23**(4), 385–389.

Small, R., Yelland, J., Lumley, J., Liamputtong Rice, L., Cotronei, V., & Warren, R. (1999b). Cross-cultural research: Trying to do it better, 2. Enhancing data quality. *Australian and New Zealand Journal of Public Health* **23**(4), 390–395.

Smith, G. H. (1992). *Research issues related to Māori education.* Auckland Research Unit for Māori Education, University of Auckland, New Zealand.

Smith, L. T. (1999). *Decolonising methodologies: Research and indigenous peoples.* London and Dunedin: Zed Books and University of Otago Press.

(2000). Kaupapa Māori research. In M. Battiste (Ed.), *Reclaiming indigenous voice and vision* (pp. 225–247). Vancouver, BC: University of British Columbia Press.

(2005). On tricky ground: Researching the native in the age of uncertainty. In N. K. Denzin & Y. S. Lincoln (Eds.), *Sage handbook of qualitative research,* 3rd edition (pp. 85–108). Thousand Oaks, CA: Sage Publications.

(2006a). On tricky ground: Researching the native in the age of uncertainty. In N. K. Denzin and M. D. Giardina (Eds.), *Qualitative inquiry and the conservative challenge: Confronting methodological fundamentalism* (pp. 85–107). Walnut Creek, CA: Left Coast Press Inc.

(2006b). Researching in the margins: Issues for Māori researchers. A discussion paper. *AlterNative: International Journal of Indigenous Scholarship,* Special Supplement, S5-S27.

(2008). On tricky ground: Researching the native in the age of uncertainty. In N. K. Denzin & Y. S. Lincoln (Eds.), *The landscape of qualitative research,* 3rd edition (pp. 113–143). Thousand Oaks, CA: Sage Publications.

Song, M., & Parker, D. (1995). Commonality, difference, and the dynamics of disclosure in in-depth interviewing. *Sociology* **29**, 241–256.

Spalek, B. (2005). A critical reflection on researching black Muslim women's lives post-September 11th. *International Journal of Social Research Methodology* **8**(5), 405–418.

Spicer, N. J. (2005). Sedentarization and children's health: Changing discourses in the northeast Badia of Jordan. *Social Science & Medicine* **61**(10), 2165–2176.

Spira, G. (2008). Chaicuriri through the lens: Envisioning community-based development through photovoice. Unpublished Masters of Arts thesis, Royal Roads University, British Columbia, Canada.

Spivak, G. (1992). The politics of translation. In M. Barrett & A. Phillips (Eds.), *Destabilizing theory: Contemporary feminist debates* (pp. 177–200). Cambridge: Polity Press.

Stake, R. E. (2008). Qualitative case studies. In N. K. Denzin & Y. S. Lincoln (Eds.), *Strategies of qualitative inquiry,* 3rd edition (pp. 119–150). Thousand Oaks, CA: Sage Publications.

Stanko, E. (Ed.) (2002). *Violence.* Dartmouth: Ashgate.

Stephenson, P. (2007). *The outsiders within: Telling Australia's indigenous-Asian story.* Sydney: University of New South Wales Press.

Stevens, P. E., & Pletsch, P. K. (2002). Informed consent and the history of inclusion of women in clinical research. *Health Care for Women International* **23**(8), 809–819.

Stewart, D. W., Shamdasani, P. N., & Rook, D. W. (2007). *Focus groups: Theory and practice*, 2nd edition. Thousand Oaks, CA: Sage Publications.

Stone, M., Pound, E., Pancholi, A., Farooqi, A., & Khunti, K. (2005). Empowering patients with diabetes: A qualitative primary care study focusing on South Asians in Leicester, UK. *Family Practice* **22**(6), 647–652.

Strack, R., Magill, C., & McDonagh, K. (2004). Engaging youth through photovoice. *Health Promotion Practice* **5**(1), 49–58.

Streck, D. R. (2007). Research and social transformation: Notes about method and methodology in participator research. *International Journal of Action Research* **3**(1), 112–130.

Streng, J. M., Rhodes, S. D., Ayala, G. X., Eng, E., Arceo, R., & Phipps, S. (2004). *Realidad Latina*: Latino adolescents, their school, and a university use photovoice to examine and address the influence of immigration. *Journal of Interprofessional Care* **18**(4), 403–415.

Strickland, C. J. (1999). Conducting focus groups cross-culturally: Experiences with Pacific northwest Indian people. *Public Health Nurse* **16**(3), 190–197.

Struthers, R. (2000). The lived experience of Ojibwa and Cree women healers. *Journal of Holistic Nursing* **18**(3), 261–279.

Struthers, R., & Eschiti, V. S. (2005). Being healed by an indigenous traditional healer: Sacred healing stories of Native Americans, Part II. *Complementary Therapies in Clinical Practice* **11**, 78–86.

Struthers, R., & Peden-McAlpine, C. (2005). Phenomenological research among Canadian and United States indigenous populations: Oral tradition and quintessence of time. *Qualitative Health Research* **15**(9), 1264–1276.

Stuttaford, M., Bryanston, C., Hundt, G. L., Connor, M., Thorogood, M., & Tollman, S. (2006). Use of applied theatre in health research dissemination and data validation: A pilot study from South Africa. *Health: An Interdisciplinary Journal for the Social Study of Health, Illness and Medicine* **10**(1), 31–45.

Subedi, B. (2006). Theorizing a 'halfie' researcher's identity in transnational fieldwork. *International Journal of Qualitative Studies in Education* **19**(5), 573–593.

(2007). Recognizing respondents' ways of being and knowing: Lessons un/learned in researching Asian immigrant and Asian-American teachers. *International Journal of Qualitative Studies in Education* **20**(10), 51–71.

Suite, D. H., La Brill, R., Primm, A., & Harrison-Ross, P. (2007). Beyond misdiagnosis, misunderstanding and mistrust: Relevance of the historical perspective in the medical and mental health treatment of people of color. *Journal of National Medical Association* **99**(8), 879–885.

Swadener, B. B., & Mutua, K. (2008). Decolonizing performances: Deconstructing the global postcolonial. In N. K. Denzin, Y. S. Lincoln, & L. T. Smith (Eds.), *Handbook of critical and indigenous methodologies* (pp. 31–43). Thousand Oaks, CA: Sage Publications.

Swantz, M-L., Ndedya, E., & Masaiganah, M. S. (2006). Participatory action research in southern Tanzania, with special reference to women. In P. Reason & H. Bradbury (Eds.), *Handbook of action research: Concise paperback edition* (pp. 286–296). London: Sage Publications.

Takahashi, M., & Kai, I. (2005). Sexuality after breast cancer treatment: Changes and coping strategies among Japanese survivors. *Social Science & Medicine* **61**(6), 1278–1290.

Tandon, S. D., Keyy, J. G., & Mock, L. O. (2001). Participatory action research as a resource for developing African American community leadership. In D. L. Tolman & M. Brydon-Miller (Eds.), *From subjects to subjectivities: A handbook of interpretive and participatory methods* (pp. 200–217). New York: New York University Press.

Tedlock, B. (2008). The observation of participant and the emergence of public ethnography. In N. K. Denzin, and Y. S. Lincoln (Eds.), *Strategies of qualitative research,* 3rd edition (pp. 75–118). Thousand Oaks, CA: Sage Publications.

Temple. B. (1997). Watch your tongue: Issues in translation and cross-cultural research. *Sociology* **31**(3), 607–618.

(2002). Crossed wires: Interpreters, translators, and bilingual workers in cross-language research. *Qualitative Health Research* **12**(6), 844–854.

(2006). Being bilingual: Issues for cross language research. *Journal of Research Practice* **2**(1), Article M2. http://jrp.icaap.org/content/v2.1/temple.html Accessed: 8 March 2009.

Temple, B., & Edwards, R. (2002). Interpreters/translators and cross-language research: Reflexivity and border crossings. *International Journal of Qualitative Methods* **1**(2), Article 1. Available at: www.ualberta.ca/~ijqm Accessed 9 October 2005.

Temple, B., Edwards, R., & Alexander, C. (2006). Grasping at context: Cross language qualitative research as secondary qualitative data analysis [46 paragraphs]. *Forum: Qualitative Social Research* **7**(4), Article 10. www.qualitative-research.net/index.php/fqs/article/view/176/393 Accessed: 8 March 2009.

Temple, T., & Young, A. (2008). Qualitative research and translation dilemmas. In P. Atkinson & S. Delamont (Eds.), *Representing ethnography,* Vol. 3 (pp. 90–107). London: Sage Publications.

Tharao, E., & Massaquoi, N. A. (2002). Black women and HIV/AIDS: Contexualizing their realities, their silence and proposing solutions. *Canadian Woman Studies* **21**, 72–80.

Thomas, G. (1990). *Afro-Caribbean elderly people: Coping with ageing.* Coventry Social Care Practice Centre, Department of Applied Social Studies, University of Warwick.

Tillman, L. C. (2002). Culturally sensitive research approaches: An African-American perspective. *Educational Researcher* **31**(9), 3–12.

(2003). Mentoring, reflection, and reciprocal journaling. *Theory Into Practice* **42**(3), 226–233.

(2005a). Culturally sensitive research and evaluation: Advancing an agenda for black education. In J. E. King (Ed.), *Black education: A transformative research and action agenda for a new century* (pp. 313–321). Mahwah, NJ, Lawrence Erlbaum.

(2005b). Mentoring new teachers: Implications for leadership practice in an urban school. *Educational Administration Quarterly* **41**(4), 609–629.

(2006). Researching and writing from an African-American perspective: Reflective notes on three research studies. *International Journal of Qualitative Studies in Education* **19**(3), 265–287.

Tindana, P. O., Kass, N., & Akweongo, P. (2006). The informed consent process in a rural African setting: A case study of the Kassena-Nangana district of northern Ghana. *IRB: Ethics and Human Research* **28**(3), 1–6.

Tipene-Leach, D., Everard, C., & Haretuku, R. (1999). Taking a strategic approach to SIDS prevention in Māori communities – An indigenous perspective. Occasional paper. Auckland: Department of Māori and Pacific Health, University of Auckland.

Topp, R., Newman, J. L., & Jones, V. F. (2008). Including African Americans in health care research. *Western Journal of Nursing Research* **30**(2), 197–203.

Trask, H. K. (1993). *From a native daughter.* Munroe, ME: Common Courage Press.

Trimble, J. E., & Fisher, C. B. (2006a) Our shared journey: Lessons from the past to protect the future. In J. E. Trimble & C. B. Fisher (Eds.), *The handbook of ethical research with ethnocultural populations and communities* (pp. xv–xxix). Thousand Oaks, CA: Sage Publications.

(2006b) (Eds.). *The handbook of ethical research with ethnocultural populations and communities.* Thousand Oaks, CA: Sage Publications.

Trimble, J. E., & Mohatt, G. V. (2006). Coda: The virtuous and responsible researcher in another culture. In J. E. Trimble & C. B. Fisher (Eds.), *The handbook of ethical research with ethnocultural populations and communities* (pp. 325–334). Thousand Oaks, CA: Sage Publications.

Troyna, B. (1998). 'The whites of my eyes, nose, ears …': A reflexive account of 'whitenes' in race-related research. In P. Connolly & B. Troyna (Eds.), *Researching racism in education: Politics, theory, and practice* (pp. 95–108). Buckingham: Open University Press.

Tsai, J. H.-C., Choe, J. H., Lim, J. M.C., Acorda, E., Chan, N. L., Taylor, V. M., & Tu, S.-P. (2004). Developing culturally competent health knowledge: Issues of data analysis of cross-cultural, cross-language qualitative research. *International Journal of Qualitative Methods* 3(4), Article 2. www.ualberta.ca/~iiqm/backissues/3_4/pdf/tsai.pdf Accessed: 9 October 2005.

Tsey, K., & Baird, B. (2004). A microanalysis of a participatory action research process with a rural Aboriginal Men's Health Group. *Australian Journal of Primary Health* **10**(1), 64–71.

Tsey, K., & Every, A. (2000). Evaluating aboriginal empowerment programs – The case of family wellbeing. *Australian and New Zealand Journal of Public Health* **24**, 509–514.

Tsey, K., Patterson, D., Whiteside, M., Baird, L., & Baird, B. (2002). Indigenous men taking their rightful place in society? A preliminary analysis of a participatory action research process with Yarrabah Men's Health Group. *Australian Journal of Rural Health* **10**(6), 278–283.

Turnbull, B., Martínez-Andrade, G., Klünder, M., Carranco, T., Duque-López, X., Ramos-Hernández, R. I., Conzález-Unzaga, M., Flores-Hernández, S., & Martínez-Salgado, H. (2006). The social construction of anemia in school shelters for indigenous children in Mexico. *Qualitative Health Research* **16**(4), 503–516.

Twine, F. W. (2000). Racial ideologies and racial methodologies. In F. W. Twine & J. W. Warren (Eds.), *Racing research: Researching race. Methodological dilemmas in critical race studies* (pp. 1–34). New York: New York University Press.

Twinn, S. (1998). An analysis of the effectiveness of focus groups as a method of qualitative data collection with Chinese populations in nursing research. *Journal of Advanced Nursing* **28**(3), 654–661.

Umaña-Taylor, A. J., & Bámaca, M. Y. (2004). Conducting focus groups with Latino populations: Lessons from the field. *Family Relations* **53**, 261–272.

Unger, J. B., Kipke, M. D., Simon, T. R., Montgomery, S. B., & Johnson, C. J. (1997). Homeless youths and young adults in Los Angeles: Prevalence of mental health problems and the relationship between mental health and substance abuse disorders. *American Journal of Community Psychology* **25**(3), 371–394.

Usunier, J. C. (1999). The use of language in investigating conceptual equivalence in cross-cultural research. http://marketing.byu.edu/htmlpages/ccrs/proceedings99/usunier.htm Accessed: 22 October 2007.

Van Manen, M. (1990). *Researching the lived experience: Human science for an action sensitive pegagogy.* London, ON: Althouse.

Vannini, A., & Gladue, C. (2008). Decolonised methodologies in cross-cultural research. In P. Liamputtong (Ed.), *Doing cross-cultural research: Ethical and methodological perspectives* (pp. 137–159). Dordrecht: Springer.

(2009). Moccasin on one foot, high heel on the other: Life story reflections of Coreen Gladue. *Qualitative Inquiry* **15**(4), 675–720.

Varas-Diaz, N., Serrano-Garcia, I., & Toro-Alfonso, J. (2005). AIDS-related stigma and social interaction: Puerto Ricans living with HIV/AIDS. *Qualitative Health Research* **15**(2), 169–187.

Vickers, M. (2005). Action research to improve the human condition: An insider–outsider and a multi-methodology design for actionable knowledge outcomes. *International Journal of Action Research* **1**(2), 190–218.

Villenas, S. (1996). The colonizer/colonized Chicana ethnographer: Identity, marginalization, and co-option in the field. *Harvard Educational Review* **66**, 711–731.

Vinokurov, A., Geller, D., & Martin, T. L. (2007). Translation as an ecological tool for instrument development. *International Journal of Qualitative Methods* **6**(2), Article 3. 1–13. www.ualberta.ca/~iiqm/backissues/6_2/vinokurov.pdf Accessed: 20 October 2007.

Vissandjée, B., Abdool, S. N., & Dupéré, S. (2002). Focus groups in rural Gujarat, India: A modified approach. *Qualitative Health Research* **12**(6), 826–843.

Vo-Thanh-Xuan, J., & Liamputtong, P. (2003). What does it takes to be a grandparent in a new country?: The lived experiences and emotional well-being of Australian-Vietnamese grandparents. *Australian Journal of Social Issues, Refugees and Migrant Issues, Special issue* **38**(2), 209–228.

Walker, S., Eketone, A., & Gibbs, A. (2006). An exploration of kaupapa Māori research, its principles, processes and applications. *International Journal of Social Research Methodology* **9**(4), 331–344.

Wallace, S. A. (2006). Addressing health disparities through relational ethics: An approach to increasing African American participation in biomedical and health research. In J. E. Trimble & C. B. Fisher (Eds.), *The handbook of ethical research with ethnocultural populations and communities* (pp. 67–75). Thousand Oaks, CA: Sage Publications.

Wallerstein, N., & Duran, B. (2008). The theoretical, historical, and practice roots of CBPR. In M. Minkler & N. Wallestein (Eds.), *Community-based participatory research for health: From process to outcomes*, 2nd edition (pp. 25–46). San Francisco, CA: Jossey-Bass.

Walsh-Tapiata, W. (2003). A model for Maori research: *Te whakaeke i te ao rangahau o te Maori.* In R. Munford & J. Sanders (Eds.), *Making a difference in families: Research that creates change* (pp. 55–73). Sydney: Allen & Unwin.

Wang, C. C. (1999). Photovoice: A participatory action research strategy applied to women's health. *Journal of Women's Health* **8**, 185–192.

(2003). Using photovoice as a participatory assessment and issue selection tool: A case study with the homeless in Ann Arbor. In M. Minkler & N. Wallerstein (Eds.), *Community based participatory research for health* (pp. 179–196). San Francisco, CA: Jossey-Bass.

Wang, C. C., & Burris, M. A. (1994). Empowerment through photo novella: Portraits of participation. *Health Education Quarterly* **21**, 171–186.

(1997). Photovoice: Concept, methodology, and use for participatory needs assessment. *Health Education and Behavior* **24**, 369–387.

Wang, C. C., Burris, M. A., & Ping, X. Y. (1996). Chinese village women as visual anthropologists: A participatory approach to reaching policymakers. *Social Science & Medicine* **42**(10), 1391–1400.

Wang, C. C., Morrel-Samuels, S., Hutchison, P., Bell, L., & Pestronk, R. (2004). Flint Photovoice: Community building among youths, adults, and policymakers. *American Journal of Public Health* **94**(6), 911–913.

Wang, C. C., & Pies, C. (2008). Using photovoice as a participatory assessment and issue selection tool. In M. Minkler & N. Wallerstein (Eds.), *Community-based participatory research for health: From process to outcomes*, 2nd edition (pp. 179–196). San Francisco: Jossey-Bass.

Warren, C. (1988). *Gender issues in field research*. Newbury Park, CA: Sage Publications.

Webster, C. (1996). Hispanic and Anglo interviewer and respondent ethnicity and gender: The impact on survey response quality. *Journal of Marketing Research* **33**(1), 62–73.

Weeks, M. R., Abbott, M., Liao, S., Yu, W., He, B., Zhou, Y.-J., Wei, L., & Jiang, J.-M. (2007). Opportunities for woman-initiated HIV prevention methods among female sex workers in Southern China. *Journal of Sex Research* **44**(2), 190–201.

Weinfurt, K., & Maghaddam, F. (2001). Culture and social distance: A case study of methodological cautions. *Journal of Social Psychology* **121**(1), 101–110.

Weis, L. (1992). Reflection on the researcher in a multicultural environment. In C. A. Grant (Ed.), *Research and multicultural education: From the margins to the mainstream* (pp. 47–57). London: Routledge.

Wendler, D., Kington, R., Madans, J., Van Wye, G., Christ-Schmidt, H., Pratt, L. A., Brawley, O. W., Goss, C. P., & Emanuel, E. (2006). Are racial and ethnic minorities less willing to participate in medical research? *PLoS Medicine* **3**(2), e19–29.

Wendler, D., & Rackoff, J. E. (2001). Informed consent and respecting autonomy. *IRB: Ethics & Research* **23**, 1–4.

Wilkin, A. (2008). Aboriginal voice and vision: Aboriginal women's experience of working in the Victorian health care system. Unpublished honours thesis, School of Public Health, La Trobe University, Melbourne, Australia.

Wilkin, A., & Liamputtong, P. (2009). The photovoice method: Researching the experiences of female Aboriginal health workers through photographs. Unpublished paper submitted to *Australian Journal of Primary Health*.

Wilkinson, S., & Kitzinger, S. (Eds.) (1996). *Representing the other*. London: Sage Publications.

Willgerodt, M. A., Kataoka-Yahiro, M., Kim, E., & Ceria, C. (2005). Issues of instrument translation in research on Asian immigrant populations. *Journal of Professional Nursing* **21**(4), 231–239.

Williams, C., Newman, P. A., Sakamoto, I., & Massaquoi, N. A. (2009). HIV prevention risks for black women in Canada. *Social Science & Medicine* **68**(1), 12–20.

Willis, E., Pearce, M., & Jenkin, T. (2005). Adapting focus group methods to fit Aboriginal community-based research. *Qualitative Research Journal* **5**(2), 112–123.

Winslow, W. W., Honein, G., & Elzubeir, M. A. (2002). Seeking Emirati women's voices: The use of focus groups with an Arab population. *Qualitative Health Research* **12**(4), 566–575.

Wolcott, H. F. (1994). *Transforming qualitative data: Description, analysis, and interpretation.* Thousand Oaks, CA: Sage Publications.

Yow, V. R. (2005). *Recording oral history: A guide for the humanities and social sciences,* 2nd edition. Walnut Creek, CA: AltaMira Press.

Yu, D. S. F., Lee, D. T. F., & Woo, J. (2004). Issues and challenges of instrument translation. *Western Journal of Nursing Research* **26**(3), 307–320.

Yu, E. S., & Liu, W. T. (1986). Methodological problems and policy implications in Vietnamese refugee research. *International Migration Review* **20**(2), 483–502.

Zinn, M. B. (2001). Insider field research in minority communities. In R. M. Emerson (Ed.), *Contemporary field research: Perspective and formulations* (pp. 159–166). Prospect Heights, IL: Waveland Press.

Index